Education and Social Mobility

The study of education and social mobility has been a key area of sociological research since the 1950s. The importance of this research derives from the systematic analysis of functionalist theories of industrialism. Functionalist theories assume that the complementary demands of efficiency and justice result in more 'meritocratic' societies, characterised by high rates of social mobility. Much of the sociological evidence has cast doubt on this optimistic, if not utopian, claim that reform of the education system could eliminate the influence of class, gender and ethnicity on academic performance and occupational destinations.

This book brings together sixteen cutting-edge articles on education and social mobility. It also includes an introductory essay offering a guide to the main issues and controversies addressed by authors from several countries. This comprehensive volume makes an important contribution to our theoretical and empirical understanding of the changing relationship between origins, education and destinations. This timely collection is also relevant to policy-makers as education and social mobility are firmly back on both national and global political agendas, viewed as key to creating fairer societies and more competitive economies.

This book was originally published as a special issue of the *British Journal of Sociology of Education*.

Phillip Brown is Distinguished Research Professor in the Cardiff School of Social Sciences, Cardiff. Since the late 1990s he has been studying economic globalisation and the new division of labour including comparative studies that fundamentally challenged Western policy debates around education, skill formation, social justice, and the knowledge economy. He also has a longstanding interest in graduate employability, social mobility, and the sociology of talent. He is the co-author of *The Global Auction: The Broken Promises of Education, Jobs and Incomes* (2011) and is currently writing a book with colleagues on the death of human capital.

Diane Reay grew up in a working class, coal mining community before becoming an inner city primary school teacher for 20 years. She is now Professor of Education at the University of Cambridge, UK, with particular interests in social justice issues in education, Pierre Bourdieu's social theory, and cultural analyses of social class. She has researched extensively in the areas of social class, gender and ethnicity across primary, secondary and post-compulsory stages of education. Her most recent book (with Gill Crozier and David James) is *White Middle Class Identities and Urban Schooling* (2011). She is currently writing a book on *Education and the Working Classes in the 21st Century*. As well as being an executive editor of the *British Journal of Sociology of Education*, she is on the editorial boards of the *Journal of Education Policy* and *Cultural Sociology*.

Carol Vincent is Professor of Education at the Institute of Education, University College London, UK. She has written and researched extensively on families' relationships with educational institutions, and, in particular, how these are shaped by race and class. She co-authored *The Colour of Class* (2015) which explores the educational strategies of Black Caribbean-origin middle classes. Other research interests include parenting, especially mothering, education policy and 'super-diversity'. Her current ESRC project focuses on 'Children and Adults' Friendships across Social Class and Ethnic Difference'.

Education and Social Mobility

Edited by
Phillip Brown, Diane Reay and
Carol Vincent

LONDON AND NEW YORK

First published 2016
by Routledge
2 Park Square, Milton Park, Abingdon, Oxon, OX14 4RN, UK

and by Routledge
711 Third Avenue, New York, NY 10017, USA

Routledge is an imprint of the Taylor & Francis Group, an informa business

© 2016 Taylor & Francis

All rights reserved. No part of this book may be reprinted or reproduced or utilised in any form or by any electronic, mechanical, or other means, now known or hereafter invented, including photocopying and recording, or in any information storage or retrieval system, without permission in writing from the publishers.

Trademark notice: Product or corporate names may be trademarks or registered trademarks, and are used only for identification and explanation without intent to infringe.

British Library Cataloguing in Publication Data
A catalogue record for this book is available from the British Library

ISBN 13: 978-1-138-11957-4

Typeset in Times New Roman
by RefineCatch Limited, Bungay, Suffolk

Publisher's Note
The publisher accepts responsibility for any inconsistencies that may have arisen during the conversion of this book from journal articles to book chapters, namely the possible inclusion of journal terminology.

Disclaimer
Every effort has been made to contact copyright holders for their permission to reprint material in this book. The publishers would be grateful to hear from any copyright holder who is not here acknowledged and will undertake to rectify any errors or omissions in future editions of this book.

Contents

Citation Information	vii
Notes on Contributors	xi
Dedication	xvii

1. Introduction: Education and social mobility 1
   Phillip Brown, Diane Reay and Carol Vincent

2. Reflections on education and social mobility 8
   A.H. Halsey

3. Social mobility, a panacea for austere times: tales of emperors, frogs, and tadpoles 24
   Diane Reay

4. Education, opportunity and the prospects for social mobility 42
   Phillip Brown

5. 'Class work': producing privilege and social mobility in elite US secondary schools 65
   Lois Weis and Kristin Cipollone

6. Higher education, social class and the mobilisation of capitals: recognising and playing the game 87
   Ann-Marie Bathmaker, Nicola Ingram and Richard Waller

7. Social mobility and post-compulsory education: revisiting Boudon's model of social opportunity 108
   Ron Thompson and Robin Simmons

8. The changing relationship between origins, education and destinations in the 1990s and 2000s 130
   Fiona Devine and Yaojun Li

9. Framing higher education: questions and responses in the British Social Attitudes survey, 1983–2010 156
   Anna Mountford-Zimdars, Steven Jones, Alice Sullivan and Anthony Heath

10. Interrupted trajectories: the impact of academic failure on the social mobility of working-class students 176
    Tina Byrom and Nic Lightfoot

CONTENTS

11. Rural students' experiences in a Chinese elite university: capital, habitus and practices   193
    He Li

12. Cultural capital and distinction: aspirations of the 'other' foreign student   212
    I Lin Sin

13. Meritocracy and the *Gaokao*: a survey study of higher education selection and socio-economic participation in East China   232
    Ye Liu

14. Educational expansion and field of study: trends in the intergenerational transmission of educational inequality in the Netherlands   252
    Gerbert Kraaykamp, Jochem Tolsma and Maarten H.J. Wolbers

15. The role of the school curriculum in social mobility   271
    Cristina Iannelli

16. Three generations of racism: Black middle-class children and schooling   293
    Carol Vincent, Stephen Ball, Nicola Rollock and David Gillborn

17. Resettling notions of social mobility: locating refugees as 'educable' and 'employable'   311
    Jill Koyama

    Index   331

Citation Information

The chapters in this book were originally published in the *British Journal of Sociology of Education*, volume 34, issues 5–6 (September–November 2013). When citing this material, please use the original page numbering for each article, as follows:

Chapter 1
Introduction: Education and social mobility
Phillip Brown, Diane Reay and Carol Vincent
British Journal of Sociology of Education, volume 34, issues 5–6 (September–November 2013) pp. 637–643

Chapter 2
Reflections on education and social mobility
A.H. Halsey
British Journal of Sociology of Education, volume 34, issues 5–6 (September–November 2013) pp. 644–659

Chapter 3
Social mobility, a panacea for austere times: tales of emperors, frogs, and tadpoles
Diane Reay
British Journal of Sociology of Education, volume 34, issues 5–6 (September–November 2013) pp. 660–677

Chapter 4
Education, opportunity and the prospects for social mobility
Phillip Brown
British Journal of Sociology of Education, volume 34, issues 5–6 (September–November 2013) pp. 678–700

Chapter 5
'Class work': producing privilege and social mobility in elite US secondary schools
Lois Weis and Kristin Cipollone
British Journal of Sociology of Education, volume 34, issues 5–6 (September–November 2013) pp. 701–722

CITATION INFORMATION

Chapter 6
Higher education, social class and the mobilisation of capitals: recognising and playing the game
Ann-Marie Bathmaker, Nicola Ingram and Richard Waller
British Journal of Sociology of Education, volume 34, issues 5–6 (September–November 2013) pp. 723–743

Chapter 7
Social mobility and post-compulsory education: revisiting Boudon's model of social opportunity
Ron Thompson and Robin Simmons
British Journal of Sociology of Education, volume 34, issues 5–6 (September–November 2013) pp. 744–765

Chapter 8
The changing relationship between origins, education and destinations in the 1990s and 2000s
Fiona Devine and Yaojun Li
British Journal of Sociology of Education, volume 34, issues 5–6 (September–November 2013) pp. 766–791

Chapter 9
Framing higher education: questions and responses in the British Social Attitudes survey, 1983–2010
Anna Mountford-Zimdars, Steven Jones, Alice Sullivan and Anthony Heath
British Journal of Sociology of Education, volume 34, issues 5–6 (September–November 2013) pp. 792–811

Chapter 10
Interrupted trajectories: the impact of academic failure on the social mobility of working-class students
Tina Byrom and Nic Lightfoot
British Journal of Sociology of Education, volume 34, issues 5–6 (September–November 2013) pp. 812–828

Chapter 11
Rural students' experiences in a Chinese elite university: capital, habitus and practices
He Li
British Journal of Sociology of Education, volume 34, issues 5–6 (September–November 2013) pp. 829–847

Chapter 12
Cultural capital and distinction: aspirations of the 'other' foreign student
I Lin Sin
British Journal of Sociology of Education, volume 34, issues 5–6 (September–November 2013) pp. 848–867

CITATION INFORMATION

Chapter 13
Meritocracy and the Gaokao*: a survey study of higher education selection and socio-economic participation in East China*
Ye Liu
British Journal of Sociology of Education, volume 34, issues 5–6 (September–November 2013) pp. 868–887

Chapter 14
Educational expansion and field of study: trends in the intergenerational transmission of educational inequality in the Netherlands
Gerbert Kraaykamp, Jochem Tolsma and Maarten H.J. Wolbers
British Journal of Sociology of Education, volume 34, issues 5–6 (September–November 2013) pp. 888–906

Chapter 15
The role of the school curriculum in social mobility
Cristina Iannelli
British Journal of Sociology of Education, volume 34, issues 5–6 (September–November 2013) pp. 907–928

Chapter 16
Three generations of racism: Black middle-class children and schooling
Carol Vincent, Stephen Ball, Nicola Rollock and David Gillborn
British Journal of Sociology of Education, volume 34, issues 5–6 (September–November 2013) pp. 929–946

Chapter 17
Resettling notions of social mobility: locating refugees as 'educable' and 'employable'
Jill Koyama
British Journal of Sociology of Education, volume 34, issues 5–6 (September–November 2013) pp. 947–965

For any permission-related enquiries please visit:
http://www.tandfonline.com/page/help/permissions

Notes on Contributors

Stephen Ball is a Professor at the Institute of Education, University College London, UK, and is affiliated to the Centre for Critical Education Policy Studies. His main areas of interest are in education policy analysis and social theory, with a focus on changes in governance and new state modalities, the Global Education Reform Movement, and the relationships between education and education policy and social class.

Ann-Marie Bathmaker is Professor of Vocational and Higher Education in the School of Education, at the University of Birmingham, UK. She is particularly interested in understanding and addressing in/equalities in educational provision in vocational and higher education. Her work has focused on HE and social class, the FE/HE interface, teaching and learning in vocational and higher education, and professionalism and professional identities in further education.

Phillip Brown is Distinguished Research Professor in the Cardiff School of Social Sciences, Cardiff. Since the late 1990s he has been studying economic globalisation and the new division of labour including comparative studies that fundamentally challenged Western policy debates around education, skill formation, social justice, and the knowledge economy. He also has a longstanding interest in graduate employability, social mobility, and the sociology of talent. He is the co-author of *The Global Auction: The Broken Promises of Education, Jobs and Incomes* (2011) and is currently writing a book with colleagues on the death of human capital.

Tina Byrom is the Academic Team Leader for Undergraduate and Professional Education in the School of Education, at Nottingham Trent University, UK. She is currently involved in exploring the interventions used by a housing association to encourage homeless young people back into education, and an evaluation of their peer mentoring scheme. Her additional research activities include exploring the higher education experiences of non-traditional students.

Kristin Cipollone is a Lecturer in the Department of Sociology, at the State University of New York at Buffalo, NY, USA. She holds a PhD in the Sociology of Education from the same institution. She is the co-author (with Lois Weis and Heather Jenkins) of *Class Warfare: Class, Race, and College Admissions in Top-Tier Secondary Schools* (2014).

Fiona Devine is Professor of Sociology, and Head of the Manchester Business School, at the University of Manchester, UK. Her research interests are in the fields of social stratification and mobility, work and employment, and politics and participation from a comparative US/UK perspective. She is the author of *Class Practices: How Parents*

NOTES ON CONTRIBUTORS

Help Their Children Get Good Jobs (2004), *Sociological Research Methods in Context* (with S. Heath, 1999), and *Social Class in Britain and America* (1997).

David Gillborn is Professor of Critical Race Studies in the School of Education, and Director of the Centre for Research in Race and Education, at the University of Birmingham, UK. His research focuses on race inequalities in education, especially the role of racism as a changing and complex characteristic of the system. He is editor-in-chief of the journal *Race, Ethnicity and Education*, and is the author of *Racism and Education: Coincidence or Conspiracy?* (Routledge, 2008), which was the winner of the Book of the Year Award from the Society for Educational Studies.

A.H. 'Chelly' Halsey was a sociologist, and Emeritus Professor of Social and Administrative Studies in the Department of Social Policy and Intervention, at the University of Oxford, UK, where he was also a Fellow of Nuffield College. His books include *A History of Sociology in Britain* (2004) and *Twentieth-Century British Social Trends* (2000). In 1978, he presented the BBC's annual Reith Lectures on the theme of 'Change in British Society', exploring class, status, the rise of organisations, the nuclear family, and fraternity in contemporary Britain.

Anthony Heath is Emeritus Professor of Sociology, and Emeritus Fellow of Nuffield College, at the University of Oxford, UK. His research interests include social mobility, class and educational opportunity, and nationalism and identity. He is the author of *The Rise of New Labour: Party Policies and Voter Choices* (with Jowell and Curtice, 2001), and co-editor of *Labour's Last Chance* (with Jowell and Curtice, 1994).

Cristina Iannelli is Professor of Education and Social Stratification, at the University of Edinburgh, UK, and Co-Director of the Applied Quantitative Methods Network Centre in Scotland. She was the principal investigator of the ESRC project *Education and Social Mobility in Scotland in the 20th Century* which provided an up-to-date picture of social mobility patterns in Scotland. She is currently involved in a further two major initiatives, Edinburgh Q-Step and the Administrative Data Research Centre in Scotland.

Nicola Ingram is a Lecturer in the Department of Social and Policy Sciences, at the University of Bath, UK. Her research focuses on social class, masculinity, and education. She is a co-investigator on the Paired Peers project, focusing on the classed gendered differences in experiences of post-university transitions; a co-investigator on 'Who wants to be an engineer?', looking at post-16 vocational transitions, and focusing on engineering; and is working with Bristol City Council and Avon and Somerset Police, evaluating their 'Bright Outlooks' programme.

Steven Jones is a Senior Lecturer at the Manchester Institute of Education, University of Manchester, UK. He is a member of the Sutton Trust Research Group, and has given papers at major international conferences, as well as appearing on television and radio to discuss Higher Education research and language use. He is the author of *Antonymy: A Corpus-Based Perspective* (2002) and *Antonyms in English: Construals, Constructions and Canonicity* (with M. Lynne Murphy, Carita Paradis, and Caroline Willners, 2015).

Jill Koyama is Associate Professor in the College of Education, at the University of Arizona, Tucson, AZ, USA. She is the co-editor (with Mathangi Subramanian) of *US Education in a World of Migration: Implications for Policy and Practice* (Routledge, 2014). Her most recent research focuses on the ways in which accessing a variety of social, medical, and legal services impacts the educational opportunities for refugees in the USA.

Gerbert Kraaykamp is Professor of Empirical Sociology, at Radboud University, Nijmegen, The Netherlands. He has published articles in a variety of journals on educational issues, inequality in health and well-being, and on cultural consumption.

He Li works in the School of Foreign Languages, at Renmin University of China, Beijing, China. She engages in empirical investigation with a social justice agenda, and is also strongly interested in social theories. She has a PhD from the Faculty of Education, University of Cambridge, UK, where her thesis was entitled 'Educational trajectories of rural students in an elite University: English learning experience and beyond', and explored issues of rural education in transitional China.

Yaojun Li is Professor of Sociology, and is based in the Cathie Marsh Institute of Social Research, at the University of Manchester, UK. Her research focuses on social mobility, social capital, and ethnic integration in Britain, China, the USA, Australia, and Qatar. She has published articles in journals such as *International Review of Social Research*, *Comparative Social Research*, *Social Inclusion*, and the *British Journal of Sociology of Education*.

Nic Lightfoot is Principal Lecturer in the Department of Education, Childhood and Inclusion, at Sheffield Hallam University, UK. His current group leader role involves supporting staff delivering Education Studies, Foundation Degree, BA Top Up in Education, and Learning Support, as well as staff from The Autism Centre. He has published articles in journals such as the *Journal of Social Science* and *Education Policy in a Comparative Perspective*.

Ye Liu is a Lecturer of International Education and Development, at Bath Spa University, UK. Her research is primarily focused on the role of education in shaping a transitional society with regard to social inequality, life chances, social mobility, and social harmony. Her analysis has paid particular attention to contextual causes and consequences of shifting socio-political circumstances in the People's Republic of China and how they shape the life chances and life courses of various social groups.

Anna Mountford-Zimdars is a Lecturer in Higher Education, at King's College, London, UK. She teaches and researches topics in higher education policy, especially concerning fairness in access to elite education and employment. Her completed projects have included a study of admissions and degree performance at the University of Oxford; a study of fair entry to the legal Bar of England and Wales; and an analysis of continuities and changes in attitudes to higher education among the British public.

Diane Reay grew up in a working class, coal mining community before becoming an inner city primary school teacher for 20 years. She is now Professor of Education at the University of Cambridge, UK, with particular interests in social justice issues in education, Pierre Bourdieu's social theory, and cultural analyses of social class. She has researched extensively in the areas of social class, gender and ethnicity across primary, secondary and post-compulsory stages of education. Her most recent book (with Gill Crozier and David James) is *White Middle Class Identities and Urban Schooling* (2011). She is currently writing a book on *Education and the Working Classes in the 21st Century*. As well as being an executive editor of the *British Journal of Sociology* *of Education*, she is on the editorial boards of the *Journal of Education Policy* and *Cultural Sociology*.

Nicola Rollock is Senior Lecturer in the School of Education, and Deputy Director of the Centre for Research in Race and Education, at the University of Birmingham, UK. She is interested in practices that enable and challenge the continued manifestation of race inequity in contemporary societies. Understanding the role of privilege and power which are often overlooked in race debates is a key aspect of her work. She is especially interested in the ways in which racially minoritised groups survive, strategise, and work to create legitimate, meaningful modes of existence, belonging and notions of self within mainly white spaces. She is the co-author of *The Colour of Class: The Educational Strategies of the Black Middle Classes* (with David Gillborn, Carol Vincent, and Stephen J. Ball, Routledge, 2015).

Robin Simmons is Professor of Education, at the University of Huddersfield, UK. His teaching and research interests include education policy, the political economy of education, and education and social justice. He has acted as principal investigator and co-investigator on a range of significant research projects, and is interested in using critical policy analysis and ethnography to examine the lived experience of teachers, learners, guidance workers, and other practitioners, particularly those working with young people on the margins of education and the labour market. He is the author of *NEET Young People and Training for Work: Learning of the Margins* (2011) and *Education, Work and Social Change: Young People and Marginalization in Post-industrial Britain* (2014).

I Lin Sin is based in the School of Social and Political Science, at the University of Edinburgh, UK, receiving a PhD from the same institution after defending the thesis, 'Cultural Capital and Distinction: Malaysian Students and Recent Graduates of UK International Tertiary Education'.

Alice Sullivan is Professor in the Department of Quantitative Social Science, at the Institute of Education, University College London, UK. Her research focuses on social and educational inequalities in the life course, making extensive use of secondary data analysis of large-scale longitudinal data sets, with a particular focus on the British birth cohort studies of 1958, 1970 and 2000.

Ron Thompson is Head of the Division of Lifelong Learning in the School of Education and Professional Development, at the University of Huddersfield, UK. His current research interests lie in two main areas: social class and educational inequality, and teacher education for the lifelong learning sector. These two interests are united by the persistent undervaluing of vocational education in the UK, and associated perceptions of the further education sector in England as largely for 'other people's children'.

Jochem Tolsma is Assistant Professor in the Department of Sociology, at Radboud University, Nijmegen, The Netherlands. His fields of interest include ethnic hostility, ethnic educational differentials, and criminology.

Carol Vincent is Professor of Education, at the Institute of Education, University College London, UK. She has written and researched extensively on families' relationships with educational institutions, and, in particular, how these are shaped by race and class. She co-authored The *Colour of Class* (2015) which explores the educational strategies of

NOTES ON CONTRIBUTORS

Black Caribbean-origin middle classes. Other research interests include parenting, especially mothering, education policy, and 'super-diversity'. Her current ESRC project focuses on 'Children and Adults' Friendships across Social Class and Ethnic Difference'.

Richard Waller is Associate Professor of Sociology of Education, at the University of the West of England, Bristol, UK. His research interests include post-compulsory education, student experiences, social class, gender, and adult education teacher training. He has published articles in journals such as the *Journal of Further and Higher Education*, the *British Journal of Sociology of Education*, and the *Journal of Education and Work*.

Lois Weis is a Distinguished Professor of Educational Leadership and Policy, at the State University of New York at Buffalo, NY, USA. She is the author of *Class Reunion: The Remaking of the American White Working Class* (Routledge, 2004), and *Working Method: Research and Social Justice* (with Michelle Fine, Routledge, 2004). She is Past President of the American Educational Studies Association.

Maarten H.J. Wolbers is Head of Educational Research, at the Institute for Applied Social Sciences, Radboud University, Nijmegen, The Netherlands. He has published articles in journals such as *Research in Social Satisfaction and Mobility*, *Economic and Industrial Democracy*, and *School Effectiveness and School Improvement*.

Dedication

In memory of A.H. Halsey (1923–2014) who played a major role in establishing the sociology of education in Britain and beyond.

INTRODUCTION
Education and social mobility

The study of education and social mobility has been a key area of sociological research since the 1950s. The importance of this research derives from the systematic analysis of functionalist theories of industrialism. Functionalist theories assume that the complementary demands of efficiency and justice result in more 'meritocratic' societies, characterized by high rates of social mobility. Much of the sociological evidence has cast doubt on this optimistic, if not utopian, claim that reform of the education system could eliminate the influence of class, gender and ethnicity on academic performance and occupational destinations.

Today, the sociological study of social mobility could be characterised as an established or 'mature' field of investigation. There are well established ways of defining intergenerational social mobility, often associated with the contribution of Goldthorpe, Halsey and colleagues at Nuffield College, Oxford. The distinction between *absolute* and *relative* intergenerational mobility, has been developed to explain why social mobility since World War II is primarily attributable to changes in occupational (class) structure rather than being the result of increasing equality of opportunity. In other words, it has been the growth in technical, managerial and professional occupations, along with the decline in elementary jobs in agriculture and manufacturing, which account for the historical pattern of intergenerational social mobility.

This field of sociological inquiry also enjoys an established methodology. There have been detailed attempts to define social class in terms of employment relations – a necessary precursor to the study of both family class origins and occupational destinations. Advances in statistical techniques enable sophisticated analyses, including comparative research, which have taken the study of social mobility to new levels of complexity and insight. However, the significant accomplishments of sociological research in this field raise a number of issues relevant to this Special Issue.

Firstly, the transformation of education, work and the labour market, in both developed and emerging economies is having profound consequences for our understanding of the (re)production of life-chances. Therefore, to what extent are existing theories of education and social mobility fit for purpose in a rapidly changing world? What does the latest empirical evidence reveal about national and international patterns of mobility? The enduring significance of social class is established, but what role do gender, ethnicity and race play and how do we understand their intersection with social class?

Secondly, research in the sociology of education has played a marginal role in respect to advances in the sociological study of social mobility. Where there has been an interest in education it has focused on class differences in education attainment in mediating the relationship between origins and destinations. The mass of research on student identities, aspirations and experiences of school, college and university has been overlooked, partly because it is primarily based on qualitative rather than quantitative methods of data collection. While this points to a weakness in mainstream mobility studies it also points to a failure of the sociology of education to engage in broader debates around intergenerational mobility, notwithstanding its engagement with wider debates on social inequalities and social justice. It also raises questions as to whether the next generation of education researchers will have the training in quantitative methods and techniques to engage in future mobility debates.

The Editors of this Special Issue have been greatly encouraged by the level of interest from potential contributors and by that fact that the call attracted enough high quality articles to justify a double-issue. We were also delighted to include an article by A.H. Halsey, Emeritus Professor at Nuffield College, Oxford. A.H. Halsey was a key advisor to the Labour government during the post-war period and gave the Reith Lectures on 'Change in British Society' (1978). He is widely known to the readers of this Journal as a key figure in shaping the sociology of education in Britain. He maintained a keen awareness of the need to tackle wider social inequalities, whilst emphasizing the potential of education to transform the relationship between origins and destinations, arguing that education 'remains a friend of those who seek a more efficient, more open, and more just society'.

This judgement on the role of education is not only informed by sociological evidence but by Halsey's own biography. His article in this volume, testifies to the extraordinary period of educational, social and economic change since his birth in 1923. He acknowledges that his family history was not typical of the working classes in the 1950s and 1960s. He also points to the importance of a scholarship and experiences in the RAF during World War II in determining his fate. He came to realize that recruits from private schools, who often talked about return to study in Oxbridge after the war, were no smarter that he was. The inclusion of these personal reflections in this volume, show the importance of both quantitative and qualitative methods in understanding education and social mobility, past and present. In his conclusion, Halsey turns to the ideals of the ethical socialist R.H. Tawney, as a consistent reminder that social justice can not be reduced to measuring the relative life-chances of people from different class backgrounds entering professional or managerial positions. There is much more to 'fairness' than social mobility.

Tawney's insights also inform the personal reflections of Diane Reay. In a similar vein to Halsey, she includes the follow quotation from Tawney, '...individual happiness does not only require that men [sic] should be free to rise to new positions of comfort and distinction; it also requires that they should be able to lead a life of dignity and culture, whether they rise or not.' Reay offers a commentary on recent accounts of education and social mobility, arguing that they obscure wider questions of educational purpose and social justice. Despite the differences in generation and gender which separate Reay and Halsey, both came from working class backgrounds to become Oxbridge professors.

While these articles draw on personal reflections the article by Brown offers an analytical account of education and its relationship to social mobility. Brown claims that much of today's policy rhetoric has ignored the lessons of sociological evidence. This consistently shows that intergenerational social mobility is not the result of a more meritocratic society but of changes in the occupational structure contributing to a growing middle class. However, he also argues that the current sociological agenda needs to be extended in order to account for the fact that the lives of many students and job seekers are not characterized by social mobility but greater social congestion, as they struggle to match the promise of the opportunity bargain to labour market realities.

The 'application frenzy' to which social congestion in the job market has given rise, is developed in the article by Weis and Cipollone. Drawing on ethnographic research with affluent and elite students in U.S. secondary schools, they examine the 'class work' now required to stay ahead of the crowd. Although this involves considerable time, effort and resources it makes it more difficult for those from less privileged backgrounds to stay in the competition, given a lack of material and cultural assets that reinforce social class differences in educational outcomes.

The article by Bathmaker, Ingram and Waller, complements this account through an examination of class differences in capital mobilization and acquisition by students and their families to enhance their prospects in the graduate labour market. Through an innovative research design which matches 'paired peers' from high and low ranking universities within the same city, they offer an intriguing account of how the 'class work' cited in Weis and Cipollone's study plays out in English higher education, in ways that compound rather than alleviate social inequalities.

Thompson and Simmons also investigate the intensification of positional competition within educational systems, drawing on the work of Boudon and his model of social opportunity. This focus on Boudon's contribution is particularly timely given the dominant position of Bourdieu within the sociology of education today (his contemporary in Paris). Boudon offered an early explanation of why educational expansion was unlikely to lead to higher rates of social mobility. Based on an analysis of post-compulsory education in England they conclude that Boudon's ideas are of considerable value in assessing the impact of educational reforms on wider social opportunities.

Boudon's contribution to the study of education and social mobility demonstrates the importance of quantitative methodologies noted above. The article by Devine and Li presents statistical data on the changing relationship between origins, education and destinations in the 1990s and 2000s. They highlight some of the complexities of assessing the hypothesis of merit-selection discussed in a number of articles in this Special Issue. Despite current concerns about declining rates of intergenerational social mobility, they find some evidence of a weakening relationship between family origins and educational performance (measured by academic attainment) for both women and men. They also find a weakening relationship between family origins and occupational destinations, again offering some support to the hypothesis of merit-selection. However, they argue that the role of qualifications in determining occupational outcomes has not strengthened as hypothesized by merit-selection, suggesting that other factors such as social networks play a key role in determining labour market outcomes in a context of mass higher education.

Mountford-Zimdars, Jones, Sullivan and Heath present evidence from the British Social Attitudes Survey since 1983, to assess how people perceive the changing role of higher education and its relationship to social mobility. They discuss the changing policy context within higher education, highlighting a greater emphasis on the private, rather than public, benefits of going to university – an important justification for the introduction of a 'user pays' model of funding. Drawing on questions such as, 'How important is it for working class people to go to university?' and 'Do you think that students leaving university have better or worse job prospects nowadays than they had 10 years ago?' they found that the negative media headlines concerning the 'value' of higher education, had not resulted in a negative shift in social attitudes. People continue to recognize the individual value of higher education and its public worth. They also found some evidence of people becoming more worried about the state of the graduate labour market.

In examining the perceived value of a university education and its relationship to future life-chances, the next three articles present qualitative evidence that draw on Bourdieu's conceptual framework based on habitus, cultural capital and field. Byrom and Lightfoot offer an account of how students from working class backgrounds respond to failing course modules and whether this leads them to re-think their career plans. Despite lacking the cultural capital associated with middle class academic achievement, Byrom and Lightfoot found high levels of resilience towards completing their respective courses. They also found that family members played an important role in encouraging those they interviewed to keep going in their pursuit of an academic degree and better future.

He Li adopts a similar conceptual approach to investigate how academic 'stars' from rural neighbourhoods in China, experienced the transition to an elite university in a major metropolitan district. Based on a detailed qualitative analysis, He Li reveals how the habitus that had contributed to educational success in rural China, led to feelings of alienation and anomie as rural students struggle to cope with prejudice and material disadvantage whilst studying alongside urban elites. This article raises interesting questions concerning the applicability of 'western' class analyses to the urban-rural divide in China. How these matters are conceptualized equally raise important issues for understanding education and social mobility, as this article shows that despite the rural exodus to the cities, those originating in the countryside continue to experience prejudice and inequalities within education and the labour market.

The importance of Bourdieu's appeal within the sociology of education is again revealed in I Lin Sin's ethnographic study of Malaysian middle class students and the use of foreign education to enhance their occupational prospects. A distinction is drawn between 'foreign' and 'local' cultural capital to capture the complexities involved in using Bourdieu's conceptual framework when engaged in comparative analyses. The article suggests that Bourdieu's concept of cultural capital needs to be extended to take account of education in different social and geographical contexts, especially in the conversion of cultural capital into economic and social advantage.

The question of origins and its relationship to educational performance is the focus of Ye Liu's quantitative study of the Gaokao (National College Entrance Examinations) in China. The article shows how the Chinese government has placed considerable emphasis on the Gaokao as an expression of the country's commitment to meritocratic competition. A survey of almost 1000 university students in two Chinese provinces did not reveal a 'strong socioeconomic selection' but the importance of parental education, as those with parents in professional occupations scored highly. The study is also consistent with He Li's study given that 'the Gaokao punishes those from rural areas for lacking equal educational opportunities and resources at the school stage, and justifies their inferior status with demonstrable outcomes in the examinations.'

Sociological research aimed at understanding the intergeneration transmission of inequalities rarely focus on field of study or the school curriculum. Kraaykamp, Tolsma and Wolbers present a quantitative analysis of intergenerational transmission of educational inequalities in the Netherlands, based on survey data between 1992–2009. They extend existing studies of social class backgrounds by investigating parental 'field of study' and what impact this has on the subject choices of their offspring. The authors suggest that while there has been an increasing tendency for men to follow 'economic' specialisms, women are opting for medical, economic and sociocultural fields of study. However, they also contend that the intergeneration transmission within specific high status fields of study has become more important within a mass system of higher education. This may also reflect differences in labour market structure between the Netherlands, which has an 'occupational' labour market as opposed to the 'flexible' labour markets found in Britain and the United States.

The article by Iannelli contributes to this line of inquiry by seeking to assess the role of curricular content on patterns of social mobility. Drawing on the British National Child Development Study, Iannelli examines subjects studied in secondary education and occupational destinations. It is shown that studying high status subjects is particularly important for gaining access to a high ranked university, enhancing opportunities within the graduate labour market. It is also claimed that most of the advantages associated with a selective school education are accounted for by the curriculum studied. This invites further research on the hierarchy of school knowledge as manifest in the organization of the curriculum and its subsequent impact on access to higher education. It also raises questions about the signifiers of cultural capital and their impact on patterns of social mobility.

The next two articles shift the focus back to ethnographic studies of ethnicity, race and the education of refugees. Vincent, Ball, Rollock and Gillborn present the findings of their study of middle class Black Caribbean families. They examine family histories that typically involved migration from the Carribean in the 1950s and 1960s. Interviews with second generation parents highlight the importance of education to their own social mobility but also its role in securing middle class status for their children, as they still perceived their families' social standing to be insecure. This not only reflects current labour market conditions but 'the racism that still exists in education and employment, albeit manifesting itself now in more subtle, but still insidious, ways.' In conclusion, they argue that race cannot be 'added on' to class analysis because it changes how class works, how it is experienced, and how it impacts on social identities.

The article by Koyama highlights the new realities of transnational movements of people that present a challenge to existing theories of education and social mobility based on 'methodological nationalism'. Koyama examines the experiences of a small sample of refugees in the United States to argue that the usual ways of measuring social mobility are less applicable as some of those entering the United States are highly educated but underemployed because their academic and professional qualifications are not recognised or valued in the US labour market. She points to issues of language proficiency, initial job placement, access to networks, and entrepreneurial activity, as possible indicators of social mobility for refugees. She concludes that the personal struggles of these refugees to make their way in the world may appear to fit the trajectory associated with the American Dream but that this misses the precarious realities of life of many refugees and their families.

Finally, the editors would like to note that the articles in this Special Issue were not commissioned and are not intended to constitute the state of the field. But they do offer an insight into the range of ideas, theories and research evidence that exists with the sociology of education. They also tell a more complicated and nuanced story about the role of education in social mobility to that espoused by the current Secretary of State for Education, Michael Gove, who takes the view that reforming the school curriculum and lifting aspirations will help achieve a fully meritocratic system, as 'bright' children from disadvantaged backgrounds succeed academically and secure well paid positions in the labour market.

The purpose of this Special Issue is to generate debate both within mainstream sociology (if such a thing exists) and the sociology of education, at the same time as recognising the invaluable contributions of other cognate disciplines within the social sciences. What this double-issue of the Journal demonstrates is the continuing importance for the sociology of education to take a leading role in researching education and social mobility, a task which in many respects began with the work of A.H. Halsey.

Phillip Brown, Diane Reay and Carol Vincent

Reflections on education and social mobility

A.H. Halsey

Nuffield College, University of Oxford, Oxford, UK

This article is a brief personal reflection on the state of research into the relation between education and social mobility. Quantitative methods are both essential and advancing in this field. Sociologists seek scientific solutions but achieve ethical neutrality only with difficulty because all are tempted to bias from social and political background. I commend the political arithmetic tradition but summarise possible sources of distortion in my own biography. Finally I go beyond the boundaries of scientific social science to advocate social policies which might result in a fairer and more equal society.

Introduction

The Nature/Nurture controversy has always lain at the heart of the study of mankind. The social sciences and the life sciences have remained in collaborative and competing search for its solution. Both have made advances since Darwin and in the process have developed disciplines such as sociology and biology, fragmented into sub-disciplines occupying an ever enlarging space in the academic territory of the modern universities.

My task in this article, while acknowledging the wider developing context, is to reflect on education and social mobility as one of the major research consequences. A complete review of the research ramifications of the relation between these two social features is beyond the scope of a short essay. What I can do, however, is to comment on my personal experience of that relation in a long career in sociology and an even longer life in British society.

Method

Everyone is prejudiced by both genetic inheritance and environmental circumstance. I am no exception, although I was brought up, especially at the London School of Economics, in the tradition of so-called 'political arithmetic', which seeks truth by empirical methods in the service of passionate issues of social policy – a tradition fostered by Max Weber in Germany, Emile Durkheim in France, Vilfredo Pareto in Italy and Richard Tawney in Britain. My interest in sociology has, in part, been focused on education and social mobility – a great social issue that is amenable to 'arithmetic' analysis but is also liable to be inflamed by deeply moral and political passions. Sociology, perhaps especially in this context, is threatened by ideological intrusion into its neutral scientific aspirations. Words such as social exclusion, meritocracy or phrases like 'the pool of ability' have ideological overtones. Even the seemingly innocent and practically usable statistical model of 'perfect' mobility may be morally suspect (as stated by Adam Swift).[1] In order to provide an objective framework of measurement it assumes random mobility and labels that condition as perfect. Some moralists would object on the grounds that such a 'perfect' condition of society would entail the disappearance of the family – a widely valued and, some would argue, indispensible institution.

To generalise, sociology only attains ethical neutrality with great difficulty. We must always attempt to do so while claiming to be a science. To particularise, in this article I try to use sociology as a science but also go beyond scientific sociology into advocacy of a social policy. Consequently I also draw attention to the various possible sources of bias in my personal history.

Education is normally thought of as formal schooling; social mobility is assumed to be climbing up some kind of fixed social ladder of income or style of life. Neither of these notions is sufficiently exact for serious scientific analysis. Sociologists might now be expected to follow Max Weber in distinguishing between class, status and power and in recognising that all social institutions offer education – the family, the street, the gang, the pub, the television, and so on, in one complicated interacting set of influences.

Moreover, social mobility as an object of study depends on datasets that, although they have multiplied in my lifetime, still have to be analysed in terms of the threefold distinction between period, age, and cohort effects that are now also widely recognised to be imprecise, overlapping and interactive. These methodological difficulties continue to beset sociological enquiry so that scepticism seems to me to be warranted in the face of any assertion of movement up or down in any country, any period and within or between any cohorts or generations.[2] This is not to deny that the class structure of the United Kingdom has changed or that education has been reconstructed, especially since World War II. Indeed, these changes only serve to make analysis more difficult.

The determinants of education and social mobility are now widely recognised to be the outcome of extremely complicated interactions between and within genetic inheritance and cultural evolution. My own inheritance and life history illustrate some of the intricacies of these interactions.

At the London School of Economics it was taken for granted that any undergraduate in the social sciences had to be taught at least the elements of statistics. So no-one should be surprised that my PhD in 1954 included a simple regression analysis of the varying rates of selection for grammar schools at the 11+ among primary schools in South West Hertfordshire. Yet few, if any, British sociologists had hitherto used such methods. Quantitative work is, in my view, essential to making advances in social science. It is especially so in studies of social mobility. In 1958 I published an article under the title 'Genetics, Social Structure and Intelligence' in the *British Journal of Sociology* and was astonished to be asked by the editor to explain the meaning of 'p' where I had used the Hardy–Weinberg formula and difference equations to explore class differences in the inheritance of intelligence.

Conflicts between advocates of quantitative and qualitative methods still rage in sociology. I can claim to be among the pioneer supporters of quantitative methods but also to have been friendly towards qualitative work. Nevertheless, the neglect of statistical training still seems to me to be a barrier, not only to sociological understanding but also to the supply of competent teachers of the subject.

Personal career

I was born in Kentish Town in 1923. As a family we were temporarily welfare dependants or 'on the parish' as my Cockney mother would have said in those far-off days ... Although still perhaps the leading imperial and industrial nation, Britain was also poverty stricken, rigidly stratified and socially rather than politically organised in its schooling, housing and welfare provision. My father was a railway porter on the London, Midland and Scottish Railway (LMS) but ill from his First War wounds. In 1926 the LMS sent him back to the country to work and regain his health as a porter-signalman at one of its whistle-stops in Rutland. All these personal and familial facts have been elaborated in my autobiography and in a book entitled *Changing Childhood*.[3] These reflections draw briefly on both these books. I am now 90 years of age and have spent the last 50 years as a fellow of Nuffield College, Oxford and an emeritus professor of the university.

My own career is largely explained by four factors. First was the 11+ examination, which made a tiny bottleneck of educational opportunity for working-class children to escape from elementary education into grammar schools and thereby to be released from the manual labour to which the great majority of their peers were fated. Second was the local Rowlett Scholarship, which paid for the required cap and blazer and the travel expenses. But third, and in the circumstances crucial, was the War, in which

I unlearned the attitude to university as 'not for the likes of us' by noticing that some of my fellow cadets in pilot training who had come from independent schools were a lot slower than I was in learning the theory of flight and yet were already planning to go on to one Oxford or Cambridge College or another after the War. I therefore resolved to take the entrance examination to the London School of Economics. The London School of Economics experience was the fourth factor. It launched me into a career in academia.

The Halseys had lived for centuries in Hertfordshire until my great grandfather had run away from the Halsey estate, leaving shepherding to take up a pick and shovel with the navvies and dig his way through Primrose Hill into St Pancras. He became a foreman platelayer in the 1860s and settled in Kentish Town. For the rest of the nineteenth century and until the end of the First World War, a tribal expansion of Halseys took place in that district. For the country as a whole the 1920s were an unprecedented low point in fertility, not to be reached again until after the baby boom following the Second World War. But not for my mother and father. They were firmly placed in the perverse tail of the distribution that still dogged the fortunes of the manual labourers and placed fertility in inverse relation to family income – the lunatic system of the nineteenth century. Much later, during the Second World War, I was on leave from the RAF when my mother picked up a plain brown envelope of birth control propaganda that came through the letter box. 'No use flying in the face of nature', she said, and threw it away with a wry smile, a dismissive sniff, and her characteristic flick of the thumb across her second and first fingers. She had recently been brought to bed with Anne, her eighth child (one, a boy, lived only for a few hours). Her husband had died soon after Anne's birth, from wounds going back to the First World War.

The basic reason for our migration out of London and back to the countryside was that my father was ill from having been gassed in the First War. He came back to London in 1919 to join his father's firm (another typical feature of working-class as well as middle-class life in those days) – the LMS. In late Victorian and Edwardian times, Kentish Town was full of railway servants and full of 'Halseys' too. They spread out into the streets described by Gillian Tindall (*The Fields Beneath*) north of King's Cross and St Pancras Stations. Grandpa was a famous 'aristocrat of labour' – an express train driver who held the Thames-Forth record for years. My father had distinguished himself as an early winner of the scholarship (to St Pancras Grammar School). His brother Bob had then won the LMS medal for loading with his hands after breaking his shovel in one of the many attempts on the speed record. Still later my brother John played football for England as a schoolboy and went on to the Arsenal squad.

None of all this matters except that I thereby acquired a particular form of family pride. It was not exactly what Karl Kautsky had in mind when he wrote of 'the proletarian clad in the pride of his class'. I doubt whether proletarian pride existed in the 1920s in Britain in that sense. I mean rather that there was plenty to talk about in our council-house kitchen, plenty of family folklore. For example, it used to be said that Grandpa once came through Bedford station so fast (there was an incline for some miles between Bedford and Luton) that he swept all the books and magazines from W.H. Smith's stall. And it is characteristic that John was persuaded by our mother to come back from Arsenal to finish his apprenticeship as a carpenter so as to be secure for the whole of his life rather than be famous for 15 minutes.

My memories are of a wholly manual inheritance: of hordes of skilled uncles and, of course, of aunts in aprons. The definition of a man was that he could mend anything, raise crops, and provide for his family while his wife was a wizard of cooking and childcare. The description from ancient Jewish sources in the Old Testament (Proverbs 31:10–31) was true of the woman and wildly untrue of the man. On Christmas day morning 1931 the uncles and my father took me to Highbury for a match against Preston North End. Most of them had had something to drink. The terrace crowd was thick. A man from outside the family was drunk and had begun to use sexual oaths. My uncle Bert told him that if he did not clean his mouth he would clean it for him: 'Can't you see that there is a woman over there?' She was just visible but outside of earshot. Nevertheless the drunkard did shut up: and we boys were taken down to the boy's pen, not to protect our innocence but to give us a fair sight of the game.

In any case, pride was severely modified by the culture of respectability that I have just illustrated and which led so many to Methodism and nonconformity. The same culture also fostered pride in the institutions of their own creation such as the trade union, the cooperative society, and above all the Labour Party: but also such strictly local associations as the football club, the parish church, the pub, the Christmas club, and the children's cinema club. So we children absorbed a complex set of values favouring both cohesion and conflict, cooperation and competition, equality and excellence.

Our return to the countryside was of great material importance. We were on average two or three inches taller and half a stone heavier than our Cockney cousins. Richard Hoggart, the urban northerner, seems to have suffered horribly in Hunslet from the fear of failure of the food supply. We had no such dread. My father gardened assiduously behind the council house and his allotment; the woods and fields were ours for foraging. The male children were regularly sent out with their go-carts to fetch sticks and, apart from 'stickin'', there were regular seasonal outings to bring in mushrooms and blackberries as well as irregular raids on the swedes and apples grown on local farms. We were, moreover, allied to the poaching faction of the village. Rabbits galore as well as pheasant and partridge and venison and hare were often delivered to the back door, and our mother soon learned all the relevant culinary arts; indeed she had already learnt them at one of the posh

EDUCATION AND SOCIAL MOBILITY

houses in Hampstead where she served as a skivvy and cook's assistant after she left school at 13 and before she was married. Incidentally I was amused many years later to find that the menu at the Athenaeum was pretty much the same as our own in my mother's kitchen, including bubble and squeak on Mondays when the washing was done and the sumptuous Sunday dinner had to be fried up for final disposal.

The 1911 Census tells us about two families, one in Kentish Town and the other a few streets away in Hampstead. The first records a William Halsey, aged 15, and the other an Ada Draper, aged 10, who were later to marry and to produce a large family of which I am the oldest living survivor. Bill and Ada themselves belonged to large Cockney working-class families. Nothing much is known about their ancestors. Family legend tells us that Bill's was Norman, arriving in England with William the Conqueror's army in 1066 and settling on the Halsey estate in Hertfordshire. Ada's stock was the Irish peasantry, driven out by the potato famine of 1842 and settling among the London Irish.

Poverty and country life must be the twin themes of both Bill's and Ada's ancestry. Their childhoods are now beyond accurate capture, although my siblings and I can, from our youthful memories, put together a sketch of these two crucial forebears of the four generations that have subsequently lived. The family tree, centred on myself, is represented in Figure 1.

For my *Changing Childhood*, I interviewed 23 relations and affines. For them the end of childhood is roughly identified with leaving school and entering some form of work or further education or training. Adolescence and adulthood are therefore thought of as processes rather than stages of life. Even so the variations are dramatic. My mother, Ada, left school at age

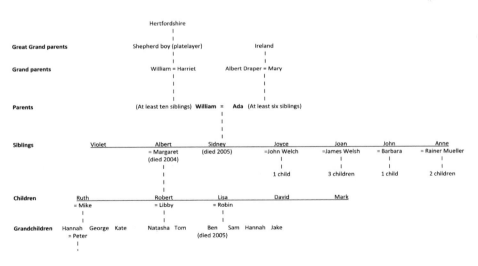

Figure 1. Halsey Family Tree in 2011.

13 for full-time domestic service. Among my siblings, Vi and Sid left school at age 14 for jobs in a factory or a farm while Joyce went on to university and teacher training until she was 21.

There, in terms of class and social status, is perhaps the essential turning point. Joyce and myself in Generation 1 were the first to clear the traditional barrier to working-class ambition – the aspiration to rise to the top of the class but to see the university as 'not for the likes of us'. In her case, teaching had already become a possible career for bright working-class girls. In my case it was the experience of the wartime RAF that changed my outlook. For both of us the barrier was removed only by the provision of public funding. For my younger siblings, Joan, John and Anne, apprenticeships to nursing or carpentry led to middle-class status through emigration. Later, for Generation 2 the exception of higher education became the rule, and for Generation 3 the rule became the expectation.

It is also noticeable that while education lengthened steadily through the generations, so did economic dependence. For John in Generation 1 the wage from a newspaper round gave strong feelings of proud independence. Generation 3, by contrast, looks forward with some equanimity to acquiring debt and receiving parental support before entering the labour force as graduates or postgraduates. Meantime, politically, such measures as the age of conscription and the right to vote have the opposite tendency and there is now even a demand that voting should begin at age 16. And finally, sexually, knowledge about 'the facts of life' and permitted sexual activity seem to occur earlier for the younger generations. It might be said that longer education and later earning tend to prolong childhood while politics, biology and mass communication accelerate the passage to adulthood. The Halsey story echoes these general social tendencies.

However, whatever may emerge from wider demographic enquiry, obviously *Changing Childhood* has serious limitations. It is focused on a single family, it begins and ends with an account and some inferences by myself, a single member of that family, and it covers only four generations, my parents and my grandchildren. Moreover, the method of collecting the data can easily be challenged. It could never yield a representative sample of child-rearing in the nation and far less of childhood the world over.

Yet, apart from these deficiencies and the shortcomings of the editor and his 'contributors', the book can claim some empirical interest as an attempt to give voice to the experiences of one family in the twentieth century without pretending to make any addition to the theories of a more abstract demography, sociology or psychology. Also its publication in both a spoken and a written form is rare if not unique.

Substantively the book is a family history of a branch of the Halseys from the 1920s to 2009 with a focus on childhood and with more or less detailed personal memories from myself, my siblings, my children and my grandchildren, supplemented by short essays from some of the affines who have married my siblings or my descendants. The stories begin with a few words about our antecedents, William Halsey (1896–1944) who married Ada Draper (1900–1974) in 1919. The contributors are all either descendants of this man and wife or are the spouses of their children, grandchildren or great grandchildren.

This late Victorian/Edwardian couple were born into large, Cockney, working-class families within walking distance of each other. Their family origins were in Hertfordshire and Eire. Little is known with certainty about their English or their Irish ancestry but it may safely be assumed that country life and poverty would be the dominant themes of such an account, as it would be for the vast majority of the population of Britain or indeed the world as a whole. In that sense we are dealing here with the childhood of everyman.

Nevertheless, the Halseys of the twentieth century are unusual, not so much because of their upward mobility or their fertility, nor because Generation 1 learned from their mother to see themselves as 'the best', but rather that despite being born into the working class they showed unusual intelligence and good health by comparison with their neighbours. They translated these genetic gifts into educational, occupational and social success as the century wore on and they were offered expanding opportunities through schooling, emigration[4] and, it must be added, some lucky events.

William (Bill) and Ada appear to have been remarkable individuals compared with the plebian multitude in the crowded streets of the metropolis. In any graph plotting the distribution of Edwardian Britons, they would be what statisticians neutrally call 'outlying cases'. Bill must have been an able boy to win a scholarship to St Pancras Grammar School from such a huge family (albeit fathered by a famous express train driver). He was also handicapped by war wounds, but the youthful recollections of my siblings suggest that he remained a man of high intelligence and belief in the power of education. Ada Draper must have been a child of vigour, wit and resolve. Her strength of will and character is plain from the memories of all who knew her, whether as children, grandchildren or affines. As a couple they provided a home environment and encouragement to their children that seem to have distinguished the family from other inhabitants of the council estate in which we lived. They avoided the drunkenness, fecklessness, indiscipline and dirtiness of the disreputable end of the working class. All sexual reference was expunged from their bad language. Good food, a clean house, rudimentary good manners at table, and insistence on regular attendance at school and church made up the regimen of child-rearing in the life of the respectable working class to which they belonged.

Thus they gave their children the self-confidence and the capacity to overcome the material poverty of their surroundings. Among their eight children, only one, John, seems to have had serious problems with the virtually moneyless world of their childhood. They all, including John, dealt with this problem in adult life by a combination of high earnings and left-wing politics or, as in the cases of Sidney and Violet, careful adaptation to low income. Sid, for example, after redundancy from the collapse of the Corby steelworks in the early 1980s, devoted himself to growing vegetables in his council-house garden and, his two allotments, and to relaxing with his 'lifelong mates' with dominoes and skittles in his local pub: yet he still managed to save substantial sums from his dole to leave to his family when he died in 2005. Most of the others made a comfortable living for themselves in the professions or in business in England, Canada and Germany.

So Generation 1 was already partially, if not quite wholly, transformed into a middle-class extended family, able to send its children to the universities almost as a matter of course and thereby to ease them as Generation 2 into more or less lucrative positions, as suburban home owners with safe career incomes, of a kind never dreamed of by their grandparents in Generation 0.

The transformation is partly explained by increasingly educational and opportunities, by the extension of managerial and professional jobs, and by the drop in low-paid manual work that distinguished the twentieth century, especially after World War II. Luck also played its part in the compassionate decision of the LMS to send Bill back to the countryside after World War I. But it was also due to the genetic accident of native wit and physical vigour of the two ancestors in Generation 0, who emerged from the London slums to bring up Generation 1 in habits of hard work and resolve despite their material poverty.

By 2010 Generation 0 was a dim memory and Generation 1 had largely run its course. Some older members, Violet and Sidney, were dead and the younger members were retired in England, Canada or Germany. The five living survivors were all unequivocally middle class in income and behaviour. Of course they varied in both. I am regarded as a rather reclusive academic; Joyce, the ex-headmistress, is very interested in art and literature; Joan, the retired nurse in Canada, is a steadfast Christian; John, also in Canada, is a keen athlete; and Anne, the teacher in Germany, is absorbed in family matters. All, however, are rooted in their common Northamptonshire childhood. It was a rural culture of 'belongingness' that modern life and the motor car have pretty effectively destroyed, leaving their nostalgia for the Avenue and the Village as oddly antiquated and irrelevant. Yet the childhood they had in a large and secure family, embedded in the rural community and disciplined by an expert mother and a gentle father, equipped them all to face the future. The attribute of 'belongingness' cannot be overemphasised. It remains something of a mystery and is certainly old-fashioned in the twenty-first century. It extends to patriotism but also to local loyalty and to intermediate social institutions such as schools, colleges, sports teams and places of employment. But the root of this hierarchy of attachments probably lies in the family. The Halsey family of our childhood followed working-class tradition in its habitual 'use of the prefix "our" to all our Christian names'. We talked to people outside the family in these terms but even when we spoke to each other we would say '"our Joyce, would you like a cup of tea?" or "our Ma, what's for dinner?" or "our Anne, it's time to go to school"'. A collective consciousness became second nature to all of us, originating in a poverty-stricken family but extending progressively to our village, our county, our political party, our class, our employers, our country and beyond.

I am groping here for a general causative theory as a sociologist should. But the material I have collected permits neither generalisation nor confirmation of any causative hypothesis. It can only suggest and illustrate the presently known factors at work in the special circumstances of three generations of one particular family. It certainly confirms the complexity of interactions between genetics and culture in determining social mobility

The first of these causative factors is genetic inheritance as distinct from environmental forces. Thus I can say with some confidence that Violet physically resembled her father, a Halsey, while the other siblings of Generation 1 were like the mother – genetically descended from the Drapers. My and Ruth's suggestion that the family was divided into two types of character, the Halseys and the Drapers, must be more tentative. And any suggestion of straightforward intergenerational inheritance of character from Ada to Joan and then to Ruth and on to Kate, would be very dangerous because 'character' is known to stem from the interaction of genetic inheritance with environmental circumstance. Yet, at least in my view, there are striking similarities of determination, articulation, and skill between the four women cited, although their upbringing has varied immensely. Generation 0 was raised among the Victorian and Edwardian urban proletariat. Generation 1 grew up on a rural council estate in Northamptonshire between the wars, Generation 2 came after World War II and was raised in the rich suburbs of Oxford with a likely future in the universities and professions.

There was also, however, a surrounding world of enlarging, risk-laden but above all unequal opportunity. Two black boys were adopted into Generation 2 and they, as adults, have had to face mental illness and unemployment. In childhood, David and Mark certainly suffered the racial prejudice of white North Oxford. At age 46 and 45 they are no longer firmly placed in the middle class, despite continuing to belong to what has become a secure middle-class family. David became mentally ill soon after completing his apprenticeship as a plumber, was in and out of medical care and struggling to escape from drug addiction, which started with cannabis while he was still at school. Mark left school at age 16 for a chequered series of jobs, gained no qualifications in apprenticeship or further education, and eventually left his last full-time job as a van driver for the university suffering from severe depression. These exceptions need to be explained.

Superficially the answer is simple: genetic descent. All the other members of Generation 2 became solidly middle class. The adopted sons shared the same environment. They failed to join their siblings in a university-educated professional life. So the cause must be genetic. But this argument fails. They did not in fact have the same environment as their sisters and their brother. For them, the world outside the family was very different and much more hostile. They repeatedly and at a very young age felt rejected and alien. I remember David, at age four, asking me anxiously 'when I grow up will I be red and white like you Dad?' and not being reassured by my reply that he had a most beautiful skin that was shared by millions of other boys throughout the world. No statistics can neutralise the strong desire of young children to be like all the others who enter their lives in street or school. That single fact made the environment of David and Mark a very different experience from that of their siblings. It distracted them from learning the academic subjects that might have led them into jobs. It did not stop Mark from setting new sporting records at school in various races. His physique was exceptional. But like most children, their mental capacities were quite normal, with David much more sociable and Mark much more inclined to withdraw.

This raises the questions of whether adoption was a good thing under the circumstances. When asked, however, each boy answered most emphatically that the decision to adopt them was totally justified when the alternative was to be cared for in a children's home. Neither has married but meanwhile the majority of Generation 2 has bred Generation 3 with a secure childhood as established middle-class Britons and university graduates with most of their lives before them in the twenty-first century.

Thus, I had five children. The others, unrecorded, are one to Joyce, three to Joan in Canada, one to John also in Canada, and two to Anne in Germany. All these 'foreigners' would now be called middle class, all were university graduates. Three of my own children went to British universities: Ruth to Oxford, Bob to Imperial College, London and Lisa to Birmingham. These three were brought up and remained middle class and they parented nine children as Generation 3. Ruth and Robert have brought up five of them in Lancaster. Lisa married Robin Jones and has brought up her four in Oxford where Robin is a financial advisor and she is a primary school teacher. Unhappily, their first born, Ben, was accidentally drowned in the Thames in 2005. The other three are successful pupils at the Cherwell Comprehensive School in Oxford, talented in music and sports and apparently destined to consolidate the middle-class family that the Halseys have built since Generation 0. Robert and his wife, Libby, have repeated the consolidation story with their two children. They also go to a comprehensive school at Kirby Lonsdale and are equally successful. Ruth married Mike Wright a mathematician, now holding a chair at Lancaster University. Their three children have been successful pupils at Lancaster Royal Grammar School from which they have gone on to northern universities. The first born, Hannah, is now a school teacher, married to an accountant (Peter Lamb), and living near Kendall in the Lakes. So they complete the picture of a consolidated middle-class extended family in Generation 3 and the parents of the first members of Generation 4, my great grandchildren, Faith and Joseph. Ruth's second (George) has become a journalist in Manchester and the third (Kate) a graduate midwife in Leeds.

These environmental variations cover the major part of the intergenerational as well as current conditions in England and, in some cases, in Canada and Germany. But, as already noted, genetic inheritance interacts with environment and the two combine to rule the life-chances of individuals. Thus, the effect of the genes is minimised by environmental variation, but it is not reduced to zero. The blood still counts to some uncertain extent. Our two adopted black boys demonstrate this dramatically but they also demonstrate the interaction effects.

Some further aspects of the changing environment deserve to be emphasised. These include such developments as weaker family structures, the softening of traditional attitudes towards ethnic minorities and women, the enlargement of educational opportunity begun so bravely by the Attlee government after the Second World War, emigration, immigration, and the uncertainty of Christian belief.

Of course, as the contributors to the Halsey story amply demonstrate, social class has so far been most significant among the changing environmental influences on childhood. Nevertheless the genetic occurrence of the union of Bill's intelligence to Ada's wit and rude health seems to have acted as a trigger to the subsequent history of upward mobility in Generations 1, 2 and 3. Even so, the genetic trigger was only made effective by the good fortune of LMS philanthropy along with other environmental factors including traditional Christian belief, the spacing out of a large family, the isolation of the nuclear family, contact with privately educated boys in pilot training during the War, the exceptional mixture of emancipation and subservience of women, the Rowlett Scholarship, cautious emigration to Canada, and Germany, the luck of linking to spouses in sustained marriages providing secure support to children, and so on through many happy aspects of nurture, encouraged and enlarged by the British state in the twentieth century.

It may appear that I have drawn an overly cheerful and optimistic picture of childhood in modern times. But, to repeat, this felicitous story is by no means universal. Even in Britain something like one-quarter of children are still being brought up in poverty as defined officially by the State, by international bodies like UNESCO or OECD, or by private social researchers. Moreover the statistics of teenage pregnancy, divorce and family breakdown are ominous indicators that the subjective as well as the objective conditions of childhood are widely threatened.

My great grandchildren, Faith and Joseph, and their fellow members of Generation 4 will grow up in a world of both ancient and novel problems. The ancient problem of drunkenness now takes new forms in drug abuse; the old order of discipline now takes more sophisticated expression in parental uncertainty (would my sister Anne's rhyme about 'me mother came out and gave me a clout' apply assuredly today?), and in the substitution of bribes for good behaviour in the shape of a surfeit of commercialised toys. Old selfishness persists: now it is a challenge to citizenship, an obstacle to attaining the common good. For Ada and her son John, debt was a disgrace. Now it is commonplace. Ada and John were children of poverty. My great grandchildren of Generation 4 have toys in abundance. They are children of affluence. But whether the flow of human selfishness and concern for others have changed is probably an unanswerable question. Some say that greed has increased. Others point to the enlargement of horizons of aid to Africa and the poorer parts of the world. I prefer to assume that both selfish greed and idealistic willingness to serve wider philanthropic causes are fundamentally constant. The problem is to fashion a social environment for children that maximises opportunities for altruism and minimises temptations to sin. That problem has to be seen as a moving target in public policies towards families, schools, sports, and games, learning and leisure – all the things that form the character, and predispositions of future citizens. It is a colossal challenge to all adults. Yet, as David points out, even recent racial attitudes have softened since he was a child in the 1970s.

My siblings and I grew up in a rural world of poverty and inequality. It was also a world of extraordinary security. My sisters Joan and Anne have described it lyrically, even romantically, and my sister Joyce more laconically. What they share, as does also my brother John, who is more pessimistic in his own assessment of the story of childhood, are two things from a now departed and possibly irretrievable world. These are the proud isolation and internal discipline of a large and lively family and, second, but connected, the community of a council estate and village school dominated by an Anglican Church with its cubs, brownies, scouts, guides, fetes, choir, and mission hall. These conditions, at least in Britain and Scandinavia, encouraged a collective outlook within which both the spirit of what we now call citizenship as well as the development of individual personality and personal dreams could unconsciously prosper. If those personal dreams were thwarted, as was conspicuously the case with Violet, or obstructed, as with Joan's resolve to become a nurse, or delayed, as was Anne's determination to become a teacher, or diverted, as with John's ambition to become a football superstar, there were some substantial compensations. Vi became the best loved of my siblings for her devoted care of the younger children. Sid's presents of vegetables and flowers were gratefully recognised by the neighbours, John, Joan and Anne were successful emigrants, spouses and parents. And, a precious inheritance from village childhood, Christian belief was retained by Joan and passed strongly to Ruth and Lisa in Generation 2 and Kate in Generation 3 who ignored her manifest academic talents and trained as a midwife. Even as I write she is busy on a church related trip to Tanzania, climbing Kilimanjaro and extending her midwifery training.

Looking back over the Halsey history I realise that my atavistic tendency to glorify my kin has to be watched. Moreover, there is a general tendency to exaggerate the effects of family structure. Nevertheless, I am impressed by the recorded views of the affines and particularly by the opinions of Torsten, the German son of Anne, who deliberately changed his name to Halsey. It is, by and large, a happy familial history. Yet I also know that the so-called 'Halsey spirit' is not unique. It will almost certainly die and even more certainly become diluted by our patrilineal system of passing surnames to each new generation through the male line. Women marry out and thereby cleave to other names, Lisa Halsey-Jones notwithstanding.

The language used to express either social or personal dreams of future life has changed over the generations. Belief in Christian religion and the importance of the Labour Party as means to the attainment of 'the New Jerusalem' or of 'socialism' were taken as beyond question by Generations 0 and 1. Loyalty to both Church and party has persisted in Generations 2 and 3. But both have weakened. Even in Generation 2, my son Robert identifies fairness to others as the common underlying ethic and Ruth, while remaining devoutly Anglican, married a declared atheist who was even more strongly a supporter of the Labour Party. Generation 4 may be neither Christian nor socialist but may believe just as fervently in equality for all children and public service for all adults. The language scarcely matters.

Only within the context of social policy can the Halsey tale serve as a minor guide from the irretrievable past. The story encourages the belief that childhood can be supported by public policies. Belief in the state, what Tawney always referred to as a 'servicable drudge', has declined sharply, especially since the 1980s when Thatcherism came to dominate Westminster and later Whitehall. Like most working-class people of her generation, my mother saw Lloyd George as a champion of ordinary people with a programme of social reform culminating in post-war Attleean socialism. Decency was commonly taught by parents, priests and teachers to millions of children in every generation. But it also depended on stable families, the prime agencies of collective solidarity. Together these families, churches, chapels and schools, combined to rear children as responsible adult citizens: freedom, humour and respect informed the local streets, shops, pubs and workplaces and extended to national even international government. The ends were settled: only the means were disputed. They have turned out to be much more complicated, more than ever liable to be corrupted.

The respectable working-class family that was exemplified by the Halseys of Generations 0 and 1 certainly worked: but at a high cost in imprisoning mothers and daughters in the kitchen, in the taboo on male participation in 'women's work', and in the systematic denial of educational opportunity to its children. These traditional conflicts and confinements are no longer needed. Positive social opportunities are now open to a richer country. For children, more serious investment in comprehensive schooling by well-paid and well-respected teachers, supported by moral mentors drawn from the upper forms of schools, colleges and the burgeoning 'third-age' of grandparents, and backed by generous public services for education and leisure. These are possible and affordable investments in child-rearing in a rich new society.

In any case, nothing must be allowed to dislodge the improvement of childhood from its high place in social policy. It can remain to make both government and the voluntary sector our 'serviceable drudge'.

As the oldest survivor of the departing Generation 1, I would challenge Generation 3 to complete the making of the reformed world dreamt of, striven for, but never fully realised by their ancestors.

Conclusion

We can summarise the modern history of rich countries as one of expanding education and contracting of what our grandparents would confidently call the working class. The same historical period has also seen a widespread growth of equalising opportunity to acquire both learning and power. Women, ethnic minorities and above all the lower classes have been seen as the victims of traditional inequality. In the past 50–80 years progress has been made towards equalising the chances of women and ethnic minorities. But class chances, measured in relative terms, seem to have remained stable.

After the acceptance of the Robbins Report in the 1960s the social sciences began to flourish in the expanding British universities. Nuffield College was a minor part of that expansion. At the same time, the British class system was changing towards more 'room at top' with the expansion of the salariat and the shrinkage of the working class of manual workers. Consequently there was an *absolute* rise in upward mobility, although, as our 1972 study showed, no change in *relative* rates.[5]

All over the world there is a search for educational reform towards equality of opportunity. With respect to gender and ethnicity these efforts have succeeded. With respect to class they have failed. Not everything has been done in Europe or America to establish *greater equality of condition*. I am here repeating the criticism of capitalist society that R.H. Tawney formulated in his classic books of 1921 and 1931, *The Acquisitive Society* and *Equality*.[6] Could we go further along the Tawney path?

A significant number of sociologists, including Phillip Brown at Cardiff University, Hugh Lauder at the University of Bath and Adam Swift at Oxford University, would now seek to *reduce the variability of social rewards*; for example, by returning to seriously progressive taxation of the rich and raising the level of minimum wages or extending the provision of citizen incomes. Such strategies would help to ease our endemic race towards competitive market success, reduce the widespread search by the middle and upper class for new and old defensive expenditure on education as a positional good for their children and loosen the pressure on schools and colleges from preparing the next generation for livelihood rather than living. A fair, free and contented society lies in that direction.

It is essential that the aim of social policy has to be not only to maximise gross national product but also to protect the well-being of individuals in a secure society. Herein lies the modern challenge: to social science, for a complex research programme aimed at solving the age-old problem of social inequality; and to politics, to discover the means to reach such a noble goal.

Notes

1. Swift, A. (2004) Would perfect mobility be perfect? *European Sociological Review*, 20, 1, 1–11.
2. I am impressed by an intervention written by E. Bukodi and John Goldthorpe on intergenerational mobility ("Class Origins, Education and Occupational Attainment in Britain: Secular Trends or Cohort Specific Effects?" *European Societies* 13: 345–73. Oxford University Department of Social Policy, 2011). An excellent and illuminating new analysis of birth cohort data that demonstrates the methods now available and which, *inter alia*, substantively contradicts the basis of current political panic over alleged declining intergenerational mobility. It shows that there is no evidence of change in rates of mobility (relative or absolute) among recent British birth cohorts.
3. A.H. Halsey's *No Discouragement* (Basingstoke: Macmillan, 1995) and *Changing Childhood* (Oxford: Nuffield College, 2009).
4. It seems to me that further research would show that emigration to the colonies was an important causative factor in promoting upward mobility from working-class origins among Britons in the nineteenth and twentieth centuries.
5. See A. Heath and C. Payne in A.H. Halsey & J. Webb's *Twentieth Century British Social Trends* (Basingstoke: Macmillan, 2002).
6. R.H. Tawney's *The Acquisitive Society* (London: G. Bell & Sons, 1921) and *Equality* (London: George Allen & Unwin, 1931).

Social mobility, a panacea for austere times: tales of emperors, frogs, and tadpoles

Diane Reay

Faculty of Education, University of Cambridge, Cambridge, UK

> This paper problematizes dominant discourses of social mobility. It begins by discussing social mobility from a philosophical perspective before examining current policies on social mobility in the United Kingdom, drawing on data from both recent mobility studies and the contemporary labour market. I then broaden out the discussion by exploring subjective aspects of social mobility, juxtaposing my own personal history with Jackson and Marsden's classic study 'Education and the Working Class' in order to exemplify the complexities of mobility journeys. Finally, I argue for better ways of achieving a socially just society, ones that, echoing Tawney, make a case for less distance and greater parity between social classes.

Introduction

> There's room at the top, they are telling you still/But first you must learn how to smile as you kill/If you want to live like the folks on the hill. (John Lennon)

In this paper I attempt to problematize dominant discourses of social mobility. There is a long history of problematizing social mobility, as the John Lennon lyrics above and the R.H. Tawney quotes below indicate. I begin by discussing social mobility from a philosophical perspective before examining current policies on social mobility in the United Kingdom, drawing on data from both recent mobility studies and the contemporary labour market. I then broaden out the discussion by exploring subjective aspects of social mobility, juxtaposing my own personal history with Jackson and Marsden's classic study 'Education and the Working Class' in order to exemplify the complexities of mobility journeys. Finally, I argue for better ways of achieving a socially just society, ones that, echoing Tawney, make a case for less distance and greater parity between social classes.

Taking an egalitarian perspective, I argue that whilst social mobility is increasingly seen to be a major source of social justice in contemporary society, a strong version of social justice requires much more than the movement of a few individuals up and down an increasingly inequitable social system. In order to make a case for the need to focus more on increasing equality and less on increasing social mobility, I draw on philosophical debates around social mobility, and, in particular, the insights of R.H. Tawney's political philosophy.

Tawney's egalitarian philosophy and the failure of social mobility

For Tawney social mobility was little more than the recycling of inequality. He wrote:

> Social well-being depends upon cohesion and solidarity. It implies the existence, not merely of opportunities to ascend, but of a high level of general culture, and a strong sense of common interests, and a diffusion throughout society of a conviction that civilization is not the business of an elite alone, but a common enterprise which is the concern of all. And individual happiness does not only require that men [sic] should be free to rise to new positions of comfort and distinction; it also requires that they should be able to lead a life of dignity and culture, whether they rise or not (Tawney 1964a, 108)

For Tawney, the vision of a fair and just society needed to be much bolder and brighter than one which saw social mobility as the solution. Tawney viewed a socially just society as one in which education is seen as an end in itself, a space that 'people seek out not in order that they may become something else but because they are what they are' (1964a, 78). In contrast, social mobility was 'merely converting into doctors, barristers and professors a certain number of people who would otherwise have been manual workers' (Tawney 1964b, 77), a crude means of getting ahead of others, of stealing a competitive edge.

I have gone back to Tawney because so much of what he writes about society at the beginning of the twentieth century is still strikingly relevant at the beginning of the twenty-first century. There is still a crude appetite for money and power among the few, and a reverence for success in obtaining these among the many. People still respect each other for what they own rather than what they are. He also wrote of a society saturated with inequalities that derived from the influence of a long tradition of educational inequality, and argued that as a consequence British society had become wedded to the idea that what is obtained by one class without question is only conceded to another class on proof of special capacities. Tawney did not write a lot about social mobility, he was much more interested in how Britain could become an equal society. However, in one of his few extended reflections on mobility he used the analogy of 'The Tadpole Philosophy':

> It is possible that tadpoles reconcile themselves to the inconveniences of their position, by reflecting that, though most of them will live and die as tadpoles and nothing more, the more fortunate of the species will one day shed their tails, distend their mouths and stomachs, hop nimbly onto dry land, and croak addresses to their former friends on the virtues by means of which tadpoles of character and capacity can rise to be frogs. This conception of society may be described, perhaps, as the Tadpole Philosophy, since the consolation which it offers for social evils consists in the statement that exceptional individuals can succeed in evading them. (Tawney 1964a, 105)

Tawney is writing here of the ability of a few to achieve highly within a capitalist system, as though it was some consolation for social evils that 'exceptional individuals can succeed in evading them,' and that the noblest use of their talents 'were to scramble to shore, undeterred by the thought of drowning companions' (1964a, 106). What Tawney particularly takes issue with is the individual nature of social mobility. He argues that what the middle and upper classes neither understood nor admired but often feared and despised were aspirations that found their expression not in individual advancement but ' in collective movements to narrow the space between valley and peak' (1964a, 105). Tawney viewed this as the key moral objective for 'a good society', one which encouraged and enabled collective rather than individual advancement, and the narrowing of social and economic differences (see also Wilkinson and Pickett [2009] for a modern application of Tawney's egalitarian philosophy). Social mobility, on the other hand, he viewed as neither compensating for large structural inequalities nor acting as a substitute for a more equal society.

Today, just as much as when Tawney was writing in the first half of the twentieth century, social mobility appears to be a mirage, a source of immense collective hopes and desires for those in the bottom two-thirds of society but in reality it is largely a figment of imagination brought to life in policy and political rhetoric. But it is also, as Tawney argued, a hollow justification for educational and wider social inequalities.

The contemporary landscape of social mobility in the United Kingdom

Despite the insights of Tawney and others (Parkin 1972), social mobility retains an iconic place in contemporary British political discourse. It appears as if the less mobility there is, the more it becomes a preoccupation of politicians and policy-makers (Payne 2012). In January 2010 the then Prime Minister Gordon Brown gave a speech in which he said 'Social mobility will be our focus, not instead of social justice, but because social mobility is modern social justice'. As I will argue later, this view of social mobility as a proxy or even co-terminous with social justice is part of the degradation and sidelining of social justice in contemporary British society.

Then there is Michael Gove, the current Education Secretary who told the House of Commons in December 2010: 'Social mobility went backwards under Labour, and it is the mission of this Coalition Government to reverse that melancholy and make opportunity more equal so we can become an aspiration nation once more'. I want to come back later to aspirational Britain, which I will argue is yet another problematic aspect of UK society. Finally, we have Nick Clegg who in his speech 'Putting a Premium of Fairness' spelt out three understandings of fairness – fairness in terms of equal treatment, fairness in terms of equal shares, and fairness as equal chances – before asserting that 'we need to put much greater emphasis on the third conception of fairness, namely, on fairness in terms of social mobility and life chances'. He concluded that 'social mobility is the central social policy objective for the Coalition Government'. Here social mobility is revealed yet again as a pale insipid version of social justice. As Geoff Payne concludes in his analysis of political policy documents on social mobility:

> Social mobility has been changed from an account in which it is inevitable that there will always be winners and losers – because that is built into the bones of the analysis – into bland reassurances that everyone can be winners, provided the right policies are in place. There is no room in this bright new social mobility future for the embarrassing fact of downward mobility or any need to dismantle the entrenched positions of the most advantaged classes. (Payne 2012, 15)

As all of these political speeches demonstrate, any attempt to combat growing economic inequalities has been sidelined. Redistribution is no longer on the agenda unless it is the covert (and recently not so covert redistribution from the poor to the rich). Neither equal chances nor equal opportunities are important considerations. Welcome instead to the twenty-first century version of the rat race in which social mobility operates as a very inadequate sticking plaster over the gaping wound social inequalities have become in the 2010s. Social mobility, rather than the ailments it is supposed to cure, has become the main focus of attention, a politically driven distraction that diverts our attention from the real problems that need to be addressed. Governmental insistence on its commitment to social mobility and equal opportunities clearly distracts attention from larger systemic processes that are making hierarchies steeper and opportunities more restricted. It also operates as a powerful mechanism of unconscious denial, but I shall come to naked emperors next.

In 2013 we have the much trumpeted Coalition government's social mobility strategy, while the previous Labour government oversaw the Panel for Fair Access to the Professions among other initiatives. Both have been aiming to increase mobility against a background of economic austerity, and, in the case of the Coalition government, savage public sector cuts. How can this shift from the real problem, wide and growing social inequalities, to a process that is designed to leave the unequal *status quo* totally untroubled, have happened? Social mobility has a totemic role in UK society not just figuring powerfully in the strategic policies of our political elites but also capturing the popular imaginary. But I want to argue that it represents the twenty-first-century version of the emperor with no clothes. It is not only attributed with mythical qualities, namely creating a socially just society when it is simply a means of redistributing inequality, it appears, from the evidence of a majority of contemporary research reports (Cabinet Office 2011; Causa and Johansson 2009; OECD 2010a), to be in and of itself largely a myth. However, at the same time it is an extremely generative and productive myth that does an enormous amount of work for neoliberal capitalism.

The actual level of social mobility in the United Kingdom is a contested area. There is dispute and disagreement about the extent of social mobility both within groups of sociologists and economists, and between them (Blanden, Gregg, and Macmillan 2007; Goldthorpe and Jackson 2007; Erikson and Goldthorpe 2010; Saunders 2010). In particular, women are perceived to have experienced higher levels of both absolute and relative social mobility over the last 50 years compared with men. Yet even apparently optimistic findings regarding women's greater levels of absolute and relative upward mobility in the second half of the twentieth century may be largely illusory, mainly attributable to a classification of routine service sector jobs that does not accurately reflect their pay, conditions and status (Manning and Petrongolo 2008). Also, despite the wrangling between UK academics, the OECD, since 2000, has consistently drawn on international data to make cross-national comparisons that place the United Kingdom either at or very near the bottom of social mobility league tables (Causa and Johansson 2009; OECD 2010b). Research has found that in the United Kingdom 50% of children can expect to find themselves in the same class position as their parents while the comparable figure for the Nordic countries and Canada is less than 20% (OECD 2010b; Trades Union Congress 2010).

Despite the low levels of mobility in the United Kingdom relative to a majority of OECD countries (OECD 2010b) the idea of social mobility has become pivotal in the legitimation of British society. The promise of mobility allows capitalist societies like the United Kingdom to maintain a system of firmly entrenched inequalities. In direct contradiction to Gordon Brown's assertion that social mobility is equivalent to social justice, it is a key justification for social inequalities, a crucial lynchpin in neoliberal ideology. Frank Parkin's assertion made over 40 years ago is just as true today:

Elevation into the middle class represents a personal solution to the problems of low status, and as such tends to weaken collectivist efforts to improve the lot of the underclass. (Parkin 1972, 50)

Britain in the 2010s is more unequal than Britain in the 1970s. And social mobility becomes even more important symbolically as inequalities worsen in societies. In deeply unequal societies such as the United Kingdom and the United States it operates as an effective form of symbolic violence, as a justification for growing levels of inequality. In the 2010s a majority of British people acquiesce in sharp distinctions of wealth and power on the basis that as individuals they are free to scale the heights.

Fairy tales and socially mobile princesses

I want to briefly take the example of the Royal Wedding of 2011 as an example of the symbolic power of mobility myths. In April 2011 I gave over 10 interviews to international and British media. All wanted me to comment on 'the rags to royalty' tale that was the Middleton family. They were all obsessed with Kate Middleton's (now the Duchess of Cambridge) maternal antecedents. I tried to point out that it had taken five generations for Kate's mother, Carole's family to move from coal mining stock to millionaire, Malborough-educated princess, but what everyone wanted was the fairy-tale myth – a glittering fantasy of social mobility. So France24 reported 'Descended from coal miners, the family of royal bride-to-be Kate Middleton is a shining example of social mobility' while Korean News celebrated 'Kate Middleton is Cinderella come to life'. As the *Financial Times* chimed:

> It has it all: love, pageantry and palaces; as every fairy tale should. When Kate Middleton and Prince William exchange their marriage vows on Friday in Westminster Abbey's gothic golden arcade, watched by lords and ladies, hailed by crowds from Buckingham Palace to Admiralty Arch, it will be proof that fairy tales can come true. Not just for the royal bride, whose nickname at school was reportedly 'princess in waiting' due to her crush on Prince William. But also for those who see the union between a royal and a 'commoner', descended from a miner in the north-east England, as a glorious symbol of social mobility – testimony that the rise from colliery to castle is no myth. (Timmins and Jacobs 2011)

Only much further down in all these articles, if at all, are we told that the Middleton parents are millionaires who sent their children to Marlborough, one of Britain's top public schools.

In the days when education was about knowing your place in society, religion used to be the opium of the masses. Now that education has been reinvented as an aspirational project for the self, social mobility has taken its place and we are all supposed to aspire to becoming doctors and lawyers, or even princesses, footballers, celebrities and billionaire entrepreneurs. In the aspirational society that Britain has become, there is intense competition for the fair chances Nick Clegg spoke of. And what all the research shows is that middle-class and upper-class parents heavily invest and constantly strategize to ensure that their children have a better chance of a fair chance than other people's children (Reay, Crozier, and James 2011). As Weis and her colleagues argue in this issue, the middle/upper-middle classes are engaged:

> in a very specific form of 'class warfare,' one in which the middle/upper-middle class individually and collectively mobilizes its embodied cultural, social, and economic capital both to preserve itself in uncertain economic times while simultaneously attempting to instantiate a distinctly professional and managerial upper-middle class through access to particular kinds of postsecondary destinations in a now national and increasingly competitive marketplace for postsecondary education. (Weis and Cipollone 2013, this issue)

I would argue that such informed and resourced 'class warfare' leaves precious little room at the top for working-class upward mobility. However, the orthodoxy is that the working classes do not need increased levels of economic and social capital as long as they develop sufficient dominant cultural capital in the form of middle-class-type attitudes and behaviours in relation to their children's education.

Yet research (Hartas 2011, 2012) indicates that working-class parents' attitudes and actions have far less influence on their children's educational outcomes than family income and parental education. So while parenting is increasingly held up as a way of compensating for social and economic disadvantage, the means of enabling working-class social mobility, research on 9500 seven year olds surveyed as part of the Millennium Cohort Study shows that:

> Parents, no matter how good or effective they are cannot overcome structural problems of poverty to maximise their children's educational opportunities and life chances (Hartas 2012, 3)

This research concludes that social mobility requires political not individual solutions, most likely to be achieved through redistribution and tax policies. What we also need, as the study makes clear, is far more information and an open and honest debate about structural inequality and the workings of social class in order to combat the symbolic violence that underpins commonsense understandings of the causes of working-class underachievement.

Embedded in the myth of social mobility is a further myth that we can all become middle class (or, at its most fantastical, very rich). Such fantasies estrange the working classes from any sense of personal worth or feelings of value if they remain as they are (Reay 2006). As a free school meal pupil in the 1950s and 1960s I know from personal experience there is nothing enobling about poverty, only a permanent sense of dread, fear and anxiety about having to go without, never having enough, and constantly making do. But in very unequal societies like our own, having a great deal more than others diminishes the self just as much as having too little. We only have to consider the recent history of banking and bankers. And making the transition from one end of the social hierarchy to the other is always painful, whether underpinned by socio-awareness or by denial and disidentification. Melvyn Bragg in his 2012 BBC series on class and culture describes himself as 'a class mongrel', indicating some of the sense of displacement and identity confusion felt by even the most successfully socially mobile. Social mobility is a wrenching process. It rips working-class young people out of communities that need to hold on to them, and it rips valuable aspects of self out of the socially mobile themselves as they are forced to discard qualities and dispositions that do not accord with the dominant middle-class culture that is increasingly characterized by selfish individualism and hyper-competition.

An American research study has found that the higher up the class system you are the more likely you are to lie, cheat and break the law. Paul Piff and his colleagues (Piff et al. 2012) write, in a recent issue of the *Proceedings of the American National Academy of Sciences*, that the research discovered a set of culturally shared norms among upper-middle-class individuals that facilitates much higher levels of unethical behaviour than that found among their working-class and lower-middle-class counterparts. We need to seriously question what we are aspiring to.

Underpinning the emphasis on parents as key to social mobility, pervasive among our political elite, is a belief that a lack of mobility is the result of either bad parenting or beyond that bad working-class culture (Reay 1998). Even the emphasis on failing schools frequently implicates working-class parents alongside inadequate teachers. When we interrogate the messages underlying the assertion that failing schools lead to low social mobility, it is as much if not more about bad working-class culture as about poor teaching. The solutions to low social mobility are seen to be greater working-class industry and better teaching. An example is a speech by Michael Gove:

> Led by inspirational heads and teachers, every day, these schools are proving the pessimists and fatalists wrong. They show us all that there need be no difference in performance – none whatsoever – between pupils from disadvantaged backgrounds and those from wealthier homes. They show us that a difficult start in life can be overcome, with hard work and good teaching. And that it is entirely possible for children to break free of the bonds of poverty and disadvantage, transforming a deprived start into a bright future. (Michael Gove speech to Brighton College, 10 May 2011)

As the speech makes clear, the main barriers to social mobility are predominantly seen to lie in a lack of aspiration and hard work among the working classes, and inadequate teaching in state schools. The actual causes of low social mobility lie elsewhere, in wider systemic inequalities, neoliberal hegemony and the workings of free-market capitalism. As Becky Francis and Val Hey point out:

> The pithy sign of 'aspiration' is, in the discursive context of neoliberalism and socio-economic inequality, overwhelmed by the moral charge of its reviled signified: that of the feckless, parasitic individual who has failed to grasp the opportunities open to them. (Francis and Hey 2009, 226)

Yet, in contradistinction to the political orthodoxy that the working classes lack aspiration, there are now a plethora of studies that show the working classes across ethnicities are highly aspirational. An Ipsos MORI (2010) survey found 64% of young people in high deprivation areas said they were very or fairly likely to go to university, while a DCSF (2009) study of 610 Year Seven pupils found a higher percentage of free school meal students wanted to go to university than their non-free school meal peers (78.5% versus 75%). As Stefan Collini (2010) asserts, it will serve early twenty-first-century Britain right if it becomes known as 'the aspirational age'.

There is evidently no lack of aspiration among the working classes. Yet aspirations tell only a fraction of the murky and difficult tale of social mobility. Far more influential are the reproductive strategies of the already privileged, the constraints facing working-class young people, and the changing economic and social landscapes. As Richard Hatcher (2011, 19) points out, and the Millennium Cohort study (Hartas 2012) confirms, 'if you want to know how well a child will do at school, ask how much its parents earn'. The aspirations the working classes are constantly enjoined to embrace are not realisable. The fact remains, after more than 50 years of the welfare state and several decades of comprehensive education, that family wealth is the single biggest predictor of success in the school system. So to borrow from Stephen Ball (2010), 'education policy is looking in the wrong place' when it focuses concertedly on social mobility. And particularly so when it focuses on social mobility in an age of austerity. As Heath and Zimdars (2011) argue, access to elite positions is likely to become more self-reproducing in tougher economic times, and it is to the economy that I now turn.

'It's the economy, stupid'

We are still far too caught up in Tony Blair's imperative to focus on 'Education, Education, Education' when the focus of our attention should be on another 'E' – the Economy. Then we would realize, as John Lennon sang, that people 'must learn how to smile as they kill/If they want to live like the folks on the hill' – there just is not enough space at the top of the hill for more than a fraction of us. In the second half of the twentieth century the rise of middle-class employment led to a predominance of upward over downward mobility measured in absolute terms (Savage 2007). Since then the growth in middle-class occupations has stalled. According to the TUC in 2001 low-paid service sector work made up 42% of labour-market occupations while 'high skill' white-collar work made up less than 40%, and that percentage is set to fall in the wake of public-sector job cuts. In the first quarter of 2012 the number of workers in professional jobs fell by 221,000 while the number on lower level occupations rose (Blanchflower 2012). There is no longer 'room at the top' for all those who aspire to professional and managerial jobs, as is evident in the statistics from the Office for National Statistics (2012). Thirty-six per cent of recent graduates are in non-graduate jobs and 20% of new graduates are unemployed. Rather, labour-market expansion has been in low-paid, service occupations.

The Wolf (2011) report found that the fastest growing jobs over the first decade of the twenty-first century were educational assistants (91% increase between 2001 and 2009) and care assistants (28% increase between 2001 and 2009). So one of the reasons that education cannot solve problems of inequality and become a vehicle of social mobility is that most jobs do not require high levels of education. Far from becoming a society of hyper-rational and high-powered 'knowledge workers', as theorists of post-industrial society predicted, the United Kingdom is becoming a society of care workers, cashiers, computer technicians and educational support staff while the size of the professional-managerial section of the labour market is falling slightly. In such a competitive context, the highly educated children of the middle and upper classes will find ways to keep all but the most determined children of the working classes out.

In the next section I draw on my own personal history as a case study of one such determined working-class child in order to further problematize narratives of social mobility as straightforward meritocratic tales of rewards for intellect and industry; that social mobility is centrally about 'the best and the brightest achieving their rightful place in society'. My story is one inflected by a curious mixture of progressive social policy, luck, political consciousness, serendipity, psychological redress and a stubborn single-mindedness. It also raises questions about the gloss that is routinely given to social mobility as uniformly positive and enhancing.

A frog's tale

My own family history provides a counterpoint to the many statistical analyses of social mobility, and a challenge to views that it is middle-class dispositions and attitudes in working-class families that facilitate and enable social mobility. It suggests instead that a strong oppositional working-class value system and political consciousness has a powerful efficacy; that valuing and strengthening working-class communities might work better than expecting them to mimic the middle classes. It also raises questions about the emphasis placed on dominant cultural capital for working-class educational success. My maternal grandmother was the illegitimate daughter of a Romany woman cast out from her community for getting pregnant by a man who was not her husband. Her disgraced mother, while still pregnant, became the housekeeper of a recently widowed coal miner with three children of his own, and later became his common-law wife. My grandmother, the person who was to have the greatest and most positive influence on my life, went into service in Crewe at age 13 but came back home to her coal-mining village in the midlands to marry a young coal-face worker from the adjacent village when she was 19.

My father's family were cockney working class, he was one of 13 children, only nine of whom survived. His mother too had been in service and his father was a brewer's drayman, but from most accounts spent large periods of time drunk and beating either his wife or one or other of his children. My father left school at age 13, doing a series of odd jobs until the war intervened when he was 19 and he found himself parachuted into the officer training scheme on the basis of his IQ test results. This was where and how he learnt that the upper and middle classes were no better than himself (see also A.H. Halsey [2013] in this issue). He constantly told his children that he and they 'were just as good as anyone else' although, as Carolyn Steedman (1986) found in relation to her own working-class father, that was no protection against humiliation and social powerlessness in the wider world. He became a navigator and flew all over the world but at the end of the war married my mother, moved into my grandparents' council house with her and became a coal-face worker like all the men in her family had been for the previous four generations.

My parents had eight children in rapid succession (four in the first five years then after a break of four years a further four over five years). With a growing number of children came poverty and over-crowding. We were always on free school meals and my abiding childhood memory was of money being counted over and over again on the kitchen table and it never adding up to enough. Even on our 'sink' council estate we were seen as one of the 'rougher' families. I knew very early on that I was the one singled out to 'raise the family', to make good the slights and humiliations of social class both my parents felt so keenly, by succeeding educationally. For one thing I was allowed to read, my younger sisters had their books burnt on the coal fire if they got distracted from their chores. I was also growing up in a tough, fiercely oppositional working-class culture, anti-monarchist, non-conformist and strongly trade unionist. There was always a potent sense of righteous indignation about the way things were, and that 'the bosses and the aristocrats were to blame for our deprivations'.

So how would I explain my own social mobility from disreputable, poor working class to Cambridge professor. In their classic study of 'Education and the Working Class', Brian Jackson and Dennis Marsden (1966) found that the successful working-class students came largely from the sunken middle classes or the upper strata of the working classes, were overwhelmingly from small families, and lived in socially mixed districts, mostly in owner-occupied housing. None of these categories applied to me. However, they do write about the salience of the thwarted educational aspirations of parents who passed scholarships but then were either not allowed to take them up or else had to leave school early because of economic constraints. To some extent I am the product of my parents' failed ambitions. My mother was a scholarship girl at the local grammar school who, despite doing well academically, had to leave school at age 16 in order to contribute to the family income. My father had had a whole new social world suddenly opened up to him at the beginning of the war that was just as rapidly snatched away from him when the war ended. Steedman (1986, 6) writes eloquently of how her mother's longing for more haunted her childhood. My parents' longing propelled my social mobility. They longed to have value, to be seen to be of value in a society that afforded my father little, and my mother even less. But what energized their longing and made it particularly potent in their children's lives was the sense of righteous indignation they both had at the 'way things were' that came through a strongly politicized working-class consciousness. My childhood was filled with rich and vivid narratives of working-class fortitude, survival and resistance. In common with many other mining communities, the one that I grew up in had at its core a distinctly radical value system: 'a moral framework that promoted an oppositional interpretation of class inequalities' (Parkin 1972). What was important was 'to rise with your class not out of it' (McLean in Bell 1944, 124).

I believe that was the main reason that I developed a habitus of recalcitrance (Skeggs 2004, 89) in relation to my social fate, a stubborn determination, a refusal to accept what the educational system seemed to be offering me, which was very little. Schooling for me became a battlefield from my first day in the Reception class when I angrily resisted the class teacher's attempts to seat me at the bottom table with all the other children from my council estate. From that first day when I obstinately refused to colour in the alphabet sheet because I could read, my primary school days were a series of confrontations with authority, ritual humiliations (I regularly got to wear a dunce's hat in the classroom or stand outside the head teacher's office for insubordination), and intense, undeclared competitions. A further major influence was the social class mix in the school; there was a significant minority of middle-class children and I began to secretly pit myself against the highest achieving boys in my class. I never did do better than the son of the headmaster of the boys' grammar school but by the end of primary school I had become a close second, and an unexpected success in the 11+ examination. One of my most vivid memories from the day we were given the results is one of the middle-class girls exclaiming 'there must be a mistake, Diane can't have passed'.

Six years on schooling was still a battlefield when I struggled in the sixth form of my girls' grammar school to reject the united efforts of my head teacher and deputy head teacher to get me to withdraw my application to read politics at university in favour of a primary teacher training course at a women's college. As they both explained, 'girls like me didn't go to university'. So education has always been a heady mixture of enormous pleasure and incalculable fears, struggles and anxieties in which learning has never been an easy straightforward process but a constant fight, a facing up to the terrifyingly unfamiliar.

I did go to university despite my teachers' advice and there was plunged into a middle-class world that was even more alienating than my school experiences had been. After coming top in my first-year examinations I ended up doing a joint honours degree in Politics and Economics. I was both the only female and the only student from a working-class background on the course. I became ill first with anorexia, then bulimia, and left university with a second-class degree and a strong sense of being bruised and battered by the whole experience. The psychic damage education can lead to in terms of classed identities was also evident in Jackson and Marsden's working-class boys who succeeded academically. They wrote eloquently about the group of nine working-class boys who, in aiming for Oxbridge, appeared like Icarus to fly too high. Seven of the nine took thirds or lower seconds. They note that 'this small group seem to be sensitively recording a crumbling away' felt through much of their wider sample (Jackson and Marsden 1966, 168). A number reflected on 'what was it all for', a question Jackson and Marsden (1966, 169) argue was 'born of the difficult and the obscure social rifts and struggles which for them had become part of the process of education itself'. In my case, instead of the political researcher both my father and I had aspired to, I became the primary school teacher my grammar school teachers had advised me to become. But I was now middle class, at least in terms of income and occupation, and set about helping my family financially and supporting my sisters in becoming middle class too. As well as encouragement, this support primarily came through providing them with free accommodation in London so they had access to, and could afford to undertake, further study.

So what general themes and insights can be drawn from my specific history – that social mobility can often be a difficult, alienating process alongside its more positive aspect of educational success and fulfilment. It can tear community and sometimes even the family out of the heart of individuals. I struggled to keep my family close despite moving so far away in terms of social space, to avoid what Jackson (1966, 207) calls 'the gap of non-understanding that opens between parent and child'. While I wanted to do well academically I did not want to leave my family behind. As Val Walsh (1997, 164) wryly comments, a common problem for those of us who are socially mobile and politically left leaning is that you 'get out' of one class but you do not want 'to get into' another. Bourdieu, writing of upward social mobility, argued that the movement of habitus across class fields can result in:

> [a] habitus divided against itself, in constant negotiation with itself and its ambivalences, and therefore doomed to a kind of duplication, to a double perception of the self, to successive allegiances and multiple identities. (Bourdieu 1999, 511)

I have spent over 50 years trying to reconcile the working-class girl I was with the middle-class woman I have become.

Social mobility in my case started out as an act of reparation, a making good of the slights and humiliations heaped on working-class parents – a stab at the structural injustices that hang over the working classes, a fighting back. It was not uncomplicatedly about escape, a desire both for a better life and 'bettering the self' (Lawler 2000), although, of course, it was about those things as well, shot through with a determination to restore pride and dignity to parents, and grandparents, who deserved much more than they had been allowed. But the individualized nature of the mobility process inevitably means separation and growing distance from those its success is meant to redeem. It is difficult to avoid a sense of treachery and overwhelming guilt. As a result, despite immense relief and gratitude at my privilege, I have an enduring ambivalence about what I have and who I have become that characterizes many of the upwardly mobile (Hey 1997; Walkerdine and Lucey 1989).

Social mobility is also, as my narrative reveals, about frequently being outside your comfort zone. It means developing a heightened awareness of threats and dangers to the extent you risk becoming permanently adrenalized, constantly attuned to possible attacks and a resurgence of the humiliations and shames that populated a working-class past. While the always middle class are primarily 'fish in water' what many of us from working-class backgrounds bring to middle-class fields is a heightened self-awareness and self-consciousness, and highly developed practices of self-monitoring and self-vigilance (Reay 2005; Reay, Crozier, and Clayton 2009).

I was also lucky enough to grow up during the early years of the welfare state. I felt, as Carolyn Steedman (1986, 122) did, 'that being a child when the state was practically engaged in making children healthy and literate was a support against my own circumstances'. An expanding welfare state and a pervasive rhetoric of providing services and homes fit for working-class war heroes in the two decades following the Second World War raised the sense of pride and entitlement among the working classes. It also softened some of the judgemental superiority of significant numbers of the middle and upper classes towards those they traditionally viewed as inferior. Also, entering the labour market during a period of large-scale expansion of professional jobs meant gaining a middle-class job was much more likely than it is in the economically austere 2010s. Such economic and social circumstances were far more favourable to working-class upward mobility than the current situation, and eased what was still a difficult trajectory for many working-class children like myself.

The roots of my social mobility lay in a complex synergy between the impact of a very specific family history on the values and ethos of the home in which I grew up, an atypical working-class community, characterized by an oppositional and explicitly socialist political consciousness, and a very particular historical juncture. Without any one of these three predisposing factors, my social mobility would not have occurred. I certainly would not have been socially mobile as a child growing up in the early twenty-first century.

Conclusion

> 'Class' could be something in the blood, in the very fibre of a man or woman: a way of growing, feeling, judging, taken out of the resources of generations gone before. Not something to be shuffled off with new possessions, new prospects, new surroundings; to be overlaid perhaps, or felt in new ways. (Jackson 1966, 192)

At the collective level, social mobility is no solution to either educational inequalities or wider social and economic injustices. But at the individual level it is also an inadequate solution, particularly for those of us whose social mobility was driven by a desire 'to put things right' and 'make things better' for the communities we came from and the people we left behind. In very unequal hierarchical societies like our own, chasms open up between those in very different economic positions, despite the best efforts of individuals. And Tawney's tadpole analogy is particularly apposite in austere times, as we frogs on the shore have to watch those we left behind drowning in a tsunami of economic cuts and the decimation of the welfare state. The powerful sense of loss that comes through unwanted social and psychological distance is rarely recognized under the positive gloss that encompasses the myth of social mobility. And as the earlier Jackson and Marsden quote illustrates, class is powerfully and enduringly embodied. We need to ensure that the contemporary working classes internalize a positive sense of their working-classness, one secured through pride, dignity and a strong sense of personal worth. This would involve not simply reducing the social and economic distance between individuals in UK society, but much wider social and personal change. Such social and individual transformation requires a revaluing of not just what it means to be working class but also a reworking of what it means to be middle and upper class, one that places social responsibility, caring and empathy at the heart of privilege. Only with a reduction of the psychic, as well as the social and economic, distances between the classes, and a rebirth of a collective sense of 'all being in it together', can social class finally lose its power to oppress and dominate. This is a far more important task than increasing social mobility in a deeply unequal society like the United Kingdom. So to conclude, social mobility is the stuff of tadpoles, frogs and naked emperors. I feel frozen in a world that from my vantage seems to have lost the plot; where most of us are still desperately pretending a naked emperor is decked out in finery; that social mobility is not a sham. What I see is that he is in the buff, it is not a pretty sight, and we need to start looking somewhere else.

References

Ball, S. 2010. "New Class Inequalities in Education: Why Education Policy May Be Looking in the Wrong Place! Education Policy, Civil Society and Social Class." *International Journal of Sociology and Social Policy* 30 (3/4): 155–166.

Bell, T. 1944. *John Maclean: A Fighter for Freedom*. Communist Party Scottish Committee.

Blanchflower, D. 2012. "Let's Call Up Vince to Get us Out of this Mess." *The Independent* 30th July 2012, p. 45.

Blanden, J., P. Gregg, and L. Macmillan. 2007. "Accounting for Intergenerational Income Persistence: Noncognitive Skills, Ability and Education." *Economic Journal* 117: 43–60.

Bourdieu, P. 1999. "The Contradictions of Inheritance." In *Weight of the World: Social Suffering in Contemporary Society*, edited by P. Bourdieu et al. 507–513. Cambridge: Polity.

Cabinet, Office. 2011. *Opening Doors, Breaking Barriers: A Strategy for Social Mobility*. London: Cabinet Office.

Causa, O., and A. Johansson. 2009. "Intergenerational Social Mobility." (OECD Economics Department Working Papers No 707).

Collini, S. 2010. Blahspeak. *London Review of Books* April 2010.

DCSF. 2009. "How Young People Formulate their Views about the Future." Research Report No DCSF – RR152. London: Department for Children, Schools and Families.

Erikson, R., and J. Goldthorpe. 2010. "Has Social Mobility in Britain Decreased? Reconciling Divergent Findings on Income and Class Mobility." *The British Journal of Sociology* 61 (2): 211–230.

Francis, B., and V. Hey. 2009. "Talking Back to Power: Snowballs in Hell and the Imperative of Insisting on Structural Explanations." *Gender and Education* 21 (2): 225–232.

Goldthorpe, J., and M. Jackson. 2007. "Intergenerational Class Mobility in Contemporary Britain: Political Concerns and Empirical Findings." *The British Journal of Sociology* 58 (4): 525–546.

Gove, Michael. 2011. "The Moral Purpose of School Reform." Speech given to The National College for School Leadership Birmingham 16th July 2011.

Halsey, A. H. 2013. "Reflections on Education and Social Mobility." *British Journal of Sociology of Education* 34 (6): this issue.
Hartas, D. 2011. "Families' Social Backgrounds Matter: Socio-Economic Factors, Home Learning and Young Children's Language, Literacy and Social Outcomes." *British Educational Research Journal* 37 (6): 893–914.
Hartas, D. 2012. "The Achievement Gap: Are Parents or Politicians Responsible?" *Bera Insights* Issue 2 Summer 2012.
Hatcher, R. 2011. "Liberating the Supply. Managing the Market." In *No Country for the Young*, edited by R. Hatcher and K. Jones, 18–36. London: The Tufnell Press.
Heath, A., and A. Zimdars. 2011. "Social Mobility: Drivers and Policy Responses Revisited British Academy." *Review* 17: 8–10.
Hey, V. 1997. "Northern Accent and Southern Comfort: Subjectivity and Social Class." In *Class Matters: Working-Class Women's Perspectives on Social Class*, edited by P. Mahony and C. Zmroczek, 140–151. London: Taylor and Francis.
Ipsos MORI. 2010. *Young People Omnibus 2010: A Research Study among 11–16 Year Olds on behalf of the Sutton Trust*. London: Ipsos MORI.
Jackson, B., and D. Marsden. 1966. *Education and the Working Class*. London: Penguin Books.
Lawler, S. 2000. *Mothering the Self: Mothers, Daughters, Subjects*. London: Routledge.
Manning, A., and B. Petrongolo. 2008. "The Part-Time Pay Penalty for Women in Britain." *The Economic Journal* 118 (526): F28–F51.
OECD. 2010. *OECD Factbook*. Paris: OECD.
OECD. 2010. *Economic Policy Reforms: Going for Growth*. Paris: OECD.
Office for National Statistics. 2012. *Graduates in the Labour Market 2012*. London: Office for National Statistics.
Parkin, F. 1972. *Class Inequality & Political Order*. London: Paladin.
Payne, G. 2012. "A New Social Mobility? the Political Redefinition of a Sociological Problem." *Contemporary Social Science* 7 (1): 55–71.
Piff, P., D. Stancato, S. Cote, R. Mendoza-Denton, and D. Keltner. 2012. "Higher Social Class Predicts Increased Unethical Behavior." *Proceedings of the American National Academy of Sciences* 109 (11): 4086–91.
Reay, D. 1998. "Rethinking Social Class Qualitative Perspectives on Gender and Social Class." *Sociology* 32 (2): 259–275.
Reay, D. 2005. "Beyond Consciousness?: The Psychic Landscape of Social Class." *Sociology* 39 (5): 911–928.
Reay, D. 2006. "The Zombie Stalking English Schools: Social Class and Educational Inequality." *British Journal of Educational Studies* 54 (3): 288–307.
Reay, D., G. Crozier, and J. Clayton. 2009. "'Strangers in Paradise': Working Class Students in Elite Universities." *Sociology* 43 (6): 1103–1121.
Reay, D., G. Crozier, and D. James. 2011. *White Middle Class Identities and Urban Schooling*. London: Palgrave.
Saunders, P. 2010. *Social Mobility Myths*. London: Civitas: Institute for the Study of Civil Society.
Savage, M. 2007. "Changing Social Class Identities in Post-War Britain: Perspectives from Mass-Observation." *Sociological Research Online* 12 (3): 6. http://www.socresonline.org.uk/12/3/6.html. doi:10.5153/sro.1459.
Skeggs, B. 2004. "Exchange, Value and Affect: Bourdieu and 'the Self'." In *After Bourdieu*, edited by L. Adkins and B. Skeggs, 75–89. Oxford: Blackwell.

Steedman, C. 1986. *Landscape for a Good Woman: A Story of Two Lives*. London: Virago.
Tawney, R. H. 1964a. *Equality*. London: Unwin Books.
Tawney, R. H. 1964. *The Radical Tradition*. Harmondworth: Penguin Books.
Timmins, N. and E. Jacobs. 2011. Britain: The Fairy-tale Fantasy. *The Financial, Times* 25th April 2011.
Trades Union Congress (TUC). 2010. 'Social Mobility.' http://www.tuc.org.uk/extras/Social_Mobility.pdf (accessed 23 August 2012).
Walkerdine, V., and H. Lucey. 1989. *Democracy in the Kitchen: Regulating Mothers and Socialising Daughters*. London: Virago.
Walsh, V. 1997. "Interpreting Class: Auto-Biographical Imaginations and Social Change." In *Class Matters: Working-Class Women's Perspectives on Social Class*, edited by P. Mahony and C. Zmroczek, 152–174. London: Taylor and Francis.
Weis, L., and K. Cipollone. 2013. "Class Work: Producing Privilege and Social Mobility in Elite U.S. Secondary Schools." *British Journal of Sociology of Education* 34 (6): this issue.
Wilkinson, R., and K. Pickett. 2009. *The Spirit Level*. London: Allen Lane.
Wolf, A. 2011. *The Wolf Report – Review of Vocational Education*. London: DfE.

Education, opportunity and the prospects for social mobility

Phillip Brown

School of Social Sciences, Cardiff University, Cardiff, UK

> There has been renewed policy interest in intergenerational social mobility as a route to a fairer society, but in ignoring the sociological evidence this article will argue that the current policy agenda will fail to achieve its goal. Based on an analysis of 'social congestion', 'social exclusion', and 'social justice', it also argues that existing sociological research on education and social mobility needs to be extended. In the early decades of the twenty-first century, the experiences of working-class and middle-class students and families are not defined by intergenerational social mobility, but by social congestion and an opportunity trap.

Introduction

The creation of a 'fairer' society through social mobility is high on the political agenda in the United Kingdom (Cabinet Office 2011; Heath and Zimdars 2011), and in other developed economies (OECD 2010). This article will assess the prospects for social mobility, especially through initiatives to improve the life-chances of those from less advantaged backgrounds (Payne 2012). It will be argued that the way the 'problem' of intergenerational mobility is framed in public policy neglects key lessons from sociological studies, including the pioneering work of Glass (1954), Halsey, Heath, and Ridge (1980), and Goldthorpe, Llewellyn, and Payne (1980). While acknowledging the contribution of these and more recent sociological studies,[1] significant changes in the fields of education, employment and the labour market call for a revised and extended approach.

This article begins by showing how the current policy agenda of 'fairness as social mobility' (Payne 2012) results in a 'deficit' model of working-class achievement (Valencia 1997). This ignores sociology's 'inconvenient truth' that explains why social mobility now depends on narrowing inequalities in education and individual life-chances. It then explains why we need to think beyond the hypothesis of 'increasing merit-selection' (IMS) (Jonsson 1992; Marshall, Swift, and Roberts 1997), a major focus of mobility studies. Rather than a route to a fairer society, the study of social mobility highlights a crisis in the neo-liberal 'opportunity bargain' (Brown, Lauder, and Ashton 2011), that can no longer bear the weight of social and political expectations. This calls for a wider definition of social justice that takes account of inequalities in class position, along with inequalities in access to such positions. In conclusion, it calls into question wider issues of quality of life and the role of education beyond that of a 'great sorting machine'.

Fairness as social mobility

Increasing intergenerational social mobility is a central tenet of the functionalist theory of industrialism (Parsons 1961; Goldthorpe 2007b, 158). Within this account, the education system assumes a major role in training the future workforce to meet the growing demand for technical, managerial, and professional workers. This includes recruiting the most talented to key occupations regardless of social origins, believed to negate the conflict between efficiency and justice. In his classic study of the rise of post-industrial society, Daniel Bell (1973) describes how the class structure is reshaped by a new technical elite recruited through a 'meritocratic' competition rather than by the hereditary principle of succession, transforming the role of education as it becomes 'the arbiter of class position' and the university gains 'a quasi-monopoly in determining the future stratification of the society' (1973, 410).

The hypothesis of IMS (Jonsson 1992; Marshall, Swift, and Roberts 1997) has been used to evaluate some of the central claims of the functionalist theory of industrialism (see Figure 1). It predicts that educational

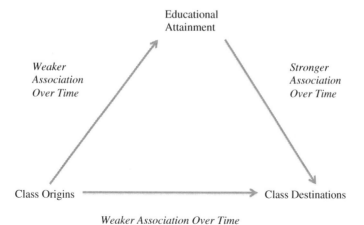

Figure 1. The hypothesis of increasing merit-selection.

attainment will become more meritocratic over time, leading to a weakening relationship between class origin and academic performance. The hypothesis also predicts that the link between academic performance and occupational destinations strengthens as employers recruit on grounds of technocratic expertise, contributing to an overall weakening in the relationship between origins and destinations.

Sociological evidence has consistently refuted the basic tenets of the IMS hypothesis (Halsey, Heath, and Ridge 1980; Marshall, Swift, and Roberts 1997). There is a vast literature highlighting social inequalities in origins, education and destinations, based on social class, gender, race and ethnicity (Crompton 2008; Heath and Chueng 2006). However, before examining sociology's contribution to the study of education and social mobility, it is important to consider the renewed policy interest in social mobility because it represents a departure from the functionalist theory of industrial and post-industrial development.

Today, the politics of social mobility is premised on neo-liberal theory that views 'market' rather than 'meritocratic' competition as the route to an efficient, fair and competitive economy (Hayek 1960; Marshall, Swift, and Roberts 1997, 97). Within neo-liberal theory, fairness as social mobility involves giving those from disadvantaged backgrounds an opportunity to compete with those from more privileged backgrounds in a market competition (Peters 2011). Neo-liberalism is consistent with the privatisation of education (Ball 2012), as we will go on to argue, but both functionalist and neo-liberal theories view the economy as continuing to create mobility opportunities for those from disadvantaged backgrounds through a general upgrading of the workforce. This assumption is equally prevalent in recent government documents aimed at addressing concerns about the lack of working class social mobility.

'Unleashing Aspiration' (Cabinet Office 2009), published under a Labour government, acknowledged the need for policies to address inequalities in housing, childrearing, education and occupational recruitment. Nevertheless, these inequalities in opportunity were discussed in the context of a 'second great wave of social mobility', which predicted a significant increase in the demand for university graduates. The Conservative-led Coalition government endorsed this approach in 'Opening Doors, Breaking Barriers: A Strategy for Social Mobility' in 2011, despite cutting financial support to people from poorer backgrounds, raising university tuition fees and abandoning any attempt to narrow income inequalities as a route to a fairer society. Whilst recognising low levels of social mobility both by international standards and compared with the immediate post-war period, and despite reporting official figures that one in five 18–24 year olds are not in education, employment or training, it concluded 'the demand for skilled workers is currently outstripping supply, which suggests that there is "room at the top" for highly qualified graduates from all backgrounds' (Cabinet Office 2011, 11).

Consequently, the policy focus is on lifting aspirations and increasing opportunities for those from socially disadvantaged backgrounds to take advantage of 'room at the top', rather than addressing inequalities in life-chances in a positional struggle for a livelihood (Payne 2012).[2] In short, this approach rests on improving the 'absolute' performance of children from lower socio-economic groups, rather than tackling the thorny political questions of 'relative' mobility that requires more of those from working-class backgrounds entering middle-class occupations and more of those from middle-class backgrounds being downwardly mobile, entering lower status occupations.

In neo-liberal theory, fairness remains a question of breaking the 'cycle of deprivation' from the early years through to the world of work because 'too many struggle to get on in the labour market, held back by low qualifications or a welfare system that does not sufficiently incentivise work' (Cabinet Office 2011, 7). Therefore, social mobility can be increased by 're-incentivising' disadvantaged families to take advantage of existing employment opportunities. But this 'deficit' model, based on blaming the victim, ignores much of the sociological evidence.[3]

Sociology's inconvenient truth

An extensive body of sociological research shows that intergenerational social mobility – the relationship between class origins and destinations – can result from two sources. Firstly, due to the 'absolute' rate of mobility reflecting changes in the occupational or class structure. Here, new job openings may become available to those of working-class origins in circumstances when there are not enough labour-market entrants from middle-class backgrounds to meet a rising demand for managerial or professional jobs. Secondly, social mobility can also result from narrowing class inequalities in life-chances. Here, the focus is on 'relative' mobility, often measured in terms of 'social fluidity' (Goldthorpe 2007b, 164) or 'odds ratios' (Marshall, Swift, and Roberts 1997, 40) that measure the relative chances of (im)mobility of those born into different social classes, regardless of how the class or occupational structure may change over time.

Sociology's inconvenient truth is that the high rates of mobility achieved in the second half of the twentieth century are explained by 'absolute' changes in the occupational structure, rather than from a narrowing of inequalities in life-chances. As Goldthorpe concludes:

> First, absolute rates of intergenerational class mobility display considerable variation, both over time within national societies and across these societies. But, second, this variation *is to an overwhelming extent produced by structural rather than by fluidity effects* – in other words, by differences in the ways in which class structures have evolved rather than by differences in underlying relative rates. Relative rates appear to be characterised by a rather

surprising degree of *in*variance: that is, by a large measure of temporal stability and also by a substantial cross-national commonality at least in the general pattern of fluidity that they imply.[4] (2007b, 157; emphasis in the original)

Therefore, high levels of 'absolute' social mobility do not confirm the hypothesis of merit-selection because they do not depend on narrowing inequalities in education or the labour market; 'high levels of absolute social mobility can go hand in hand with a society in which background has an unfair influence on life chances' (Cabinet Office 2011, 15; Breen 2010a). Despite this insight, its implications for the future of social mobility are neglected in much of the policy debate. The result is a 'fallacy of fairness' as policies to increase educational standards, including the student premium, or widened access to higher education, have little impact on 'relative' mobility.[5]

The fallacy of fairness results from the well-known limitations of methodological individualism (a major flaw in neo-liberal economic theory). When the individual is the unit of analysis it commonly results in an 'adding up' problem (Hirsch 1977), in failing to recognise that what some achieve, all cannot: while everyone can do their best, not everyone can be the best.

Policies aimed at increasing relative mobility need to begin from the fact that individual achievements are not judged in isolation, but in a positional competition that typically privileges those from higher social classes, due to their superior material and cultural assets (Bourdieu 1984). Inequalities in class, status and power are a defining feature of the struggle for 'positional goods' including credentials, incomes and high-status jobs. Unlike absolute mobility, 'relative' mobility is based on a positional competition that determines one's standing (or position) in a hierarchy of academic performance or hierarchy of labour-market entrants, where the key to personal welfare is an ability to stay ahead of the crowd because if everyone advances together it 'increases the crush' (Hirsch 1977, 7; Brown 2006).

In the absence of a positional (relational) theory of 'relative' social mobility, policy debate is reduced to a 'deficit' model of what working-class students and families lack – credentials, incentives, internships or employability skills. It assumes that by giving them more of what the middle classes already have, this 'deficit' can be reduced without disturbing the privileges of the middle classes because there is more room at the top. It also leads to exaggerated claims about the efficacy of educational reforms, despite its limited impact on the pattern of social mobility since the 1950s (Goldthorpe and Jackson 2007, 542). Sociological studies point to an inherent 'conflict' in the competition for positional assets, which are often zero-sum. Without addressing class inequalities in opportunity, there is little prospect of increasing rates of intergenerational social mobility.

Today, addressing inequalities in relative life-chances is even more important. There is little prospect of repeating the 'absolute' rate of mobility driven by the rising demand for managers and professionals within public and private-sector organisations. Indeed, there is tentative evidence of more downward mobility even though Bukodi, Goldthorpe and Waller show that there has been little change in the overall rate of intergenerational social mobility (2013). Again, this downward mobility is not the result of middle-class families making way for high-achievers from working-class backgrounds but due to changes in the occupational structure that we will outline below (Li and Devine 2011).[6]

Although sociological studies have made an invaluable contribution to explaining patterns of social mobility, the IMS hypothesis needs to be extended to account for significant ideological and structural changes in the relationship between education, jobs and rewards. Despite evidence of little change in 'odds ratios' (fluidity) over time, it would be surprising if market reforms in education and the labour market had little impact on life-chances or the way people experience the competition for a livelihood. To achieve a better understanding of the prospects for social mobility we will examine issues of *social congestion*, *social closure* and *social justice*.

Social congestion

In the early decades of the twenty-first century the experiences of many working-class and middle-class families are not defined by intergenerational social mobility but by the realities of social congestion. The lack of capacity within the economy to deliver on the opportunity bargain has led to labour-market crowding, along with wider congestion problems, as people seek to use the education system to 'stand out from the crowd'. The failure of the labour market to meet the social demand for professional occupations is particularly acute in developed economies with large middle classes, mass higher education, and wide income inequalities. Social congestion is also exacerbated by neo-liberal policies that make people more dependent on waged employment to support themselves and their families. The study of social congestion is therefore central to a sociological account of social mobility as the neo-liberal opportunity bargain has turned into an 'opportunity trap' (Brown 2003, 2006) for many students and workers.

The opportunity trap results from contestants seeking to gain a positional advantage over other contestants. This leads to a trap because the actions used to get ahead often contribute to the very congestion people are trying to avoid. If only a few adopt the same tactics to gain an advantage it may stand a chance of success, but if everyone adopts the same tactics no one gets ahead (Hirsch 1977). It simply leads schools, universities and employers to raise entry requirements, or to increase the number of hurdles, such as the need for work experience alongside a bachelor's degree on leaving university (Collins 1979).

A proper understanding of social congestion requires a multi-causal explanation. It is the result of a confluence of factors including structural, cyclical, and demographic factors (Breen 2010b). It could be argued that it is a temporary phenomenon resulting from the 2008 financial crisis and the subsequent recession. However, increasing problems of social congestion were evident well before the financial crisis and clearly relate to capacity problems within the labour market.

We have already seen how absolute mobility depends on the capacity for occupational upgrading. This is easier to achieve when professional and managerial jobs constitute a relatively small proportion of the overall workforce such as in the 1950s and 1960s. When these occupations already constitute a significant proportion of job openings, it is more difficult to achieve a 'second great wave of social mobility' (Cabinet Office 2009). Goldthorpe and Jackson observe that:

> the very substantial growth in demand for professional and managerial personnel ... was created by an historic shift in the scale of public administration, of health, education and social welfare provision, and of industrial and commercial organization that could scarcely be repeated. (2007, 541)[7]

There are at least two other trends that explain why there are limited prospects for 'absolute' intergenerational mobility resulting from a rise in the demand for technical, managerial and professional personnel. Firstly, emerging economies including China and India now compete with western companies and employees for high-skilled work, as well as intermediate and low-skilled work. Globally, the numbers enrolled in higher education since the mid-1990s has more than doubled from 76 million to 179 million by 2009. While this is partially explained by the expansion of tertiary education in OECD countries, there has also been significant growth within emerging economies. China now has significantly more people in higher education than the United States, with plans to add a further 95 million graduates to its workforce by 2020. When this rapid increase in the global supply of 'educated' labour is combined with the 'quality-cost revolution' that enables workers and companies to compete with the West on quality as well as cost, the barriers to competition assumed to protect the middle classes in western countries are in a state of collapse (Brown, Lauder, and Ashton 2011).

Secondly, faith in the next wave of social mobility rests on knowledge, innovation and the creativity of employees. However, Bell (1973), along with many others, failed to understand that the more 'knowledge' work becomes important to companies the more they would look for innovative ways to control and reduce the price of educated labour, along with ways to eliminate it altogether (Head 2003; Brynjolfsson and McAfee 2011). Transnational companies are attempting to apply knowledge to work in services along with manufacturing. If the twentieth century brought what can be described as mechanical Taylorism characterised by the Fordist production line, where the knowledge of craft workers was captured by management, codified and re-engineered in the shape of the moving assembly line, the twenty-first century is the age of digital Taylorism (Brown, Lauder, and Ashton 2011, 72). This involves translating knowledge work into working knowledge through the extraction, codification and digitalisation of knowledge into software prescripts, templates and platforms, which can be transmitted and manipulated by others regardless of location. The result is the standardisation of functions and jobs, including an increasing proportion of technical, managerial and professional roles that raise fundamental questions about the future of 'knowledge' work (Livingstone and Guile 2012). These changes are having a profound impact on middle-class occupations at the same time that western governments depend on a rising demand for 'knowledge' workers to deliver social mobility (Lauder et al. 2012).

If a lack of middle-class job opportunities has contributed to social congestion, it has also resulted from official government policies that have peddled the myth of the knowledge economy and occupational advancement for all. Within the neo-liberal opportunity bargain, 'learning equals earning' is promoted as the route to individual prosperity, leading to record numbers of students entering the job market prior to the cuts in university funding introduced by the Coalition government in 2010.

The rhetoric of 'learning equals earning' enticed people in, heightening their sense of expectation and personal responsibility. In neo-classical economic theory, congestion problems of this kind are regarded as temporary phenomena assumed to return to a state of equilibrium following the laws of supply and demand. But the market has not cleared because of a lack of freedom (choice) over how to make a living. While individuals have varying degrees of freedom within the market place, all but the seriously wealthy are compelled by the cash nexus to compete within education and the labour market (Simmel 1978).

People are also being forced to play for higher stakes. In highly unequal societies such as Britain, a finely calibrated hierarchy of credentialised achievement has been flattened into winners and losers. The merits of a few are celebrated at the expense of the majority, leading to a winner-takes-all competition for the 'best' schools, colleges, universities, and employment opportunities (Frank and Cook 1996).

Moreover, Boudon (1973) predicted that students from middle-class backgrounds would need to run faster to stand still. He recognised that as more students came from backgrounds where family members were in managerial or professional occupations, it would make it more difficult for them to reach a higher social status than their parents (1973, 6). This prediction has become a reality given a large middle class and a significant change in gendered patterns of educational performance and labour-market participation (Francis and Skelton 2005; Arnot and Mac an Ghaill 2006). A contest between men has been transformed as female students and employees compete for a livelihood with males, often with higher academic credentials because they outperform male students at virtually every level of the education system (Penny 2010).

The study of social congestion adds an important dimension to existing accounts of social mobility because it reveals how the costs of positional competition continue to mount for individuals and families as they are forced to redouble their efforts to win a livelihood. This has left many working-class families increasingly excluded as the 'social distance' between what is required to do a job, as opposed to what is required to get a decent job, widens (Reay, Crozier, and Clayton 2009). Conversely, middle-class families find themselves in a positional struggle – increasing expensive in time, effort and money – with little certainty of reproducing their class location. The middle classes are therefore engaged in a 'secret war' in the struggle for positional advantage, reflected in a 'legitimation crisis' as the ideology of merit-selection is jettisoned in a market competition for middle-class survival.

Social closure: from the ideology of meritocracy to the ideology of performocracy[8]

The hypothesis of IMS, which has been the focus of research on education and social mobility, reflects the political priorities of the post-war era, including the aspiration to create an education-based meritocracy (Young 1961; Halsey 1975). This literature has clearly demonstrated the myth of meritocracy, but it has not explained its political abandonment or subsequent impact on the relationship between class origins and educational attainment. This is surprising as much of the research within the sociology of education since the early 1980s has examined the nature and consequences of neo-liberal reforms in education (Halsey et al. 1997; Whitty, Power, and Halpin 1998). Research within the sociology of education points to declining prospects for 'fairness' in the competition for a livelihood, due to a fundamental shift in the rules of inclusion and exclusion over a 30-year period (Brown 1990).

This shift is captured in the move from the 'ideology of meritocracy' to the 'ideology of performocracy'. In societies based on meritocratic ideology there is a formal requirement to reduce inequalities in opportunity even if odds are stacked in favour of children from the middle classes (Halsey, Heath, and Ridge 1980). The state is expected to perform a key role in levelling the playing field through building 'common' schools, using standard curricula and formal examinations open to all, aimed at eliminating inequalities in the external conditions of conflict (Durkheim 1933). Differences in educational attainment are then used to judge whether the contest is fair. If the best jobs consistently go to those from higher social classes, while those from disadvantaged backgrounds get locked into low-status occupations with little prospect of advancement, governments can be held to account for failing to achieve a more meritocratic society.[9] This is what the IMS model was developed to analyse.

In a 'performocracy' the competition for a livelihood is 'socially blind'. It is based on a market ideology where it is a winning performance that counts. The goal is to 'achieve' a competitive advantage, whether for individuals in the competition for credentials, jobs or income; for companies in the competition for profits; or for nations in the competition for productive growth (Cerny 1997). There is less emphasis on how success is achieved because it accepts the injustices of market competition as a necessary evil in an increasingly competitive world, where the demands of global competition typically over-ride issues of social justice (Polanyi 1944). There is therefore no attempt to create a level playing field but policy measures may legitimately be aimed at those who have failed to make the most of market 'opportunities'. Therefore, the approach of the Conservative-led Coalition government in the United Kingdom is consistent with the ideology of performocracy, premised on a model of market individualism (Hayek 1960; Gamble 1996).

The Coalition government talks of 'fairer access' to education, at the same time that market rules have become more entrenched in English education with renewed efforts to give schools greater freedom from local state control through the creation of 'academy' and 'free' schools (Department of Education 2011). The role of market competition has also been extended to the university sector (Olsson and Peters 2005). Previously, this was restricted to the fight for resources, reputation and research excellence, where British domiciled students paid no or low fees. However, the Browne Review of Higher Education advocated a market for students based on differential fees making the ability to pay a more important facet of student 'choice', although a £9000 per annum cap was imposed for undergraduate English domiciled students.

Consequently, inequalities in educational opportunities will become more entrenched, as students from middle-class backgrounds are the primary beneficiaries of university expansion (Elias and Purcell 2012). But market choice for parents does not mean that middle-class families get things all their own way. Competition is not dampened by privatisation and parental choice because performance becomes even more important as market reforms contribute to an intensification of positional competition for access to the 'best' schools, universities and employers (Ball 1996; Power et al. 2003). The meritocratic 'ideal' of neutralising the impact of class origins in education selection has not only been abandoned in the competition for credentials, but also in the labour market.

Credentials: a declining currency of opportunity

As a currency of exchange, credentials have always been different from money (Collins 1979; Simmel 1978), but when credentials are relatively scarce there is a higher level of social tolerance in the gap between the hirer and the hired. Indeed, one of the aims of an education-based meritocracy is to create a competition played out in purpose-built arenas (schools, colleges, and universities) where social differences are removed to reveal innate character and ability. Credentials were then supposed to communicate such differences to employers irrespective of the prospective candidates or employee's class background, gender or ethnicity. This is why the IMS hypothesis assumes a strengthening relationship between educational attainment and occupational destinations.

But within a mass system of higher education, credentials lose much of their value to employers in screening potential applicants, especially at a time when companies have become 'impatient' – they demand new recruits to 'hit the ground running'. There is a greater emphasis on competency-based recruitment, combining the 'hard currencies' (credentials, sporting achievements, work experience, etc.), along with the 'soft currencies' of personality, character and social confidence (Brown and Hesketh 2004; Jackson, Goldthorpe, and Mills 2005). While this is aimed at eliminating direct discrimination, the candidates 'performance' over-rides all considerations of class privilege in the selection process.

This change in the rules of the game makes it more difficult for those from less privileged backgrounds to hide their cultural inheritance behind the mask of technical expertise (Rose 1999; Skeggs 2004). It is also more difficult for them to demonstrate the appropriate 'economy of experience' (Brown and Hesketh 2004) that involves translating everyday life into a narrative of employability. It highlights the importance of capitalising on 'extracurricular' activities (Roulin and Bangerter 2013) and social networks that demonstrate the range of behavioural competences employers benchmarked as indicative of employability. It requires access to 'learning' opportunities beyond the classroom and lecture theatre in the form of foreign travel, internships, and extra-curricula activities, taken for granted by students from privileged backgrounds (Bourdieu 1984).

Yet even for those from more affluent backgrounds, the economy of experience is no longer a passive consequence of living a privileged life, or coming from a privileged background (Bourdieu 1984). It has to be 'worked at' as a reflexive project of the self, where everyday life has to be captured in a narrative of individual employability, often at the expense of intrinsic human experience (Brown and Hesketh 2004). Rather than lacking the appropriate credentials, candidates are excluded for lacking the personal qualities that constitute employability. In such circumstances we should anticipate a weaker, rather than stronger, relationship between educational attainment and class destination.

Opportunity and the war for talent

The ideology of performocracy is not limited to legitimating inequalities in education and occupational selection. It is also being used to re-evaluate the relationship between education, jobs and incomes. Leading consultancy companies, most notably McKinsey & Co., advise companies that they are in a 'war for talent' (Michaels, Handfield-Jones, and Axelrod 2001). They are encouraged to differentiate employees on performance given that company profits are assumed to depend on the contribution of top performers. To remain competitive it is recommended that employers identify their 'high potentials' and top talent, rewarding them significantly more than other employees. Accordingly, the selection and retention of top talent is said to matter much more than having vast ranks of graduate employees (Brown and Tannock 2009). Indeed, mass higher education makes it even more important to identify, recruit and develop the 'best of the best' because from this perspective it is not certified knowledge that matters but outstanding performance (Michaels, Handfield-Jones, and Axelrod 2001). Therefore, at the same time as companies are trying to reduce their labour costs they are also trying to attract and retain a talented elite, 'so a larger share of the wage bill is going to those judged as top performers' (Wooldridge 2006).

This emphasis on the scarcity of talent, despite unprecedented numbers entering the labour market with a bachelor's degree, can be understood as a 'positional' power struggle as those in executive positions attempt to legitimate widening income inequalities within the ranks of managers and professionals. The 'war for talent' is also consistent with shareholder models of corporate governance, with the interests of senior executives aligned to shareholders, often at the expense of other employees. This alignment is achieved through share options and other incentives where performance is measured in terms of short-term increases in dividends and rising share prices (Lazonick and O'Sullivan 2000). It has also been a feature of public-sector organisations as the salaries of senior managers have pulled away from the rest (Hutton 2011). Therefore, the war for talent offers executives in both public and private organisations a convenient way of legitimating widening income inequalities at a time when large numbers of university graduates are entering the job market.

This disjunction in the relationship between education, jobs and incomes highlights the need for caution in treating occupational categories as a proxy for class relations (Lockwood 1958; Holmes and Mayhew 2012), which reflected a period in the 1960s and 1970s, characterised by a rapid expansion of white-collar employment in private and public-sector bureaucracies. Today, the rhetoric of a 'war for talent' is used to signify a changing relationship between education, occupation and income. It rejects the bureaucratic model of incremental pay based on expertise and experience. A finely calibrated hierarchy of occupational roles and careers is flattened into winners and losers, as noted above (Frank and Cook 1996).

The achievements of a few are recognised at the expense of the majority, fuelling positional conflict within the middle classes (Devine 1997; Savage 2000). They compete in 'ranking' competitions (resources in the market place), such as getting selected to a top-ranked university or appointed by a leading employer. But it also involves inequalities in power as elite class fractions use 'rigging' tactics (influences over markets), to legitimate significant wage hikes through the re-definition of talent and performance (Brown 2000).

This account of social closure in education and the labour market highlights enduring inequalities in social class opportunities, but also a 'crisis' of reproduction within the middle classes (Savage 2000). The changing rules of social exclusion show that Britain and the United States remain far from the promise of the IMS hypothesis, despite unprecedented numbers entering the job market with graduate qualifications.

Social justice: extending the research agenda

This analysis raises broader questions of social (in)justice. In political and policy debate, social justice is often reduced to fair access. Here, inequalities are only viewed as injustice, 'when they are fixed; passed on, generation to generation. That's when societies become closed, stratified and divided' (Clegg 2010). But this is far removed from Rawls's formulation of justice as fairness that includes issues of distributional justice in conjunction with equality of opportunity (Rawls 1971).

In focusing on the IMS hypothesis – reflecting functionalist debates about industrial and post-industrial development – mobility studies often perpetuated a narrow version of social justice as fairness (Swift 2004; Fevre 2003). As Marshall et al. acknowledge, 'it should be clear that our focus on data relating to (in)equality of access ... manifests a concern with only a particular subset of issues that might be thought relevant to social justice' (1997, 16).

Consequently, odds ratios (social fluidity) have been used as a standard measure of mobility rates between classes, but as Swift has argued this 'tells us solely and specifically about the distribution of chances, as between those of different class origins, of achieving and voiding particular class destinations. They tell us nothing about the distribution of opportunities in any more general sense' (Swift 2004, 3). Therefore, while leading mobility theorists such as John Goldthorpe claim that odds ratios have remained constant, social class inequalities (measured by occupational income) have increased (Hills et al. 2010; Mishel et al. 2012). This calls for new analyses of how inequalities in income and wealth reinforce inequalities in the competition for a livelihood, for example, by determining who can afford the rising costs of private education, university admissions and internships (often unpaid).

In short, mobility studies need to be extended from the current focus on inequalities in life-chances (based on origins and destinations via education) to include inequalities in condition (the nature of class positions). Social justice is as much about how societies distribute rewards to those in different occupational 'destinations', as how societies organise the competition for a livelihood. This takes on added significance with widening income inequalities *within* occupational categories, such as lawyers, engineers, and managers, along with those traditionally found *between* occupational categories.

Sociologists and economists need to work more closely together to develop new job classifications, aimed at capturing widening income disparities within the same occupational categories (Li and Devine 2011), and to get a better picture of how workplace relations and rewards are changing (Blyton, Heery, and Turnbull 2011).

A wider conception of social justice in the study of education and social mobility should also include quality-of-life issues (often found within the pages of this journal), without jettisoning quantitative analyses of origins and destinations, which remain a core part of the sociological enterprise. This wider research agenda would help overcome education being treated as a 'black box' in a lot of the social mobility literature, with an almost exclusive focus on class differences in education attainment. Issues of curriculum, pedagogy and student experiences are largely absent because the education system is treated as a monolithic sorting machine within which class inequalities shape the opportunities and rational responses of students (Goldthorpe 2007a). Indeed, when education is reduced to credential performance and league tables (Ball 2003), we move further away from a view of education as a means to improve the quality of life for all.

This wider focus on social justice calls for new empirical studies of how people are responding to changes in education, employment and the labour market. How, for instance, is the competition for a livelihood understood by members of different class fractions (Devine et al. 2005)? Equally, how do women and men in different class locations perceive income inequalities and to what extent are these judged legitimate (Heath, de Graaf, and Li 2010)? Consideration of the politics of social mobility is important in this context because previous assumptions about social mobility as an insurance policy against political instability must also be called into question. Dahrendorf observed that:

> wherever possible, people will try to make headway by their own efforts. In the United States, this has long been the dominant mode of conflict. Today the same is true in most countries. Individual mobility takes the place of the class struggle. (1990, 159)

Wilensky (1960), however, argues that industrial societies have much to fear from a well-educated population frustrated and discontented, as the 'Arab Spring' testified. This raises the issue of whether high youth unemployment and underemployment are likely to breed new forms of class politics or expressions of opposition. It is too early to answer such questions but the responses of young people to stagnant, if not declining, career prospects, in conjunction with higher college and university debts, should be a key area of comparative sociological investigation, especially in a European context where close to one-half of young people in Greece and Spain are reported to be unemployed (Allen and Ainley 2010; International Labour Organisation 2011).

Some of the implications of the above analysis could also be missed by existing mobility studies because the focus on class relations underplays Boudon's observation that 'change often stems from a dislocation between customs and institutions and, consequently, from a conflict between institutions and social groups rather than from conflict between opposed social groups. In this case conflict signifies incompatibility not confrontation' (1982, 13).

Today, the sources of conflict as experienced by middle-class youth, may not be expressed in class or gender terms (middle class versus working class; men versus women) but as a conflict around the institutions of education, employment and the job market. Conflict takes the form of a clash between expectations and institutional realities where a growing number of aspiring working-class and middle-class families are becoming 'institutionally disappointed'. This can be experienced as a prolonged struggle with and within institutions, where there is no identifiable enemy or opponent (akin to a traffic jam), just other people wanting to do the best for themselves and their families. It is for this reason that positional conflict is often experienced as a form of 'personal' frustration or in some cases anomie (Merton 1957, 161).

Without understanding change in the fields of education, employment and the labour market, it is difficult to understand how policies aimed at increasing social mobility have led to unintended consequences in fuelling social congestion. Today, the clash between expectations and institutional realities is the dominant form of conflict in developed economies and a major question is whether in a context of austerity it may develop into other forms of oppositional conflict based on class, gender, race, ethnicity or nationalism. Moreover, austerity measures leading to public-sector cuts will have more adverse consequences for the young, combined with the rising costs of higher education that will adversely affect the 'new' universities, within which working-class and ethnic-minority students are concentrated.

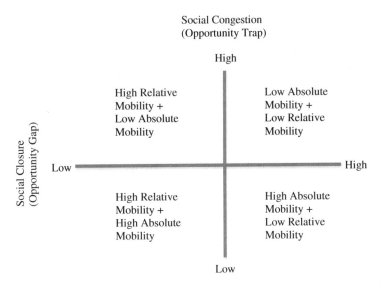

Figure 2. Prospects for social mobility and the structure of competition.

Conclusion

There is nothing inherent in twenty-first-century societies that lead them to become fairer or more socially mobile. If anything, efficiency and justice are pulling in opposite directions, especially when neo-liberalism and the ideology of performocracy dominate the political agenda. Britain has not only failed to achieve IMS, but has abandoned it as a political project (Payne 2012). The relationship between origins and destinations is now determined by a market competition that restricts the role of state intervention, severely limiting its capacity to reform educational opportunities aimed at weakening the relationship between origins and educational attainment.

There is little prospect of increasing social mobility without the political courage to address underlying sources of social congestion and inequalities in the competition for a livelihood. In the current policy context, social mobility has become part of the problem rather than the solution to a fairer society because the neo-liberal opportunity bargain cannot resolve the central problem of educational and social inequalities (Hutton 2010; Stiglitz 2012).

Indeed, existing studies of intergeneration social mobility show how difficult it is for education to equalise relative life-chances because it cannot compensate for wider social inequalities. This is why a 'deficit model' of working-class (im)mobility will inevitably fail. In periods of rapid employment growth, education can qualify people for new occupational positions but, as today, when the prospects for 'absolute' mobility are extremely limited, social mobility depends on breaking the middle-class stranglehold on education and professional employment.[10]

This article has drawn attention to increasing social congestion, which reflects a deeper crisis in liberal democratic societies (see Figure 2). It reveals the social limits of the neo-liberal opportunity bargain to resolve inequalities in condition, as well as opportunity (Brown, Lauder, and Ashton 2011; Souto-Otero 2010). There are too many contestants wanting the same things, often involving middle-class families competing with similar resources (including cultural assets), adding to congestion throughout the education system and job market that is ultimately self-defeating and socially wasteful.

This crisis will only be addressed when there is a political commitment to confront longstanding questions of distributional justice and social inequalities in life-chances. What is now required from the next generation of sociologists (including those within the sociology of education) is the same leap in sociological imagination that gave rise to the nascent studies of education and social mobility that played a major role in defining the discipline in the second-half of the twentieth century.

Acknowledgements

I would like to thank Chelly Halsey, Ian Jones, Hugh Lauder, and Gareth Rees for their invaluable comments on earlier drafts of this article.

Notes

1. More recent studies by Erikson and Goldthorpe (1993) and by Breen (2004) have extended our understanding of comparative differences in mobility rates; Marshall, Swift and Roberts (1997) reveal the 'myth' of an education-based meritocracy; Crompton (1989) and Walby (1997) focused on the importance of gender inequalities; while other sociologists have examined class cultures, identities and lifestyles in shaping inequalities in life-chances (Savage et al. 1992; Devine et al. 2005).
2. Even where there is an over-supply of qualified people it is viewed as a temporary problem as employers seek to take advantage of available skills (Acemoglu 2002).
3. The hypothesis of IMS remains of value despite the limitations examined in this article. It still has a role in assessing neo-liberal models because they claim that market competition is a more efficient way of delivering social mobility than state-managed alternatives.
4. However, there is evidence based on recent income data to show that inequalities in life-chances may be growing (Blanden, Gregg, and Machin 2005; Blanden and Machin 2007), although this is contested by Erikson and Goldthorpe (2010).
5. Even if they could contribute to absolute rates of mobility at times of increased demand for workers in intermediate and professional occupations. For further details about the pupil premium. see 'Consultation on School Funding Reform: Proposals for a Fairer System' available online: https://www.education.gov.uk/consultations/downloadableDocs/July%2011%20Consultation%20on%20School%20Funding%20Reform%20FINAL.pdf. For more on efforts to promote fair access to university, go to: http://www.offa.org.uk/.

6. There are also gender differences observed in both studies by Bukodi et al. and Li and Devine, which highlight concerns about the future mobility prospects for males from working-class backgrounds.
7. Performance within global capitalism, moreover, does not conform to the view of an ever-increasing demand for high-skilled, high-waged employees within western economies. Many companies continue to make decent profits based on a low-skilled workforce (Keep and Mayhew 2010). And the 'boom and bust' nature of capitalism, exemplified by the 2008 financial crisis, leads to fluctuations in the demand for skilled labour as austerity measures are introduced to reduce budget deficits (created by the nationalisation of private debt in the banking sector). Recent austerity measures have resulted in a decline in public-sector employment, previously expanded in the early 2000s by New Labour in Britain to compensate for weak labour-market demand in the private sector (Buchanan et al. 2009).
8. Social closure (Weber 1945; Parkin 1979; Brown 2000) refers to way social elites define the rules of the game to their own advantage. Although the focus is primarily on exclusionary tactics, it can also include consideration of inclusionary tactics to usurp the power base of privileged classes or social groups. Although ostensibly open to all, market competition primarily benefits those with the assets or capital (financial, cultural, social) to enable individuals or classes to preserve their privileges through restricting or out-performing others (individuals, groups or classes) within the competition for credentials, jobs or incomes. The concept of performocracy draws heavily on Lyotard's (1984) work on the performativity of knowledge. Within the field of education it also draws on the work of scholars including Ball (2003) and Ollsen and Peters (2007). Here, however, it is used in border societal terms also drawing on the work of scholars including Hayek (1960), and especially Polanyi's (1944) writings on the self-regulating market. In short, it is akin to the idea of a market-based, commodity-driven 'achieving' society dominated by 'use value', 'positional advantage' and 'competitive success'.
9. Based on the assumption that intelligence is randomly distributed throughout the population. However, some – including Herrnstein and Murray (1994) and Saunders (2006) – believe that the existing class structure does reflect the distribution of intelligence.
10. As noted above, giving working-class students more of what their middle-class peers had yesterday will do little to improve their chances in today's labour market, because achievements in education are relative. The 'deficit' does not narrowed by giving those from disadvantaged backgrounds access to 'more' education. The problem is not a working-class 'deficit' but middle-class access to capital (financial, cultural, and social), giving them an unfair advantage in education and the labour market (Bourdieu 1984).

References

Acemoglu, D. 2002. "Technical Change, Inequality and the Labor Market." *Journal of Economic Literature* 40: 7–72.
Allen, M., and P. Ainley. 2010. *Lost Generation? New Strategies for Youth and Education*. London: Continuum.
Arnot, M., and M. Mac an Ghaill. 2006. *The Routledge Falmer Reader in Gender and Education*. Abingdon: Routledge.

Ball, S. 1996. "School Choice, Social Class and Distinction: The Realization of Social Advantage in Education." *Journal of Education Policy* 11: 89–112.

Ball, S. 2003. "The Teacher's Soul and the Terrors of Performativity." *Journal of Education Policy* 18: 215–228.

Ball, S. 2012. *Global Education Inc.: New Policy Networks and the Neoliberal Imaginary.* London: Routledge.

Bell, D. 1973. *The Coming of Post-Industrial Society.* Harmondsworth: Penguin.

Blanden, J., P. Gregg, and S. Machin. 2005. "Social Mobility in Britain: Low and Falling, Centre Piece." Spring, 18–20. Available at: http://cep.lse.ac.uk/centrepiece/v10i1/blanden.pdf.

Blanden, J. and S. Machin. 2007. "Recent Changes in Intergenerational Mobility in Britain, Sutton Trust." Available at: http://www.suttontrust.com/reports/mainreport.pdf.

Blyton, P., E. Heery, and P. Turnbull. 2011. *Reassessing the Employment Relationship.* Basingstoke: Palgrave.

Boudon, R. 1973. *Education, Opportunity and Social Inequality.* New York, NY: John Wiley and Sons.

Boudon, R. 1982. *The Unintended Consequences of Social Action.* London: Macmillan.

Bourdieu, P. 1984. *Distinction: A Social Critique of the Judgement of Taste.* London: Routledge.

Breen, R. 2004. *Social Mobility in Europe.* Oxford: Oxford University Press.

Breen, R. 2010a. "Social Mobility and Equality of Opportunity, Geary Lecture Spring 2010." *The Economic and Social Review* 41 (4): 413–428.

Breen, R. 2010b. "Educational Expansion and Social Mobility in the 20th Century." *Social Forces* 89: 365–388.

Brown, P. 1990. "The 'Third Wave': Education and the Ideology of Parentocracy." *British Journal of Sociology of Education* 11: 65–85.

Brown, P. 2000. "The Globalisation of Positional Competition?" *Sociology* 34: 633–653.

Brown, P. 2003. "The Opportunity Trap: Education and Employment in a Global Economy." *European Educational Research Journal* 2: 141–177.

Brown, P. 2006. "The Opportunity Trap." (Revised and Abridged). In *Education, Globalization and Social Change*, edited by H. Lauder, P. Brown and J. A. Dillabough. Oxford: Oxford University Press.

Brown, P., and A. Hesketh. 2004. *The Mismanagement of Talent: Employability and Jobs in the Knowledge Economy.* Oxford: Oxford University Press.

Brown, P., H. Lauder, and D. Ashton. 2011. *The Global Auction: The Broken Promises of Education, Jobs and Incomes.* New York: Oxford University Press.

Brown, P., and S. Tannock. 2009. "Education, Meritocracy and the Global War for Talent." *Journal of Education Policy* 24: 377–392.

Brynjolfsson, E., and A. McAfee. 2011. *Race against the Machine.* Lexington, KY: Mass. Digital Frontier Press.

Buchanan, J., J. Froud, S. Johal, A. Leaver, and K. Williams. 2009. "Undisclosed and Unsustainable: Problems of the UK National Business Model." CRESC Working Paper 75, University of Manchester.

Bukodi, E., J. H. Goldthorpe, and L. Waller. 2013. "Has Social Mobility in Britain declined? New findings from Cross-Cohort Analyses." Oxford Institute of Social Policy and Nuffield College, available at: http://paa2013.princeton.edu/papers/130693.

Cabinet Office. 2009 "Unleashing Aspiration: The Final Report of the Panel on Fair Access to the Professions." Available at: http://www.bis.gov.uk/assets/biscore/corporate/migratedd/publications/p/panel-fair-access-to-professions-final-report-21july09.pdf.

Cabinet Office. 2011. *Opening Doors, Breaking Barriers: A Strategy for Social Mobility.* London: HM Government.

Cerny, P. G. 1997. "Paradoxes of the Competition State: The Dynamics of Political Globalization." *Government and Opposition* 32: 251–274.

Clegg, N. 2010. "Inequality becomes Injustice when it is Passed on, Generation to Generation." *The Guardian*, 23 November, 32.

Collins, R. 1979. *The Credential Society: An Historical Sociology of Education and Stratification.* New York, NY: Academic Press.

Crompton, R. 1989. "Class Theory and Gender." *The British Journal of Sociology* 40: 565–587.

Crompton, R. 2008. *Class and Stratification.* 3rd ed. Cambridge: Polity.

Dahrendorf, R. 1990. *The Modern Social Conflict.* Berkeley: University of California.

Department of Education. 2011. "The Importance of Schooling: School's White Paper." Available at: http://www.education.gov.uk/b0068570/the-importance-of-teaching.

Devine, F. 1997. *Social Class in Britain and America.* Edinburgh: Edinburgh University Press.

Devine, F., M. Savage, J. Scott, and R. Crompton. 2005. *Rethinking Class: Culture, Identities and Lifestyle.* Palgrave: Basingstoke.

Durkheim, E. 1933. *The Division of Labor in Society.* New York, NY: Macmillan.

Elias, P. and K. Purcell. 2012. "Higher Education and Social Background." In *Understanding Society*, ESRC/Institute for Social and Economic Research. https://www.understandingsociety.ac.uk/research/publications/findings/2012.

Erikson, R., and J. H. Goldthorpe. 1993. *The Constant Flux: The Study of Class Mobility in Industrial Societies.* Oxford: Oxford University Press.

Erikson, R., and J. H. Goldthorpe. 2010. "Has Social Mobility in Britain Decreased? Reconciling Divergent Findings on Income and Class Mobility." *The British Journal of Sociology* 61: 211–230.

Fevre, R. 2003. *The New Sociology of Economic Behaviour.* London: Sage.

Francis, B., and C. Skelton. 2005. *Reassessing Gender and Achievement.* London: Routledge.

Frank, R., and P. Cook. 1996. *The Winner-Take-All Society.* New York, NY: Penguin.

Gamble, A. 1996. *Hayek: The Iron Cage of Liberty.* Cambridge: Polity Press.

Glass, D. V. 1954. *Social Mobility in Britain.* London: Routledge and Kegan Paul.

Goldthorpe, J. H. 2007a. *On Sociology: Volume One – Critique and Program.* 2nd ed. Stanford: Stanford University Press.

Goldthorpe, J. H. 2007b. *On Sociology: Volume Two – Illustrations and Retrospect.* 2nd ed. Stanford: Stanford University Press.

Goldthorpe, J. H., and M. Jackson. 2007. "Intergenerational Class Mobility in Contemporary Britain: Political Concerns and Empirical Findings." *The British Journal of Sociology* 58 (4): 525–546.

Goldthorpe, J. H., C. Llewellyn, and C. Payne. 1980. *Social Mobility and Class Structure in Modern Britain.* Oxford: Clarendon Press.

Halsey, A. H. 1975. "Sociology and the Equality Debate." *Oxford Review of Education* 1: 9–23.

Halsey, A. H., A. F. Heath, and J. M. Ridge. 1980. *Origins and Destinations: Family, Class and Education in Modern Britain.* Oxford: Clarendon Press.

Halsey, A. H., H. Lauder, P. Brown, and A. S. Wells, eds. 1997. *Education: Culture, Economy and Society*. Oxford: Oxford University Press.

Hayek, F. A. 1960. *The Constitution of Liberty*. London: Routledge.

Head, S. 2003. *The New Ruthless Economy: Work and Power in the Digital Age*. New York, NY: Oxford University Press.

Heath, A. and S. Y. Chueng. 2006. "Ethnic Penalties in the Labour Market: Employers and Discrimination." Research Report No.341, Department of Work and Pensions, http://statistics.dwp.gov.uk/asd/asd5/rports2005-2006/rrep341.pdf.

Heath, A., N. D. de Graaf, and Y. Li. 2010. "How Fair is the Route to the Top? Perceptions of Social Mobility In *British Social Attitudes, the 27th Report*, edited by A. Park and C. Bryson. London: Sage.

Heath, A., and A. Zimdars. 2011. "Social Mobility: Drivers and Policy Responses Revisited." *British Academy Review, Issue* 17: 8–10.

Herrnstein, R. J., and C. Murray. 1994. *The Bell Curve: Intelligence and Class Structure in American Life*. New York, NY: Free Press.

Hills, J. et al. 2010. "An Anatomy of Economic Inequality in the UK." Report of the National Equality Panel (London: Centre for the Analysis of Social Exclusion, LSE). http://sticerd.lse.ac.uk/dps/case/cr/CASEreport60_summary.pdf.

Hirsch, F. 1977. *Social Limits to Growth*. London: Routledge and Kegan Paul.

Holmes, G., and K. Mayhew. 2012. "The Changing Shape of the UK Job Market and its Implications for the Bottom Half of Earners (London: Resolution Foundation)." Available at: http://www.resolutionfoundation.org/media/media/downloads/The_Changing_Shape_of_the_UK_Job_Market_1.pdf.

Hutton, W. 2010. *Them and Us: Changin Britain – Why We Need a Fair Society*. London: Little Brown.

Hutton, W. 2011. "Hutton Review of Fair Pay in the Public Sector: Final Report." Available at: http://www.hm-treasury.gov.uk/indreview_willhutton_fairpay.htm.

International Labour Organisation. 2011. *Global Employment Trends for Youth: 2011 Update*. Geneva: ILO.

Jackson, M., J. H. Goldthorpe, and C. Mills. 2005. "Education, Employers and Class Mobility." *Research in Social Stratification and Mobility* 23: 3–33.

Jonsson, J. O. 1992. *Towards the Merit-Selective Society?* Stockholm: Swedish Institute for Social Research, University of Stockholm.

Keep, E., and K. Mayhew. 2010. "Moving beyond Skills as a Social and Economic Panacea." *Work, Employment & Society* 24: 565–577.

Lauder, H., M. Young, H. Daniels, M. Balarin, and J. Lowe. 2012. *Educating for the Knowledge Economy: Critical Perspectives*. London: Routledge.

Lazonick, W., and M. O'Sullivan. 2000. "Maximizing Shareholder Value: A New Ideology for Corporate Governance." *Economy and Society* 29: 13–35.

Li, Y. and F. Devine. 2011. "Is Social Mobility Really Declining? Intergenerational Class Mobility in Britain in the 1990s and the 2000s." *Sociological Research Online*, 16, (3) 4. Available at http://www.socresonline.org.uk/16/3/4.html.

Livingstone, D. W., and D. Guile. 2012. *The Knowledge Economy and Lifelong Learning: A Critical Reader*. Rotterdam: Sense Publishers.

Lockwood, D. 1958. *The Blackcoated Worker: A Study in Class Consciousness*. London: Unwin.

Lyotard, J. F. 1984. *The Postmodern Condition: A Report on Knowledge*. Manchester, NH: Manchester University Press.

Marshall, G., A. Swift, and S. Roberts. 1997. *Against the Odds? Social Class and Social Justice in Industrial Societies*. Oxford: Oxford University Press.

Merton, R. 1957. *Social Theory and Social Structure*. New York, NY: Free Press.

Michaels, E., H. Handfield-Jones, and B. Axelrod. 2001. *The War for Talent*. Boston, MA: Harvard Business School Press.

Mishel, L., J. Bivens, E. Gould, and H. Shierholz. 2012. *The State of Working America*. 12th Ed. Washington: Institute of Economic Policy/ Cornell University Press.

OECD. 2010. "A Family Affair: Intergenerational Social Mobility Across OECD Countries." In *Economic Policy Reforms: Going for Growth*, Available at: http://www.oecd.org/document/24/0,3746,en_2649_34117_41665624_1_1_1_1,00.html.

Olssen, M., and M. Peters. 2005. "Neoliberalism, Higher Education and the Knowledge Economy: From the Free Market to Knowledge Capitalism." *Journal of Education Policy* 20 (3): 313–347.

Ollsen, M., and M. Peters. 2007. "Neoliberalism, Higher Education and the Knowledge Economy: From the Free Market to Knowledge Capitalism." *Journal of Education Policy* 20: 313–345.

Parkin, F. 1979. *Marxism and Class Theory: A Bourgeois Critique*. London: Tavistock.

Parsons, T. 1961. "The School Class as a Social System." In *Education, Economy and Society*, edited by A. H. Hasley , et al.. New York, NY: Free Press.

Payne, G. 2012. "A New Social Mobility? the Political Redefinition of a Sociological Problem." *Contemporary Social Science* 7: 55–71.

Penny, L. 2010. "Girls, Exams and Employment: A Race to the Bottom." *New Statesman*, 29 August. Available at: http://www.newstatesman.com/blogs/laurie-penny/2010/08/young-women-girls-market.

Peters, A. M. 2011. *Neoliberalism and after?* New York, NY: Peter Lang.

Polanyi, K. 1944. *The Great Transformation*. Boston, Mass: Beacon Books.

Power, S., T. Edwards, G. Whitty, and V. Wigfall. 2003. *Education and the Middle Class*. Buckingham: Open University Press.

Rawls, J. 1971. *A Theory of Justice*. Oxford: Clarendon Press.

Reay, D., G. Crozier, and J. Clayton. 2009. "'Strangers in Paradise?': Working-Class Students in Elite Universities." *Sociology* 43: 1103–1121.

Rose, N. 1999. *Governing the Soul: The Shaping of the Private Self*. 2nd edn. London: Free Association Books.

Roulin, N., and A. Bangerter. 2013. "Students' Use of Extra-Curricular Activities for Positional Advantage in Competitive Job Markets." *Journal of Education and Work* 26 (1): 21–47.

Saunders, P. 2006. "Meritocracy and Popular Legitimacy." In *The Rise and Rise of Meritocracy*, edited by G. Dench. Oxford: Blackwell/The Political Quarterly.

Savage, M. 2000. *Class Analysis and Social Transformation*. Buckingham: Open University Press.

Savage, M., J. Barlow, A. Dickens, and T. Fielding. 1992. *Property, Bureaucracy and Culture: Middle Class Formation in Contemporary Britain*. London: Routledge.

Simmel, G. 1978 [1907]. *The Philosophy of Money*, Edited by David Frisby (London, Routledge).

Skeggs, B. 2004. *Class, Self, Culture*. London: Routledge.

Souto-Otero, M. 2010. "Education, Meritocracy and Redistribution." *Journal of Education Policy* 25 (3): 397–413.

Stiglitz, J. E. 2012. *The Price of Inequality*. London: Allen Lane.

Swift, A. 2004. "Would Perfect Mobility Be Perfect?" *European Sociological Review* 20: 1–11.

Valencia, R. R. 1997. *The Evolution of Deficit Thinking: Educational Thought and Practice*. London: Routledge.
Walby, S. 1997. *Gender Transformations*. London: Routledge.
Weber, M. 1945. In *From Max Weber*, edited by H. Gerth and C. W. Mills. London: Routledge.
Whitty, G., S. Power, and D. Halpin. 1998. *Devolution and Choice in Education: The School, the State, and the Market*. Philadelphia, PA: Open University Press.
Wilensky, H. 1960. "Work, Careers, and Social Integration'." *International Social Science Journal* 12: 543–560.
Wooldridge, A. 2006. "The Battle for Brainpower." *Economist*. October 7, 1–14.
Young, M. 1961. *The Rise of the Meritocracy*. Harmondsworth: Penguin.

'Class work': producing privilege and social mobility in elite US secondary schools

Lois Weis and Kristin Cipollone

Department of Educational Leadership and Policy, State University of New York, University at Buffalo, Buffalo, New York, USA

> Drawing upon two ethnographic studies of affluent and elite co-educational secondary schools in the United States, Weis and Cipollone spotlight the explicit 'class work' of a now highly insecure middle/upper middle class, as they attempt to maintain advantage via entrance to particularly located post-secondary destinations. Affirming the notion that class position must now be 'won' at both the individual and collective level, rather than constituting the 'manner to which one is born,' the authors track and theorize intensified preparation for and application to particular kinds of post-secondary destinations in an increasingly segmented national and international marketplace for higher education. Although the US media have taken note of such 'application frenzy,' little scholarly work tracks and theorizes this 'frenzy' as a distinctly 'class process,' one that represents intensified 'class work' at one and the same time as class 'winners' and 'losers' become ever more apparent in the larger global arena.

Introduction

Since the 1960s there has been a robust research program linked to issues of education and social mobility in both the United States and the United Kingdom (Goldthorpe 1987, 1992; Sewell and Hauser 1975). In the United States, status attainment models have predominated. Using statistical techniques and relying on quantifiable data to determine the relationship between individual socio-economic status of origin (usually measured by father's occupation and education), measured IQ, educational attainment, and occupational status and income, among other variables, models attempt empirical description of society. As Kerckhoff 1995, 2001) points out, however, such models ignore the relationship between institutional arrangements and processes of stratification. As such, they are unable to 'take into account the structural locations in the social organization that constitute the society's sorting machine' (Kerckoff 1995, 326).[1]

Here we take Kerckhoff's observations seriously, giving specific attention to the extent to which student location within the structure of educational opportunities in secondary schools – both as hierarchically ranked and as providing varied opportunities for later moves and access to various kinds and levels of attainment – empirically limits their possible locations at the next level (Kerckoff 1995). Long considered a pathway to ensure upward mobility, recent shifts within the higher education system in the United States (Hoxby 2004; Mullen 2010; Thomas and Bell 2008) complicates the ways in which education confers social advantage. In brief, intensified massification of the post-secondary sector, as coupled with a relatively constant number of available slots in the most valued post-secondary destinations, renders the 'access to what' question increasingly paramount. In response to the limitations of 'political arithmetic' approaches, we highlight the value of developing an institutional dimension to studies of social stratification. In so doing, we provide insights into the ways in which the day-to-day actions by students, parents, and school personnel result in normative practices and subsequently work to pattern inequality.

Access to particularly located post-secondary institutions has become a space of intensified struggle, especially for more socially and economically privileged groups, who are poised to take advantage of their position to maximize opportunity for their offspring. Such struggle is linked to the now globalized knowledge economy, in which competition for jobs has increased while economic security, particularly for the middle/upper middle class, has become less stable (Brown, Lauder, and Ashton 2011; Ehrenreich 1990; Harvey 2005; Reich 2007). Given massification and accompanying intensified stratification of the post-secondary sector in the United States, middle-class and upper-middle-class parents/families work to maximize their advantage via access to particularly located post-secondary destinations (Gamoran 2008; Lucas 2001).

We draw upon data from two ethnographic studies of relatively elite co-educational secondary schools (elite is defined as high ranking with regard to the educational sector of the nation) located in tier-two, 'non-global' cities in the northeastern United States. Such cities are marked by substantially less concentration of capital and wealth than tier-one cities, such as New York City, wherein schools draw from a far wealthier clientele. This has clear implications for allowable tuition costs at differentially located schools ('what the market can bear'), as well as relative endowment levels over time.[2] Data were collected over a one and one half-year time period at two different types of schools: a secular private co-educational day institution (National Association of Independent Schools); and an affluent, suburban, co-educational State school located in a comparable geographic area.

Data were collected during the 2009/10 academic school year and each researcher was embedded within her respective site for this entire year with some limited engagement before this year.[3] At the State school, 37 participants were interviewed and participated in three focus group sessions. Study participants include: students (nine in the top 10% of the class), parents ($n = 11$), school counselors ($n = 8$), counseling support staff ($n = 2$), 11th-grade and 12th-grade core subject teachers ($n = 5$), and administrators ($n = 2$).[4] All participants were interviewed between one and three times. Additionally, 200 hours were spent in the field observing classes, counselor sessions, college-related presentations, course advisement, parent information meetings, SAT test administration and many other less-formal occurrences (i.e. spending time in the College Center while students researched schools). Relevant school documents were also collected and analyzed.

Data collection at the private school was conducted similarly. A total of 38 individuals were interviewed, including students (13 in the top 20% of the class), Head of the Upper School, Head of College Counseling (one of two counselors in the school), parents ($n = 18$), and teachers of core junior and senior year subjects ($n = 5$). All participants were interviewed between one and three times. Additionally, a total of 100 hours were spent in the field observing classes, college-related presentations, parent information meetings, and other less formal interactions such as time spent in the senior lounge while students engaged the college process, and so forth. As with the State school, relevant school documents were collected and analyzed.[5]

Engaging the Weis and Fine (2012) method of *critical bifocality* – a dedicated theoretical and methodological commitment to a bifocal design that simultaneously documents the linkages and capillaries of structural arrangements and the discursive practices by which youth and adults make sense of their circumstances – we reveal the ways in which and the extent to which similarly capitalized parents and children in two different types of secondary school position for advantage amidst altered economic context that threatens the stability which once marked the middle-class/upper-middle-class experience (Ehrenreich 1990). Critical bifocality offers a theory of method wherein researchers make visible the linkages or circuits through which structural conditions are enacted in policy and institutions, as well as the ways in which such conditions are woven into community relationships and metabolized by individuals.[6]

Class productions in new time and space

Reay, Crozier, and James suggest that:

> Despite the advent of the 'age of anxiety', the emergence of the 'super rich', and economic upheavals (Apple 2010), it appears that the white middle

classes continue to thrive, their social position strengthened and consolidated. However, there are also growing signs of unease, the exacerbation of anxiety, and a lack of ontological security, 'the sense of continuity and order in events, including those not directly within the perceptual environment of the individuals (Giddens 1991, 243). (Reay, Crozier, and James 2011, 2)

'These insecurities,' as Reay, Crozier, and James (2011, 2) argue, 'are particularly evident in their children's education.' Anxieties surface in relation to where their children go to school; what they learn in school in contrast to what other people's children learn in other schools; and, as we argue here, how parents and children linked to specific secondary schools work to position their children for the now global knowledge economy in which access to highly valued post-secondary destinations is scripted as increasingly paramount.[7]

Given charges of impending class dislocation of the relatively privileged, our research is instructive. We pry open critical discussion with regard to the explicit 'class work' involved in maintaining advantage under shifting global conditions and attendant rearrangement of the US post-secondary sector by exploring the specifically located and largely unacknowledged reworking of the professional and managerial upper middle class. Simultaneously, we focus on the mechanisms through which observed, macro-level, globally induced phenomena are produced and reproduced at the lived level on a daily basis, whether by explicit design/work, or by virtue of what Bourdieu refers to as '"habitus" – a system of lasting and transposable dispositions which, integrating past experiences, functions at every moment as a matrix of perceptions, appreciations and actions and makes possible the achievement of infinitely diversified tasks' (Bourdieu and Wacquant, as cited in Bourdieu 1982, 18). Affirming the notion that class position must now be 'won' at both the individual and collective level, rather than constituting the 'manner to which one is born,' data enable us to track and theorize the intensified preparation for, and application to, specific post-secondary destinations in relatively privileged secondary schools as parents and children attempt to hold onto social (and economic) advantage.

Our data suggest that there is increasing pressure for children in top curricular tracks (Advanced Placement [AP] and International Baccalaureate) to attend the most selective post-secondary institutions in the United States – in this case, those classified as Most Competitive (including, but not exclusively, Ivy League schools) and Highly Competitive+private institutions.[8] Marked as 'distinctive' by virtue of secondary school curricular track placement, students and parents script themselves as highly competitive in the post-secondary admissions process. However, the intensifying national marketplace for higher education, coupled with relatively stable entering classes at the most selective institutions, renders competition for entrance to these schools increasingly intense (Hoxby 1997). In point of fact, as more students from a broader range of secondary schools apply to and, to some extent at least, gain admission to the best post-secondary institutions in the United States (Bowen and Bok 1998; Cookson and Persell 1985), the acceptance rate to these institutions plummets, rendering competition for admission ever more fierce while simultaneously raising the status of these schools in the ubiquitous institutional rankings.[9]

Within this context, similarly privileged parents and children in both school sectors work hard to position for continued advantage. Importantly, however, our data suggest that it is the particular *sector* of secondary school – private versus State – that encourages distinct forms of class positioning 'work,' which then sets the stage for differential post-secondary attendance patterns, and, perhaps, future class position. We turn to the State secondary school first.

Class/ed practices and the post-secondary process: a State school example

Ball (2003, 28) tells us that 'classes, and here specifically the middle class, are to a great extent, constituted through their practices.' In other words, much of what earns a particular person or group the moniker of middle class has as much to do (or more) with the particular day-to-day practices and social and cultural experiences one engages, as it does the types of careers one pursues and the attached income and prestige; or, as Walkerdine, Lucey, and Melody put it, 'the social and psychic practices through which ordinary people live, survive and cope' (2001, 27).

In the footsteps of Ball and of Walkerdine, Lucey, and Melody, among others, we understand that much of what it means to be middle class or upper middle class in Canalside, an affluent, suburban community, is inextricably connected to ways of behaving and acting.[10] While certainly related to income, these ways of acting and being are heavily influenced by other families and their practices, and by schools (Ball 2003; Weis 2008). The acts of preparing for and applying to college, then, are practices that are influenced by 'classed' ways of being (and *habitus*) and shaped by what others in this social class category consider to be appropriate choices and actions.

Explicit 'class moves' among parents in Canalside begin early, revolving largely around locating a place of residence tied to their already born, or anticipated, children's attendance at particular State schools. Canalside has been rated as one of '100 Best Places to Live' in the United States and is recognized as having some of the strongest schools in the larger Tech City metropolitan area. The median income places the community squarely in the fourth economic quintile, with the majority of study participants earning enough to place them in the top quintile.[11] Median home prices are some of the highest in the area and the majority of Canalside residents (over 70%) own their own homes.[12] Canalside exceeds national averages in all areas in regards to educational attainment, and approximately 53% of the civilian employed population works in professional and managerial occupations, and about 80% work for private employers.[13] The community is almost exclusively White (95% of the population is White), and less than 3% of families fall below the poverty line. Given these descriptive statistics, Canalside qualifies as one of the most exclusive communities in the greater Tech City metropolitan area. It also has a reputation as a district with strong schools, which is a major selling point for real-estate agents, further entrenching its reputation as a good place for affluent people to live and send their children to school.

It is not uncommon for parents in the United States to purchase homes in particular neighborhoods in order to gain access to valued State schools. Recent studies by Holme (2002), Brantlinger (2003), Andre-Bechely (2005), Lawrence (2009) and others highlight the ways in which middle-class and upper-middle-class parents make very specific housing choices directly related to school reputations. Similar to Holme's (2002) findings, Canalside parents relied primarily upon their social networks of families, friends, colleagues, and acquaintances who are similarly situated (financially), as well as their knowledge of the area, to assess the relative reputation of the educational sector. As parent Allison Gruzina tells it, part of why they opted to purchase a new home (which they needed for their growing family) was because 'people said "Oh, the schools were good and blah, blah, blah," stuff like that.'

Significantly, parents begin to position their children for post-secondary entrance when children are very young. Beyond purchasing a home in what is perceived to be one of the most highly advantageous school catchment areas, parents engage in particular positioning work with an eye toward marking their children with 'distinction' at a very young age. For example, Canalside parents discuss working to ensure placement in gifted and talented programs in elementary school and linked accelerated curriculum in middle school. Given that the US post-secondary selection process is driven by full dossier review (the dossier, at minimum, includes: grade point average; teacher and counselor recommendations; SAT test and subject area scores/ACT[14], as relevant; sport and additional extracurriculars, and volunteer work) rather than a unitary set of secondary school-leaving examination scores and/or university entrance examination scores, the explicit move to mark children as distinctive at a very young age is noteworthy. Parents operate under the assumption that such distinction travels with their children through secondary school, and into the post-secondary entrance process.

Watching, waiting, and deciding when to intervene

In her chapter entitled 'Watching, Waiting, and Deciding when to Intervene', Lareau (2008) – drawing from her study of middle/upper-middle-class and working-class families' childrearing patterns across class and race in the United States (Lareau 2003) – analyzes the ways in which Black, middle-class parents utilize their class-based resources to ensure advantage for their children *vis-à-vis* the education system.[14] Lareau suggests that parents 'were *selective* in their activation of cultural capital' ((2008, 128), opting to choose their battles rather than intervene constantly on behalf of their children.

Participants from Canalside express and enact similar sentiments, particularly in regard to secondary school experiences and the post-secondary entrance process. Based upon parent and counselor interview data, participants note that while there are a few hyper-involved parents, these so-called 'helicopter' parents are, for the most part, few and far between.[15] Comments made by Nadine, a school counselor, which are representative of the counselors as a whole, suggest that 'some parents are over involved [in the process] but for the most part, parents are pretty actively involved,' mostly, she explains 'by driving the process.' Rather than micro-manage the process at all relevant points, in discursive contrast to the popular rendition (and as will be seen, in contradistinction to Matthews Academy), Nadine indicates that parents prompt their children to make their *own* critical decisions: 'Ok, we are going to visit some colleges over Columbus Day weekend; tell me what campus you want to visit.'

In point of fact, parent and counselor accounts indicate that direct intervention by parents on behalf of students drops off in high school rather than intensifies at the point of post-secondary entrance, suggesting that parents are much more directly involved at the elementary and middle school levels, a finding supported by Lareau (2003), Brantlinger (2003) and others. Canalside focal parents, like Sandra Whitcombe, for example, recount stories of approaching the principal of her son Brad's elementary school after she felt his second-grade teacher passed him over for the gifted and talented program. Requesting that he be *formally* tested for admission rather than simply relying upon the teacher's (perceived to be incorrect) subjective judgment, the gifted designation was ultimately granted. Placement in the gifted program set in motion an educational trajectory that traveled with Brad into middle and secondary school, ultimately positioning him in particular ways *vis-à-vis* the post-secondary search process. Mrs Penn, in similar fashion, intentionally sought a teaching position in the district when her children were young – in fact she went back to school to become a teacher explicitly to teach in Canalside – so that she could 'have [her] hands in everything,' thereby attempting to ensure her children's future rather than leave it entirely up to the school.

Abby, a Canalside school counselor who has spent some time working at the middle school level in the district, shares her perspective on parental involvement in relation to positioning work at the middle school:

Well, they have this accelerated and twice exceptional [label] and they label them in elementary school, whether they are advanced or not, and that kind of sticks with them.[16] And the parents are constantly [knocks on table to simulate knocking on a door] 'My kid has been labeled twice exceptional' and it's constantly like 'What can I do to get my kid ahead?' And, it's constant, you know, 'What can I do?' You see it in the Honor-thing in middle school, it's like math and science are the only places where they are going to be able to get ahead high school-wise, so parents are always wanting to, you know, 'I want my kid in honors, I want my kid in honors!' There is a lot of that pressure from parents.

Jamie, another school counselor, affirms Abby's comments, indicating that parents push for their children to be classified as exceptional and/or gifted early on and placed in Honors-level classes in middle school because they are interested in 'what's going to make their kid competitive when they apply to college.' Parents intervene, particularly in the younger grades, to ensure academic advantage for their children by way of positioning for presumed access to high-level, gatekeeping courses in secondary school. By secondary school, however, direct intervention of this type becomes far less frequent, and parents trust the school to work in the best interest of those positioned at the top of the academic hierarchy (and/or work directly with the students) so as to obtain entrance into the most valued and prestigious post-secondary institutions in the nation.

Course selection

Once in secondary school, while parents certainly appear to encourage children to build upon their already marked 'distinction,' students themselves drive the push for high-level courses, wherein admission to a highly selective four-year post-secondary institution becomes an integral part of student identity among those students in the top 10% of the class. Building on prior schooling experiences, and parental advocacy in regards to earlier placement in gifted and talented programs and accelerated curriculum in middle school, as well as the normalization of parental (and community) expectation about college attendance, secondary school students come to take ownership of their *own* academic careers, making choices that continue the positioning work that was once the exclusive domain of parents:

Kristin (interviewer): And Kelly took a number of APs, right?

Sue (parent): She took a few, yes.

Kristin: Is that something that you and your husband encouraged?

Sue: Well, yeah, we did encourage her, just because of her ability. You know, we'd rather see her struggle a little bit than coast through.

Sue states that she and her husband encouraged Kelly to enroll in advanced coursework, including several AP classes during her junior and senior year. Kelly attests that while she took a number of advanced courses, this is something she might not have done had she not aspired to attend a highly selective college. Due to Kelly's initial designation as gifted and talented, as accompanied by logical subsequent enrollment in high level courses in middle and secondary school, Kelly is now in a position to *choose* to take APs and do well in them, clearly not an option open to all students. While Kelly is certainly intelligent and hard working, this sheds light on the ways in which schools, as middle-class and/or upper-middle-class institutions, praise and reward family practices that are in line with their values (Hochschild and Scovronick 2003).

Further, as Canalside, like virtually all secondary schools in the United States, employs a system of academic tracking, we can see how Kelly, who was placed in the gifted program in elementary school, is able to convert such placement into later academic advantage with regard to course selection. While other students may work equally hard or even harder than Kelly, because she had been previously placed in the accelerated track she now has access to higher-level courses, and is now deemed to have greater 'ability' than most of her peers at Canalside. Importantly, and in addition to Kelly's intelligence, such ultimate advantage often rests on parental intervention at an early age. This, coupled with the available opportunity structure, such as gifted and talented programs in given districts, serves to shape school outcomes, both offering more to certain students while designating them as more 'accomplished' by the end of secondary school.

Most notably, by the time Canalside students reach secondary school, parents exert a somewhat 'hands off policy' with regard to the highly intensified post-secondary admissions process. Canalside parents tend to engage a very distinct form of 'up front class work,' as they take great care to purchase homes in particular catchment areas and subsequently work to position their children for accelerated/gifted and talented programs at the elementary and middle school levels. Such 'up front' work is engaged under the assumption that, once marked 'distinction' is accomplished, schools themselves, and particularly the secondary school, will work to position their now appropriately designated children (the top 10% of the class; those taking the AP and/or International Baccalaureate courses) for entrance to the most highly valued post-secondary institutions in the nation.

At the point of secondary school entrance, then, parents in this State secondary school largely abdicated *explicit* and constant intervention with regard to driving towards the post-secondary admissions process, instead placing this task in the hands of the school and, ultimately, the students themselves. In contrast to explicit and direct intervention as evidenced in earlier grades, parents adopt more of a 'lead from behind' approach once children enter secondary school. Parents spend a great deal of 'up front' effort laying a foundation for their children that emphasizes academic achievement, high expectations, and selective college admissions. Additionally, they put a tremendous amount of effort into cultivating particular identities and skill sets early on (often before children were even born; i.e. housing choices), which results in the normalization of these values and identities, and, ultimately, the adoption of selective college-oriented identities that students embrace *as their own*. This, along with the organizational *habitus* of the school (McDonough 1997), which ensures the privileged status of the participant students by isolating them in advanced tracks with students like themselves, and thereby insulating them in a selective college-going culture, allows parents to take a step back.[17] This is in contrast to the shape and form of positioning work engaged in the elite private sector, a sector to which we now turn.

Fractures in the middle/upper middle class: the case of Matthews Academy

Like parents in elite State schools, parents who send their children to elite private schools similarly invest 'up front' in their children's future class position. Attending a private school reflects parental work involved in accessing such schools, as well as the underlying work and accompanying sacrifices of having enough disposable income to pay for them. However, two points are relevant here with regard to the sites under consideration. To begin with, the class circumstances of the parents in these two schools are, by and large, quite similar, comprised of families with largely equivalent tertiary-level educational backgrounds, levels of disposable income, and occupational locations. Rather than upper class in the sense of being able to live off investments, families at both the private and State schools under study are largely professional and/or upper managerial, constituting the top 20% of the US class structure, with enough disposable income to invest in their children's future.

At both Canalside and Matthews Academy, families and children are comparably *highly privileged* in relation to the larger metropolitan context in which they are located. So too, they are comparably *less privileged* in relation to comparably located families in cities (such as New York City) of far greater concentrations of capital and wealth. Canalside and Matthews residents and school children, then, are *relatively and objectively both more and less privileged* in the same kinds of ways, depending on the reference point; the most meaningful difference between the two populations lies with the schools their children attend, a point that has critical implications for the nature of class positioning and likely future relative class location in new national and global context.

In similar fashion, although gaining entrance into particularly located private nursery, elementary, and secondary schools in wealthier cities has become hyper competitive, this is not the case in tier-two cities of far less concentration of wealth, where far fewer people can afford the price of attendance. For this reason, competition for entrance into private institutions in the geographic area under consideration is not particularly intense. Rather than turn large numbers of prospective applicants away by virtue of a rigorous admissions process, private schools in tier-two cities work hard to *entice* residents to send their children to their respective institutions. For this reason, students in the top academic tracks at elite private and State schools, such as those under consideration here, are largely similar with regard to academic ability.

There are, however, differences in the nature of the 'class' work in the two institutional sectors, in spite of the fact that they serve comparably capitalized students and parents.[18] What is not starkly revealed in terms of background characteristics is exposed clearly with regard to forms and duration of class positioning, wherein private school parents *intensify* their efforts at class positioning at one and the same time as parents in the privileged State sector largely *retract/redirect* their direct involvement in the process. Our data below suggest the extent to which parents in privileged privates markedly expand their involvement at the point of the post-secondary admissions processes, a response that is shaped by the *organizational habitus* of the school.

Leaving nothing to chance: micromanaging the college process

The post-secondary search and application process begins in junior year when initial lists of prospective institutions are drawn up, quickly followed by on-site college visits in spring semester and into the summer, and then intensifies in the early fall of senior year. This is, by and large, the same *formal* process followed at Canalside. Although college counselors warn parents at Matthews Academy that 'your child must drive the process, not you,' parents remain integrally connected to each stage of the process, often micromanaging the process as if they were their children's personal college counselor.

At the most basic level, privileged parents across both sites pay for and facilitate college visits, and ultimately pay, in most cases, for the cost of attendance, which is exceptionally steep, even at State institutions in the United States. Parents prod, strategize, remind their children to meet deadlines, stay on top of their college essays, and get feedback on their essays, study for the SAT/ACT and SAT subject tests, as relevant, and so forth. Perhaps most importantly, they support their children emotionally as they go through the increasingly long and arduous admissions process that spans approximately two years, culminating in decision letters from the myriad colleges to which they apply.[19] As many parents note, 'breakdowns' are common, and it is a rare student, male or female, that goes through the process emotionally unscathed.

While these practices are largely the same across the two schools, the extent to which parents actively direct this process differs. While Canalside parents typically took a 'lead from behind approach,' granting their children greater autonomy in putting together an initial list of colleges to which they might apply, arranging college visits, assembling application materials, and making application decisions, Matthews parents (in most cases) did not leave these decisions to their children or the college counselors, in spite of the fact that the in-school college counseling process at Matthews was more intense than at Canalside. For example, each Matthews child is expected to meet with the counselor and their parents at the end of junior year. From that point on, children are expected to meet with the counselor on their own, as necessary. However, it was not at all uncommon for Matthews' parents to schedule additional and not infrequent one-on-one meetings with the school counselor, and from there to take over the process.[20]

In line with what Matthews students are themselves expected to do, Matthews parents often meticulously monitor and assess their children's strengths and weaknesses, with an eye towards their chances of acceptance at particular institutions based on grades, course load and the like. Such vigilance extends beyond those parents in the private sector who are themselves highly educated. Ron Tomlinson, a White working-class parent who has no prior connection with private schools, is, according to Head of Counseling Dave Henderson, 'hunting big game' (most specifically Harvard, Yale, Princeton), after which comment Dave notes: 'He is not going to get it.' The struggle between son and parent is palpable, as Matt wants to go to Rensselaer Polytechnic Institute, as this is where he personally sees his strengths, and Ron wants him to apply to the Ivies, Harvard in particular.[21]

The desire of Mr Tomlinson to situate his child in an Ivy League school is understandable, especially in light of the sacrifices that Mr Tomlinson had to make in order to send his son to Matthews, but Matt wants to no part of this scenario, making it clear that he wants to go to Rennselaer Tech. In response, Mr Tomlinson drives even harder towards college visits, a push that is largely ignored by Matt who has already made up his mind that he was interested in Rensselaer Polytechnic Institute:

> Ron: Take your pick [of colleges to visit]. Here's my schedule. And I offered it before the application process. I said, you know, when he was at Harvard over the summer, he really didn't get to see the school. You know, cuz at first he's like, 'I'm not sure [why I didn't look at the school]. I was at practices [soccer].' Why don't I take you back there in the regular school year? ... Nothing ever, you know, and I was trying not to pressure him too much, and there were times where I as like, pulling my hair out! ... One of the reasons why I told him I was hoping he would apply to Harvard was income-wise, it's free for me to send him there [tuition pricing is tied to income levels and Matt, by his father's calculation, would attend tuition-free].

Thinking, plotting, planning

As mentioned earlier, for highly ranked students at relatively elite schools, there is a great deal of pressure to gain admission to the most highly selective colleges and universities. Students (and their parents) perceive themselves as the 'best of the best' and strive to gain entry to the most prestigious post-secondary institutions that will confer this status (Gatzambide-Fernandez 2009; Stevens 2007). In response, parents at Matthews, in collaboration with their children, work to intensify their strategizing. Susan and Robert Larkin cast their 'outsider' eye on the process, as they experienced their own schooling in Europe and their two older children attended higher education there:

> Susan: [...] So I would say the last 8–10 years that I've heard parents talking about it [college application process and entry]. Parents of the older children, I would say, maybe even into middle school, parents are contriving or conniving.
>
> Robert: From my point of view, in a real sense, it [the conniving and contriving] started in sophomore year.
>
> Susan: It intensified certainly.
>
> Robert: Became much more apparent. So we had heard, Susan probably more than I had. We'd heard the noise, some of the sure things, but it didn't have anything to do with us, things that we had to do. And I think it was at that level, we began to realize that it was competitive, and ... maybe you could've started sending your child to this place [a specific institution] to do extracurriculars and you would tell your colleagues [other parents of children in the class] afterwards, to show how good you are, but you wouldn't actually bring them all up and say, 'Why don't we all send our children to [the local cancer research facility] to do cancer research ... because everyone wanted to get a step ahead with their children, was my impression. ... So I think that sophomore year onwards, we began to realize it was a game, and that we were perhaps a bit late in the game, and that we're still a bit late in the game and we're realizing that. Even if you put down your name for mock trial and you don't even appear or do anything, at least you can put on the form ... I did mock trial at sophomore level, even if you had only turned up to one meeting, and we go 'shoot', we didn't do that because we thought honor was pure ... It's just a bit unfair, you know, that sort of, well most people probably behaving entirely honorably, but there's some sense of competition and do anything to get your child well positioned, and I think we've been swept up in it because at the end of the day, the person who loses if we stand our ground is Stephanie.

Succumbing to the US normative private school processes around post-secondary admissions, Susan and Robert begin to encourage Stephanie to maximize her international roots, thereby distinguishing herself from others in the college competition:

> Susan: I did say to Stephanie, it's all well to say you've traveled, but further down the line, this may be mistaken for colleges thinking here's a rich kid, driving around in expensive cars, you know, [staying at] the Best Western overseas. I said maybe you have to demonstrate you can do more than that. I mean, I knew she could. So I put it to her to volunteer at this home in Bogotá. And it was started and run by a former colleague of mine from [the firm] because otherwise it might have been hard for us to get there because of her age. But there were 170 boys of all ages and just under 20 girls. She spent two weeks with them and was a little tearful when she left. And she did say that if she should take a job here that she might well go back and volunteer. And I thought again that if one wanted to demonstrate her adaptability that it was the perfect testing ground for her.

As the above example demonstrates, parents actively encourage and facilitate the building of a dossier through targeted extracurricular activities. Even when parents do not fully support such 'game playing,' they ultimately 'connive and contrive' to ensure that their children seek out activities that will mark them as 'distinctive.' In Susan's case, she activates her social capital so as to enable Stephanie to work in a children's home in Bogotá, with an eye towards helping her daughter stand out in the college admissions process.

Like Canalside parents, Matthews parents encourage their children to search for relevant college and university information on the Internet and write their essays, and advise them to seek additional feedback from their teachers and the college counselor. Some parents are more active than others, of course, but for the most part parents are *highly* engaged in the post-secondary search process – for example, reading and revising their children's essays – in contrast to parents in the relatively elite State school sector, who were generally more laid back. Rather than adhering to Mr Henderson's advice to let students 'drive the process,' Matthews parents tend to do the opposite:

Donna Kenney, for example, states the following:

> I don't know how many other parents feel this way, or who you already talked to, but it was really hard to get the kids to focus and to get off of their rear ends and pay attention to it. So I was doing all the stuff on the Internet, and before we would plan a trip we would figure out which schools and which we could handle on a [college visiting] trip. And there were schools we had to eliminate because we couldn't get to all of them. And then, I do sheets with getting the most important information. I get language about their Anthropology Department, whether they have them, whether there is squash. At some point, she seemed interested in sororities. We wrote down whether they had them and what percentage [joins], so that we could see at a glance as she was going through. Then we would have information on how to find the admissions offices at each school and directions, and then Jeremy (husband) would take it and MapQuest ... you know ...

The Larkins, the Kenneys, and Mr Tomlinson are all engaged heavily in the post-secondary preparation and application process. In Mr Tomlinson's case, he is a class outsider; in the case of the Larkins, they were outsiders to the US post-secondary admissions process, having only had experience with continental European institutions prior to moving to the United States 12 years ago. In the case of Donna Kenney, two aspects appear to drive her intense management of Briana's process. On the one hand, she is not entirely happy with the level of assistance provided by the Matthews college counselor, and works to 'own' the process herself. On the other, her own college choices had been quite limited, and she wants to ensure that her daughter's experience is different.

While the parents discussed in the previous examples exhibit different motivations, they similarly feel the necessity to take a *very* strong hand in positioning their children for the post-secondary entrance process. Despite the counselor's edict to be more 'hands off,' parents in this sector are in fact involved every step of the way, from helping their children to conceptualize and carve out 'distinction' *as an applicant*, to proofing college essays, planning and executing road and/or plane trips to visit potential colleges, and weighing in and facilitating final decisions once accept, reject and waitlist letters are received. The receipt of such final dispensations from the colleges/universities involves a *second* full round of college visits, where students generally spend several days at each college, with parents inevitably hovering in range of the school, preparing to 'grill' them as to pluses, minuses, and generalized thoughts with regard to 'their decision.'[22]

The above scenario is predicated upon a certain level of parental privilege – which, at a place such as Matthews, is exacerbated by the normalization of certain college positioning strategies within the given space – and an ability to actualize social and cultural capital in relation to the post-secondary linking process. It is certainly the case that such privileged capital is linked to educational attainment of the parents in the first place, as parents who are not highly educated would be less likely to be able to engage this process at the normative level in this particular sector of schools. Importantly, however, the space itself presses towards particular kinds of moves with regard to 'class positioning,' and what *comes to be seen as normative parental engagement* in fact differs by sector.

For example, the planning and execution of college visits rests on parental time and money, wherein they can devote both time and money to accompany their children on expensive visits. The simple possession of such capital is not enough, however, as capital must be conceptualized and 'activated' (Lareau 2000) as an investment in their children's post-secondary options, and the activation of such capital in particular kinds of ways becomes more or less normative in particularly located secondary schools. As we see here, parents in private and State schools individually and collectively head in distinct directions in this regard, wherein the

State-linked parents put in more work 'up front,' and ultimately hand over the reins at a key moment when parents in the private school intensify their efforts.

In so arguing, we do not mean to suggest that parents in the State secondary school are not tied to the post-secondary process, as this is most certainly not the case. What we do suggest, however, is that parents in the State sector largely invest in class positioning 'up front' so as to position their children for secondary school, under the assumption that the school and their children will do the rest. Parents in the private sector do no such thing – in fact, they dramatically intensify their efforts at class positioning at one and the same time as those in the State sector leave it up to the institution to do the work. In the final analysis, despite the fact that both groups are similarly capitalized, occupying largely comparable occupational, economic, geographic, and cultural space, data from the two sites differ in fundamental ways. Confident that they have selected a strong school and that students are well positioned within that school, State parents take a step back in a way that the private school parents do not. In this way, the school itself (and its organization *habitus*) appears to play a critical role in shaping the class practices of each group.

Conclusion

In this article we track the fundamental 'class work' embedded in two secondary schools – one private and one State – as parents, students and schools work to position children for access to the most highly valued post-secondary destinations in the nation as a hedge against 'losing class ground' in the now global knowledge economy. As noted throughout, although both groups mobilize their social, cultural, and economic capital to position the next generation for advantage, they engage this 'class work' in perceptively different ways and to different extents. In spite of largely equivalent backgrounds in the geographic context in which the two schools are located, parents mobilize their cultural and economic capital differently in the two sectors, with those in the private sector actively 'pushing and prodding' their children up until the very end of the race for post-secondary admissions, in contrast to those in the State sector who invest 'up front' and then grant their children greater autonomy in driving the process.

Notably, although the motivation *within* sector may vary to some extent, dependent on parental connection to valued cultural, economic, and academic capital (for example, the case of Mr Tomlinson), the class practices (Ball 2003; McDonough 1997) coalesce *within the space itself*, ultimately becoming normative. At Matthews, for example, there is more explicit focus on the role of the college counseling office with regard to post-secondary admissions. Such focus enables and encourages parents to center on college counseling as a valued good, thereby latching onto it in a markedly different way than parents at the State school. Although they are continually instructed by the counselor that 'college is a match to be made, not a prize to be won,' Matthews parents bulldoze through this statement in an attempt to situate their children at the very top of available post-secondary options. This distinct class practice is forged within the private school itself, as the organizational *habitus* works toward encouraging this particular class form in spite of attempts on the part of teachers, counselors and even students to interrupt what is seen to be parental over-involvement. Largely ignoring the dictums of the on-site college counseling staff to 'let the students drive the process,' parents respond in their own way to the broadened marketplace for US higher education and accompanying swelling applications to the most valued institutions.

Although we cannot conclude on the basis of our study that the strategies of one group versus the other necessarily renders students in the two sites more or less successful in the college admissions process, the post-secondary entrance outcomes differ in notable ways. Focal students at both Canalside and Matthews overwhelmingly apply to the most selective colleges and universities in the United States, and are strategic in their approaches, yet acceptance patterns vary such that Matthews students have higher acceptance rates at the most prestigious institutions – a finding that holds, given that participants from Canalside were drawn from the top 10% of the class while participants at Matthews were selected from the top 20%.[23] Canalside students, accustomed to being the 'best of the best,' often feel burned by the process once acceptance outcomes are known. For example, none of the focal students were accepted to Ivy League institutions (four applied). Of the nine focal students, five opted to attend schools ranked as 'Most Competitive,' two enrolled at 'Highly Competitive+' institutions, one matriculated in a 'Very Competitive' college, and one other attended a non-ranked, local school. While such outcomes are laudable, and considered quite impressive when considered in relation to the greater population of college-going students in the United States, these outcomes do not map neatly onto Canalside's expectations nor do they match the outcomes at Matthews.

Focal students at Matthews overwhelmingly applied to the most selective schools in the country, applying to elite Ivy League and elite liberal arts institutions in greater numbers than students from Canalside (11 out of 13 focal students applied to Ivy League schools). Matthews students engage the process in a highly strategic manner, with continued counselor and parental prodding as to the range of colleges they should target, including 'reaches,' 'probable admits,' and 'safeties.' Like their children, Matthews parents continually assess their child's chances of being accepted at particularly located institutions, and they are involved in the application process every step of the way as students prepare upwards of 10 full application packets to strategically chosen destinations.

Although parents at Canalside are involved in the process as well, they are not involved to the degree that Matthews parents are, where such involvement *becomes* normative practice within the site itself. In the final analysis, all but two of the Matthews 13 focal students are attending institutions ranked as the best in the nation (rated 'Most Competitive' by Barron's), with three enrolled at Ivy League schools (one Princeton, two Harvard).

As noted at the beginning of this article, Kerckoff (1995) argues that *where* students are located in the structure of educational opportunities at each stage limits their possible locations at the next stage. In so stating, he stresses the importance of adding an institutional/structural dimension to studies of social stratification. Although remarkably little empirical work has been conducted in response to Kerckhoff's call over 15 years ago, our data largely affirm his point. Data also suggest that we must take into account the ways in which and the extent to which current and future inequalities are produced by the day-to-day actions and activities of parents, teachers, and school personnel as they collectively forge and enact normative practice within specific and differentially located educational institutions.

The above two points speak to the importance of altering our frameworks with regard to issues of education and social mobility, as well as class structural/cultural productions more broadly. In light of a massively altered global context and attendant rearrangement of the post-secondary sector in the United States, we must acknowledge the ways in which and the extent to which highly capitalized groups in the United States now explicitly work to maximize advantage via access to particularly located post-secondary destinations. As it is arguably the case that such destinations are tied to the production of a new brokering professional and managerial upper middle class, we will gain important insight into future class structure and potential individual and collective positions in relation to new class structural forms.[24]

Acknowledgements

This research was supported by The Spencer Foundation and the Baldy Center for Law and Social Policy, University at Buffalo, USA. The authors thank the funding agencies for supporting this work and two anonymous reviewers who provided very helpful comments on an earlier version of this paper. Interpretation rests solely with the authors.

Notes

1. This particular form of the 'political arithmetic' approach (Heath 2000) also cannot account for the movement of groups in relation to one another, as its focus is on individual social mobility.
2. We explore this point at greater length in our forthcoming book (Weis, Cipollone, and Jenkins 2014).

3. The specific academic year has been altered so as to further maintain anonymity of participants.
4. The sample at the state school was limited to the top 10% because of the large class size (over 600 students in the grade).
5. All data were coded and analyzed in accordance with standards released by the American Educational Research Association (2006). These standards are guidelines, and do not prescribe detailed movement with regard to coding procedures or structure of argument. Details of coding and so forth will be reported in full in Weis, Cipollone, and Jenkins (2014).
6. For further elaboration of critical bifocality, please see Weis and Fine (2012) and Weis and Fine (2013).
7. These insecurities may have begun earlier; Barbara Ehrenreich (1990), for example, called attention to a version of psychic distress associated with such perceived disintegration in the early 1990s. However, the strong economy of the mid-to-late 1990s mitigated this anxiety somewhat until more recently.
8. For classification purposes, we rely on the Barron's (2009) profiles of American Colleges.
9. This argument is fleshed out in full in Weis, Cipollone, and Jenkins (2014).
10. All names of schools and participants are pseudonyms.
11. According to the 2010 Census Bureau report on *Income, Poverty, and Health Insurance Coverage in the United States: 2010*, households in the lowest quintile had incomes of $20,000 or less. Those in the second quintile had incomes of $20,001–38,043; those in the third quintile had incomes of $38,044–61,735; and those in the fourth quintile had incomes of $61,736–100,065. Households in the highest quintile had incomes of $100,066 or more. It is important to note that the top quintile (or top 20%) represents a much greater range in income than the other four quintiles. While the top quintile includes the very wealthy (the 1%), our focus is the professional and managerial upper middle class (Apple 2006).
12. The housing market in the United States is largely tied to geographic location and cost of living (which is also geographically specific). While housing prices in Canalside pale in comparison with prices outside 'tier-one' cities such as New York or Boston, the median prices in Canalside relative to the surrounding metropolitan area demonstrate the extent to which it is indeed affluent.
13. This is a term derived from the Census Bureau and it refers to anyone who is legally able to work – 16 years of age and older.
14. ACT originally stood for 'American College Testing' but the official name is now ACT. The ACT is a college entrance examination similar to the SAT. See act.org for further information.
15. A common critique of Lareau (2003) is that she was too generous with her classification of middle class, including families that would more frequently be referred to as upper middle class.
16. The conception of the 'helicopter parent' must itself be contextualized. Unlike stories in the *New York Times* about the suburbs surrounding New York City in which parents employ a cadre of professionals to manage their children's college entrance process and at times actually do the work associated with application, parents in Canalside are comparatively laid back.
17. A student who is classified as 'twice exceptional' has been identified as capable of advanced level work in both mathematics and English-language arts.
18. Organizational habitus is an extension of Bourdieu's notion of habitus, which can be understood as 'an ensemble of durable and transposable dispositions that

internalize the necessities of the extant social environment, inscribing inside the organism the patterned inertia and constrains of external reality' (Bourdieu and Wacquant 1992). Habitus shapes individual actions and aspirations, and sets the terms for what falls within the realm of possibilities and what is appropriate behavior. The organizational habitus of a school 'limits the universe of possible college choices into a smaller range of manageable considerations' (McDonough 1997, 10). In other words, schools, through their organizational culture, shape and mediate college aspirations for students.
19. There are of course some quite wealthy families in the private sector, but such 'trust fund' children are few and far between.
20. It is not uncommon for this group of children to apply to 9–16 post-secondary institutions. Students at Canalside generally applied to fewer schools – six being the average.
21. At Canalside, all students meet individually with their counselor for a 'junior review' in which they discuss coursework for the upcoming year as well as post-secondary plans. The counseling department orchestrates several group meetings about college but there is no requirement that students and parents meet with counselors individually (although many students, particularly those in the top 10% do meet with their counselors regularly). During students' senior year, counselors will schedule a 'senior review' to check in with students individually and assess whether they need any assistance planning for post-secondary life.
22. All post-secondary institution names have been changed and have been substituted with equally ranked schools as per Barron's (2009), as have relevant personal details of the parents and students.
23. Once students receive letters from all institutions, generally by 1 April of their senior year, a great deal of work goes into thinking through which schools should remain on their list—in other words, which schools should they visit again, generally staying overnight on campus. Interviews suggest that parents are engaged in this crucial set of 'cuts' every step of the way.
24. We specifically refer to those schools rated as 'Most Competitive' and 'Highly Competitive +' as per Barron's (2009).
25. The long-term outcomes here are, of course, unknown. However, given broader economic constriction in the United States, it is at least plausible that such 'class work' as linked to institutional location will have long-range class structural consequences.

References

American Educational Research Association 2006. "Standards for Reporting on Empirical Social Science Research in AERA Publications." *Educational Researcher* 35 (6): 33–40.
Andre-Bechely, L. 2005. "Public School Choice at the Intersection of Voluntary Integration and Not So Good Neighborhood Schools: Lessons from Parents' Experiences." *Educational Administration Quarterly* 41 (2): 267–305.
Apple, M.W. 2006. *Educating the "Right" Way: Markets, Standards, God and Inequality*. 2nd ed. London and New York: Routledge.
Ball, S. 2003. *Class Strategies and the Education Market*. London and New York: RoutledgeFalmer.
Barron's. 2009. *Compact Guide to Colleges*. 16th edition New York, NY: College Division of Barron's Educational Series, Inc.

Bourdieu, P., and L. J. D. Wacquant. 1992. *An Invitation to Reflexive Sociology.* Chicago, IL: University of Chicago Press.

Bowen, W., and D. Bok. 1998. *The Shape of the River: Long-Term Consequences of Considering Race in College and University Admissions.* Princeton, NJ: Princeton University Press.

Brantlinger, E. 2003. *Dividing Classes: How the Middle Class Negotiates and Rationalizes School Advantage.* New York and London: RoutledgeFalmer.

Brown, P., H. Lauder, and D. Ashton. 2011. *The Global Auction: The Promise of Education, Jobs, and Income.* New York, NY: Oxford University Press USA.

Cookson, P., and C. Persell. 1985. *Preparing for Power: America's Elite Boarding Schools.* New York, NY: Basic Books.

Ehrenreich, B. 1990. *Fear of Falling: The Inner Life of the Middle Class.* New York, NY: Harper Collins-First Harper Perennial Edition.

Gamoran, A. 2008. "Persisting Social Class Inequality in U.S. Education." In *The Way Class Works: Readings on School, Family, and the Economy*, edited by L. Weis, 169–179. New York and London: Routledge.

Gatzambide-Fernandez, R. 2009. *The Best of the Best: Becoming Elite at an American Boarding School.* Cambridge, MA: Harvard University Press.

Goldthorpe, J. 1987. *Social Mobility and Class Structure in Modern Britain.* Oxford: Clarendon Press.

Goldthorpe, J. 1992. *The Constant Flux: A Study of Class Mobility in Industrial Societies.* Oxford]: Clarendon Press.

Harvey, D. 2005. *A Brief History of Neoliberalism.* New York, NY: Oxford University Press.

Heath, A. 2000. "The Political Arithmetic Tradition in the Sociology of Education." *Oxford Review of Education* 26 (3-4): 313–331.

Hochschild, J., and N. Scovronick. 2003. *The American Dream and Public Schools.* Oxford: Oxford University Press.

Holme, J. 2002. "Buying Homes, Buying Schools: School Choice and the Social Construction of School Quality." *Harvard Educational Review* 72 (2): 177–205.

Hoxby, C. M. December 1997. *How the Changing Market Structure of U.S. Higher Education Explains College Tuition* (Working Paper 6323). Cambridge, MA: National Bureau of Economic Research.

Hoxby, C.M. 2004. *College Choices: The Economics of Where To Go, When To Go, and How To Pay for It.* Chicago and London: University of Chicago Press.

Kerckhoff, A. 1995. "Institutional Arrangements and Stratification Processes in Industrial Countries." *Annual Review of Sociology* 21: 323–347.

Kerckhoff, A. 2001. "Education and Social Stratification Processes in Comparative Perspective." *Sociology of Education* 74: 3–18.

Lareau, A. 2000. *Home Advantage: Social Class and Parental Intervention in Elementary Education.* 2nd ed. Lanham, MD: Rowman & Littelfield Publishers.

Lareau, A. 2003. *Unequal Childhoods: Class, Race and Family Life.* Berkeley, CA: University of California Press.

Lareau, A. 2008. "Watching, Waiting, and Deciding When to Intervene: Race, Class, and the Transmission of Advantage." In *The Way Class Works: Readings on School, Family, and the Economy*, edited by L. Weis, 117–133. New York and London: Routledge.

Lawrence, T. 2009. "Private Spaces in Public Places: Class in a Suburban, Public High School." (Unpublished doctoral dissertation). State University of New York at Buffalo, Buffalo, NY.

Lucas, S. 2001. "Effectively Maintained Inequality: Education Transitions, Track Mobility, and Social Background Effects." *American Journal of Sociology* 106 (6): 1642–1690.

McDonough, P. 1997. *Choosing Colleges: How Social Class and Schools Structure Opportunity*. Albany, NY: State University of New York Press.

Mullen, A. 2010. *Degrees of Inequality: Culture, Class, and Gender in American Higher Education*. Baltimore, MD: The Johns Hopkins University Press.

Reay, D., G. Crozier, and D. James. 2011. *White Middle Class Identities and Urban Schooling*. Basingstoke, UK: Palgrave.

Reich, R. B. 2007. *Supercapitalism: The Transformation of Business, Democracy, and Everyday Life*. New York, NY: A.A. Knopf.

Sewell, W., and R. Hauser. 1975. *Education, Occupation, and Earnings: Achievement in the Early Career*. New York, NY: Academic Press.

Stevens, M. 2007. *Creating a Class*. Cambridge, MA: Harvard University Press.

Thomas, S. L., and A. Bell. 2008. "Social Class and Higher Education: A Reorganization of Opportunities." In *The Way Class Works: Readings on School, Family, and the Economy*, edited by L. Weis, 273–287. New York and London: Routledge.

Walkerdine, V., H. Lucey, and J. Melody. 2001. *Growing up Girl: Psycho-Social Explorations of the Gender and Class*. New York, NY: NYU Press.

Weis, L. 2008. *The Way Class Works: Readings on Schools, Family and the Economy*. New York, NY: Routledge.

Weis, L., K. Cipollone, and H. Jenkins. 2014. *Class Warfare: Class and Race in Affluent and Elite Secondary School*. Chicago: University of Chicago Press.

Weis, L., and M. Fine. 2012. "Critical Bifocality and Circuits of Privilege: Expanding Critical Ethnographic Theory and Design." *Harvard Educational Review* 82 (2): 173–201.

Weis, L., and Fine, M. 2013. "A Methodological Response from the Field to Douglas Foley: Critical Bifocality and Class Cultural Productions in Anthropology and Education." *Anthropology and Education Quarterly*. 44 (3): 222–233

Higher education, social class and the mobilisation of capitals: recognising and playing the game

Ann-Marie Bathmaker[a], Nicola Ingram[b] and Richard Waller[c]

[a]*School of Education, University of Birmingham, Birmingham, UK;* [b]*Department of Social and Policy Sciences, University of Bath, Bath, UK;* [c]*Department of Education, University of the West of England, Bristol, UK*

> Strategies employed by middle-class families to ensure successful educational outcomes for their children have long been the focus of theoretical and empirical analysis in the United Kingdom and beyond. In austerity England, the issue of middle-class social reproduction through higher education increases in saliency, and students' awareness of how to 'play the game' of enhancing their chances to acquire a sought-after graduate position becomes increasingly important. Using data from a longitudinal study of working-class and middle-class undergraduates at Bristol's two universities (the Paired Peers project), we employ Bourdieu's conceptual tools to examine processes of capital mobilisation and acquisition by students to enhance future social positioning. We highlight middle-class advantage over privileged access to valued capitals, and argue that the emphasis on competition, both in terms of educational outcomes and the accrual of capital in the lives of working-class and middle-class students, compounds rather than alleviates social inequalities.

Introduction

Education as a route to social mobility, and economic prosperity remains a key tenet of twenty-first-century UK government policy. This includes higher education (HE), which under both the previous Labour (1997–2010) and current Conservative–Liberal Democrat Coalition governments is promoted as extremely important for both individuals and national prosperity in a high-skills globalised economy. In England, young peoples' participation in HE increased from some 15% in 1988 (Chowdry et al. 2010) to 47% by 2010/11 (Department for Business, Information and Skills 2012). However, successful transition into well-paid employment in graduate labour markets remains uncertain. Brown and colleagues' work argues that labour markets have not kept up with the increasing number of graduates, resulting in ever greater competition for graduate jobs (Brown 2003; Brown and Hesketh 2004; Brown and Tannock 2009; Brown, Lauder, and Ashton 2011). Getting a degree is no longer enough, and students are urged to mobilise different forms of 'capital' during their undergraduate study to enhance their future social and economic positioning (Tomlinson 2008).

Whilst the study reported here is based in England, its findings resonate far more widely, the issues discussed being of relevance not just within the United Kingdom and European countries, but also beyond. Social mobility, HE and graduate employability are concerns in all developed nations, and increasingly so as the impact of globalisation intensifies and much of the world confronts a period of severe austerity. Brown and his collaborators (Brown and Tannock 2009; Brown, Lauder, and Ashton 2011) talk of a 'global war' for the most talented graduates, acknowledging the increasingly international character of the career market for today's highest achieving young people.

Our focus in this paper is on how students from different class backgrounds respond to an increasingly competitive environment. As the 'rules of the game' in the HE field shift and adapt, how do students respond, how aware are they of the changing nature of 'the game', and what resources and strategies do they use to enable them to succeed? We draw on data from a three-year study[1] of working-class and middle-class undergraduates at Bristol's[2] two universities; one a research-intensive university, the other a more teaching-oriented institution. We use Bourdieu's (1986) conceptual tools to examine processes of capital mobilisation and acquisition by students and their families aimed at enhancing future social positioning.

We begin the paper by considering debates and research concerning the need to enhance employability in order to compete in changing graduate labour markets. We then outline the methods of the project from which the data are drawn, before presenting the data in three sections. The first considers how 'knowing the game' helps some students maintain social advantage, and the second and third consider extra-curricular activities (ECAs) and internships as instances of how different forms of capital may be mobilised and generated, distinguishing between 'active' and 'internalised' behaviours and strategies. The paper concludes with a discussion of how 'knowing' and 'playing the game' generally further advantage those with the greatest accumulated capital.

Changing graduate labour markets and the need to enhance 'employability'

UK public and policy discourse around HE study has been dominated by the understanding that participation leads to long-term financial benefit, with graduates enjoying increased earnings over their working life compared with their non-graduate peers. This argument, cited as justification for recent changes transferring the major cost of university study from the taxpayer to the student, is known by economists as 'a graduate premium'. While some economists including Chowdry et al. (2010) acknowledge differential returns based on degree subject studied and university attended, others (for example, O'Leary and Sloane 2011) emphasise that, despite substantially increased numbers, graduates retain a salary premium over their non-graduate peers. Using Labour Force Survey data from 1997 to 2006, and Elias and Purcell (2004), they maintain that the earnings advantage of graduates has remained largely stable across this period, for both men and women, across all subject areas and across the 'ability distribution', and continue to do so during the current economic downturn. Even if the graduate premium does exist there are still differences in the occupational attainment by class. Bukodi and Goldthorpe (2011) show that significant class differences in relative occupational outcome have persisted over the past 60 years despite increased absolute mobility.

Brown et al.'s work (Brown 2003; Brown and Hesketh 2004; Brown and Tannock 2009; Brown, Lauder, and Ashton 2011), in contrast, proposes that an explosion of HE across the world is driving changes in graduate labour markets. Brown, Lauder, and Ashton (2011, 132) argue that the competition for 'good, middle-class jobs' is increasingly a global struggle, with middle-class families in particular adopting increasingly desperate measures to 'stay ahead' of the competition for future employment. However, as Brown (2003, 142) comments elsewhere, 'if all adopt the same tactics, nobody gets ahead', yet 'if one does not play the game, there is little chance of winning'. This is Brown's *opportunity trap*, something he considers an inevitable and defining feature of contemporary society. The consequences of this are efforts by upper-class and upper-middle-class families 'to position their children in the most prestigious schools and programmes, to become one of the select members of the internationally sought after, high skill elite' (Brown and Tannock 2009, 384). We acknowledge that the focus of these authors' work is oriented towards competition for elite jobs, and therefore particularly applicable to some but not all of the present study's participants. Nevertheless, the overall argument that a degree is no longer enough in the competition for graduate jobs has increasing authority across HE provision. In this paper we explore how such arguments may result in strategies aimed at capital acquisition and *curriculum vitae* (CV) building by undergraduates. Drawing upon Bourdieu (1990), we refer to this strategic enhancing of graduate employment opportunities as 'having a feel for the game'.

To 'play the game' successfully, students are encouraged to enhance their 'employability' through additional activities including work experience and internships, and by exploiting the skills gained through ECAs (Tomlinson 2008). Lareau's (2011) work suggests that working on the self in these ways may be taken-for-granted practice amongst middle-class students, as a result of what she calls 'concerted cultivation' in the family, which involves the continual working on the child to create an individual with the right capitals to succeed in life. For many middle-class families this involves a high degree of engagement in structured ECAs. This may entail increasingly overt and conscious strategising; firstly to accrue 'valuable' capitals, and secondly to mobilise these capitals to gain advantage in both education and labour markets.

Following this view, once in HE, how students spend their non-study time may be of growing importance in determining future life-chances. However, as Stuart et al. 2009 emphasise in their study of students' involvement in ECAs in English HE, students' lifestyles and activities are shaped and constrained by level of income, social background, and so on, and media coverage of internships suggests that similar constraints apply here too (for example, Chakrabortty 2011). Studies of students from different social backgrounds (Redmond 2010; Stevenson and Clegg 2010; Tomlinson 2008) find differences not only in their engagement in ECA and internship or work experience opportunities, but in their capacity and orientation towards mobilising additional experience into valuable capitals in the transition to the labour market. Whereas Tomlinson (2008) found that middle-class students at an elite university increasingly saw the need to add value to their 'hard' academic credentials through the addition of 'soft credentials' gained through various forms of ECA, Redmond's study of mature 'widening participation' students at a post-1992 English university found that these students 'tended to conceptualise higher education in terms of academic achievement'. There was 'an almost non-existent engagement in any non-academic related, extra-curricular activities' (Redmond 2010, 128), partly due to constraints including family responsibilities.

Other research indicates the highly complex process of mobilising different experiences into 'valuable' capital. Stuart et al. 2009 cite contradictory evidence of the value employers placed on different forms of ECA, and Tchibozo's (2007) study of UK graduates found although ECAs had a significant effect on graduates' transition into the labour market, different types of activity had different effects, with activities demonstrating leadership capabilities particularly beneficial. While Tchibozo argues that students need to understand and exploit the 'strategic potential of extra-curricular activity' for transition to the labour market (2007, 55), this requires both tacit and explicit know-how of how to package ECAs into valuable 'personal capital' (Brown, Lauder, and Ashton 2011; Tomlinson 2008). Moreover, certain students can more readily mobilise several forms of capital simultaneously, for example combining cultural capital in the form of 'what they know' with social capital in the form of 'who they know'.

In contrast to more broadly defined forms of ECA, studies focusing specifically on internships and work experience suggest they play a significant role in gaining access to graduate labour markets, as highlighted in a UK government report on accessing the professions (Millburn 2009). Browne's (2006) research into recruitment to the UK's financial services industry provides an example of this. She found that employers recruited an elite cohort to their fast-track leadership programmes specifically via internships. However, there are clear patterns of inequality in students' experience of such opportunities (Allen et al. 2012; Browne 2006; Lehmann 2012), which raise concerns about the implications for social mobility. Allen et al.'s study of undergraduate work placements in arts and creative disciplines in England found that students needed a fund of social, cultural and economic capital to successfully access placements in the creative industries. Lehmann's research found a similar pattern amongst working-class students in Canada, where relative lack of financial resources and social networks were barriers to accessing career-relevant internships and work experience. Other studies demonstrate the salience of these issues in a wider international context, including Jonsson et al. (2009) in the United States, Sweden, Germany and Japan, and Swartz (2008) also in America.

While developing capitals appropriate to future employability through various forms of ECAs, internships and work experience has generated increasing research interest, students do not spend all their time at university strategising for the future. Students may also be oriented to the present (Stevenson and Clegg 2010), and constructing a viable identity and sense of belonging at university (Stuart et al. 2009). Amongst working-class and non-traditional students in particular, for whom HE is not a taken-for-granted stage in a trajectory to adulthood (Quinn et al. 2005), successful attainment and progression during HE study involve a constant fashioning and re-fashioning of the self (Reay, Crozier, and Clayton 2009), in order to fit in or stand out (Reay, Crozier, and Clayton 2010). Decisions about involvement in different forms of ECA may therefore be about finding like-minded people, and spending time doing things that 'a person like me' does. On this view, concerted cultivation of valued capitals through structured ECA may fit more with middle-class notions of 'the worthy individual' than the values of students from working-class backgrounds (Lehmann 2009).

This paper builds on the research discussed above by considering in more detail the processes of capital acquisition and mobilisation by middle-class and working-class students while at university. We focus on the potential generation of 'valuable' capital through two types of activity: first, social and cultural activities that we refer to as ECAs; and second, internships and work experience. Whilst we acknowledge arguments for a broad understanding of ECA that reflects the diversity of student experience in mass HE (Stevenson and Clegg 2010; Stuart et al. 2009), we use a narrower definition of ECAs here and treat internships/work experience separately, because we found that students in our study oriented themselves in particular ways to these different types of activity. As we show, internships and work experience were clearly understood as important for generating capital useful in the transition to the labour market. Students' orientations to ECAs in the form of social and cultural activities were more varied, with only some of these second-year students clearly strategic in relation to their involvement in ECAs. Moreover, the majority described how they spent leisure time as involving the construction of a viable identity and a sense of belonging as a student (Stuart et al. 2009), by engaging in the sorts of things that 'a person like me' does.

Methods

The data used here are taken from the first two years of a longitudinal study, exploring the progress of a cohort of students through their three-year undergraduate degree course in England (2010–2013). The study aimed to compare systematically the experiences of pairs of students from different social classes, attending the traditional 'elite' University of Bristol (UoB) and the 'new' more teaching-focused University of the West of England (UWE), in the same English city. Pairs were matched in three ways: by class, by institution and by discipline. Our objectives were to identify the various kinds of capital that students from different classes brought into their university experience (economic, social, cultural, etc.), and to explore the types of capital they acquired over the three years. In this way we aimed to examine differing processes of capital mobilisation and acquisition by students that may enhance future social positioning.

Our target was to follow a sample of 80 students from 10 disciplines taught at both universities, involving 40 students from UWE and 40 from UoB, eight from each subject, comparing the experiences of students from differing class backgrounds. This presented both theoretical and operational problems, especially given the fact that students could be seen as partially removed from any class nexus in a moratorium between their class of origin and their class of destination (Brake 1980). Such problems are not easy to resolve. Our predominant concern was the need to operationalise class, which necessitated a simplification of its complexities. We sought to classify students using a number of indicators, including: occupations of both parents, type of school/college attended, parents' experience of HE, and self-reported class. On this basis we divided all responses into three groups: clearly working class, clearly middle class and 'in between' – a division that might correspond to Bourdieu's (1984) three-class model of dominant, dominated and intermediate. We only included 'young' (18–21 years old) students, to avoid the additional complexities of comparing mature and younger students. All students were enrolled on three-year degree programmes, however, in engineering at both universities, and in geography at UoB there was an option to follow a four-year track depending upon grades achieved at the end of year two.

We found 40 students who pretty clearly belonged to the dominant classes, as defined by Bourdieu, but the paucity of unambiguously working-class students in some disciplines led us to draw from the intermediate grouping. Inevitably during interviews, some of our original classifications appeared inaccurate. Eventually it seemed to us that students' backgrounds fell into four clusters: unambiguously middle class; ambiguously middle class (including, for example, some self-employed people, teachers, nurses, graduates in low-paid work); ambiguously working class (similar occupations, but lacking qualifications or having climbed up from lower echelons); and unambiguously working class (manual and unskilled occupations). We would argue, however, in Bourdieusian terms that those students we designate as working class fall within the dominated groupings, not the dominant, and they do display differentiated patterns of attitudes, experiences and behaviours, as we go on to discuss later in this paper.

In this paper we focus on social class. There were insufficient students in our sample from Black and minority ethnic backgrounds to discuss 'race' in a meaningful way, but we do refer to some emerging differences in the experiences of male and female students. However, a more detailed consideration of gender alongside class will be the subject of future papers. We also concur with Sayer (2005), who argues that on occasions it is both important and legitimate to focus explicitly on social class in developing understandings of how class as a source of inequality works.

Our study also concerns how attending an elite university versus a more teaching-focused university may affect students' movement through and progression beyond HE. This paper does not give a detailed account of such differences, because they were only beginning to emerge at this stage in the study. We identify some examples of unambiguously middle-class students at UWE, the teaching-focused university, who sought to stand out and distinguish themselves from other students there, but at this point in the study we more typically found middle-class students in both universities enjoying advantages over their working-class peers.

The paper is based on data from four interviews undertaken during the first two years of the study. At this point there were 81 students in the study, 40 working class and 41 middle class (see Table 1). Of these, eight lived 'at home' for one or both years, five working class (four from UWE, one from UoB) and three middle class (two from UWE and one from UoB).

All interview data were analysed and coded using NVivo data analysis software, employing broad, thematic codes. Specifically relevant to this paper were data coded under ECAs, internships and work experience. Other activities, including paid employment and family roles and relations were coded separately and are not considered here.

Table 1. Class background of participants.

	UWE	UoB	Total
Working-class females	6	15	21
Working-class males	13	6	19
Middle-class females	10	11	21
Middle-class males	8	12	20
Total working class	19	21	40
Total middle class	18	23	41
Total	37	44	81

'Knowing the game': playing the higher education game to maintain advantage

Our analysis draws on the work of Pierre Bourdieu, and specifically his concept of capital (Bourdieu 1986) and his analogy of 'playing the game', to explore ways middle-class university students may maintain their advantages through the acquisition, maintenance, development and mobilisation of cultural, social and economic resources. Using the analogy of 'playing the game' we consider the extent that students mobilise capitals in both 'active' and 'internalised' ways to position themselves advantageously for a future career, whilst seeking to avoid a dichotomy between 'agentic' and 'determined' players, recognising that people are 'neither fully determined nor fully willed' (McNay 1999, 100). Some students may have a *more* active self-awareness about acquiring and mobilising their resources than others. However, regardless of the degree of perceived agency or internalised action, students may still operate within the game in a way that secures advantage. That is, some middle-class students have an internalised understanding of the game and play it well without actively considering the mechanisms of their own operations while others operate in a more intentional way. We concur with Bourdieu that '[O]ne can refuse to see strategy as the product of an unconscious program without making it the product of a conscious and rational calculation' (Lamaison 1986, 112). Although this paper identifies some students as more active in their acquisition and mobilisation of capitals, others are less active and appear to have a more internalised or taken-for-granted orientation to the mobilisation of capitals; we stress that our conceptualisation precludes neither structure nor agency from the equation of individual practice.

We have found Bourdieu's (1990) notion of 'the feel for the game' helpful in thinking about ways in which certain students ensure their advantage through the development of capitals and put themselves in the best position to win the game. Bourdieu (1990, 64) writes: '(W)hoever wants to win this game, appropriate the stakes, catch the ball ... must have a feel for the game, that is, a feel for the necessity and the logic of the game'. The majority of our participants — both working class and middle class — demonstrated an awareness of 'the game' of obtaining a much-sought-after graduate position, including how the rules of the game had changed. Garry for instance suggested:

> Going back a few years ... a degree in anything ... was a statement in itself about someone, [but now] ... more and more people do go on to higher education and have degrees, [which] ... seems to, perhaps unfairly, water down what a degree is or how it's regarded ... It's ... market forces ... if there's more of something, that something becomes less valuable. (Working class, UoB)

Middle-class students in particular emphasised the status of different universities, as outlined by Liam:

> It just ... seems to be first of all what classification of degree you get – you have to get a 2:1 or above – and *where* you get it from. You know ... basically you've got the top tier, then you've got the rest of the Russell Group.[3] The kind of stuff they do, they do take into account where you've got it from and the reputation the university has, how hard it is to get into that university. (Middle class, UoB)

Harvey, a working-class student, recognised, like Liam above, that attending UoB was advantageous for him. He chose to study economics, a subject he assumed would further his ambitions for a lucrative job in a City bank, but he lacked the necessary capitals to secure a desirable internship:

> I've realised that, especially when it comes to university, that where you went is a lot more important than what you did. And there's people now that are doing ... like they've got the internships that I'd love and they're doing sort of Sociology degrees! (Harvey, working class, UoB)

Harvey's disappointment that his strategically chosen degree subject – which he claimed not to enjoy – had not conferred the advantages he had anticipated in terms of securing an internship in a City bank, indicates how 'playing the game' is not simply about making strategic choices about university and course, but being able to mobilise additional resources as well.

In contrast, Nathan enjoyed the social networks so helpful in getting the 'foot in the door' that eluded Harvey, and enthusiastically exploited them fully:

> I'm sure my networking helped as well, I'm absolutely convinced ... I have one family member in an investment bank in London who ... my dad put me in contact with and said 'oh yeah do you know such and such ...'. So I met with him in London, which was a useful contact, and if I'd got to the final stages of the interview process there that probably would have been quite helpful. As regards other contacts ... [I] ... worked for my mum and dad's accountant ... spending a few days with him, whacked it on the CV and they think 'oh look he's done some accounting' – 'tick box'. (Nathan, middle class, UoB)

Whilst Nathan's strategising was by no means universal amongst our participants, the following sections provide numerous examples of strategising to accumulate and mobilise capital amongst some, and they were disproportionately found amongst particular sub-sections of the sample: middle-class students generally, and male students in particular.

Generating capital through extra-curricular activities
Active and internalised generation of capitals through ECAs

Fifteen students (10 middle class and five working class) engaged in what we define as the active generation of capitals through ECAs. These students were involved in a range of societies and activities, but additionally they were assuming positions of responsibility, including joining committees, becoming secretary of their sports society, or becoming vice-president or president of a specialist subject society.

For two middle-class students at UWE, ECAs were a means of standing out from their peers. Both were very conscious of being from different social backgrounds to their perceptions of 'typical' students at a post-1992 university. Amina had become a student peer tutor and applied to be a student ambassador (helping out on open days and welcome weekends), partly because these activities would be useful on her CV but also as a means of finding 'the right circle of people' in an environment where she felt out of place. Oscar differentiated himself through his involvement in music, explaining:

> I play trumpet, bass guitar, guitar, drums, all that kind of stuff, and I've done lots of stuff playing in orchestras, big bands, rock bands, in plays, musicals, all that kind of thing. Drumming is my big thing, I've played drums in Japan, Italy, France, America, played in the Royal Albert Hall lots of times. (Middle class, UWE)

Another middle-class student at UWE emphasised how she continued with ECAs to cultivate her CV:

> I'm ... carrying on really, trying to do well in academic side of it but also keep up like the sports and stuff, because ... so many people have good academic skills and academic qualifications. And also you're up against pretty much a lot of people from other countries as well, because I always forget it's not just like English unis. (Francesca, middle class, UWE)

However, these students were unusual in their *active* generation of capital through ECAs. More typical were students for whom ECAs involved the internalised generation of valuable capitals.

We categorised 33 students as generating capitals in a taken-for-granted way, building on practices apparently internalised through childhood experiences. Of these, the majority ($n = 25$) were from middle-class backgrounds. Some middle-class students had a conscious awareness of the cultivation of capital that occurred in the family, including moral judgements of which activities counted as worthwhile. When asked about the money his parents invested in their children, Jack explained:

> Oh just making sure we've got something that we can have for the future, like windsurfing, surfing, trumpet, climbing, I've done so many activities when I was little it's just stupid ... my sister's now working all round the world doing windsurf teaching and stuff like this, and I've taught break dancing and stuff like that. So kind of setting us up for the future rather than just giving us [computer games]. (Middle class, UWE)

We found similar processes amongst some working-class students, all of whom studied at UoB, with interview data suggesting these students mainly came from aspirational working-class families, who encouraged and supported their children's development in ways redolent of more middle-class families. An additional important aspect of internalised generation involved finding a group where an individual student felt they belonged, which was not necessarily at their place of study. This applied to middle-class as well as working-class students. For seven middle-class students at UWE, in particular (including one who played football for his brother's team at the city's *other* university), ECAs appeared to be a means of dis-identifying with their place of study.

Barriers to the mobilisation of capitals through ECAs

Eleven students, all from working-class backgrounds, explained that they did not engage in structured ECAs due to financial or time constraints, or because they wanted to prioritise their studies. This was often a source of regret, as Henry suggested:

> I love to meet new people so it was a bit disappointing ... but this year unfortunately I couldn't really afford to join any societies or anything. But I have been playing football and stuff with my mates just down the local park and stuff. (Working class, UWE)

and similarly by Zoe:

> I physically don't have time ... I'd love to get involved but I physically can't. Which is another frustrating thing then because I feel like I am not making the most out of my time here. (Working class, UoB)

Three students were not involved in ECAs because they sensed social class differences between themselves and members of the societies they attempted to join. Here Rob attempted to explain why he was not involved in his subject society:

> the person who runs the society isn't one we'd ... generally ... include in our social group ... The sort of vocabulary he uses and things like that, sort of

very well spoken vocabulary whereas ... we use sort of more relaxed vocabulary as we're good friends, because when you're with friends you don't use a form of vocabulary like you would for example in an interview or something. (Working class, UWE)

A serious concern for this group of students is that through non-engagement they were precluded from any opportunity to use ECAs as a means of mobilising capital for the future.

Engaging in activities unlikely to generate 'valuable' capitals

A final group of 22 students described how, rather than engage in structured ECAs, they invested in spending time with people like themselves. Some activities named by students in this group would not be deemed worthwhile by middle-class students such as Jack above. A number of male, working-class students talked of playing X-box, and one young woman, Sariah (working class, UWE), said she spent her time 'going out clubbing and stuff and, you know, shopping, every girl likes to shop'. Other students invested energy in cultivating friendships and the social aspects of their lives. Jade, for example, explained:

> There's like four of us in my flat especially that get on really well, we just sit in the kitchen, make food together, have a chat. It's nice to like catch up after like a day, because we all go like our separate ways in the day and then come back. It's quite like a little family. (Working class, UoB)

These various activities arguably involve the generation of capitals, but they do not easily translate into something for a CV.

These different orientations towards ECAs suggest that a considerable number of students (33 out of 81) engaged in processes of internalised generation of capitals, which could allow them to package their experience as valuable 'personal capital' (Brown, Lauder, and Ashton 2011) when they began looking for employment. A further 15 were already beginning to use ECAs strategically to develop potential capitals that could be mobilised in the future. In contrast, 33 students were not engaged in activities that could be easily repackaged as valuable capital in the future, and of these 27 were from working-class backgrounds.

Generating capital through internships
Students' attitudes to internships

Students' awareness of the increasingly competitive nature of the graduate employment market and the limited opportunities in a period of financial recession perhaps intensifies their commitment to acquiring as many 'extras' as possible whilst completing their studies (Tomlinson 2008). Another way for students to generate forms of capital that may help them in the future graduate employment market is through internships. Most participants had, by the end of second year, secured (or were actively pursuing) an internship relating to their future aspirations, regardless of social class or institution, although differences emerged in the types of internships gained and the success of their applications. An overview of the experience of applying for internships can be seen in Tables 2 and 3.

Clearly, there are class and gender differences regarding who was applying for and securing internships. Overall, 10 working-class students had secured internships compared with 23 middle-class students. In terms of gender there are interesting institutional differences, which also intersect with class, and while this paper focuses on class differences, we acknowledge the need to further explore gender issues. The types of internships applied for varied across subjects, with students taking more 'professional' courses such as law, accounting and engineering applying to jobs in their respective sectors. Other students were attempting to secure broader experience in teaching, the media, retail, and the creative industries.

For some working-class students, the importance of internships needed to be made explicit, as Isabel's comments illustrate:

Table 2. Internship experiences of UWE students.

UWE	Secured / completed	Rejected	Actively seeking	Not looking	Total
Working-class males	1	3	0	2	6
Middle-class males	4	0	3	2	9
Working-class females	1	0	2	4	7
Middle-class females	7	0	1	0	8
Total	13	3	6	8	30

Table 3. Internship experiences of UoB students.

UoB	Secured / completed	Rejected	Actively seeking	Not looking	Total
Working-class males	2	2	1	1	6
Middle-class males	8	0	1	2	11
Working-class females	6	0	2	4	12
Middle-class females	4	0	0	5	9
Total	20	2	4	12	38

I need to start volunteer work pretty soon or some sort of work experience, 'cos they've been drilling it into us from the start that like it's all well and good that you've got qualifications, but employers are looking for something else now because everyone's got the same qualifications, like there's going to be however many of us, hundreds of us graduating with this degree, we need something to make us stand out. (Working class, UWE)

For other middle-class students, being competitive might be better read as their taken-for-granted dispositions towards university and career advancement. Nathan was one example, whose interviews from the outset showed clear career strategising, as well as a world-view where competition was inevitable, desirable and also cut-throat, as demonstrated in the following comment:

Everyone has A's at GCSEs, you've just got to try and differentiate yourself by doing something extra like Investment Society, or an internship, or do mooting ... Because you see some of these people – particularly if you want to become a barrister – it's ridiculous, you see these people who, you know, run a soup kitchen in their spare time, got a First Class Honours in their degree, been to Africa and saved a school from famine, you know, it's absolutely ridiculous how much they have. So you've got to try and aim for that or try to match it, try and build up your CV because it's so competitive. (Nathan, middle class, UoB)

However, not all students were actively seeking internships. For many of the middle-class females this was because they were unsure what they wanted to do. In contrast, the reason that some working-class students gave for not seeking internships was that they were concentrating on what might be considered the 'old' rules of the game, focusing their energies on the quality of their degree:

I think that I'd just rather focus on the degree ... obviously internships and stuff like that are useful, I think I'd rather focus on getting the work done and improving essentially the grade of the work, for now, and then consider other stuff later. (Samantha, working class, UoB)

It may be the case that, for some working-class students, going to university in itself has taken them far enough from their comfort zone, and that acquiring 'more than a degree' requires excessive energy and generates extra levels of discomfort.

Active and internalised mobilisation of capitals
Middle-class students in both institutions were more successful than their working-class counterparts in gaining access to internships, particularly in high-status areas such as law or banking, even though many working-class

students had clear internship goals and were achieving top grades on their courses. Largely this was down to middle-class social capital advantage. While working-class students were unlikely to have contacts in big companies to help them, middle-class students could frequently draw on significant connections to secure the best internships. It was striking how the social capital most often employed was firmly embedded in family networks, as the following examples show:

> It's a case of who you know not what you know in some cases. So I am trying to pull in any family ties ... like my dad's quite friendly with one of the traders at [bank name] ... he was head of the internship scheme ... [and] my mum's a governor at my old school and one of the governors was a trader at [bank name], so I am trying to pull some strings there [too]. (Dylan, middle class, UWE)

And

> My dad's quite high up in engineering so like advises the government, so a lot of people owe him a lot of favours around the country ... [or] ... if everything doesn't go well this summer, I can pretty much go to France and study in Lyon for a couple of months, because people owe him a lot of favours [there]. (Nicholas, middle class, UWE)

In both cases, these students had an awareness of the capital they possessed and were predisposed to utilising this fully. They knew how to 'pull strings' and capitalise on 'favours' owed to family members.

While some students actively mobilised available capital to secure internships, others simply took such advantages for granted. David (middle class, UoB), for example, talked about his work experience without mentioning the role his family connections played in the process. However, when probed he revealed the extent of the help received:

> Well I guess this interview I had over Easter was through a family friend who is the partner of the firm so hopefully that would help ... Saying that, my previous work experience last summer was ... through one of my dad's contacts ... so I guess there's always the chance [of finding] ... something through them. (David)

Elliot, a middle-class student at UoB who wanted to work in journalism, was casual about the help his parents could provide:

> Well my dad worked for the BBC, but ... I don't know, actually ... he does do a job every year. He runs a conference, oh no, streams a conference ... so ... he might get me a job there this time in the kind of PR, just doing press releases all the time, which would be tedious and quite hard work, but it's only for a week and it's in Abu Dhabi so ...

These students' lack of recognition of their privileged position appeared to stem from a taken-for-granted disposition towards opportunity, considering such opportunity their entitlement.

In addition to social capital, economic capital played a significant role in acquiring experience likely to promote chances of success in graduate labour markets for middle-class students. Economic capital meant they could afford to work in different geographical locations even when the internship was unpaid, and did not need to earn money to cover their living costs. Francesca, for example, a highly motivated UWE student, secured a very competitive internship in an Australian law firm, funded by her parents:

> I'm working for six weeks … although the company asked me if I would do twelve weeks, but I didn't want to and I'm paying them … [the] … company don't pay interns anyway … I have to pay for the flights, I have to pay for my accommodation, I have to pay for food, I pay for the privilege of working for the company, and paying the insurance, visa, everything … My parents are funding it all ….

Francesca could only conceive of applying for such internships because of her family's economic capital (and their contacts). The financial expense alone closes off this sort of opportunity to students from poorer backgrounds.

Barriers to Internships

Many working-class students cannot access the same resources as their middle-class counterparts. Their families simply did not have the connections to draw upon to offer advantages in the competitive world of student internships. The following examples contrast starkly with the examples of pulling strings and pulling-in favours above:

> I find it so weird when people have parents that are lawyers or doctors and they can get you work experience in a hospital or … I just think 'that's crazy' that's like something I've never experienced. Because my parents do just ordinary jobs. I don't know how they would help me. I don't think they would be able to. (Anna, working class, UoB)

> It's not that they won't give me help, my parents are the most helpful people I could ever imagine. It's just I don't know whether they've got the skills to be able to find me what I want, because I know what I'm looking for, it's not really a 'them' sort of thing. (Zoe, working class, UoB)

Although working-class students seldom had access to high-value social capital helpful in gaining internships, they were often aware of the advantages of their middle-class peers. Garry, a working-class history student, talked at length about his observations of the privileged students at UoB:

> Two of the girls that live above us ... one is going to do a work placement with the other's dad 'cos she does Geography and he's something to do with some sort of environmental management thing ... Law's another one ... my flatmate Pete ... got a placement shadowing a solicitor for two weeks in London this year because of someone he got to know from a placement last year [who] sort of referred him.

However, simple awareness of differential capacities for developing, and importantly mobilising, social capital did not help working-class students compensate for their lack of privilege. In fact it would appear that it was quite frustrating for them to see their peers continue to exploit the advantages they had already acquired through privileged backgrounds.

In addition, Marcus was not alone in highlighting working-class preclusion from unpaid internships because of a lack of economic capital, and the need for paid employment:

> I often worked during the summers but it's never kind of related to any kind of career I want. Last year I did a lot of sport and this year I've decided not to and I'm focussing on myself and trying to get good grades, so there's still I'm trying to get a job and then I might try and maintain some kind of job next year – hopefully it might be one that's relevant to a future career, or if not just a standard job for financial reasons. (Marcus, working class, UoB)

Marcus, in emphasising his need to earn money to live with any degree of comfort, highlights how students from economically disadvantaged backgrounds might not have the 'luxury' of seeking an unpaid internship, despite being aware of its obvious usefulness to longer-term career aspirations. Marcus knew the rules of the game, but could not compete equally in it.

These working-class students, although perhaps very successful at university, were often disadvantaged when it came to mobilising capitals to improve employment prospects. In particular, their families, whilst supportive and willing to help, did not have access to privileged and valued social capital, as well as having less economic capital, creating an uneven playing field where middle-class students were much better positioned to appropriate the stakes of the game (Bourdieu 1990). University thus does not become a social leveller, but rather it becomes another site for the middle classes to compound and exploit their advantages.

Discussion and conclusions

We found both working-class and middle-class students in this study were aware of arguments that a degree is no longer enough, and that to gain positional advantage in the graduate recruitment 'game' they would need to mobilise additional capitals that might be gained through a variety of activities beyond their formal curriculum. However, although there was a general awareness that a degree is not enough among working-class and middle-class participants alike, it is our argument in this paper that awareness of these limitations (in terms of future employment) is not the same as having a 'feel for the game' of constructing employable selves.

Using Bourdieu's tools to understand the mobilisation and generation of different forms of capital as contributing prospectively to a particular game, which allows 'players' to gain advantage for their future transition to graduate labour markets, enables us to consider the processes by which advantage may accrue during the course of undergraduate study, and the potential for classed advantages in 'playing the game', even without any conscious or active strategising. For some students in our study, the privileged middle classes, this advantage was something internalised through their pre-university experiences in their social milieu; these players internalised the logic of the game and played accordingly. As Bourdieu remarks in an interview on the rules of the game: 'The good player, who is as it were the embodiment of the game, is continually doing what needs to be done, what the game demands and requires' (Lamaison 1986 112). In *Weight of the World*, Bourdieu (1999) describes how the middle-classes 'make themselves' and how 'the game' is established to middle-class advantage. To illustrate this we could say that the middle classes are not only dealt the better cards in a high-stakes game, but they have internalised the knowledge, through economic and cultural advantages, of when and how best to play them.

This propensity for 'playing the game' was clearly visible with internships, with numerous examples of class differences in the capacity to mobilise social and economic capital to considerable advantage. In the case of some middle-class students the strategies employed in this mobilisation clearly demonstrated an active recognition of their advantages and how they might be exploited. For other middle-class students, capital was mobilised without conscious acknowledgement of its value – what we have termed an internalised approach to capital mobilisation. These differences were more subtle in the context of ECAs. Here, apart from a small number of students who understood their activities as a conscious form of strategising towards future goals, ECA was not (yet) an acknowledged part of the 'game'. However, the differences we found in orientation to and engagement in ECAs appeared to be generating what would translate into valuable personal capital in the transition to graduate labour markets for some students, and more than three-quarters of these students were middle class. It could therefore be argued that such students were indeed 'playing the game' in a way that ensured that they would appropriate greater stakes. Their capacity to play the game could appear to be almost instinctive. However, Bourdieu's work on habitus (1984) shows that what happens is not instinctive but learned through prolonged, managed and planned socialisation. The dispositions of mind, taste and body that are read as 'instinctive' thus become so habitual that they appear instinctive, but are in practice 'internalised' through what Lareau (2011) calls 'concerted cultivation'.

In contrast, working-class students in our study were disadvantaged through not being ready for the game in the same way as their middle-class peers, with a limited pre-disposition towards accumulation of additional capitals. Moreover, some had a pre-disposition towards trying to play a meritocratic game fairly, putting extra effort into securing a higher class of degree rather than securing an internship for instance. Also, while only a minority of students ($n = 11$) said that they did not engage in ECA because of financial and/or time constraints, all of these students were working class.

The capacity of middle-class students to play the game in both a conscious and internalised manner suggests that in the construction of 'personal capital' for graduate employability (Brown, Lauder, and Ashton 2011), social inequalities are compounded rather than alleviated. Those in dominant and dominated positions are likely to remain so based on the capacity to generate and exploit differing capitals, with middle-class advantage over privileged access to capitals (through economic support from parents, through privileged networks, through long-term investment in leisure activities), meaning they can mobilise these to further weight the game to their advantage.

There are important implications for such an analysis. McLeod (2005, 24) argues that the 'pressing political and analytical challenge' at the present time is 'attempting to theorize both change and continuity, invention and repetition, and understanding the forms they take today'. Whilst previously the arguments on social reproduction through education have focused on differential educational outcomes, it is our argument that with shifts in access to education, when the playing field appears to have been levelled for some people (i.e. even when working-class young people make it into HE), advantage is maintained through a shift in the rules of the game. The game is no longer just about educational advantage based on quality of degree. The stakes have been raised and the privileged seek ever-increasing ways of securing their position and coming out on top. This has implications for HE policy and widening participation strategies, and suggests a need for universities to address maximising the experience of university and actively providing opportunities to have 'more than just a degree' in order to begin to address the equity challenges currently facing working-class young people.

Notes

1. The Paired Peers study, funded by the Leverhulme Trust. See http://www.bristol.ac.uk/spais/research/paired-peers/.
2. Bristol is a medium-sized city in the South West of England.

3. The Russell Group consists of 24 leading UK universities, which emphasise research as well as outstanding teaching and learning. See http://www.russell-group.ac.uk/home/.

References

Allen, K., J. Quinn, S. Hollingworth, and A. Rose. 2012. "Becoming Employable Students and 'Ideal' Creative Workers: Exclusion and Inequality in Higher Education Work Placements." *British Journal of Sociology of Education* iFirst.

Bourdieu, P. 1984. *Distinction: A Social Critique of the Judgement of Taste*. London: Routledge and Kegan Paul.

Bourdieu, P. 1986. "The Forms of Capital." In *Handbook of Theory and Research in Education*, edited by J. Richardson, 241–258. Westport, CT: Greenwood.

Bourdieu, P. 1990. *The Logic of Practice*. Stanford: Stanford California Press.

Bourdieu, P., et al. 1999. *Weight of the World: Social Suffering in Contemporary Society*. Cambridge: Polity.

Brake, M. 1980. *The Sociology of Youth Culture and Youth Subcultures*. London: Routledge and Kegan Paul.

Brown, P. 2003. "The Opportunity Trap: Education and Employment in a Global Economy." *European Educational Research Journal* 2: 142–180.

Brown, P., and A. J. Hesketh. 2004. *The Mismanagement of Talent*. Oxford: Oxford University Press.

Brown, P., H. Lauder, and D. Ashton. 2011. *The Global Auction, the Broken Promises of Education, Jobs and Incomes*. Oxford: Oxford University Press.

Brown, P., and S. Tannock. 2009. "Education, Meritocracy and the Global War for Talent." *Journal of Education Policy* 24: 377–392.

Browne, L. 2006. "As UK Policy Strives to Make Access to Higher Education Easier for All, is Discrimination in Employment Practice Still Apparent?" *Journal of Vocational Education and Training* 62: 313–326.

Bukodi, E., and J. H. Goldthorpe. 2011. "Class Origins, Education and Occupational Attainment in Britain." *European Societies* 13: 347–375.

Chakrabortty, A. 2011. 'The Business Podcast: Interns and Internships' *The Guardian online* 1 June. Accessed September 29, 2012. http://www.guardian.co.uk/business/audio/2011/jun/01/business-podcast-interns-internships?INTCMP=SRCH

Chowdry, H., C. Crawford, L. Dearden, A. Goodman, and A. Vignoles. 2010. *Widening Participation in Higher Education: Analysis Using Linked Administrative Data*. London: IFS.

Department for Business, Information and Skills. 2012. *Participation Rates in Higher Education: Academic Years 2006/2007 – 2010/2011 (Provisional)*. London: Department for Business, Innovation and Skills.

Elias, P. and K. Purcell. 2004. *The Earnings of Graduates in Their Early Careers*, Research Report No. 5, IER/ESRU.

Jonsson, J., D. Grusky, M. Di Carlo, R. Pollak, and M. Brinton. 2009. "Microclass Mobility: Social Reproduction in Four Countries." *American Journal of Sociology* 114: 977–1036.

Lamaison, P. 1986. "From Rules to Strategies: An Interview with Pierre Bourdieu." *Cultural Anthropology* 1 (1): 110–120.

Lareau, A. 2011. *Unequal Childhoods: Class, Race and Family Life. Second Edition with an Update a Decade Later*. Berkeley: University of California Press.

Lehmann, W. 2009. "Becoming Middle Class: How Working-class University Students Draw and Transgress Moral Class Boundaries." *Sociology* 43: 631–647.

Lehmann, W. 2012. "Extra-Credential Experiences and Social Closure: Working-class Students at University." *British Educational Research Journal* 38: 203–218.

McLeod, J. 2005. "Feminists Re-Reading Bourdieu: Old debates and new questions about gender habitus and gender change." *Theory and Research in Education* 3 (1): 11–30.

McNay, L. 1999. "Gender, Habitus and the Field: Pierre Bourdieu and the Limits of Reflexivity." *Theory, Culture and Society* 16 (1): 95–117.

O'Leary, N., and P. Sloane. 2011. "The Wage Premium for University Education in Great Britain During A Decade of Change." *The Manchester School* 79: 740–764.

Panel on Fair Access to the Professions (the Millburn Report). 2009. *Unleashing Aspiration. The Final Report of the Panel on Fair Access to the Professions*. London: Cabinet Office.

Quinn, J., L. Thomas, K. Slack, L. Casey, W. Thexton, and J. Noble. 2005. *From Life Crisis to Lifelong Learning. Rethinking Working-Class 'Drop Out' from Higher Education*. York: Joseph Rowntree Foundation.

Reay, D., G. Crozier, and J. Clayton. 2010. "'Fitting in' or 'Standing out': Working-class Students in UK Higher Education." *British Educational Research Journal* 32: 1–19.

Reay, D., G. Crozier, and J. Clayton. 2009. "'Strangers in Paradise?': Working Class Students in Elite Universities." *Sociology* 43, 1103–1121.

Redmond, P. 2010. "Outcasts on the inside: Graduates, Employability and Widening Participation." *Tertiary Education and Management* 12: 119–135.

Sayer, A. 2005. *The Moral Significance of Class*. Cambridge: Cambridge University Press.

Stevenson, J., and S. Clegg. 2010. "Possible Selves: Students Orientating Themselves towards the Future through Extracurricular Activity." *British Educational Research Journal* 37: 231–246.

Stuart, M., C. Lido, J. Morgan and S. May. 2009. *Student Diversity, Extra-Curricular Activities and Perceptions of Graduate Outcomes*. Higher Education Academy Grant 2007–08. Accessed August 2012. http://www.heacademy.ac.uk/assets/documents/resources/publications/Stuart_ECA_Final.pdf.

Swartz, D. 2008. "Social Closure in American Elite Higher Education." *Theory and Society* 37: 409–419.

Tchibozo, G. 2007. "Extra-curricular Activity and the Transition from Higher Education to Work: A Survey of Graduates in the United Kingdom." *Higher Education Quarterly* 61: 37–56.

Tomlinson, M. 2008. "'The Degree is Not enough': Students' Perceptions of the Role of Higher Education Credentials for Graduate Work and Employability." *British Journal of Sociology of Education* 29: 49–61.

Social mobility and post-compulsory education: revisiting Boudon's model of social opportunity

Ron Thompson and Robin Simmons

School of Education and Professional Development, University of Huddersfield, Huddersfield, UK

> This paper uses Raymond Boudon's model of educational expansion to examine the relationship between education and social mobility, paying particular attention to post-compulsory education – an important site of social differentiation in England. The paper shows how Boudon focuses explicitly on the consequences of educational expansion, and argues that his work helps us understand why widening access to post-compulsory education does not necessarily lead to higher rates of social mobility. We investigate Boudon's key theoretical insights and assess the contemporary relevance of his model. The paper argues that the fundamental assumptions of Boudon's model not only remain valid, but have been intensified by systemic changes in English post-compulsory education, and its articulation with the labour market.

Introduction

For much of the twentieth century, widening access to education was seen in western societies as *the* legitimate means of increasing social mobility. More recently, discourses of neo-liberalism and globalisation have intensified this focus and positioned educational expansion as central to economic competitiveness and social cohesion (Avis 2007). Emphasising equality of opportunity as opposed to equality of outcome, greater social mobility has become something of a holy grail for successive UK governments. However, despite such aspirations, the relationship between social origins and destinations in the United Kingdom displays a remarkable degree of stability (Erikson and Goldthorpe 2010; Goldthorpe and Mills 2008). Although there is evidence that countries with higher levels of income inequality have lower social mobility, and that redistributive policies can have a positive impact on mobility (Blanden 2009; Ermisch, Jäntti, and Smeeding 2012), successive

UK governments have promoted education and training as a panacea for a range of social and economic ills (Keep and Mayhew 2010). Improving schools and raising the aspirations of young people from disadvantaged backgrounds, rather than direct measures to reduce inequality, continue to be presented as the chief means of increasing social mobility (see, for example, Cabinet Office 2012a, 67–78).

Attempts to educationalise social questions in this way are underpinned by what Goldthorpe (1996) describes as a liberal–industrial theory of the decline of class. According to this theory, a logic of industrialism demands increasingly efficient utilisation of human resources, reflected in the expansion and reform of education, greater equality in educational attainment, and consequent increases in social mobility as class-linked inequalities of opportunity are reduced. However, although educational attainment remains an important determinant of achieved status, evidence suggests that its contribution to social mobility in the United Kingdom has not increased as liberal theory predicts. There are two key reasons for this: firstly, class-based inequalities in education have persisted rather stubbornly; and secondly, the influence of educational attainment on achieved status has remained stable, or even diminished, between cohorts born since the mid-twentieth century (Bukodi and Goldthorpe 2011; Jackson, Goldthorpe, and Mills 2005). Similar trends are evident in other OECD nations (Shavit and Blossfeld 1993; Breen 2004; OECD 2011), calling into question the assumption that western societies will increasingly be transformed into education-based meritocracies.

In spite of significant increases in participation over the last 40 years, educational opportunities continue to be structured by gender, ethnicity and, above all, social class – albeit to differing degrees in different countries (Ermisch, Jäntti, and Smeeding 2012; Strand 2011; Jackson 2013). In Britain, Sullivan, Heath, and Rothon (2011) find evidence for equalisation in post-compulsory education, but conclude that class-based inequalities remain significant and are greater at higher levels of attainment. In UK higher education we see clear continuities of advantage and disadvantage: in 1961, around 25% of undergraduates were from manual or routine backgrounds, compared with 28% in 2008 (Bolton 2010). Moreover, there is no guarantee that an individual's educational attainment will translate unproblematically into achieved social status. In many western societies, an 'opportunity trap' (Brown 2006) appears to exist as labour-market opportunities have failed to keep pace, not only with increased participation in education but also with the implications of an expanded middle class, whose children must now consolidate their position if they are to avoid downward mobility. The resulting social congestion has led to intensified positional competition in education.

The persistence of educational inequality is perhaps unsurprising, given the extensive empirical and theoretical evidence contesting the notion that education can straightforwardly interrupt patterns of advantage and disadvantage. In the sociology of education, the work of Pierre Bourdieu has been particularly influential, offering a powerful critique of the effects of inequality on educational outcomes and arguing that an important function of educational systems is to legitimise and strengthen the position of those already possessing the greatest concentrations of economic, cultural and social capital. Bourdieu proposes a cultural theory of social reproduction, in which individual habitus is simultaneously a product and a constituent of social and cognitive relations characterising a field of unequal positions. In this account, both the performance of an individual in the educational system and their orientation towards it are unified within the habitus. However, whilst Bourdieu's analysis has much to offer, it finds difficulty in accounting for the realities of educational expansion. If differences in habitus explain both performance and orientation, class inequalities in educational attainment would widen, as advantaged groups take up new educational opportunities at a greater rate than their disadvantaged peers; as Goldthorpe (1996, 489) points out, this contradicts the evidence for stability outlined above.

Nearly 40 years ago Bourdieu's contemporary and great rival, Raymond Boudon, offered an alternative perspective in his seminal work *Education, Opportunity and Social Inequality* (Boudon 1974). Here Boudon focuses directly on the consequences of educational expansion and demonstrates that, even in a meritocratic society, increasing levels of participation in post-compulsory education do not necessarily increase social mobility. Although educational expansion may benefit people from disadvantaged backgrounds, it also increases competition at all levels and erodes the labour-market value of qualifications. In a society where opportunities to achieve higher social positions grow less rapidly than the supply of qualified individuals, expanding educational participation may have little effect. Boudon's approach is to build an explanatory model that shows how the actions and choices of individuals engaging in positional competition make intelligible observed patterns of educational and social inequality:

> [I]n order to analyse the system of macroscopic data which social mobility represents, it was vital to take it for what it in fact *is* – the statistical imprint of the juxtaposition of a host of individual acts ... [by] individuals who are socially *situated*, in other words people who are part of a family and other social groups, and who have resources which are cultural as well as economic. Moreover, the choices which these individuals face are not abstract, but are choices the terms of which are fixed by specific institutions – for example, in the field of education; or by constraints – for example, the supply of and demand for skills in the context of career choices. (Boudon 1989, 6–7)

This paper takes up the central question of Boudon's problematic: how is it that the benefits of education have been extended to more and more people, without consequent increases in social opportunity? It investigates

Boudon's theoretical insights and considers their applicability to the contemporary UK context, paying particular attention to the role of post-compulsory education in England. The paper begins by discussing the nature of this sector, highlighting its importance as a site of social differentiation. The conceptual framework underpinning Boudon's model of educational expansion and social mobility is then critically discussed, followed by a detailed account of the model and its implications. We argue that the fundamental assumptions of Boudon's model not only remain valid, but are intensified by systemic changes in education and its articulation with the labour market. In contrast to contemporary discourses emphasising the individual and social benefits of continued participation, post-compulsory education therefore operates as a positional rather than an intrinsic good, reproducing and strengthening inequality and social division.

As Nash (2006) points out, the sociology of education has largely forgotten Boudon's contribution – apart from notable exceptions such as Hatcher (1998) and Brown's work on positional competition (see, for example, Brown 2006). By contrast, Boudon's ideas on primary and secondary effects of social stratification have retained great importance in the study of social mobility. An indication of their continuing vitality is given by an important recent volume bringing together new contributions from eight countries (Jackson 2013). One of the aims of this paper is to re-emphasise the continued relevance of Boudon's insights at a time when some of the questions that provoked his work are particularly pressing.

Transitions from school to post-compulsory education in England

This section considers the nature of post-compulsory education in England, where a diverse range of providers, including further education colleges, sixth-form colleges, school sixth forms and specialist colleges, deliver a wide range of academic, vocational and pre-vocational education and training. Private and voluntary providers are also an important part of this landscape and, since the 1980s, successive governments have driven the commercialisation and marketisation of English post-compulsory education, which is now effectively a mixed economy of public, voluntary and private-sector organisations operating in an educational quasi-market (Fisher and Simmons 2012, 34–35). This system – if system is an appropriate term – is more differentiated not only than those found in most other European countries but also in comparison with the other nations of the United Kingdom, where, for example, in Scotland there are fewer private providers, further education colleges tend to have a more focused remit and sixth-form colleges do not exist (Avis et al. 2012).

Certain forms of vocational and pre-vocational learning, particularly those located in further education colleges, have traditionally been seen as an 'alternative route' to success for early school-leavers (Raffe 1979). Even today, such forms of participation are claimed to provide a fresh start for both young people and mature students. However, in England especially, patterns of participation in post-compulsory education depend significantly but subtly on social class. On the surface, the highly comprehensive nature of further education colleges means that, at an institutional level, they are not selective. Although often described as being for 'other people's children', social class inequalities are in fact quite low in terms of attendance at such colleges (Sullivan, Heath, and Rothon 2011). However, this broad feature conceals deeper inequalities. Firstly, further education has been viewed rather differently by children from different backgrounds (Thompson 2009): as a route to mobility for relatively successful working-class children, but as a remedy for failure by the middle class. Secondly, further education colleges are not the whole story: on the one hand, elite schools and sixth-form colleges attract students from middle-class backgrounds, whilst private and charitable work-based learning providers cater for learners from largely working-class backgrounds deemed to be disaffected or disengaged from academic study. Even within further education colleges, there is evidence of social stratification by academic level. Although highly diverse, the post-compulsory sector is therefore stratified in ways that schools, and even universities, are not (Thompson 2009).

Participation and attainment have always been significantly greater for the higher social classes, and they have also tended to access high-status forms of learning and attend more prestigious institutions, but recent policy decisions have exacerbated such inequalities (Ball 2012). As Ball (2003) argues, in an educational marketplace those from higher social classes are better able to manipulate ostensibly neutral mechanisms of educational selection and allocation. Notions of diversity and choice are highly stratified according to social class and other forms of difference and effectively the number of transition points which young people are required to negotiate has multiplied. However, whilst elite forms of education continue to offer social and economic advantages for those able to access such opportunities, other forms of provision may actually reproduce and reinforce disadvantage. Wolf (2011, 21) highlights the 350,000 16–19 year olds on low-level vocational programmes whose engagement fails either to promote progression into stable employment or to help them access higher level education and training. Simmons (2009) argues that the stigmatising effects of certain forms of work-related learning make progression into decent employment or more prestigious forms of education especially difficult for people on the margins of participation. The traditional image of the young person gaining incremental progression at work facilitated by study at their local college seems increasingly outdated. These considerations support Boudon's contention that educational expansion alone cannot prevent young people with lower-level qualifications being exposed to the effects of positional competition.

Educational opportunity and social mobility

This section is concerned with the conceptual basis of Boudon's model of social opportunity. Following Boudon (1974, xi), we define inequality of educational opportunity (IEO) as differences in educational attainment according to social background, whilst inequality of social opportunity (ISO) is defined as differences in achieved social status according to social background. Although the term 'opportunity' is used in these definitions, the focus is on outcomes rather than a narrower conception of opportunity in terms of access to education or employment. ISO is not simply the converse of social mobility – for example, positive discrimination in favour of those in lower social positions could lead to a situation in which both ISO and social mobility were high. However, in practice it is assumed that in contemporary societies ISO tends to favour those in higher social positions, so that ISO and social mobility are inversely related – high ISO implies that those already advantaged are more likely to retain this advantage. Furthermore, specific levels of IEO are not necessarily associated with specific levels of ISO or social mobility. As discussed above, Boudon argues that although liberal–industrial theory proposes that reductions in IEO should decrease ISO, there is no necessary relation between the two. The structure of labour-market opportunities need not correspond to the supply of people with particular educational credentials.

The definitions of ISO and IEO raise a number of methodological problems. Firstly, social background can be measured in various ways – for example, by social class, income, occupational status, or educational level – so that the generic concept of social mobility decomposes into more specific measures, which are not necessarily equivalent. Choosing between these measures is not simply a practical issue based on the availability of data, but also embodies more fundamental distinctions – for example, between analysing correlations involving continuous variables such as income, and a more sociological approach in which the focus is on patterns of association between categories with specific social meanings, notably social class (Erikson and Goldthorpe 2002). Indeed, the way in which social background is operationalised can significantly affect the conclusions drawn from empirical data, with recent evidence pointing to decreases in social mobility when social background is measured by income, but stability when class is used as the indicator (Blanden and Machin 2007; Erikson and Goldthorpe 2010).

Secondly, it is necessary to distinguish between absolute and relative mobility. Changes in the social structure, such as the growth in professional and managerial positions in the 30 years following the Second World War, will inevitably increase social mobility as the distribution of available positions changes. However, the relative chances of people from different social backgrounds achieving higher or lower social positions need not change in the same way. A classic finding of social mobility research in the United

Kingdom is that, whilst significant absolute upwards mobility existed in the post-war period, analysis of relative mobility showed great advantages in favour of those originating in the highest social classes (Goldthorpe 1980). Since then, whilst the class structure has continued to change (albeit more slowly than hitherto), relative mobility between social classes in the United Kingdom has remained essentially constant (Goldthorpe and Mills 2008). The distinction between absolute and relative mobility draws attention to a point rarely mentioned by politicians – that, in the absence of general increases in social opportunities, for an individual to move up, someone else has to move down. It is therefore more appropriate to think of ISO as related to both absolute and relative social mobility, rather than absolute mobility alone.

Similar considerations apply to IEO, and the effects of educational expansion must be considered when discussing inequalities in educational opportunity (Mare 1981; Sullivan, Heath, and Rothon 2011). Although in most industrialised countries access to higher levels of education has increased substantially, this does not necessarily lead to greater equality. If educational reform and expansion really are effective in reducing IEO, social background effects on educational attainment should weaken. Conversely, if educational expansion takes place largely through increased participation at higher levels of children from more advantaged backgrounds, social background effects may strengthen. Again, relative rates are the most useful here, in the form of ratios expressing the differential likelihood of educational outcomes according to social origin (Jackson et al. 2007).

The model of social opportunity that Boudon develops consists of two components: a model of changing IEO under conditions of educational expansion, and a model of ISO under conditions in which the supply of educated individuals grows more rapidly than the availability of social positions. An essentially meritocratic society is assumed, in which the highest social positions tend to go to those with the highest levels of education; although Boudon discusses the potential impact of dominance effects, in which the chances of obtaining a high-status position for a given educational level increase with social background, his model explicitly excludes such effects. The IEO component of the model will be discussed first, examining some of its basic assumptions; the ISO component and the main conclusions from the model will be considered in the next section.

Primary and secondary effects of social stratification

Perhaps the most crucial element of the IEO component is Boudon's distinction between the primary and secondary effects of social stratification on educational inequality. In a recent formulation of this distinction, Jackson et al. (2007) define primary effects as those expressed through the association between children's social backgrounds and their educational performance, whilst secondary effects are expressed through the educational choices made by children from differing social backgrounds but with similar levels of performance. Unlike Bourdieu, for whom IEO results from a unitary cultural process in which habitus and field condition one's whole experience of education, Boudon explicitly distinguishes between cultural (primary) effects and positional (secondary) effects:

> IEO is generated by a two-component process. One component is related mainly to the cultural effects of the stratification system. The other introduces the assumption that even with other factors being equal, people will make different choices according to their position in the stratification system. In other words, it is assumed (1) that people behave rationally in the economic sense ... but that (2) they also behave within decision fields whose parameters are a function of their position in the stratification system. (Boudon 1974, 36)

Although Boudon uses the language of choices, aspirations and ambitions, this should not be seen as essentialising secondary effects – producing a discourse of low aspirations reminiscent of the 'value theory' that Boudon (1974, 22–23) was at such pains to reject. Secondary effects comprise influences on transitions deriving not only from individual preferences, but also from social position, economic and cultural resources, and local opportunity structures. Drawing on Keller and Zavalloni (1962), Boudon relates secondary effects to a positional theory of educational progression, in which young people's aspirations are seen as relative to their social background. This theory rejects the notion that differing aspirations between social groups arise from different value systems; instead, similar processes operate across all social classes, but because the costs and benefits of particular educational decisions vary with social position, behavioural outcomes may differ (Boudon 1974, 23). As we have seen, Boudon regards people as behaving rationally, but the rationality involved is bounded – or perhaps, more accurately, situated – and one's current position is an important factor in evaluating the satisfactions associated with individual mobility. Those from higher social classes must aspire to a high position merely to avoid downward mobility; conversely, more modest aspirations may still provide a measure of upward mobility to someone from a lower social class. A more meritocratic society may actually increase secondary effects, in that those from the highest social classes must strive through education to achieve the strongest possible labour-market position (Brown 2006).

In Boudon's formulation, both costs and benefits may have socio-cultural as well as economic dimensions: for example, through the impact of choices on family solidarity or the risk of losing touch with peers. More recently, there has been considerable debate on the relative importance of cultural and economic factors in the evaluation of costs and benefits; in particular, Goldthorpe rejects the inclusion of socio-cultural elements in models of educational choice and emphasises the role of economic resources and benefits (see Goldthorpe 1996; Hatcher 1998; Hansen 2008). Nash (2006) proposes that the distinction between primary and secondary effects should be seen as methodological rather than theoretical, and that there is no reason why performance and choice effects should be associated with different causes, or why these causes should be identified as due to primary socialisation and rational decision-making, respectively. However, whilst these criticisms are important, there is substantial evidence that secondary effects as conceptualised by Boudon are both significant in size and theoretically valuable, particularly in accounting for variability in IEO between different educational systems (Jackson and Jonsson 2013).

Evidence for secondary effects

Empirical support for distinguishing between primary and secondary effects is provided by evidence that choices made at a particular point in an educational career – for example, whether to pursue an academic or vocational curriculum, or to continue in schooling rather than seek work – depend significantly on social background. Boudon (1974, 24–28) cites data from the United States, France and Denmark indicating a substantial class gradient in continued participation, after controlling for various measures of underlying academic ability. Since then, although participation by all social classes has increased considerably, the continued importance of secondary effects has been confirmed in a succession of more recent studies (for example, Breen and Yaish 2006; van de Werfhorst and Hofstede 2007; Jackson 2013). Thus, children from high-socio-economic status backgrounds are more likely to aspire to the highest levels of education, even at modest levels of academic ability. Furthermore, educational choices of low-socio-economic status children are more sensitive to academic ability than those from high-socio-economic status backgrounds, particularly in the mid-range of ability. For example, Jackson et al. (2007) analyse A-level transitions in England and Wales: in three cohorts, progressing from compulsory education in 1974, 1986 and 2001, respectively, transition probabilities controlled for academic attainment are consistently ordered by social class, with particularly large differences in the mid-range of attainment. Jackson et al. estimate that secondary effects account for 25–50% of overall class differentials at A-level, but declined between 1974 and 2001.

Significance of secondary effects

The significance of secondary effects for Boudon's model is that over an individual's educational career they will typically make a number of decisions affecting their ultimate level of attainment. These decisions include what to do at certain institutionalised transition points, such as whether to enter higher education, but are not limited to formal choices at specified times: they may also include frequent informal decisions concerning one's educational priorities and commitment (Nash 2006, 171). Boudon argues that primary effects become less visible in higher-status curricular tracks over the life of a school cohort, because lower-ability students from working-class backgrounds tend to leave these tracks at an earlier stage. This effect is also noted in Bourdieu's 'unequal selectedness', although for Bourdieu selectedness operates through the criteria required for progression rather than through explicit choices (Bourdieu and Passeron 1990, 72). By contrast, secondary effects 'assert themselves repeatedly over the life of a cohort' (Boudon 1974, 86), so that according to Boudon IEO is 'probably more attributable to the different systems of expectations generated by different social backgrounds than to the different cultural backgrounds that are due to the same source' (1974, 85).

Boudon emphasises the cumulative impact of secondary effects, which increases exponentially with the number of transition points. So-called 'anticipatory' decisions (Jackson 2013, 17), in which a student ceases to make a serious effort well before a formal transition point, highlight the continuously-operating nature of secondary effects and provide a challenge to their estimation. When comparing empirical studies of primary and secondary effects with Boudon's model, a distinction must be made between the multiplication of secondary effects over a sequence of transitions (formal or informal) and the magnitude of 'choice' effects at a specific transition. A cross-sectional study will typically isolate secondary effects operating at a particular transition, with reference to an estimate of primary effects based on performance at a time more or less removed from the transition. As Jackson (2013, 17) notes, secondary effects at age 16 are estimated to be much smaller relative to primary effects when a contemporaneous measure of performance is used than when based on a measure of ability at age 11 (see also Nash 2005, who finds a low contribution of secondary effects using an ability measure close to the relevant transition point).

Boudon's model of educational opportunity and social mobility

Unlike the statistical modelling techniques that were attaining a high level of sophistication at the time, Boudon does not intend his model to provide a 'fit' to the patterns of IEO and ISO in a particular society. Replying to an unsympathetic review by Robert Hauser, one of the leading proponents of statistical modelling, Boudon explains that his aim was rather to answer:

> [A] set of questions, not of the *how much* type but of the *why* type: Why does IEO remain so high in spite of all the efforts to reduce it? Why has the decline in IEO not provoked a decrease of intergenerational inheritance, even though educational attainment is a powerful determinant of status? ... Given my objective, I came to the idea of building a model roughly describing the basic mechanisms responsible for educational and social inequality ... a kind

of ideal-typical model taking into account only some simplified basic mechanisms to check whether this model could account for a set of 'qualitative' statements. (Boudon 1976, 1176–1177)

Criticism of Boudon's model on the basis of deviations from specific empirical data would therefore be misplaced. Indeed, Boudon would regard his model as being refuted only if it failed to generate the qualitative features he highlights as puzzling, or if another model, using substantively different assumptions, could account for them more effectively (1976, 1181). The model is developed by first stating a set of axioms embodying what Boudon sees as the essential mechanisms generating IEO/ISO, and then operationalising these axioms to construct an idealised quantitative system whose development can be traced over time, enabling the effects of educational expansion to be analysed. Although the operational parameters are chosen somewhat arbitrarily, Boudon argues that the features he seeks to reproduce are not particularly sensitive to their precise values.

Generating IEO and ISO

The axioms defining Boudon's ideal–typical society comprise two sets: the first set of four axioms (E1–E4) specifies the way in which primary and secondary effects of social stratification combine to produce socially differentiated educational outcomes for a cohort of students, and is therefore the IEO component of the model. The remaining two axioms (S1–S2) concern how educational attainment translates into achieved social status, and therefore provide the ISO component. The conceptual basis of these axioms has largely been discussed in the previous section; however, some additional comments are made here where necessary.

- E1: the society is stratified, and primary effects of stratification exist in which underlying academic ability is differentiated by social class from an early age. These primary effects are persistent; that is, the academic aptitude of an individual does not change over time.
- E2: the curriculum available to young people is differentiated for a substantial proportion of an educational career. Some routes offer progression to the highest levels of academic attainment, whilst others do not. At certain transition points, students must choose whether to continue with the higher curriculum. Once having left this curriculum, students are unlikely to return to it.
- E3: at any transition, secondary effects of social stratification operate, so that the probability of a particular individual continuing with the higher curriculum is an increasing function of social status as well as academic aptitude.

- E4: the society is in a state of educational expansion. The probabilities of continuing with the higher curriculum are increasing with time, although not necessarily uniformly for all social groups.

In axiom E1, the variables used to specify underlying ability are not particularly important: they may include cognitive test scores, age of reaching a particular educational level, or other dimensions – what matters is that they produce a hierarchy of academic aptitude, and predict later educational outcomes. Evidence for this axiom is plentiful; as Boudon suggests, empirical findings support the view that few, if any, school systems have been able to reduce significantly class differentials in educational attainment. For example, a recent UK study finds that by three years of age, significant differences have emerged in cognitive test scores according to family socio-economic position (Goodman and Gregg 2010, 11). Furthermore, these differences persist or even widen up to age 14, although some decrease is evident from 14 to 16. Recent research on 10 western OECD countries uncovers similar trends: none of these countries showed reductions in class-based disparities as children grew older (Ermisch, Jäntti, and Smeeding 2012).

Axiom E2 makes two claims: that the curriculum is differentiated, and that this differentiation operates long enough for progression choices to have a significant impact. Earlier in this article, we have focused on English post-compulsory education, arguing that whilst in principle it could begin to compensate for inequalities in compulsory education, in practice it is currently one of the most highly differentiated parts of the education system, with progression particularly sensitive to choice at a time when decisions are crucial to whether an individual reaches the highest levels of attainment. At earlier ages, curriculum differentiation is less overt, although still significant – particularly at age 14, when lower-status vocational tracks are often promoted as an alternative to academic learning for those deemed to be disengaged. Institutional differentiation, however, is of growing importance and is often related to family economic and cultural resources – the most obvious examples being selective and private education. Axiom E3 has, of course, been discussed in the previous section. Axiom E4 asserts that, whilst secondary effects remain important, social differentiation of transition rates may be expected to decline as more students from all social backgrounds access higher levels of education. In operationalising this axiom, Boudon introduces a ceiling effect to represent the slackening in growth to be expected as the participation of a particular social group approaches 100%.

ISO and changes in social structure

The four axioms E1–E4 have defined the IEO-generating component of Boudon's model. The central further assumptions embodied in the ISO generating component are as follows:

- S1: the social structure, in terms of the number of social positions available at each level, changes considerably less rapidly over time than the educational structure.
- S2: an individual's achieved status depends on four independent variables: social background; educational attainment; social structure; and educational structure, in terms of the number of people reaching each level of educational attainment.

The axioms S1–S2 are expressed here in the general form provided by Boudon. However, the detailed model he presents is based on two simplifications of these axioms: in S1, that the social structure remains essentially unchanged; and in S2, that social background acts only indirectly, through educational attainment. Both of these simplifications require some comment.

As the distribution of people across different occupations has changed, 'white-collar' employment has grown, at the expense of manual work. To some extent, this has driven change in the class structure; in the United Kingdom, Goldthorpe and Mills (2008, 86–87) point to a steady growth through the 1970s and 1980s in the professional and managerial salariat, while the body of manual workers – the traditional working class – has declined, particularly its skilled component. Official discourse presents de-industrialisation as part of a transformation from an economy based on largely low-skill mass production, to a 'knowledge economy' demanding highly-skilled workers able to contribute to value-added labour processes (Avis 2007, 2–4). However, a decline in manufacturing does not automatically mean there will be less unskilled work. Although, since the 1980s, there has been some increase in professional and 'hi-tech' employment, the most significant growth has been in retail, care, personal services and other relatively low-skill areas of the service sector. The UK economy remains mired in what Finegold and Soskice (1988) describe as a 'low-skills equilibrium' (Holmes and Mayhew 2012). Whilst Boudon's model assumes that the number of social positions available at each level remains stable, opportunities for young people may *worsen* as manufacturing jobs disappear and competition from displaced workers increases (Lloyd, Mason, and Mayhew 2008). Moreover, the apparent growth of professional employment needs to be treated with caution. As Boudon (1974, 157) argues, changes in the distribution of occupations lead to changes in their sociological meaning. Despite high-status titles, many apparently 'good jobs' offer mediocre pay, and underutilise the skills and abilities of an increasingly well-qualified workforce (Holmes and Mayhew 2012). As such positions have become downgraded, so the upgrading of the class structure has slowed: between 1991 and 2005 the higher salariat grew very little, and the working class largely maintained its size (Goldthorpe and Mills 2008, 87). Given the expansion of education over this period, the general form of S1 appears largely valid in contemporary Britain; however, the stronger statement that there is *no* change in the social structure may be applicable only as an idealisation – which is, after all, what Boudon intends.

The second simplification introduced above is that social dominance effects are omitted. However, there is considerable evidence that in the United Kingdom a more realistic model would be obtained by including such effects. Those from privileged backgrounds have considerable advantages over their contemporaries in labour-market entry, and are able to capitalise on them in various ways. Many middle-class parents mobilise social, economic and cultural advantages that influence not only transitions into post-compulsory education, but various other parts of their children's lives – whether using their connections to secure employment, subsidising unpaid or low-paid work experience, or assisting with property purchase. Such processes illustrate what Boudon (1984) describes as the *dominance de milieu* of social class. In other words, inequalities deriving from social background mean there is a lower probability of working-class people reaching a higher social position, even with similar levels of educational attainment to their more privileged peers. Whilst Boudon argues that dominance effects are a feature of even relatively meritocratic societies, the changing nature of the UK labour market is likely to exacerbate ISO in this way.

Extended programmes of study and poorly-paid periods of work experience have always presented a barrier for young working-class people seeking to enter professions such as medicine, architecture or law; however, the replacement of many established graduate trainee schemes with internships, where young people are often expected to work unpaid to prove themselves worthy of employment, is likely to exclude working-class young people from a wider range of occupations than hitherto (Cabinet Office 2012b). Moreover, formal qualifications are becoming a less reliable predictor of securing employment. Personal attributes gained via family or community socialisation, as much as through educational processes, are increasingly sought by some employers (Brown and Hesketh 2004; Jackson, Goldthorpe, and Mills 2005, 13). Such practices demonstrate not only the lack of any straightforward link between educational expansion and decreasing ISO, but are likely to intensify the intergenerational persistence of advantage and disadvantage. Whilst excluding social dominance effects from axiom S2 may be unrealistic, such a simplification provides an interesting test of the meritocratic ideal that open competition based on educational attainment increases social mobility. The remainder of axiom S2 is essentially a statement concerning the nature of positional competition, and enables Boudon to use the output of his IEO component as the input to the ISO part of his model, constructing a numerical model that shows over-time changes in educational inequalities and social mobility for an ideal society with three social classes. Boudon repeatedly emphasises the over-simplifications of this model, but also the robustness of its conclusions taken as qualitative answers to the *why* questions discussed earlier.

Educational change and social mobility

We illustrate the main trends of Boudon's model of social opportunity by presenting three tables briefly summarising its output. Tables 1 and 2 show over-time development of IEO, condensing the six educational levels used by Boudon to three: these broadly correspond to attending higher education, reaching upper-secondary education, and all lower levels of attainment. In Table 1, we use the proportions of children from each of three idealised social classes (C1, C2 and C3) reaching each educational level, which provides a vivid illustration of the extent of expansion and differences in uptake by social background. However, proportions conflate the effects of educational expansion with changes in the underlying association between attainment and social background, and in Table 2 odds ratios are used instead – the now standard method of isolating changes in IEO from the structural changes associated with expansion.[1] Table 3 is a mobility table showing changes in ISO over the same time intervals as Table 1. Odds ratios showing the relative chances of different classes of origin reaching different destination classes are again used to express inequality, although because Boudon assumes constant social structure there is no expansion effect to allow for.

From Table 1 we see that although increases in participation take place across all social classes, analysing these increases in different ways shows that expansion does not benefit different social groups uniformly. The most marked changes over time in the chances of reaching the highest educational

Table 1. Proportions achieving each educational level by social background.

Time	Social background	Highest	Intermediate	Lowest
t0	C1	0.2872	0.2353	0.4775
	C2	0.0736	0.1755	0.7509
	C3	0.0157	0.0772	0.9072
t1	C1	0.3266	0.2334	0.4399
	C2	0.0982	0.1944	0.7074
	C3	0.0246	0.0996	0.8758
t2	C1	0.3665	0.2292	0.4043
	C2	0.1264	0.2103	0.6633
	C3	0.0366	0.1235	0.8399
t3	C1	0.4062	0.2230	0.3707
	C2	0.1580	0.2228	0.6193
	C3	0.0522	0.1475	0.8004

Source: Boudon (1974, 146).

Table 2. Odds ratios for educational achievement by social background.

Time	Social background comparison	Educational level		
		Highest	Intermediate	Lowest
t0	C1/C3	25.26	3.68	0.09
	C1/C2	5.07	1.45	0.30
	C2/C3	4.98	2.54	0.31
t1	C1/C3	19.23	2.75	0.11
	C1/C2	4.45	1.26	0.32
	C2/C3	4.32	2.18	0.34
t2	C1/C3	15.23	2.11	0.13
	C1/C2	4.00	1.12	0.34
	C2/C3	3.81	1.89	0.38
t3	C1/C3	12.42	1.66	0.15
	C1/C2	3.65	1.00	0.36
	C2/C3	3.41	1.66	0.41

Source: Calculated from data in Boudon (1974, 146).

Table 3. Odds ratios for achieved social status by social background.

Time	Social background comparison	Achieved social status		
		C1	C2	C3
t0	C1/C3	8.12	1.26	0.29
	C1/C2	2.92	0.99	0.50
	C2/C3	2.78	1.28	0.58
t1	C1/C3	8.27	1.21	0.30
	C1/C2	2.93	0.98	0.50
	C2/C3	2.82	1.23	0.59
t2	C1/C3	8.72	1.17	0.30
	C1/C2	2.95	0.97	0.50
	C2/C3	2.95	1.20	0.60
t3	C1/C3	8.56	1.18	0.30
	C1/C2	2.93	0.98	0.50
	C2/C3	2.92	1.20	0.60

Source: Calculated from data in Boudon (1974, 152).

level, when expressed as a ratio of proportions from one time period to another, are for students from less privileged backgrounds. However, in terms of differences between proportions, the greatest increases are for students from more privileged backgrounds. Comparing the first and third rows of Table 1 at times t0 and t3, participation by class C1 increases by 11.9% whilst that by class C3 increases by 3.4%; however, this represents just over a threefold increase in proportion for class C3 compared with less than half this for class C1. Thus, although *opportunity* may be said to have increased significantly for those from class C3, the greatest benefit in numerical terms – and therefore in resources allocated to education – has been received by class C1. This point has been observed in empirical data on the expansion of UK higher education (Machin and Vignoles 2004). Part of the reason for this lies in the relative underdevelopment of the educational system modelled here: even for class C1, participation at the highest level is initially quite low, so that secondary effects are not offset by proximity to the ceiling of full participation.

A clearer picture of how inequalities have changed is provided by Table 2, which as discussed earlier uses odds ratios to allow for the effects of educational expansion. In this table, we see a steady decrease in inequalities between the highest and lowest social class, although decreases in other class comparisons are less dramatic. Taking into account Tables 1 and 2, we may conclude that inequality in educational opportunity decreases over time and with the degree of development of the educational system. However, in spite of the reductions in inequality occurring in the educational system, intergenerational social mobility is remarkably stable over time. In Table 3, which again uses odds ratios expressing the relative chances of reaching each social class by social class of origin, we see no particular trend of increasing or decreasing equality. Clearly, this is partly due to the somewhat unrealistic simplification that the social structure remains unchanged. However, another important factor is the greater uptake of education by higher social classes discussed in relation to Table 1; because of the difference in proportions reaching higher education between the classes, the market is flooded with well-qualified young people from higher classes, squeezing out those below. Unless the social structure changed *substantially*, this effect would still be present even if the simplification was dropped. Furthermore, including social dominance effects would also reinforce social immobility.

Conclusion

Despite the multi-causal nature of social mobility and the importance of underlying inequalities in shaping opportunities, the nature and form of education plays an important role in individual social achievement. As educational expansion proceeds, the later stages of education become more critical in differentiating between students, and we have therefore focused particularly on post-compulsory education. Raymond Boudon's work shows us that greater differentiation within education increases inequality of attainment, over and above that which can be attributed to socio-cultural influences on academic aptitude. In England, government policies since the 1980s have exacerbated the accumulation of secondary effects over an educational career. As we have shown, the post-compulsory sector is a site in which such policies have had a particularly negative impact.

In recent decades, neo-liberal governments have used discourses of social mobility as a means of legitimising growing social inequality. Disparities in wealth and income are presented as acceptable, provided everyone has an equal chance of climbing the ladder of success. In achieving this ideal, education is given a central role, based as we have seen on the assumptions of liberal–industrial theory on the decline of class. However, Boudon's model shows us that educationalising the issue of social mobility is untenable without concomitant changes in the structure of social opportunities, and powerfully illustrates Bernstein's famous claim that education cannot compensate for society (Bernstein 1970). In order to facilitate social mobility, a range of interventions in the labour market are necessary, alongside broader measures to reduce inequality. Boudon's analysis provides a powerful explanatory framework for understanding this: firstly, by underlining the logical disconnection between decreasing educational inequality and social mobility; and secondly, by emphasising the contribution of rationality and choice in the production and reproduction of educational inequality. Boudon's positional theory provides an important counterweight to essentialising arguments that present low aspirations as an explanatory variable, rather than mediating the relationship between broader social conditions and educational or labour-market outcomes.

Critiques of Boudon's work show the importance of elucidating the nature of secondary effects. Are they, as Goldthorpe argues, largely based on economic rationality, or do they have a socio-cultural component, as Boudon suggests? If secondary effects are at least partly socio-cultural in origin, the question of how to distinguish them from primary effects arises – a difficulty highlighted by Nash (2006). It is also important to consider how secondary effects change over time, and how we interpret evidence suggesting that high-achieving working-class young people are more likely to pursue prestigious progression routes than was the case in previous generations (see, for example, Jackson et al. 2007). A related question is how differences between the educational systems in different countries influence the relative magnitude of primary and secondary effects. Drawing on evidence from eight countries, Jackson and Jonsson (2013, 327) conclude that, whilst primary effects appear to vary little between these countries, there is considerable variation in secondary effects. Although the relationship with educational structures is not entirely clear, it is striking that where secondary effects are relatively large, so is inequality of social opportunity.

Although concepts such as bounded rationality may appear to endorse a theory of social reproduction in which different forms of consciousness are attributed to people from lower social classes, Boudon in fact proposes that the same motivations and consciousness underlie the decisions of people from all classes. Unlike Bourdieu's account, in which 'We can always say that individuals make choices, so long as we do not forget that they do not choose the principles of these choices' (Wacquant 1989, 45), the desire to 'better oneself', to achieve a higher position than one's parents or at least to avoid downward mobility, is shared by all. What is different, according to Boudon, is their social, cultural and economic situation, which any rational person must take into account when considering their future. Although Ichou and Vallet (2013, 143) warn that differences between Boudon and Bourdieu should not be exaggerated, by ascribing a greater level of consciousness and intentionality to the individual, Boudon's approach avoids a cultural determinism that tends to deflect attention from the possibility that changes in the social structure could contribute to reducing inequalities in both educational and social opportunity.

Note

1. Odds are calculated by dividing the probability of an event occurring (e.g. someone from class C1 reaching educational level E1) by the probability of it not occurring. However, odds taken in isolation can be misleading – if educational opportunities increase for all, the odds of reaching a high level will also increase for all, but the odds of one class relative to another may not change to the same extent. An odds ratio is the odds for one class divided by the odds for a comparison class (Sullivan, Heath, and Rothon 2011). Large odds ratios indicate high degrees of inequality; if an odds ratio remains constant over time, this implies that any reduction in inequality is due to expansion alone.

References

Avis, J. 2007. *Education, Policy and Social Justice: Learning and Skills*. London: Continuum.
Avis, J., B. Morgan-Klein, R. Canning, R. Simmons, and R. Fisher. 2012. "Teacher Education for Vocational Education and Training: a Comparative Study of the Scottish and English Systems Set within a European Context." *Scottish Educational Review* 44 (2): 14–23.
Ball, S. J. 2003. *Class Strategies and the Education Market: The Middle Class and Social Advantage*. London: RoutledgeFalmer.
Ball, S. 2012. "The reluctant state and the beginning of the end of state education." *Journal of Educational Administration and History* 44 (2): 89–103.
Bernstein, B. 1970. "Education Cannot Compensate for Society." *New Society* 15 (387): 344–347.
Blanden, J. 2009. *How Much Can We Learn from International Comparisons of Intergenerational Mobility?* London: Centre for Economics of Education.
Blanden, J., and S. Machin. 2007. *Recent Changes in Intergenerational Mobility in Britain*. London: Sutton Trust.
Bolton, P. 2010. *Higher Education and Social Class. SN/SG/620*. London: House of Commons Library.

Boudon, R. 1974. *Education, Opportunity and Social Inequality: Changing Prospects in Western Society.* London: John Wiley.
Boudon, R. 1976. "Comment on Hauser's review of Education, Opportunity and Social Inequality." *American Journal of Sociology* 81 (5): 1175–1187.
Boudon, R. 1984. *L' inegalité Des Chances.* Paris: Hachette.
Boudon, R. 1989. *The Analysis of Ideology.* Cambridge: Polity Press.
Bourdieu, P., and J.-C. Passeron. 1990. *Reproduction in Education, Society and Culture.* 2nd ed London: Sage.
Breen, R., ed. 2004. *Social Mobility in Europe.* Oxford: Oxford University Press.
Breen, R., and M. Yaish. 2006. "Testing the Breen-Goldthorpe Model of Educational Decision-making." In *Mobility and Inequality: Frontiers of Research in Sociology and Economics*, edited by S. L. Morgan, D. B. Grusky, and G. S. Fields. Stanford: Stanford University Press.
Brown, P. 2006. "The Opportunity Trap." In *Education, Globalization and Social Change*, edited by H. Lauder, et al. Oxford: Oxford University Press.
Brown, P., and A. Hesketh. 2004. *The Mismanagement of Talent: Employability and the Competition for Jobs in the Knowledge Economy.* Oxford: Oxford University Press.
Bukodi, E., and J. Goldthorpe. 2011. "Class Origins, Education and Occupational Attainment in Britain." *European Societies* 13 (3): 347–375.
Cabinet Office. 2012a. *Opening Doors, Breaking Barriers: a Strategy for Social Mobility.* London: Cabinet Office.
Cabinet Office. 2012b. *Fair Access to Professional Careers: a Progress Report by the Independent Reviewer on Social Mobility and Child Poverty.* London: Cabinet Office.
Erikson, R., and J. Goldthorpe. 2002. "Intergenerational Inequality: a Sociological Perspective." *Journal of Economic Perspectives* 16 (3): 31–44.
Erikson, R., and J. Goldthorpe. 2010. "Has Social Mobility in Britain Decreased? Reconciling Divergent Findings on Income and Class Mobility" *British Journal of Sociology* 61 (2): 211–230.
Ermisch, J., M. Jäntti, and T. Smeeding. 2012. *From Parents to Children: the Intergenerational Transmission of Advantage.* New York: Russell Sage Foundation.
Finegold, D., and D. Soskice. 1988. "The Failure of Training in Britain: Analysis and Prescription." *Oxford Review of Economic Policy* 4 (3): 21–53.
Fisher, R., and R. Simmons. 2012. "Liberal Conservatism, Vocationalism and Further Education in England." *Globalisation, Societies and Education* 10 (1): 31–51.
Goldthorpe, J. 1980. *Social Mobility and Class Structure in Modern Britain.* Oxford: Clarendon Press.
Goldthorpe, J. 1996. "Class Analysis and the Re-orientation of Class Theory: the Case of Persisting Differentials in Educational Attainment." *British Journal of Sociology* 47 (3): 481–505.
Goldthorpe, J., and C. Mills. 2008. "Trends in Intergenerational Class Mobility in Modern Britain: Evidence from National Surveys, 1972–2005." *National Institute Economic Review* 205: 83–100.
Goodman, A., and P. Gregg. 2010. *Poorer children's Educational Attainment: How Important Are Attitudes and Behaviour?* York: Joseph Rowntree Foundation.
Hansen, M. 2008. "Rational Action Theory and Educational Attainment: Changes in the Impact of Economic Resources." *European Sociological Review* 24 (1): 1–17.

Hatcher, R. 1998. "Class Differentiation in Education: Rational Choices?" *British Journal of Sociology of Education* 19 (1): 5–24.
Holmes, C., and K. Mayhew. 2012. *The Changing Shape of the UK Job Market and Its Implications for the Bottom Half of Earners*. London: Resolution Foundation.
Ichou, M., and L.-A. Vallet. 2013. "Academic Achievement, Tracking Decisions, and Their Relative Contribution to Educational Inequalities." In *Determined to Succeed? Performance versus Choice in Educational Attainment*, edited by M. Jackson. Stanford, CA: Stanford University Press.
Jackson, M., ed. 2013. *Determined to Succeed? Performance versus Choice in Educational Attainment*. Stanford, CA: Stanford University Press.
Jackson, M., R. Erikson, J. H. Goldthorpe, and M. Yaish. 2007. "Primary and Secondary Effects in Class Differentials in Educational Attainment: the Transition to A-level Courses in England and Wales." *Acta Sociologica* 50 (3): 211–229.
Jackson, M., J. Goldthorpe, and C. Mills. 2005. "Education, Employers and Class Mobility." *Research in Social Stratification and Mobility* 23: 3–33.
Jackson, M., and J. Jonsson. 2013. "Inequality of Educational Opportunity across Countries." In *Determined to Succeed? Performance versus Choice in Educational Attainment*, edited by M. Jackson. Stanford, CA: Stanford University Press.
Keep, E., and K. Mayhew. 2010. "Moving beyond Skills as a Social and Economic Panacea." *Work, Employment and Society* 24 (3): 565–577.
Keller, S., and M. Zavalloni. 1962. "Classe Sociale, Ambition Et réussite." *Sociologie Du Travail* 4: 1–14.
Lloyd, C., G. Mason, and K. Mayhew, eds. 2008. *Low-wage Work in the United Kingdom*. New York: Russell Sage Foundation.
Machin, S., and A. Vignoles. 2004. "Educational Inequality: the Widening Socio-economic Gap." *Fiscal Studies* 25: 107–128.
Mare, R. 1981. "Change and Stability in Educational Stratification." *American Sociological Review* 46: 72–87.
Nash, R. 2005. "Boudon, Realism, and the Cognitive Habitus: Why an Explanation of Inequality/Difference Cannot Be Limited to a Model of Secondary Effects." *Interchange* 36 (3): 275–293.
Nash, R. 2006. "Controlling for 'ability': a Conceptual and Empirical Study of Primary and Secondary Effects." *British Journal of Sociology of Education* 27 (2): 157–172.
OECD. 2011. "Education at a Glance 2011: OECD Indicators." Paris: OECD Publishing. Available online at http://dx.doi.org/10.1787/eag-2011-en (accessed 14 August 2012).
Raffe, D. 1979. "The 'alternative route' Reconsidered: Part-time Further Education and Social Mobility in England and Wales." *Sociology* 13: 47–73.
Shavit, Y., and H. P. Blossfeld. 1993. *Persistent Inequality. Changing Educational Attainment in Thirteen Countries*. Boulder, CO: Westview.
Simmons, R. 2009. "Entry to Employment: Discourses of Exclusion in Work-based Learning for Young People." *Journal of Education and Work* 22 (2): 137–151.
Strand, S. 2011. "The Limits of Social Class in Explaining Ethnic Gaps in Educational Attainment." *British Educational Research Journal* 37 (2): 197–229.

Sullivan, A., A. Heath, and C. Rothon. 2011. "Equalisation or Inflation? Social Class and Gender Differentials in England and Wales" *Oxford Review of Education* 37 (2): 215–240.

Thompson, R. 2009. "Social Class and Participation in Further Education: Evidence from the Youth Cohort Study of England and Wales." *British Journal of Sociology of Education* 30 (1): 29–42.

Van de Werfhorst, H., and S. Hofstede. 2007. "Cultural Capital or Relative Risk Aversion? Two Mechanisms for Educational Inequality Compared." *British Journal of Sociology* 58 (3): 391–415.

Wacquant, L. 1989. "Towards a Reflexive Sociology: a Workshop with Pierre Bourdieu." *Sociological Theory* 7: 26–83.

Wolf, A. 2011. *Review of Vocational Education – the Wolf Report*. London: Department for Education.

The changing relationship between origins, education and destinations in the 1990s and 2000s

Fiona Devine[a] and Yaojun Li[b]

[a]School of Social Sciences, Manchester University, Manchester, UK; [b]Institute for Social Change, Manchester University, Manchester, UK

> This paper examines the changing relationship between origins, education and destinations in mobility processes. The meritocracy thesis suggests the relationships between origins and education and between origins and destination will weaken while the relationship between education and destinations will strengthen. Comparing data from the 1991 British Household Panel Survey and the 2005 General Household Survey, we test these associations for men and women. We find that the relationship between origins and education and origins and destinations has weakened for both sexes. While these findings are supportive of the meritocracy thesis, they are not, however, evidence of a secular trend towards merit-based selection. Contrary to the thesis, we also find the association between education and destinations has weakened for men and women. The relationship between education and destinations is more complicated than is often assumed and the role of meritocratic and non-meritocratic factors in occupational success needs to be better understood.

Introduction

There has been growing concern among politicians and policy-makers about whether social mobility is declining and what can be done to arrest this decline (Devine 2009; Payne 2012). In 2011, the Coalition government established a new Social Mobility and Child Poverty Commission, launched by Deputy Prime Minister Nick Clegg and led by Alan Milburn, the government's independent reviewer, which unveiled its Social Mobility Strategy. The strategic document accompanying the launch, 'Opening Doors, Breaking Barriers: A Strategy for Social Mobility' (Cabinet Office: 2011), focused attention on intergenerational mobility and emphasised the importance of equal opportunities for all. The Commission has to monitor progress by way of a set of key indicators and report to Parliament on an annual basis. The strategy is based on a lifecycle framework that emphasises the importance of foundation years (ages 0–5), school years (ages 5–16) and transition years (ages 16–24) as crucial moments when social policy can make a difference to young people's life-chances in the labour market and adulthood (24 years and over).

In May 2012, various politicians spoke at a social mobility summit organised by the Sutton Trust to launch its latest report, 'Social Mobility and Education Gaps in the Four Major Anglophone Countries' (Carnegie Corporation of New York/The Sutton Trust 2012). The report noted that the United Kingdom and the United States are less mobile than Canada and Australia. It emphasised that the gap in educational attainment increases between children from poor and rich families as they move through the school system in the United Kingdom. In the same month, Alan Milburn published the first of three reports for the government, 'Fair Access to Professional Careers' (Cabinet Office 2012). He emphasised that not enough is being done to recruit people from poor backgrounds into professions such as medicine, law and journalism. Employers, for example, recruit from a small group of elite universities, who themselves recruit students from middle-class families. As a result, there have been only minor changes in the social composition of the professions and these practices are a barrier to more meritocracy in the professions.

In a recent paper, we considered the debate about whether social mobility is declining and suggested absolute upward mobility is declining among men (Li and Devine 2011; see also Lambert, Prandy, and Bottero 2008).[1] Here, we consider the role of education in the mobility process and examine the relationship between origins, education and destinations (OED) and the extent to which it has changed in current times. Firstly, we address the debate and previous evidence on meritocracy. Secondly, we draw on the 1991 British Household Panel Survey and the 2005 Household Survey to analyse this changing OED relationship. We explain the changing patterns in the association between OED in absolute and relative terms. We find that the association has declined between origins and education, between education and destinations and between origins and destinations. We suggest that further research is required on the role of meritocratic and non-meritocratic factors in inter-generational and intra-generational social mobility.

The debate on meritocracy

The term 'meritocracy' was first coined, satirically, by Michael Young in his book *The Rise of the Meritocracy 1870–2033* published in 1958. He described the growing importance attached to merit, defined as 'intelligence plus effort', in recruitment to high-level occupations. With less satire, American sociologists Talcott Parsons (1940) and Daniel Bell (1976) advanced similar theories that as societies modernised, social selection would be based on achievement and not ascription. Educational attainment would determine occupational success and the social sorting of people into positions would be fair. Although politicians now see a meritocracy in aspirational terms, Young was aware of its dystopian aspects. He was concerned about what would happen to those people who were seemingly less able and less hard working. He feared they would be miserable and disaffected. A meritocracy would not necessarily, in other words, be legitimate.

More recently, the meritocracy thesis has been operationalised in terms of an 'OED triangle' (see Figure 1). The hypothesis assumes that the association between class origins and educational attainment (OE) will decrease, the association between educational attainment and class destinations (ED) will increase and the direct association between class origins and class destinations (OD) will decrease. The 'OED triangle' is a simple measure. Sociologists have noted that sophisticated research on the relationship between OED is required to either prove or disprove the thesis since it touches on issues of fairness and justice and the domains of philosophy and politics (Marshall and Swift 1993). Rather, empirical research has focused on the role of education in the 'intergenerational transmission of class advantage and disadvantage' (Marshall, Swift, and Roberts 1997, 70–71). These caveats apply in the discussion of the empirical evidence presented here too.

Previous research on the meritocracy thesis has produced mixed results. Data gathered on men in the Oxford Mobility Study in the early 1970s by Halsey, Heath, and Ridge (1980) found class origins were increasingly associated with educational attainment (OE), there was a closer association between education and destinations (ED) and a decreasing direct influence of class origins on class destinations (OD). Thus, while there was evidence of increasing merit selection in the labour market, this trend had been counter-balanced by decreasing merit selection in the education system. Education is 'increasingly the mediator of the transmission of status between generations', although there has been no reduction in the overall influence

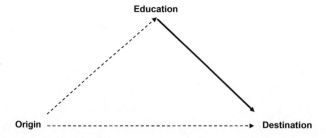

Figure 1. Stylised path diagrams on the changes in the OED relations.
Note: Dotted lines indicate weakening effects, solid line indicates strengthening effects.

of class origins on destinations. Ascriptive forces find ways of repackaging themselves as achievement. Halsey, Heath, and Ridge concluded there was little evidence of a secular trend towards meritocracy.

These conclusions – and those on social mobility (Goldthorpe, Llewellyn, and Payne 1987) – were contested by Saunders (1995, 1997, 2010; Bond and Saunders 1999). Saunders adopted a 'strong thesis' asserting that IQ, as measured through various intelligence tests, is the better predictor of occupational destinations than class or education. Drawing on longitudinal data from the National Child Development Study (NCDS), Saunders found a child's ability, as measured at aged 11, is the best predictor of occupational success. Saunders (2010, 84) concluded 'that people in Britain are getting allocated to occupational class positions mainly according to meritocratic principles'. He does not ignore the fact that 'a meritocracy can be an uncomfortable place in which to live, for it is inherently competitive, and it produces losers as well as winners' (Saunders 2010, 124). The key is that the competition (equality of opportunity) is fair and transparent.

Saunders' research was the source of much disagreement. Analysing the 1973 and 1985 General Household Surveys (GHSs), Heath, Mills, and Roberts (1992) found an unchanging relationship between origins and education (OE). They also found a weakening association between education and destinations (ED) and a slightly decreasing relationship between origins and destinations (OD). These findings were confirmed by Marshall, Swift, and Roberts (1997). In a series of responses, Breen and Goldthorpe; (1999, 2001) analysed the NCDS and found that neither merit nor education eliminate the association between origins and destinations. Class still has powerful effects on who gets ahead. Finally, Savage and Egerton (1997), also using NCDS data, found that although those who do well in ability tests from any social class background have reasonable chances of moving into advantaged jobs, class origins still have an independent effect on destinations, however.

The overall consensus is that education attainment is the major influence on occupational destinations although origins still have a direct and independent effect on destinations. Recent research has considered whether the changing relationship between OED in Britain exhibits general long-term trends or is the product of cohort-specific effects. Drawing, again, on the NCDS, Bukodi and Goldthorpe found that education has a strong effect on destinations although its effects have not increased over time. Origins affect destinations, although less strongly than education, and this association has not decreased over time. Uniquely, Bukodi and Goldthorpe look at work–life mobility and found the frequency of job changes has a strong effect, independent of both origins and education, on destinations. Thus, men in the 1958 birth cohort who entered the labour market in difficult times were affected by these difficult economic conditions in their subsequent occupational destinations.

Bukodi and Goldthorpe (2011, 370) reject the 'idea of education playing a steadily increasing role in the occupational attainment process or in mediating the influence of class origins in this process'. Cross-cohort differences 'seem often better understood in the context not of some relatively benign transition from industrialism to post-industrialism but rather in that of what we can today readily recognise as the disruptive economic cycles endemic to capitalism' (2011, 371). This examination of intra-generational work–life mobility is a welcome addition to the study of social mobility. In this paper, however, we return to the key question that informed the earlier debate on meritocracy and mobility. Has the association between class origins, educational attainment and occupational destinations changed over time? Is there any evidence that merit selection increased and the effects of class origins decreased on occupational success in the 1990s and 2000s?

Data and methods

We use the British Household Panel Survey (BHPS) for 1991 and the General Household Survey (GHS) for 2005.[2] Both are nationally representative sample surveys for respondents resident in private households in Great Britain at the time of interview and both have large sample sizes. The BHPS began in 1991 as the premier British panel study, and had 5143 households and 9912 individuals with full interviews in that year, with a response rate of 92% at the individual level. The GHS is the longest-standing government annual survey, starting in 1972, with around 20,000–30,000 respondents each year. From 1972 to 1992 the GHS contained information on the respondent's parents' class, but this information was not collected in the subsequent 12 years. In 2005, because of the integration into it of the EU Statistics on Income and Living Conditions Survey, information on parental occupation was collected again. It has a full sample size of 30,069. The overall response rate for the survey was 74%. We confine the analysis to men aged 25–65 and women aged 25–63. The age range was chosen because the GHS only collected data on parental occupation from respondents aged 25–65.

The two surveys are the only data sources currently available that have the respondents' origin and destination classes consistently coded in the National Statistics Socio-economic Classification (NS-SeC). For both origin and destination, we first constructed the 35-category-long version of the NS-SeC from the standard occupational classification, which was then coded into the seven-class NS-SeC schema (Rose and Pevalin 2003, 8–10). Following Erikson and Goldthorpe (1992, 241), men and women in lower intermediate classes were combined with the routine manual working class, which was done for both the parents' and respondents' classes. We also followed Erikson's (1984) 'dominance approach' by using father's or mother's class (whichever is higher) as the family class. It better reflects changing social reality (Goldthorpe and Mills 2008, 86; Li and Heath 2010,

85). For the samples used here, 17.9% of mothers were in a higher class than fathers in 1991 but the proportion rose to 23.5% in 2005. It also increased the effective sample sizes (by 296 for the British Household Panel Survey and 651 for the GHS). After selecting respondents with valid origin and destination classes, we have 6060 respondents for the 1991 data and 9040 respondents for the 2005 data.

The seven-class NS-SeC schema we use for both origin and destination classes is as follows: (1) higher managerial and professional and large employers, (2) lower managerial and professional, (3) intermediate, (4) small employers and own account workers, (5) lower supervisory and technical, (6) semi-routine, and (7) routine. We also refer to the first two as 'salariat' classes, the middle three as 'intermediate' classes, and the last two as 'working' classes. With regard to education, we coded a six-category variable – (1) first degree or above, (2) professional qualifications below degree such as nursing and teaching, (3) A-levels or equivalent, (4) O-levels or equivalent, (5) primary-level qualifications, and (6) no formal qualifications – which is similar to that used in Breen et al. (2009). We use standard methods for the analysis. As we are concerned with changes in the OED relations over time, we shall assess such changes in terms of absolute and relative rates, a crucial distinction long used by social mobility researchers (Goldthorpe, Llewellyn, and Payne 1987; Halsey, Heath, and Ridge 1980; Heath 1981). The models will be explained in the analysis section. All analysis in the following is based on weighted data and conducted for men and women separately.

Absolute trends

First, we look at the association between origins and education (OE), between education and destinations (ED) and between origins and destinations (OD) for men and women. As the sevenfold class and sixfold education would yield large tables making interpretation difficult, we have put the full tables in Appendix 1 and base our analysis on a condensed version as shown in Tables 1–3. To aid interpretation, we focus on the differences in the most and least desirable categories in the outcome variables between the top and the bottom origin categories.

Looking at the origin–education (OE) association in Table 1, we find three features: educational upgrading, pronounced class disparities, but also signs of declining class differentials over time for men and women. Focusing on men first, the proportion with very low or no qualifications became smaller over time. This is shown in the rows for 'all'. In 1991, 37% of men had low-level qualifications, which fell to 24% in 2005. Correspondingly, the proportion of men with secondary-level education level increased from 29 to 40% while the proportion of men with tertiary-level qualifications rose, more modestly, from 34 to 35%. The class differences are striking

Table 1. The origin–education (OE) association by sex and year (% by row).

	1991 Tert	1991 Sec	1991 Prim	2005 Tert	2005 Sec	2005 Prim
Men						
Higher salariat	68	23	10	64	29	7
Lower salariat	49	33	18	47	38	15
Intermediate	49	30	21	38	48	14
Small employer/own account	36	27	36	27	41	33
Lower supervisory/technical	28	32	40	26	43	30
Semi-routine	21	28	51	22	46	32
Routine	18	27	54	21	40	39
All	34	29	37	35	40	24
Women						
Higher salariat	61	26	13	64	29	7
Lower salariat	43	33	24	49	37	14
Intermediate	32	38	30	41	46	13
Small employer/own account	21	34	45	27	43	30
Lower supervisory/technical	19	31	49	23	42	35
Semi-routine	14	30	56	22	42	36
Routine	13	24	63	19	39	41
All	25	31	44	35	39	26

Notes: Tert = tertiary (professional qualification, degree or above); secondary = A/O-levels or equivalent; Prim = primary or no formal qualifications. Primary level of education refers to education below O-levels or equivalent or, more precisely, to commercial qualifications below O-level CSE, Grades 1–5, Scottish Grades 4–5, apprenticeships or other qualifications. Row margins in this and the following two tables are shown in the tables in Appendix 1. Source: British Household Panel Survey (1991) and General Household Survey (2005) (same below).

however. In 1991, over two-thirds (68%) of men from higher-salariat families had tertiary levels of education but less than one-fifth of their peers (18%) from routine manual families had tertiary education, with a gap of 50 percentage points. Thus, over one-half (54%) of men from routine manual families had only primary-level qualifications while 10% of their peers from higher salariat families had only primary level qualifications (a gap of 44 points). That said, a clear trend of declining class inequality in education is also in evidence. The gaps between the top and the bottom in tertiary education narrowed from 1991 to 2005, by seven points for men, and the reductions in primary/no qualifications went even further, falling by 12 points.

Turning to women, the proportion with very low or no qualifications also became smaller over time. In 1991, 44% of women had low-level qualifications, which fell to 26% in 2005. Correspondingly, the proportion of women with secondary-level education level increased from 31 to 39%. The proportion of women with tertiary-level qualifications rose from 25 to 35%. The class differences are striking for women too. In 1991, just under two-thirds

Table 2. The education–destination (ED) association by sex and year (% by row).

	1991 SAL	1991 INT	1991 WC	2005 SAL	2005 INT	2005 WC
Men						
Degree+	89	9	2	81	12	7
Sub-degree	58	29	13	64	24	12
A-levels	44	41	15	44	37	19
O-levels or equivalent	31	38	32	30	38	32
Primary	11	47	41	23	33	44
No qualifications	9	40	51	10	35	56
All	37	34	29	44	29	27
Women						
Degree+	84	11	5	80	12	8
Sub-degree	63	22	15	62	20	18
A-levels	26	48	26	34	33	33
O-levels or equivalent	21	45	34	24	31	46
Primary	11	40	49	18	36	45
No qualifications	8	27	65	8	21	71
All	29	32	39	39	24	37

Notes: SAL = salariat (Classes 1+2), INT = intermediate (Classes 3–5); WC = Working class (Classes 6–7).

(61%) of women from higher salariat families had tertiary levels of education but less than one-fifth of their peers (13%) from routine manual families had tertiary education. This is a gap of 48 percentage points and 2 points less than the gap between men from the two origin classes. Thus, nearly two-thirds (63%) of women from routine manual families had only primary-level qualifications while just more than one-tenth (13%) of their peers from higher salariat origins had this level of qualifications. The gap here is 50 points, which is six points higher than the gap between men. As with men, however, a clear trend of declining class inequality in education is also in evidence. The gaps between the top and the bottom in tertiary education narrowed from 1991 to 2005, by three points for women. The reductions in primary/no qualifications went even further, falling by 16 points.

Overall, the tables capture the continued improvements in educational attainment and the significant upgrade in levels of educational attainment, especially at degree level, for women already noted elsewhere (Devine 2010; Schoon 2010). The class differences in educational attainment for men and women in 1991 and 2005 confirm the earlier findings of critics of the meritocracy thesis (Heath, Mills, and Roberts 1992; Marshall, Swift, and Roberts 1997). That said, our *prima facie* evidence suggests that class differentials in educational attainment have declined over time. Class differences are still considerable but the decline in those differences is important to acknowledge. This finding suggests that the relationship OE remains

Table 3. The origin–destination (OD) association by sex and year (% by row).

	1991			2005		
	SAL	INT	WC	SAL	INT	WC
Men						
Higher salariat	70	19	11	68	18	14
Lower salariat	56	28	15	54	26	20
Intermediate	50	30	20	52	29	19
Small employer/own account	33	44	23	36	36	28
Lower supervisory/technical	32	35	32	38	32	30
Semi-routine	25	34	41	33	32	35
Routine	23	38	39	31	32	37
All	37	34	29	44	29	27
Women						
Higher salariat	61	25	14	56	23	21
Lower salariat	42	32	26	50	24	26
Intermediate	31	40	29	46	25	29
Small employer/own account	23	37	40	37	26	37
Lower supervisory/technical	24	35	41	31	26	43
Semi-routine	19	28	53	29	26	45
Routine	20	28	52	25	22	53
All	29	32	39	39	24	37

Notes: SAL = salariat (Classes 1+2), INT = intermediate (Classes 3–5); WC = Working class (Classes 6–7).

although it has weakened over time. Of course, the period under investigation is very short indeed – only 14 years – and it will be interesting to see whether this trend continues into the future.

Turning to the association between educational attainment and occupational destination (ED) as shown in Table 2, we note two main features here. The first is the time-honoured sociological finding of the crucial importance of education on occupational success. Thus, the overwhelming majority (89%) of men with tertiary qualifications were found in salariat positions in 1991, in sharp contrast to only 9% of men with no formal qualifications to be found in such positions (a gap of 80 percentage points). To put it another way, the majority (51%) of men with no qualifications were found in working-class positions while only 2% of men with tertiary-level education were found in such positions (a gap of 49 percentage points). The effect of education on destination is also obvious in 2005. Second, there is evidence of a declining association between education and destinations over the 14-year time period. For example, men with primary-level qualifications secured greater access to the salariat between 1991 and 2005, rising from 11 to 23%. At the same time, the class lead of those men with tertiary levels of education over those with no qualifications fell from 80 to 71 percentage points. Thus, while there has been a growth in educational attainment, there has been no corresponding growth in educational returns in terms of access to the salariat.[3]

Similar findings pertain to women. The overwhelming majority (84%) of women with tertiary qualifications were found in salariat positions in 1991, in sharp relief to only 8% of women with no formal qualifications to be found in such positions. This picture is very similar to men. To put it another way, the majority of women (65%) with no qualifications were found in routine working-class positions while only 5% of women with tertiary qualifications were found in such positions. The picture is similar to men, with educational attainment having a major bearing on occupations destinations. These effects are also evident 14 years later. That said, the figures show a declining association between education and destinations over the time period under consideration. The percentage of women with primary qualifications to be found in the salariat increased from 11% in 1991 to 18% in 2005, for example. At the same time, the class lead of those women with tertiary-level education over those with no qualification fell from 76 to 72 percentage points. The declining association between education and destinations, therefore, is somewhat less pronounced for women than men.

In summary, educational attainment is a critical factor in determining occupational destinations and remains the case between 1991 and 2005. There is no evidence, however, that the association between education and destination has strengthened over time. In fact, the bond appears to have weakened over time for men and women to a greater or lesser degree. These findings concur with others who argue that the returns to education decline as education loses its position as an exclusive good over time (Heath, Mills, and Roberts 1992). Moreover, there is further evidence to suggest that other (arguably non-meritocratic) factors (such as personal attributes or social networks) (Jackson 2001, 2008; Jackson, Goldthorpe, and Mills 2005) can influence occupational life-chances in the labour market. Moving beyond individual attributes, the wider economic context at the time of labour-market entry and its subsequent effects on work–life mobility are also influential, as noted by Bukodi and Goldthorpe (2011) and outlined earlier in this paper.

Finally, we look at the direct association between origins and destinations (OD) as shown in Table 3. Firstly, we see the familiar upgrading in the occupational structure as shown in the rows for 'all'. Unlike the educational upgrading seen above, the class upgrading occurred at the higher rather than lower ends. In 1991, 29% of men occupied routine working-class positions, which fell to 27% in 2005. The proportion of men in intermediate class positions also fell from 34 to 29% and the proportion of men in the salariat increased from 37 to 44%. Again, the relationship between class origins and destinations is strong. In 1991, over two-thirds (70%) of men from higher salariat families were found in salariat positions but just under one-quarter (23%) were from routine working-class families, with a gap of 47 percentage points. Thus, 39% of men from routine working-class families were found in routine destinations while only 11% from higher salariat origins were found in the routine working-class positions (a gap of 28 points). This association is also evident in 2005 although there is a trend of a declining association between origins and destinations over 14 years. Working-class sons secured greater access to the salariat between 1991 and 2005, rising from 23 to 31%. As the same time, the class lead of the higher salariat over routine working-class families for men fell from 47 to 37 percentage points.[4]

Women are also more likely to be found in higher positions in 2005 than in 1991. In 1991, 39% of women occupied routine working-class positions, which fell to 37%. The proportion of women in intermediate class positions also fell from 32 to 24% and the proportion of women in the salariat increased from 29 to 39%. Starting from a lower base, this is a bigger increase than that of men (by three points) although women are still less likely (five points less likely) to be in salariat positions than men. Again, the relationship between class origins and destinations is strong. In 1991, nearly two-thirds (61%) of women with higher salariat origins were found in salariat positions but only one-fifth (20%) from routine working-class origins were found in such positions, with a gap of 41 percentage points. To put it another way, over one-half (52%) of women of routine working-class origins were found in the same class destination and only 14% of women from higher salariat families were found in working-class positions. The gap here is 38 percentage points. This association is also evident in 2005 although, as with men, there is evidence of a declining association between origins and destinations over 14 years. Working-class daughters secured greater access to the salariat between 1991 and 2005, rising from 20 to 25%. As the same time, the class lead of the higher salariat over routine working-class families for women fell from 41 to 31 percentage points.

In sum, the tables confirm the upgrading of the occupational structure that has been well documented for much of the twentieth century and how this has been experienced slightly differently for men and women who have long occupied different parts of the class structure (Goldthorpe and Mills 2008; Li and Devine 2011). The evidence also shows the continuing association of origins on destinations, which is direct and independent of education, in 1991 and 2005 as others have previously argued (Heath, Mills, and Roberts 1992; Marshall, Swift, and Roberts 1997). Even so, our *prima facie* findings show that the association between class origins and occupational destinations has declined over the period under investigation. Once again, however, it is important to be mindful that 14 years is a short period of time and it is not possible to indicate, at this juncture, whether this is a general or particular trend either in support or rebuttal of the meritocracy thesis.

Relative trends

The preliminary analysis in the foregoing shows that the inequalities in all three links (OE, ED and OD) were pronounced but there were also signs of some reduction of such inequalities over time for men and women alike. As noted earlier, the analysis focused on the most salient contrasts, such as possession of tertiary qualifications, or access to the salariat, between people from higher-grade professional and managerial families on the one hand, and those from semi-skilled or unskilled working-class families on the other. While such contrasts bring into sharp relief the most unequal aspects of social life in educational and occupational attainment, they pay insufficient attention to the differences and changes in other parts of the class and the educational structures and do not fully answer the question of whether there is constant, growing or declining fluidity in the net associations in the three interrelated domains, which has captured the imagination and research attention of sociologists for decades. We now turn to this latter kind of question in the following, using relative rates.

Relative mobility rates refer to the competition of people from one rather than another origin for one rather than another destination (in terms of educational qualifications or social class) and are expressed as odds ratios. Let us assume, for the sake of simplicity, a social structure with only two origins and two destinations: middle and working classes. If one-half of the people from each origin class are found in each destination class, we have an odds ratio of one. In such a scenario, there is no difference in class mobility. The closer the odds ratio is to one, the greater the equality in the origins–destinations association; while the further away the odds ratio rises above one, the greater the inequality. In similar vein, the further away the odds ratio fall below one, the greater the equality. Relative differences thus tap the net association between origins and destinations, independent of structural changes as reflected in the heterogeneous marginal distributions.

Two statistical models are usually used for the analysis of the overall social fluidity in the relative mobility rates: log-linear and log-multiplicative layer-effect (also called 'uniform difference' or UNIDIFF) models (Erikson and Goldthorpe 1992). The former is further divided into a baseline (conditional independence) and a constant social fluidity (CnSF) model.[5] Briefly, the baseline model assumes that the distributions of both origins and destinations vary by time (survey year) but there is no association between them. In other words, all of the odds ratios or relative chances defining the origin and the destination classes are equal at a value of one. The CnSF model allows for the latter but not the three-way association, which would be a saturated model. The UNIDIFF model is a variant of the CnSF model that further allows for a uniform movement for the coefficient of one year to move above or below that of the other. In the present analysis, we use the first survey year (1991) as the reference point. The further away the z coefficient for year 2005 rises above that of 1991, the more unequal the distribution of educational/occupational opportunities is becoming, and *vice versa*.

Table 4 shows the results of fitting the log-linear and the UNIDIFF models to the OE, ED and OD tables for men and women on the basis of the full data; namely, the seven-way class and six-way education categories as shown in Appendix 1 (Tables A1–A3) rather than the collapsed forms in Tables 1–3. Although the CnSF models provide an acceptable fit to the OE

Table 4. Results of fitting the conditional independence, constant social fluidity and UNIDIFF models to the OE, ED and OD relations for the 1991 and the 2005 data.

Model	df	G^2	p	rG^2	BIC	DI
OE						
Men (n = 7252)						
1. Cond. ind.	60	1119.7	0.00	−0.0	586.4	14.2
2. CnSF	30	52.1	0.01	95.4	−214.6	3.0
3. UNIDIFF	29	27.7	0.54	97.5	−230.1	2.2
2. − 3.	1	22.4	0.00			
Women (n = 7848)						
4. Cond. ind.	60	1380.6	0.00	−0.0	842.5	15.6
5. CnSF	30	42.4	0.07	96.9	−226.7	2.8
6. UNIDIFF	29	34.2	0.23	97.5	−225.9	2.3
5. − 6.	1	8.2	0.00			
ED						
Men (n = 7252)						
1. Cond. ind.	60	2803.8	0.00	−0.0	2270.4	24.8
2. CnSF	30	65.4	0.00	97.7	−201.3	2.8
3. UNIDIFF	29	61.9	0.00	97.8	−195.8	2.8
2. − 3.	1	3.9	0.06			
Women (n = 7848)						
4. Cond. ind.	60	3155.1	0.00	0.0	2617.0	26.0
5. CnSF	30	61.2	0.00	98.1	−207.8	3.0
6. UNIDIFF	29	57.8	0.00	98.2	−202.3	2.8
5. − 6.	1	3.4	0.07			
OD						
Men (n = 7252)						
1. Cond. ind.	72	721.5	0.00	−0.0	81.5	13.1
2. CnSF	36	44.0	0.17	93.9	−276.0	2.9
3. UNIDIFF	35	30.3	0.69	95.8	−280.8	2.3
2. − 3.	1	13.7	0.00			
Women (n = 7848)						
4. Cond. ind.	72	714.6	0.00	0.0	68.9	12.2
5. CnSF	36	61.1	0.01	91.4	−261.7	2.9
6. UNIDIFF	35	54.8	0.02	92.3	−259.1	2.9
5. − 6.	1	6.3	0.01			

link for women and the OD link for men, the UNIDIFF models give a statistically significant improvement in fit over the CnSF models for both men and women in both OE and OD links. As for the ED link, we find that neither CnSF nor UNIDIFF models fit the data satisfactorily and that the UNIDIFF models do not show statistically significant improvement in fit over the CnSF models. Thus some real changes were taking place in the net associations OE and OD but non-significant changes were discerned with regard to the link between education and class destinations.

As the fit statistics in the log-linear and UNIDIFF models are not intuitive, we show in Figure 2 graphic presentations on the direction and strength of change in the three links for men and women. The data on the arrows are derived from the UNIDIFF parameters, referring to changes in the net association in the odds ratios in 2005 as compared with 1991. Turning to men, we find that the OE link declined by a factor of 4.1, which is significant at the 0.01 level; that the ED link also declined by a factor of 1.8, which is significant only at the 0.1 level; and that the OD link, fell significantly too, by 2.3. The picture for women is similar although the magnitude is of a lesser degree. We find a highly significant decline (at the 0.01 level) in the OE link by a factor of 2.4, a notable decline (at the 0.1 level) in the ED link, and again a highly significant decline (at 0.01 level) in the OD level.[6] The log-linear and UNIDIFF analysis thus confirms our analysis of absolute rates about the significant declines in origin effects in both educational and occupational mobility and the notable (albeit non-significant at the conventional 0.05 level) weakening in the education–destination links for both men and women over a 14-year period. Our findings in relative mobility via log-linear and UNIDIFF modelling thus confirm our *prima facie* analysis of the absolute rates in showing that there was a decline, albeit to varying degrees, in all

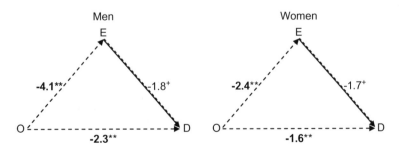

Figure 2. Changes in the OED associations (1991–2005).
Notes: dotted arrows indicate significantly weakening and solid arrows indicate uncertain effects. The figures on the arrows show the extent of changes that are derived from the UNIDIFF parameters in Table 4.
**$p < 0.01$; +$p < 0.10$.

three links (OE, ED and OD), and for men and women alike for the time period under investigation.

This analysis has been conducted at the 'global' level and we may wish to see whether this kind of decline in the three links occurred across the board or was confined to certain, more 'local', domains (Goldthorpe and Jackson 2007). For instance, Breen et al. (2009) suggest that the significant decline in class inequality in education was due to welfare protection reducing the social distance (family resources) between social groups, such as between the higher salariat and the routine working class. This, accompanied by the expansion and reform of the educational system, explains how working-class children caught up with middle-class children. An opposite view is expressed by Blanden, Gregg, and Macmillan (2011) in seeking to explain the growing effects of origins on educational and income mobility. According to these authors, the use of father's class as the family origin variable is unduly limited. Women are increasingly employed in the labour market and they bring incomes to the family. Given the increasing class homogamy (Garret and Li 2005) and the greater employment security and income stability of people in higher social positions (Goldthorpe and McKnight 2006), one could expect that middle-class families with dual and higher incomes would, over time, become increasingly more advantaged than working-class families, increasing social polarisation in class-based income disparities.

While the space limit does not allow us to engage in further explorations in this regard, we could turn to the 'local' effects in the three links; that is, changes in the effects of the same origin (class or educational) categories upon outcome variables. As our dependent variables (education and NS-SeC class) are fairly ordinal, we use ordinal logit regress analysis (we reversed the categories in the dependent variables so that higher values indicate higher positions). As our interest is in the possible changes in the 'local' effects, we also use the Wald tests[7] to see, for instance, whether the coefficients for Class 5 families in their children's education in 2005 are significantly different from, or similar to, those in 1991.

The data in Tables 5 and 6 show the coefficients from the ordinal logit regressions on the OE, ED and OD links for men and women, respectively. With regard to the ED links, we not only present the direct effects of education on class (under the ED columns), but also the indirect effects of origins on destinations; that is, the family effects on respondents' own class positions controlling for education (under the OED columns) as indicated in the diagram paths of Figure 1. The coefficients can be understood as the extent to which people from certain family or educational backgrounds obtain more advantaged and avoid more disadvantaged positions in education and class positions. With regard to the data for men as shown in Table 5, we find three main features. Firstly, there are clear family class gradients in both educational and occupational attainment (as shown under the OE and OD columns), and even stronger educational effects on class attainment (under

Table 5. Ordinal logit regression coefficients on educational and class destinations for men ($n = 2955$ in 1991 and $n = 4122$ in 2005).

	Education (OE)		Class (ED)		Class (OED)		Class (OD)	
	1991	2005	1991	2005	1991	2005	1991	2005
Parental class (routine = ref.)								
Higher salariat	2.508***	2.080***			0.681***	0.602***	1.858***	1.565***
Lower salariat	1.629***	**1.312*****			0.525***	0.319***	1.299***	**0.943****
Intermediate	1.531***	1.051***			0.383*	0.409***	1.061***	0.883***
Small employer/own account	0.821***	**0.334****			0.305**	0.197	0.642***	0.345**
Lower supervisory/technical	0.578***	0.377***			0.103	0.184	0.349***	0.324***
Semi-routine	0.143	0.222*			−0.079	−0.003	−0.017	0.099
Education (none = ref.)								
Degree			3.580***	**3.193*****	3.325***	3.022***		
Sub-degree			2.191***	2.408***	2.052***	2.333***		
A-level			1.661***	1.596***	1.528***	1.522***		
O-level			0.919***	0.933***	0.843***	0.875***		
Primary			0.247*	0.510***	0.209	0.470***		
Pseudo R^2	0.043	0.039	0.096	0.095	0.100	0.098	0.026	0.021

Notes: Coefficients in 2005 that are significantly different (at 5% or above) from those in 1991 are in bold.
The intercepts are not presented in the table but are available on request.
*$p < 0.05$, **$p < 0.01$, ***$p < 0.001$.

Table 6. Ordinal logit regression coefficients on educational and class destinations for women ($n = 2860$ in 1991 and $n = 4373$ in 2005).

	Education (OE)		Class (ED)		Class (OED)		Class (OD)	
	1991	2005	1991	2005	1991	2005	1991	2005
Parental class (routine = ref.)								
Higher salariat	2.623***	2.218***			0.644***	0.385***	1.896***	**1.419*****
Lower salariat	1.811***	1.547***			0.308**	0.400***	1.147***	1.112***
Intermediate	1.449***	1.296***			0.198	0.404***	0.847***	0.983***
Small employer/own account	0.760***	0.575***			0.094	0.368***	0.415***	0.560***
Lower supervisory/technical	0.571***	0.373***			0.161	0.179	0.388***	0.318***
Semi-routine	0.282*	0.305**			−0.061	0.107	0.065	0.230*
Education (none = ref.)								
Degree			4.037***	**3.511*****	3.817***	3.372***		
Sub-degree			2.654***	2.470***	2.534***	2.368***		
A-level			1.503***	1.509***	1.406***	1.416***		
O-level			1.225***	1.017***	1.160***	0.955***		
Primary			0.645***	**0.974*****	0.588***	0.930***		
Pseudo R^2	0.051	0.045	0.101	0.102	0.103	0.104	0.024	0.020

Notes: Coefficients in 2005 that are significantly different (at 5% or above) from those in 1991 are in bold.
The intercepts are not presented in the table but are available on request.
*$p < 0.05$, **$p < 0.01$, ***$p < 0.001$.

the ED columns). For instance, men from higher salariat families had much more favourable chances of obtaining higher (and avoiding lower) educational qualifications and class positions than those from routine working-class families in 1991, with odds being ($e^{2.508}$ and $e^{1.858}$) 12.3 and 6.4 times as high in the two respects. Those with degrees were, as compared with people with no formal qualifications, around 39 times as likely to obtain more advantaged and avoid more disadvantaged class positions ($e^{3.58}$) in 1991.

The second feature, more relevant to our present purposes, is that the weakening class effects in the OE links did not take place for men from the higher salariat families but were confined to men from the middle ranges of class hierarchy. As shown in the bold-faced figures, the origin effects declined only for men from lower salariat, intermediate and small employer/own account families in the OE link.[8] As for the ED link, we do find that it is the degree-level education that lost some of the occupational returns, a reduction of around 11% in terms of log odds. However, when origin effects were taken into account, as shown under the OED columns, there were no significant changes in any of the educational categories. Even after controlling for education, coming from more advantaged families was still associated with more favourable class positions with no significant change over time. In 1991, men from higher salariat families were nearly twice as likely to attain higher and avoid lower class positions ($e^{0.681} = 1.98$) as those equally qualified men from routine families. As noted earlier, social and cultural capital might well play a part in this regard. With regard to the OD link, there was rather little change, with only a significant decline for lower salariat sons.[9]

Turning now to the patterns for women as shown in Table 6, we find that, for the OE link, there was an overall declining class effect, although non-significant for any of the origin categories. As for the ED link, the effects fell significantly for degree holders but increased significantly for those with primary levels of education as we noted earlier. Yet when origin class effects were taken account of, there were no significant declines across the educational categories whilst coming from higher family classes still significantly affected access to more advantaged positions when the educational effects were held constant. Finally, with regard to the OD link, we find that only the higher salariat class effect was significantly reduced, from log odds of 1.896 to 1.419. Comparing men's and women's patterns, we find some similarities and some differences. For example, the degree effects were 3.58 (in terms of log odds) for men but 4.037 for women in 1991, and the coefficients were higher for women than for men at each of the corresponding educational categories (with the exception of A-levels) and that in both years. It is also noteworthy that the net origin effects (after controlling for education) were at a similar level for women as for men. It is notable that while the class effects were of a similar magnitude for men and women in education and class attainment, education was obviously playing a more salient role on class attainment for women than for men.

To sum up the evidence on local effects, our analysis shows that the reduction of origin class effects upon educational attainment and occupational destinations was fairly mild, with only significant changes for men in the middle ranges of the class hierarchy and for women from higher salariat origins. The findings are somewhat different from the suggestions of a narrowing gap between the top and the bottom by Breen et al. (2009) and of a gaping chasm of the social hierarchy by Blanden, Gregg, and Macmillan (2011).

Conclusion

In this paper, we have examined the changing relationship between OED and the role of class and education in mobility processes. We found that the relationship between origins and education and between origins and destinations have weakened between 1991 and 2005 for men and women. This is in line with two of the three assumptions underpinning the meritocracy thesis. Of course, we cannot say whether our findings are suggestive of a secular trend towards meritocracy. Such a definite statement would require data spanning a considerable time period. That said, the weakening association between origins and education and origins and destinations are interesting findings in themselves. When public anxiety about educational success is high (Devine 2004; Power 2003), the weakening relationship between education and destinations is interesting. Qualifications play a key role in social selection although more so for high-level rather than low-level occupations. Even so, the role of credentials in occupational success is more complicated than the meritocracy thesis assumes.

There are many aspects to this complexity. As Halsey, Heath, and Ridge (1980) pointed out years ago, while educational attainment is a major factor in occupational success, other non-meritocratic forces have not disappeared from view. There is strong evidence to show, for example, that non-meritocratic factors such as personality traits come into play in occupational selection and the reproduction of class inequality (Jackson 2001, 2008). Politicians, as noted in the opening remarks of this paper, are increasingly aware of the importance of social capital – individual connections and collective networks – in both educational and occupational attainment and thereby class reproduction. The extent to which education fades from view and other factors of a meritocratic (job performance) and non-meritocratic kind (developed networks) come into play over the life-course could be better understood. Describing and explaining ascription and achievement in inter-generational and intra-generational mobility could open up a very interesting research agenda indeed (Tampubolon and Savage 2012).

A research agenda of this kind could embrace many levels of analysis. The study of social mobility tends to focus on people moving between positions. Attention is directed towards individual mobility. In seeking to understand the relationship between OED, it is also imperative to understand wider institutional contexts, notably the education system and the labour market. The education system and labour market in Britain are ever changing with, for example, the growth of predominantly vocational credentials with relatively low labour-market value (Wolf 2011) and the trend towards educational qualifications becoming a declining asset in the labour market (Brown, Lauder, and Ashton 2010). Moreover, these wider changes remind us that private worries and public anxiety about declining social mobility and the importance attached to education for occupational success are a reflection of the increasing competition for good jobs in Britain and around the world.

Notes

1. In an earlier paper, we considered the recent debate between economists (Blanden and various colleagues) and sociologists (Goldthorpe and numerous other authors) about whether social mobility is declining (Li and Devine 2011). The work of the economists and the considerable attention they enjoyed has been discussed in an earlier volume of this journal (Gorard 2008).
2. The reason for using the datasets is chiefly due to the quality and consistency of the data on parental and respondent's class. For further discussion of the matters in this regard, see Goldthorpe and Mills (2008, note 6) and Li and Devine (2011, notes 5, 6, 8 and 12). It is also noted here that after the analysis for the current paper was completed, information on parental occupation in the Understanding Society survey was released but the data from the latter survey are not used in the current paper.
3. A close look at the data in Table A1 of Appendix 1 shows *prima facie* support to Breen et al. (2009) in that the reduction of class effects occurred at the lower rather than higher levels of education, and this feature is apparent in both men's and women's profiles. It is noted here that for the British data they use the GHS 1973, 1975–1976, 1979–1984 and 1987–1992 for men, and that the GHS data they used do not allow the fine-grained class measurement for father's class because Classes I, II and IVa are collapsed.
4. Similar to education, the class reduction in occupational attainment occurred at the bottom rather than at the top. As Table A2 in Appendix 1 shows, there is no change in the gap between sons from Class 1 and 7 families in gaining access to Class 1, at 28% at both time points, and that for women actually increased by five points, from a differential of 10 points in 1991 to 15 points in 2005. The differences in avoiding routine positions fell by three and six points, respectively, for men and women.
5. The models can be written as: 1: baseline (conditional independence) model, $\log F_{ijk} = \mu + \lambda_i^O + \lambda_j^D + \lambda_k^Y + \lambda_{ik}^{OY} + \lambda_{jk}^{DY}$ 2: constant social fluidity model (CnSF), $\log F_{ijk} = \mu + \lambda_i^O + \lambda_j^D + \lambda_k^Y + \lambda_{ik}^{OY} + \lambda_{jk}^{DY} + \lambda_{ij}^{OD}$ and 3: log multiplicative or uniform difference (UNIDIFF) model, $\log F_{ijk} = \mu + \lambda_i^O + \lambda_j^D + \lambda_k^Y + \lambda_{ik}^{OY} + \lambda_{jk}^{DY} + \lambda_{ij}^{OD} + \beta_k X_{ij}$ – where O stands for origin, D for destination, and Y for year. In the UNIDIFF model, X_{ij} indicates the general pattern of

the origin–destination association, and β_k the direction and relative strength of the association specific to a year. Note that the O and D in the formula are represented in different ways in the OE, OD and ED links.

6. If we use father's (rather than the dominance) class, similar findings are obtained. The changes in the OE and OD links are -3.6% ($p < 0.000$) and -2.3% ($p < 0.000$) for men ($n = 6823$), and -3.7 ($p < 0.000$) and -2.0% ($p < 0.002$) for women ($n = 7269$), in 2005 as compared with 1991 in terms of the odds ratios.
7. The Wald test is written as $t = (b_1 - b_2)/(s_1^2 + s_2^2)^{1/2}$.
8. Another way of looking at the OE relationship is to see the changing effects of parental class on gaining more advantaged and avoiding less advantaged levels of education in the way the maximised maintained inequality (MMI) thesis proposes. We carried out such an analysis with five transitions: from no qualifications to primary education or above, from primary schooling to O-levels or above, from O-levels to A-levels and above, from A levels to professional qualifications, and from professional qualifications to first degree of above. The results show that there are significant declines in the class effects at certain transitions for men, and Classes 1 and 2 daughters' transitions from sub-degree to first degree also showed significant declines. What is noteworthy is that none of the transitions showed any increased class affects, rendering no support to the MMI thesis. We need to note, however, that our data were not well placed to test the thesis fully as we not have information on the types of higher education institutions attended by our respondents. Class privileges have long played a role in gaining entry into elite universities although whether they are *increasingly* important, given that people from advantaged class backgrounds have always sought to gain access to elite universities in Britain, has yet to be fully ascertained.
9. Breen et al. (2009, 1475) show a 'wide-spread decline in educational inequality' among men in eight European countries but the decline was rather limited in the British case. Their data show (1501) that only the distance between Classes I+II+IVa and VII in the first transition (from primary to O-levels or above) was slightly reduced from the first birth cohort (1908–1924) to the last (1955–1964) and that no clear reductions were in trend in the other two transitions (from O-levels to A-levels or above; from A-levels to tertiary education). We carried out a similar analysis of the transitions and found no significant changes over time for any category of the origin class in any of the three transitions in either men's or women's case. Data are not presented but are available on request.

References

Bell, D. 1976. *The Coming of Post-Industrial Society*. London: Heinemann.

Blanden, J., P. Gregg, and L. Macmillan, 2011. *Intergenerational Persistence in Income and Social Class: The impact of Within-Group Inequality*. JRSS, JRSS-OA-SA-May-10-0087.R1.

Bond, R., and P. Saunders. 1999. "Routes of success: influences on the occupational attainment of young British males." *The British Journal of Sociology* 50: 217–249.

Breen, R., and J. H. Goldthorpe. 1999. "Class Inequality and Meritocracy: A Critique of Saunders and an Alternative Analysis." *British Journal of Sociology* 50 (1): 1–27.

Breen, R., and J. H. Goldthorpe. 2001. "Class, Mobility and Merit; the Experience of Two British Cohorts." *European Sociological Review* 17: 81–101.

Breen, R., R. Luijkx, W. Müller, and R. Pollak. 2009. "Non-Persistent Inequality in Educational Attainment: Evidence from Eight European Countries." *American Journal of Sociology* 114: 1475–1521.

Brown, P., H. Lauder, and D. Ashton. 2010. *The Global Auction*. Oxford: Oxford University Press.

Bukodi, E., and J. H. Goldthorpe. 2011. "Class Origins, Education and Occupational Attainment in Britain." *European Societies* 13 (3): 347–375.

Cabinet Office. 2011. *Opening Doors, Breaking Barriers: A Strategy for Social Mobility*. https://www.gov.uk/government/uploads/system/uploads/attachment_data/file/61964/opening-doors-breaking-barriers.pdf.

Cabinet Office. 2012. *Fair Access to Professional Careers: A Report by the Independent Reviewer on Social Mobility and Child Poverty*. London: The Cabinet Office.

Carnegie Corporation of New York/The Sutton Trust. 2012. *Social Mobility and Education Gaps in the Four Major Anglophone Countries: Research Findings for the Social Mobility Summit, May 2012*. London: The Sutton Trust.

Devine, F. 2004. *Class Practices: How Parents Help Their Children Get Good Jobs*. Cambridge: Cambridge University Press.

Devine, F. 2009. "Class." In *The Oxford Handbook of British Politics*, edited by M. Flinders, A. Gamble, C. Hay, and M. Kenny, 609–628. Oxford: Oxford University Press.

Devine, F. 2010. "Class Reproduction, Occupational Inheritance and Occupational Choices." In *Gender Inequalities in the 21st Century, Class, Employment and Family*, edited by J. Scott, R. Crompton, and C. Lyonette, 40–58. London: Edward Elgar.

Erikson, R. 1984. "Social Class of Men, Women and Families." *Sociology* 18: 500–514.

Erikson, R., and J. H. Goldthorpe. 1992. *The Constant Flux*. Oxford: Clarendon Press.

Garratt, D., and Y. Li. 2005. "The Foundations of Experimental/Empirical Research Methods." In *Research Methods in the Social Sciences*, edited by B. Somekh and C. Lewin, 198–206. London: Sage.

Goldthorpe, J. H. 2007. *On Sociology*, Vols. 1&2. Stanford, California: Stanford University Press.

Goldthorpe, J. H., and M. Jackson. 2007. "Intergenerational Class Mobility in Contemporary Britain: Political Concerns and Empirical Findings." *British Journal of Sociology* 58: 526–546.

Goldthorpe, J. H., C. Llewellyn, and C. Payne. 1987. *Social Mobility and Class Structure in Modern Britain*. Oxford: Clarendon Press.

Goldthorpe, J. H., and A. McKnight. 2006. "The Economic Basis of Social Class." In *Mobility and Inequality: Frontiers of Research in Sociology and Economics*, edited by S. L. Morgan, D. B Grusky, and G. Fields, 109–136. California: Stanford University Press.

Goldthorpe, J., and C. Mills. 2008. "Trends in Intergenerational Class Mobility in Modern Britain: Evidence from National Surveys, 1972–2005." *National Institute Economic Review* 205: 83–100.

Gorard, S. 2008. "A Re-Consideration of Rates of 'Social Mobility in Britain or Why Research Impact is Not Always a Good Thing." *British Journal of Sociology of Education* 29: 317–324.

Halsey, A., A. Heath, and J. Ridge. 1980. *Origins and Destinations: Family, Class and Education in Modern Britain*. Oxford: Clarendon Press.

Heath, A. 1981. *Social Mobility*. London: Fontana.

Heath, A. F., C. Mills, and J. Roberts. 1992. "Towards Meritocracy - New Evidence on an Old Problem." In *Social Research and Social Reform: Essays in Honour of a.H. Halsey*, edited by C. Crouch and A. F. Heath, 217–243. Oxford: Oxford University Press.

Jackson, M. 2001. "Non-Meritocratic Job Requirements and the Reproduction of Class Inequality." *Work, Employment & Society* 15: 619–630.

Jackson, M. 2008. "Personality Traits and Occupational attainment'." *European Sociological Review* 22: 187–199.

Jackson, M., J. H. Goldthorpe, and C. Mills. 2005. "Education, Employers and Class Mobility." *Research in Social Stratification and Mobility* 23: 3–33.

Lambert, P., K. Prandy, and W. Bottero. 2008. "By Slow Degrees: Two Centuries of Social Reproduction and Mobility in Britain." *Sociological Research Online*, 13(1): http://www/socresonline.org.uk/12/1/prandy/html.

Li, Y. and F. Devine. 2011. "Is Social Mobility Really Declining? Evidence from the 1990s and 2000s." *Sociological Research on Line,* 16(3), 4 Available on line at http://www.socresonline.org.ik/16/3/4/html.105153/sro2424.

Li, Y., and A. Heath. 2010. "Struggling onto the Ladder, Climbing the Rungs, Employment Status and Class Position by Ethnic Minority Groups in Britain (1972–2005)." In *Population, Heath and Well-Being*, edited by J. Sitwell, P. Norman, C. Thomas, and P. Surridge, 83–97. London: Springer.

Marshall, G., and A. Swift. 1993. "Social Class and Social Justice." *The British Journal of Sociology* 44: 187–211.

Marshall, G., A. Swift, and S. Roberts. 1997. *Against the Odds? Social Class and Social Justice in Industrial Societies*. Oxford: Clarendon Press.

Parsons, T. 1940. "An Analytical Approach to the Theory of Social Stratification, rep in Parsons, T. (1954)." *Essays in Sociological Theory*, New York: Free Press.

Payne, G. 2012. "Labouring under a Misapprehension: Politicians' Perceptions and the Realities of Structural Social Mobility in Britain, 1995–2010." In *Social Stratification: Trends and Processes*, edited by P. Lambert, R. Connelly, R. M. Blackburn, and V. Gayle, 223–242. Farnham: Ashgate.

Power, S. 2003. *Education and the Middle Class*. Buckingham: Open University Press.

Rose, D., and D. Pevalin, eds. 2003. *A Researcher's Guide to the National Statistics Socio-Economic Classification*. London: Sage.

Saunders, P. 1995. "Might Britain Be a Meritocracy?" *Sociology* 29: 23–41.

Saunders, P. 1997. "Social Class in Britain: An Empirical Evaluation of Two Competing Explanations." *Sociology*, 31: 261–288.

Saunders, P. 2010. *Social Mobility Myths*. London: Civitas.

Savage, M., and M. Egerton. 1997. "Social Mobility, Individual Ability and the Inheritance of Class Inequality." *Sociology* 31: 645–672.

Schoon, I. 2010. "Becoming Adult: The Persisting Importance of Class and Gender." In *Gender Inequalities in the 21st Century, Class, Employment and Family*, edited by J. Scott, R. Crompton, and C. Lyonette. London: Edward Elgar.

Tampubolon, G., and M. Savage. 2012. "Intergenerational and Intragenerational Social Mobility in Britain." In *Social Stratification: Trends and Processes*, edited by P. Lambert, R. Connelly, R. M. Blackburn, and V. Gayle, 115–131. Farnham: Ashgate.

Wolf, A. 2011. *Review of Vocational Education - the Wolf Report*. London: Department for Education.

Young, M. 1958. *The Rise of the Meritocracy, 1870–2023: An Essay on Education and Equality*. London: Thames and Hudson.

Appendix 1

Table A1. Educational distribution by parental class, sex and year (% by row).

	1991							2005						
	Deg	Prof	A	O	Prim	None	N	Deg	Prof	A	O	Prim	None	N
Men
1 Higher salariat	41	27	11	12	4	6	146	55	9	14	14	3	4	477
2 Lower salariat	22	28	16	17	6	11	548	36	11	17	21	5	10	1071
3 Intermediate	20	29	14	15	8	13	186	28	11	20	28	5	9	333
4 Small employer/own account	11	25	11	16	7	29	410	17	10	16	24	8	25	419
5 Lower supervisory/technical	5	23	12	19	11	29	606	16	10	16	27	9	21	681
6 Semi-routine	5	17	8	20	12	39	455	13	9	16	30	9	23	651
7 Routine	2	16	9	18	12	43	575	11	10	17	23	7	32	694
(All)	11	22	12	18	9	28		25	10	17	24	6	18	
Women
1 Higher salariat	32	29	7	19	8	5	189	49	15	13	16	4	3	488
2 Lower salariat	17	26	10	23	10	14	614	33	16	14	23	6	7	1144
3 Intermediate	11	21	11	27	17	13	218	27	14	14	32	5	8	397
4 Small employer/own account	5	16	9	25	13	32	400	13	14	16	27	7	23	450
5 Lower supervisory/technical	4	15	5	26	13	36	653	12	11	14	27	10	25	752
6 Semi-routine	3	11	6	25	12	43	516	11	10	13	29	13	24	739
7 Routine	2	12	4	20	12	51	544	9	10	9	30	8	34	744
(All)	8	17	7	24	12	32		22	13	13	26	8	18	

Notes: Deg = first degree or higher; Prof = professional qualifications below degree; A = A-levels or equivalent; O = O-levels or equivalent; Prim = primary education; None = no formal qualifications.

Table A2. Class distribution by parental class, sex and year (percentage by row).

			1991								2005					
	1	2	3	4	5	6	7	N	1	2	3	4	5	6	7	N
Men																
1	36	34	4	8	7	4	7	146	39	29	5	8	6	5	9	477
2	24	32	5	12	12	6	9	548	24	31	5	12	9	9	11	1071
3	22	27	5	11	14	7	12	186	23	30	4	12	12	8	11	333
4	16	17	4	25	14	7	16	410	15	21	3	16	17	13	14	419
5	12	20	5	13	18	14	19	606	16	22	5	12	15	13	17	681
6	8	17	3	13	17	18	24	455	13	20	3	13	16	15	20	651
7	8	15	4	13	21	16	23	575	11	20	3	13	15	15	22	694
All	15	22	4	14	16	12	17		20	25	4	12	12	11	15	
Women																
1	11	51	16	8	1	5	9	189	19	36	14	5	4	12	9	488
2	6	35	20	7	5	15	11	614	12	38	14	7	4	15	11	1144
3	5	25	27	7	6	14	15	218	12	34	16	5	4	19	10	397
4	3	20	22	10	5	20	20	400	7	30	13	7	6	22	15	450
5	3	21	21	4	9	19	22	653	5	26	15	5	6	25	19	752
6	2	17	16	4	8	28	24	516	5	25	13	6	7	25	20	739
7	1	19	17	3	8	23	29	544	4	22	11	5	7	30	23	744
All	4	25	20	6	7	19	20		9	30	14	6	5	21	15	

Note: For class categories, see Table A1 in Appendix 1.

Table A3. Class distribution by educational qualifications, sex and year (percentage by row).

	1991								2005							
	1	2	3	4	5	6	7	N	1	2	3	4	5	6	7	N
Men																
Degree	50	39	4	3	2	1	1	331	45	36	4	5	3	3	4	1073
Sub-degree	25	33	6	12	11	4	9	661	29	35	6	9	9	6	6	437
A-level	17	27	6	15	20	5	11	349	17	28	5	16	16	7	12	738
O-level	7	24	4	16	18	15	17	522	8	22	5	14	19	15	17	1024
Primary	4	7	5	17	26	16	25	278	5	17	2	18	13	17	27	283
None	2	7	3	18	19	21	30	785	1	8	2	17	16	23	33	771
All	15	22	4	14	16	12	17		20	25	4	12	12	11	15	
Women																
Degree	23	61	6	5	1	4	2	261	27	53	7	4	1	5	3	1016
Sub-degree	5	58	11	6	5	7	8	542	8	54	11	4	4	11	8	617
A-level	4	23	32	7	8	14	12	225	6	29	20	7	6	17	15	617
O-level	2	20	33	6	6	18	15	755	3	21	18	6	7	29	17	1248
Primary	1	11	30	7	4	23	25	386	4	15	23	7	6	28	17	370
None	1	7	11	5	10	31	34	965	1	6	7	6	8	37	34	846
All	4	25	20	6	7	19	20		9	30	14	6	5	21	15	

Note: For class categories, see Table A1 in Appendix 1.

Framing higher education: questions and responses in the British Social Attitudes survey, 1983–2010

Anna Mountford-Zimdars[a], Steven Jones[b], Alice Sullivan[c] and Anthony Heath[d]

[a]*King's Learning Institute, King's College, London, UK;* [b]*Manchester Institute of Education, The University of Manchester, Manchester, UK;* [c]*Institute of Education, University of London, London, UK;* [d]*Institute for Social Change, The University of Manchester, Manchester, UK and Nuffield College, Oxford, UK*

> This article focuses on questions and attitudes towards higher education in the British Social Attitudes (BSA) survey series. First, we analyse the changing BSA questions (1983–2010) in the context of key policy reports. Our results show that changes in the framing of higher education questions correspond with changes in the macro-discourse of higher education policies. Second, we focus on the 2010 BSA survey responses to investigate how attitudes towards higher education are related to respondents' characteristics. Respondents' socio-economic position predicts attitudes towards higher education. Graduates and professionals are most likely to support a reduction in higher education opportunities, but those who have so far benefitted least from higher education are supportive of expansion. One interpretation – with potential implications for social mobility – is that those who have already benefited from higher education are most inclined to pull the ladder up behind them.

1. Introduction

Higher education is viewed by both the public and policy-makers as an important route to upward social mobility (for example, Milburn 2012).[1] We use the British Social Attitudes (BSA) survey as a lens through which to view policy changes and map attitudes towards higher education. From a policy perspective, opportunities to fulfil one's potential, for example through education, need to be open and fair (National Equality Panel 2010, 4). Public perception, as documented in responses to surveys such as the BSA, considers a good education fundamental to personal achievement.

Indeed, 72% of BSA respondents in 1987 and 74% of respondents in 2009 thought education was essential or very important in 'getting ahead'.[2] Overall, education ranked second only to hard work, which was selected by 84% of respondents in both years (Heath et al. 2010).

The BSA survey series began in 1983. With the benefit of hindsight, the early 1980s can be characterised as a relatively stable time in higher education policy. The major expansion of the higher education system following the Robbins Report (1963), and the founding of the Open University in 1969, had already occurred. The division between polytechnics and universities remained, with the debates that would lead to the end of this divide in 1992 still some years away. This stability contrasts with the more rapid policy developments in higher education in the 1990s and 2000s, which saw the change from a free-tuition, grant system to an upfront tuition fee system (1998), then to higher deferred tuition fees (2004) and, finally, to fees of £9000 per year (2012) accompanied by a return to bursaries and a strong discourse of social mobility through higher education access (Milburn 2012).

We elaborate on the changing higher education policy context in England in Section 2 of this article, which is followed by a description of our research methods and hypotheses. We then analyse how changing policy discourses were mirrored in the framing of survey questions on higher education in the BSA. Furthermore, we investigate the link between current attitudes towards higher education and respondents' social position. Our combination of a linguistic content analysis of survey questions with statistical analysis of the responses allows us to bring together reflexive and empirical insights and recognises that changes in respondents' answers are in part constructed by the changing questions posed to them.

2. Higher education in England: the changing policy context

The post-war era has been characterised by expansion in student numbers, structural changes and changing funding regimes. A summary of the key changes to English higher education since Robbins is provided in Table 1.

The first notable shift in post-war English higher education was from an elite to a mass system with 3% enrolment prior to the Second World War (Halsey 1988, Table 7.2) to 7.2% in 1962 and steadily increased to reach 47% in 2010 (Department for Business, Information and Skills 2012, 2). The expansion began following the 1961 review by Lord Robbins, which established the 'Robbins principle' that: *'courses of higher education should be available for all those who are qualified by ability and attainment to pursue them and who wish to do so'* (Robbins 1963, 2:31). The principle is a classic meritocratic statement in the sense that academic ability and potential rather than other factors – such as occupational and socio-economic status – should influence opportunities for higher education (see, for example,

Table 1. Key publications and dates in English higher education, 1963–2013.

Year	What?	Impact
1963	Robbins Committee Report	• Triggering higher education expansion • 'Robbins Principle' established that university places 'should be available to all who were qualified for them by ability and attainment'
1965	Binary system introduced	• Higher education system split into universities and polytechnics
1969	Open University founded	• Aims to bring high-quality degree-level learning to people who had not had the opportunity to attend traditional campus universities • First successful distance learning university worldwide
1992	Further and Higher Education Act	• Polytechnics and colleges incorporated as universities (end of binary system) • Attempt to create a comprehensive (unitary) university system
1998	Teaching and Higher Education Act (following Dearing Report of 1997)	• Means tested up-front tuition fees of £1000 introduced • Living cost maintenance grants replaced by loans
2003	White Paper: 'The Future of Higher Education'	• Target to increase higher education participation, to re-introduce grants, and to abolish up-front fees • Recommends Access Agreements to improve access for disadvantaged students
2004	Schwartz Review	• Five admissions principles established, including selection on ability and potential
2004	Higher Education Act	• Introduction of variable fees (£0–3000) • Up-front fees replaced by income-linked deferred payment. • Establishment of Office for Fair Access
2/-11	White Paper 'Students at the Heart of the System'(based on Browne Review of 2010)	• Variable fess of up to £9000 per year introduced • Universities charging fees of over £6000 per year required to contribute to a National Scholarship programme • Sanctions for not meeting widening participation targets • Threshold for loan repayment increased from £15,000 to £21,000. • Part-time students become eligible for loans • Upfront government loans for fees and maintenance • Means tested grants for students from lower income families

Habermas 1976). Following Robbins, universities became less a preserve of the select elite and more a route for upward social mobility. Hindsight shows again that the expansion of higher education during the 1960s coincided with increased 'room at the top' and absolute upward social mobility, thus arguably hiding continued difference in relative upward mobility chances (for example, Goldthorpe and Mills 2008). Wider access to higher education was seen as an integral part of this opening up of social opportunity and the Open University was founded in this spirit in 1969.

The second landmark report, the Dearing Report of 1997, and the subsequent Teaching and Higher Education Act of 1998 introduced tuition fees and student loans while simultaneously abolishing grants. This marked a return to 'ability to pay' being a criterion for university admissions rather than the meritocratic Robbins ideal of ability to benefit.

Support for tuition fees came from the political right as well as from the political left. Higher education was increasingly regarded as having significant private benefits and economic returns in addition to public benefits (Dearing 1997, 90). Furthermore, England – even in the 2000s – did not have free universal childcare in the early years. A left-wing critique of free higher education was thus that it was a 'middle class subsidy': a society that chooses not to afford free provision in education at a stage where every child is using it (during the early years) should not then publicly subsidise a service disproportionately used by the better off. Labour thus framed the introduction of tuition fees in 1998 in terms of social justice and a commitment to increasing the proportion of people participating in higher education.

However, once the principle of charging the individual was established, the level of cost that the individual was expected to shoulder escalated. Only six years after the first introduction of tuition fees and seven years after the Dearing Report, tuition fees were raised to £3000 (US$5382). The payment mode changed from up-front fees to deferred payments in an attempt to mitigate against the drop in participation from those unable to afford up-front fees implied in charging for higher education. In 2012, following the Browne review, deferred, income-linked, variable fees of up to £9000 per annum (US$16,146) came into effect (Browne 2010, 2).

Between Robbins in 1963 and Browne in 2010, the perceived balance between the public and private benefits of higher education has shifted greatly: from emphasising societal rewards towards emphasising private returns (for example, Marginson 2007; Calhoun 2006), and from an academically selective, elitist system with no financial barriers (Robbins Report) to a mass system with up-front tuition fees (Dearing Report). This shift has often been accompanied by further policies to mitigate against the unintended or most obviously 'anti-meritocratic' effects of moves towards privatisating higher education, including the establishment of the Office for Fair Access in 2004. Meanwhile, access to higher education has been highlighted in political discourse on social mobility, and research has shown continuing inequalities in access (for example, Sutton Trust 2005).

3. Data and methods

The annual BSA survey targets 3000 British respondents and tracks their social, political and moral attitudes. New questions are added each year to reflect current issues, but many questions are repeated periodically to chart shifts in attitudes over time. Elements of the survey are often funded by government departments with an interest in learning more about public perceptions of a particular area. Therefore, question batteries are routinely alternated, introduced or removed as policy contexts change.

We analyse the BSA data in two ways. First, we provide a linguistic content analysis of the changing BSA questions over time. Second, we analyse the BSA responses over time, and the social basis of responses in the 2010 survey.

We reviewed the survey items using the BSA information system site.[3] Using the key search terms 'higher education', 'university' and 'social mobility,' we identified relevant key questions that were asked in different years. We then undertook a linguistic analysis of the questions considering the words used, the framing, and implicit assumptions within the questions. We analysed the characteristics of questions that were dropped from the survey and those of newly introduced items.

Social mobility and widening educational opportunity are usually portrayed as universally positive in public discourse, but both processes have winners and losers. We investigate whether this is reflected in the social and political basis of support for propositions regarding higher education policies that may be regarded as widening opportunities and providing routes to social mobility. We use simple descriptive techniques to show differences between groups, supplemented with multivariate analyses (logistic regression) to address questions regarding the independent significance of each of our predictor variables. The variables we use in these analyses are as follows:

- *Gender*: women tend to support welfare states including educational provision more strongly than men (Pratto et al. 1997), and we hypothesise that this will be reflected in the BSA responses.
- *Social class*: working-class political movements have traditionally supported free education and the expansion of educational opportunities, and we hypothesise that this will be reflected in the class basis of responses to the BSA questions. However, the converse hypothesis is suggested by arguments that it is the middle classes who benefit disproportionately from subsidised higher education. We use the three-category version of the National Statistics Socio-economic Classification schema, which is an occupational schema, and determines class position

in terms of employment relations. It reflects not just income, but longer term economic security, stability and prospects, determined by a person's labour-market position (Goldthorpe and McKnight 2006).
- *Education*: responses from graduates may be expected to mirror those for respondents with professional and managerial jobs, as education and class status are linked. However, our multivariate analyses will partial out whether, once class is controlled, highly educated respondents are more or less likely to support increased educational opportunities.
- *Private schooling*: this variable indicates whether the respondent or a family member has ever attended a private school. We hypothesise that respondents whose families use private schooling will express lower levels of support for state provision.
- *Children aged under 16 in the household*: rational choice theory suggests that political views should be largely determined by private interests (Hindess 1988). In this case, people with children under 16 years old should be relatively likely to support state subsidies for education and widening opportunities.

We are interested in the relationship between party affiliation and attitudes because of the salience of higher education in the previous election. Although the Conservative and Labour parties had similar policies on higher education going into the 2010 general election, with only the Liberal Democrats taking a distinctive anti-fees stance, we hypothesise that the views of Labour supporters will be relatively favourable to expanding educational opportunities. We operationalise political affiliation using respondents' self-classified support for a particular party.

4. Surveying British attitudes to higher education: questions and responses in the BSA

In this section, we draw on the questions asked in the BSA series between 1983 and 2010 to carry out a content analysis of the surveys and note changing patterns in responses. By deconstructing the survey questions themselves, we investigate how the framing of questions towards different aspects of higher education has shifted over time. We also explore how answers correlate with the changing political and policy context.

The first question we examine appeared in the 1983, 1985, 1987 and 1990 surveys: 'When British students go to university or college they generally get grants from the local authority. Do you think they should get grants as now, or loans which would have to be paid back when they start working?' In each of the four surveys, the majority answer was 'grants'. And surprisingly, in each survey the proportion of respondents giving this answer increased (from 57% in 1983 to 71% in 1990). This question, however, was dropped from the BSA survey after 1990.

Similarly, when asked whether students should contribute to their degree or the local authority pay the full amount, a majority of respondents chose the latter. Again, the trend was against students being charged: when the question was last asked, in 1995, the proportion in favour of a student contribution fell 3% on the previous year, to just 25%.

Not all 'disappearing' questions were excluded from the BSA survey permanently. Some formed part of early surveys, then stopped being used for a while before re-emerging in 2010, by which time public opinion had often shifted. For example, in 1995, 1999, 2000 and 2010, respondents were asked about student loans. In the first three of those surveys, the proportion of respondents who believed that students should be expected to take out a loan was between 26 and 31% (with a fall of 2% between 1999 and 2000). However, when the question re-emerged in 2010, this figure had jumped to 43%. Likewise, between 2003 and 2004, an increasing majority of respondents (64% and 67%) felt that tuition fees for all universities and colleges should be the same. When the question was re-introduced in 2010, however, this figure had fallen to 57%. And finally, across the same three years, a similar pattern emerged for variable tuition fees by subject (53%, 56%, 46%). It is interesting to note that fewer respondents objected to fees varying by subject than by institution; however, the key finding is that public attitudes shifted during the latter half of the decade, with the 2010 survey being the first to show public attitudes warming towards student loans and variable fees. Support for maintenance grants did not diminish greatly over the same timeframe. In 2000, the proportion of respondents saying that all or some students should receive grants was 94%; in 2010, it was 92%.

In the early 2000s, a question was included in three surveys about whether tuition costs should be repaid by graduates. Respondents could choose whether all students, some students or no students should make repayments. The proportion of those saying that all students should make repayments was 18% in 2000, 16% in 2001 and 15% in 2003. The downward trend is interesting as this was the period in which tuition fee repayments (as opposed to upfront fees) were being introduced.

In 2002 and 2003, respondents were also asked how important it was that more people from working-class backgrounds went to university. The proportion of those feeling it was 'not very' or 'not at all' important fell fractionally during the two years and did not exceed 19% in either survey. When asked in 2002 whether universities did enough to encourage working-class young people to study there, only 34% of respondents agreed or strongly agreed. The question was not asked again. Indeed, support for widening access was very notable in the BSA surveys of the early 2000s, and it is interesting to note the (admittedly very small) shift towards more progressive and inclusive responses during this period in which fees stood at £1000 but were about to rise to £3000.

In terms of the language used to frame the surveys, we first find that, until recently, it was common for questions to lead the respondent to think about higher education in a positive, progressive light. For example, in 2001, respondents were asked: whether older people should be able to go to university as easily as younger people, how important it is to give older people financial help, and whether university prepares people for the world of work. Also, as noted above, in 2002 and 2003, respondents were asked how important it is for working-class people to go to university.

Strong elements of presupposition are encoded in each of these questions. Within the field of linguistics, and pragmatics in particular, a presupposition is an implicit assumption that is taken for granted within the discourse. Two of the questions listed above, like many others in early BSA surveys, favour a 'how important is it for X to do Y' structure. This structure assumes that some degree of importance is present. In pragmatics, 'important' is said to be the unmarked antonym because it is less conspicuous than its unmarked partner, 'unimportant' (Jones 2002, p. 15). However, most linguists accept that the unmarked term still guides the listener/reader towards agreement with the proposition (Levinson 1983). Therefore, in asking how important it is for working-class people to go to university, the BSA question is implicitly assuming that respondents will indeed attach *some* degree of importance to the proposition. Note also that the question refers to 'working class people', not the 'disadvantaged' or 'non-traditional' applicants, terminology that Burke (2012) connects to 'deficit assumptions'.

It is also interesting that agree/disagree questions, such as 'older people should be able to go to university as easily as younger people' were formulated as a positive statement in the early 2000s. Instead of university entrance for mature students being constructed as a financial burden, or even a societal inequity, the statement is presented in terms of citizens' right. To reject the statement is to discriminate against older people. This does not necessarily make this, or any of the other questions, 'leading'; rather, the constructions reflect societal norms during a period in which the importance of university, and the entitlement of all people to participate, was more widely accepted.

Shortly after these questions were dropped from the BSA survey, however, a different kind of linguistic structure began to be favoured. For example, in both 2005 and 2010, respondents were asked to respond to 'a university education just isn't worth the amount of time and money it usually takes', a statement that presupposes a university degree is both lengthy and expensive. By also presenting the statement in negated form ('*not* worth the time and money'), an implicit assumption is made that participation is not of value. In order to be positive about higher education, the respondent must actively disagree with the proposition, as it is framed by the questioner.

Note also that in 2005 two new questions appeared about voluntary donations by graduates to university, with only 34% agreeing or strongly agreeing that alumni ought to do this, but 23% saying that they themselves would never donate, even if approached directly and able to afford it. A contrast is observable with earlier BSA questions, which tended to focus on values and fairness, rather than inviting individualised judgements.

As these questions indicate, 2005 saw the introduction of BSA questions relating to graduate employability. This included a statement to which the responses over time warrant close consideration: 'A university degree guarantees a good job' (see Table 2)

This question was posed in 2005 and 2010 and, at first glance, the distributions of answers could be seen as evidence that people are increasingly worried about the graduate job market: agreement is rising and disagreement falling. However, the data could be interpreted from a different angle, especially in light of the verb chosen for the statement. If taken literally, it is difficult to imagine any qualification 'guaranteeing' a good job. Had the BSA used less absolute construction, such as 'a university degree *improves the chances of getting* a good job' or 'a university degree *often leads to* a good job', responses may have been different. The selection of 'guarantee' invites rejection of the statement, again pushing respondents towards thinking of higher education as a private, not public, good and questioning its value even within an individualised, consumerist framework. Nonetheless, it is interesting to note that only 41–42% of respondents actually disagree (or strongly disagree) with the statement. Given the unqualified way in which the proposition is expressed, one might expect positive support to be very limited. In fact, the distribution of responses suggests that some respondents have refused to be literal-minded in their interpretation of the question – in effect answering a different question from the one set. This makes any substantive interpretation of the responses problematic.

Indeed, evidence of belief in the value of higher education is widespread in the BSA results. Note the distribution of answers for the question about optimum numbers of university participants, as asked in the 2010 survey (see Table 3).

Interestingly, the desired proportion of young people that respondents would like to see enter higher education actually exceeds current numbers. In total, 129 respondents' answers fell in the 31–40% bracket, the range at which participation actually lay in 2010. For every respondent who indicated

Table 2. Responses to the question 'a university degree guarantees a good job'.

	2005 (%)	2010 (%)
Agree strongly	3	2
Agree	32	29
Neither agree nor disagree	23	27
Disagree	35	35
Disagree strongly	6	6

Note: Responses in column per cent.

a preference for participation below this level, 3.25 participants wanted the proportion to be higher. This kind of support for mass higher education is rarely reflected in media discourse.

Recent BSA surveys also show that participation is indeed considered highly beneficial to young people. Fewer than 7% of respondents in 2010 disagree or disagree strongly that it is important for a young person to go on to a university or college, and fewer than 9% feel the government spends much, or much too much, on higher education.

In terms of the affordability of university, respondents grew more concerned about the costs of higher education between 2005 and 2010 even though fees rose only in line with inflation. The proportion of those agreeing or strongly agreeing with the negatively phrased statement 'the cost of going to university leaves many students with debts that they can't afford to repay' was 77% in 2005 and 79% in 2010. The proportion of those disagreeing or strongly disagreeing was 10% in 2005 and just 8% in 2010. This is strong evidence that the public were not reassured by the abolition of upfront fees or the introduction of a repayment schedule that did not begin until the graduate earned £15,000 or over per year. On the other hand, as noted earlier, a majority of respondents in both 2005 and 2010 rejected the idea that a university education is not worth the amount of time and money it usually takes (55% and 51%, respectively). This suggests that the British public simultaneously hold the view that the financial cost of participating is too high and that participation is still worth the investment of time and money. This could be interpreted as evidence of an awareness of higher education as a public good. Note also that in 2010 only 7% of respondents disagreed or strongly disagreed with the statement 'There are more advantages to a university education than simply being paid more'.

Table 3. Responses to the question: 'Out of every 100 young people in Britain, how many do you think should go on to a university or college?'(BSA 2010).

Answer	Frequency (%)
No young people should go on to higher education	0
Between 1 and 10%	1
Between 11 and 20%	6
Between 21 and 30%	11
Between 31 and 40%	15
Between 41 and 50%	16
Between 51 and 60%	17
Between 61 and 70%	10
Between 71 and 80%	9
Between 81 and 90%	3
Between 91 and 100%	4
All young people should go on to higher education	0
Don't know	6
Refusal	1

Finally in this section, it is interesting to note the BSA's 'disappearing' questions. These include a question related to perceived bias in higher education admissions, which was included in the 2002 and 2003 survey but has not appeared since:

> Suppose two young people with the same A/A2-level (or Scottish Higher) grades apply to go to university. One is from a well-off background and the other is from a less well-off background. Which one do you think would be more likely to be offered a place? (see Table 4).

Given the rise of the Widening Participation agenda in the last decade, and the attention increasingly paid to fairness in UK higher education admissions processes (Moore et al. 2013; Hoare and Johnston 2011), it may seem surprising that the BSA survey did not persist with direct questions such as this. Responses from 2002 and 2003 clearly indicate a perceived lack of equity in how the two hypothetical applicants would be treated. Although over 40% of respondents believe that no bias would arise, a slightly higher proportion anticipated unequal treatment. And where unequal treatment was anticipated, respondents were clear that it would be the 'well-off' candidate who would benefit (at a ratio of 21:1 in 2002 and 11:1 in 2003). This is in stark contrast to public discourses around the same time expressing concern that independent-school applicants would be disadvantaged by the use of contextual data (see Leathwood [2004] or the furore that followed Bristol University's policy to offer slightly lower grades to candidates from less advantaged schooling backgrounds).

In summary, early questions about widening access were arguably more explicit in early BSA surveys than in government policies or even public discourse at the time. It is possible that subsequent policies were based on the assumption that expansion would indeed widen access. However, later BSA questions placed much greater emphasis on the perceived negatives of expansion (devaluation of degrees, greater competition in the graduate market, student debt, etc.) than on possible benefits to the individual or to society.

Table 4. Responses to the question: 'This question is about two young people with the same A/A2-level (or Scottish Higher) grades applying to go to university. One is from a well-off background and the other is from a less well-off background. Which one do you think would be more likely to be offered a place at university?'

	2002 (%)	2003 (%)
Well-off person	42	43
Less well-off person	2	4
Equally offered place	43	41
Can't choose	9	9
Not answered	1	1

5. British Social Attitudes survey responses

We now turn to the analysis of responses to selected BSA questions over time and to associations between attitudes towards higher education and the social position of respondents to the 2010 BSA survey (National Centre for Social Research 2010). We chose the 2010 survey because it is relatively current but also because it included a specific battery of questions on higher education. These questions concerned university funding, including issues such as tuition fees, maintenance grants and loans, as well as probing attitudes towards participation and the value of university education. The greater number of questions about higher education in recent BSA surveys itself indicates the public salience of these issues in the context of the introduction of tuition fees. The 2010 survey was carried out just before the government confirmed the raise in tuition fees to up to £9000.

First, we look at trends over time. Second, we analyse differences in attitudes according to social status and political affiliation. We explore responses to the following question: 'Do you feel that opportunities for young people in Britain to go on to higher education – to a university or college – should be increased or reduced, or are they at about the right level now?' When respondents answered increased or reduced, they could further specify whether this should be by 'a lot' or 'a little'.

We categorised the answers as follows: 'increased' (which includes 'increased a lot' and 'increased a little'); about right; and 'reduced' (which includes 'reduced a lot' and 'reduced a little'). In 2010, 35% of respondents thought opportunities for higher education should be increased, 46% thought opportunities were 'about right' and 16% wished to see opportunities reduced.

Looking at overall trends, we note that between the start of the BSA surveys in 1983 and 2010 a growing minority of respondents thought that the number of students going into higher education should be reduced. This group was around 5% of respondents in 1983 but tripled to more than 16% in 2010. The most frequent response throughout the period (with just under 50% of respondents) was that the number of people going into higher education was 'about right'.

Responses to the BSA have also tracked the actual policy trends in higher education. When asked whether students should be expected to take out loans, fewer than one-third of respondents (27%) supported this proposition in 1995. In 2010 this had become the most common answer, with 43% supporting the idea. The increased acceptance may reflect the political reality of student loans in the post-1998 student loan era.

Perhaps even more illuminating from a sociological perspective than the frequencies and changes over time is the social basis of support. Table 5 shows that those in favour of reducing higher education opportunities are disproportionately male, from the professional and managerial class, educated to degree level or above, private school graduates, Conservative voters, and those without children in the household.

We use multivariate analysis to test the relative impact and statistical significance of these different predictors. We use multivariate logistic regression, which allows more than two discrete outcome categories. We model the predictors of responding that educational opportunities should be increased or decreased compared with the reference category of 'just right'. This allows us to highlight 'asymmetrical' patterns of response; that is, where the social basis of support for a policy is not merely a mirror image of the social basis of disagreement. For example, the first four columns of Table 6 show a strong pattern among those who are against a reduction in higher education opportunities, but we do not find an equally strong pattern of support for expansion.

Table 6 shows regressions modelling for the responses to three separate items: 'Opportunities for young people in Britain to go on to higher education – to a university or college – should be [increased/reduced/are about right]'; 'A university degree guarantees a good job' [agree/disagree/neither agree nor disagree]; and 'University education is not worth the time and money it usually takes' [agree/disagree/neither agree nor disagree].

The first four columns in Table 6 relate to the first question above. The findings replicate the findings from Table 5, showing that men were statistically significantly more likely than women to think opportunities for higher education should be reduced. This is interesting as women increasingly outperform men in educational attainment and participation (Department for Business, Information and Skills 2012). There were no statistically significant gender differences in support for increasing higher education opportunities.

Graduates were both less likely to support an increase in opportunity and also more likely to support a reduction in opportunities. In some respects, this finding is counter-intuitive. One might expect those respondents who had themselves benefited from higher education to value it most. However, as we will discuss later, self-interest might play a role as graduates seek to secure their advantage in the employment market and perhaps feel they have the financial clout to afford their offspring similar opportunities.

Similarly, those who had experience of private schooling – either themselves or in their families – were more likely to be in favour of a reduction and against an increase of higher education opportunities.

Finally, we examine how attitudes towards higher education varied by party affiliation. Compared with Conservative Party supporters, both Labour and the Liberal Democrat supporters and those with no party affiliation were more likely to be against a reduction in higher education opportunities. Labour party supporters were also somewhat more likely than Conservative supporters to favour an increase of opportunities, but Liberal Democrat and Conservative supporters were indistinguishable in their attitudes towards expansion in higher education.

Table 5. Attitudes towards higher education opportunities, by demographic characteristics.

	Higher education opportunities ...			Number of observations
	... should be increased (%)	... are about right (%)	... should be reduced (%)	
Sex				
Female	38	46	13	608
Male	34	46	19	473
Occupational status				
Professional / managerial	34	39	26	163
Intermediate	33	45	18	361
Working class	38	50	10	351
Missing	~	~	~	38
Qualification level				
Degree or higher	28	40	30	182
Below degree level	40	45	14	426
No qualifications	31	54	11	211
missing	~	~	~	94
Respondent's schooling experience				
Only state school	38	47	13	952
Some private school	24	42	30	129
Child in the household				
Yes	42	45	12	377
No	32	47	18	704
Party identification (Conservative)				
Conservative	28	46	25	299
Labour	41	47	11	315
Liberal Democrat	39	42	16	138
Other, none, missing	39	46	12	329
All	35	46	16	913

Note: All percentages are weighted to take into account of sample biases. This is a requirement for the analysis of BSA data. However, the frequencies are raw frequencies representing the actual number of observations for each category. Analysis of valid responses only. Where rows do not add up to 100% this is due to missing data or no response.

Next we turn to the responses to the question about whether a university degree guaranteed a good job. Labour supporters were more likely than Conservative supporters to think that a university degree guaranteed a good job, and those with a child in the household were less likely than those without children to disagree that university education guaranteed a good job.

Table 6. Multinomial logistic regression models predicting attitudes towards higher education participation.

BSA question 2010	Opportunities for young people in Britain to go on to higher education – to a university or college – should be						Whether a university degree guaranteed a good job						'University education is not worth the time and money it usually takes'					
Response category	... increased		... reduced				Agree		Disagree				Agree		Disagree			
Omitted reference category, response variable	... are about right						Neither agree nor disagree'						Neither agree nor disagree'					
Predictor (reference category)	B	SE	B	SE			B	SE	B	SE			B	SE	B	SE		
Intercept	−0.57	0.57	−1.95**	0.81			0.52	0.68	1.42**	0.64			−0.06	0.72	−1.18^	0.62		
Gender (female)																		
Male	−0.17	0.15	0.53***	0.20			0.14	0.19	−0.03	0.17			0.71***	0.21	0.24	0.17		
Social class (intermediate)																		
Professional	0.20	0.22	−0.15	0.26			−0.39	0.28	−0.02	0.24			−0.47	0.32	−0.05	0.25		
Working	0.16	0.17	−0.63***	0.25			−0.29	0.22	−0.28	0.21			−0.81***	0.25	−0.44**	0.20		
Qualification (some qualification)																		
Degree	−0.36^	0.20	0.61***	0.24			−0.20	0.24	0.03	0.22			0.17	0.30	0.65***	0.24		
No qualification	−0.28	0.21	−0.45	0.29			0.13	0.28	0.36	0.26			0.82***	0.31	−0.13	0.26		
Children at home (now)																		
Yes	0.00	0.16	−0.36	0.23			−0.29	0.20	−0.39**	0.19			−0.42^	0.23	−0.23	0.19		
Schooling (all state)																		
Someone private	−0.48^	0.25	0.51**	0.25			0.05	0.28	−0.02	0.26			0.76**	0.33	0.51^	0.28		

(Continued)

Table 6. (Continued).

BSA question 2010	Opportunities for young people in Britain to go on to higher education – to a university or college – should be			Whether a university degree guaranteed a good job			'University education is not worth the time and money it usually takes'		
Party identification (Conservative)									
Labour	0.31^	0.19	−0.88*** 0.25	0.58**	0.24	−0.04 0.22	0.62**	0.27	0.73*** 0.22
Liberal Democrat	0.37	0.24	−0.55*** 0.30	0.30	0.29	−0.32 0.27	0.35	0.37	0.90*** 0.28
Other, none, Missing	0.16	0.19	−0.55*** 0.24	0.27	0.25	0.03 0.22	0.34	0.26	0.12 0.22
N		1049			907			886	
Chi		135.587***			46.85**			112.01***	
Df		28			28			28	

Note: *** $p < 0.001$; ** $p < 0.05$; ^ $p < 0.10$. We also included the following response categories in the statistical model underlying the table: age and age squared, missing education information, and social class missing. None of the missing factors were statistically significant and are omitted from the table.

There were no significant differences in this model according to gender, social class or education.

Finally, we investigated responses to the negatively worded question about university pay-offs ('University education is not worth the time and money it usually takes'). We compare those who agree or agree strongly or disagree or disagree strongly with those who neither agree nor disagree.

Our analysis shows that men are more likely to think that university is not worth the time or money. Working-class respondents were relatively unlikely to agree and also likely to disagree that university is not worth the time and money. Having a degree is associated with disagreement with the statement that university is not worth the time and money. Those respondents with children at home agree less often that university is not worthwhile – and those who went to private school are more likely to agree than those who went to state school. Finally, Labour supporters are most likely to have an opinion, positive or negative, regarding the value of university, while both Labour and Liberal Democrat supporters are more likely to disagree with the negative statement regarding the value of higher education than Conservatives.

6. Discussion and conclusion

We have shown how the discussion of higher education funding and benefits shifted between the Robbins, Dearing, and Browne reports, with increasing emphasis placed on the private rather than public benefits of higher education. The Browne report in particular introduced new elements of marketisation into higher education (Mountford-Zimdars and Teulon, forthcoming 2014). Simultaneously, there has been an increasing focus on the widening participation agenda in higher education, linking this to discourses regarding social mobility.

We investigated how the changing public discourse surrounding higher education has been reflected in changed formulations of BSA survey questions over time. Our linguistic content analysis of the BSA questions illustrated how changing social and political discourses and realities determine the questions posed by researchers as much as they determine public responses to them.

The early BSA survey questions tended to carry positive presuppositions, enquire about social justice, and assume that higher education was a public good rather than a private investment. However, in more recent surveys, cynicism about higher education expansion has crept into questions, with respondents being increasingly reminded of its expense and possible devaluation as a result of massification. Questions about fairness in the admissions process have largely disappeared.

Ironically, our analyses have shown that responses to the questions neither reflect nor justify the shift in their content and tone. Despite higher education increasingly being presented in negative light, respondents still seem able to recognise its value. Even when presented as a private good, respondents remain aware of its public worth. This suggests that media discourses and also some aspects of the Browne report may not be an accurate reflection of how British society regards higher education.

In our empirical analyses of BSA questions on higher education in 2010, we found support for some of our hypotheses regarding self-interest and attitudes. Those who had themselves benefitted from a university expansion acknowledged that it had been worthwhile but opposed future expansion. Those who had attended private schools were generally also in favour of a reduction in higher education. Those with children at home were more hopeful that graduates would get a good job than those without children. However, the responses according to social class and educational qualification are more complex. On the one hand, people's attitudes reflect and reinforce the life-choices they have made. Working-class respondents are less likely to have a strong view on the actual value of a university education, perhaps because they have less personal experience of university and its benefits. Graduates thought that university was worth the time and money, whereas those with no qualifications disagreed. Many of the responses by social class and qualification status thus map onto the actual life-choices people made. Gendered attitudes to higher education expansion are also striking. Here, male respondents are significantly less positive about expansion or the benefits of higher education than female respondents. This is in line with our hypothesis, and these less positive male attitudes towards higher education may also be reflected in the lower levels of male participation in higher education.

Turning to the responses to attitudes towards expansion, it is striking that working-class respondents favour an expansion in university opportunities, whereas graduates strongly favour a reduction in opportunities. Working-class respondents might aspire for their children to have opportunities they themselves did not enjoy, whereas graduates are more in favour of pulling up the ladder behind them and decreasing opportunities

This 'pulling up the ladder' argument is supported by the private school findings. Those who attended private schools are in favour of a reduction of university places and think that universities may not be worth the time and money. In line with our hypotheses, Labour supporters were more inclined to support an expansion of educational opportunities than Conservatives. Liberal Democrats' views were similar to those of Labour supporters.

Implications for social policy are not clear-cut. The BSA survey results indicate that, according to public opinion, higher education opportunities should be more widely available, and that the optimum proportion of young people attending university should exceed its current level.

Strikingly, to win the argument for a marketised higher education system, arguments supporting the higher education as a public good tend to be downplayed. Policy decisions therefore focus on 'cost-sharing' measures, invoking the assumption that public funding disadvantages lower earners because the (participating) middle classes must be effectively subsidised by the (non-participating) working classes. What this analysis of BSA data shows is that popular support for higher education expansion is not always dulled by such self-interest. Comparisons could be made with popular support in the United Kingdom for the National Health Service, which is not necessarily predicated on self-interest (i.e. whether the respondent is in need of treatment) but rather reflects a broader sense of communal good.

In conclusion, our paper highlights the widening gap between public and policy discourses regarding higher education and social mobility on the one hand, and public opinion on the other. Support for higher education as a public good and route to opportunity remains strong, especially among those who have so far benefited least.

Notes

1. These perceptions are supported by some, but not all, empirical evidence (for example, Stuart 2012; but see Lindley and Machin 2012; cf. Goldthorpe and Mills 2008).
2. The BSA survey question (asked in 1987, 1992, 1999, and 2009) was: 'To begin with, we have some questions about opportunities for getting ahead ... Please tick one box for each of these to show how important you think it is for getting ahead in life ... important is ... coming from a wealthy family? ... having well-educated parents? ... having a good education yourself? ... having ambition? ... hard work? ... knowing the right people? ... having political connections? ... giving bribes? ... a person's ethnicity? ... a person's religion? ... being born a man or a woman?'
3. See http://www.britsocat.com.

References

Browne Report. 2010. *Securing a Sustainable Future for Higher Education – an Independent Review of Higher Education Funding and Student Finance*. London.
Burke, P. J. 2012. *The Right to Higher Education*. London: Routledge.
Calhoun, Craig. 2006. "The University and the Public Good." *Thesis Eleven* 84 (1): 7–43.
Dearing Report. 1997. National Committee of Inquiry into Higher Education.
Department for Business, Information and Skills. 2012. *Statistical First Release, Academic Year 2010/11 (Provisional)*. London: BIS.
Goldthorpe, J., and A. McKnight. 2006. "The Economic Basis of Social Class." In *Mobility and Inequality: Frontiers of Research from Sociology and Economics*, edited by S. Morgan, D. B. Grusky and G. S. Fields. Stanford: Stanford University Press.

Goldthorpe, J. H., and C. Mills. 2008. "Trends in Intergenerational Class Mobility in Modern Britain: Evidence from National Surveys." *National Institute Economic Review* 205: 83–100.

Habermas, J. 1976. *Legitimation Crisis*. London: Heinemann.

Heath, A., N. De Graaf, and Y. Li. 2010. "How fair is the route to the top? Perceptions of Social Mobility." In *British Social Attitudes - the 27th Report: Exploring Labour's Legacy*, edited by Alison Park, John Curtice, and Elizabeth Clery, 29–50. London: Sage.

Halsey, A. H. 1988. "Higher Education." In *British Social Trends since 1900*, edited by A. H. Halsey, 268–296. London: MacMillan.

Hindess, B. 1988. *Choice, Rationality and Social Choice*. London: Unwin Hyman.

Hoare, A., and Ron Johnston. 2011. "Widening Participation through Admissions Policy – a British Case Study of School and University Performance." *Studies in Higher Education* 36: 21–41.

Jones, S. 2002. *Antonymy: A Corpus-based Perspective*. London: Routledge.

Leathwood, C. 2004. "A Critique of Institutional Inequalities in Higher Education (or an Alternative to Hypocrisy for Higher Educational Policy)." *Theory and Research in Education* 2 (1): 31–48.

Levinson, Stephen C. 1983. *Pragmatics*. Cambridge: Cambridge University Press.

Lindley, J., and S. Machin. 2012. "The Quest for More and More Education: Implications for Social Mobility." *Fiscal Studies* 33 (2): 265–286.

Marginson, Simon. 2007. "The Public/Private Divide in Higher Education: A Global Revision." *Higher Education* 53 (3): 307–333.

Milburn, Alan. 2012. *University Challenge: How Higher Education Can Advance Social Mobility a Progress Report by the Independent Reviewer on Social Mobility and Child Poverty*. London: Cabinet Office.

Moore, J., A. Mountford-Zimdars, and J. Wiggans, forthcoming 2013. Contextualised Admissions: Examining the Evidence: Report of Research into the Evidence Base for the Use of Contextual Information and Data in Admissions of UK Students to Undergraduate Courses in the UK. Cheltenham: Supporting Professionalism in Admissions.

Mountford-Zimdars, A., and P. Teulon, forthcoming 2014. "AABe or not to AABe: A Very English Problem." In *International Perspectives in Higher Education Admission: a Reader*, edited by Virgina Stead. New York: Peter Lang Publishing.

National Centre for Social Research. 2010. *British Social Attitudes 2010: Face to face questionnaire*. London: National Centre for Social Research available for download at: http://www.natcen.ac.uk/media/778212/bsa28-questionnaire.pdf.

National Equality Panel. 2010. *An Anatomy of Economic Inequality in the UK: Report of the National Equality Panel*. London: Government Equalities Office.

Pratto, F., L. M. Stallworth, and J. Sidanius. 1997. "The Gender Gap: Differences in Political Attitudes and Social Dominance Orientation." *British Journal of Social Psychology* 36: 49–68.

Robbins Report. 1963. *Higher Education, Report of the Committee Appointed by the Prime Minister under the Chairmanship of Lord Robbins*. London: Her Majesty's Stationery Office.

Stuart, Mary. 2012. *Social Mobility and Higher Education: The Life Experiences of First Generation Entrants in Higher Education*. Stoke on Trent: Trentham Books.

Sutton Trust. 2005. *State School Admissions to our Leading Universities: An Update to 'The Missing 3000*. London: Sutton Trust.

Interrupted trajectories: the impact of academic failure on the social mobility of working-class students

Tina Byrom[a] and Nic Lightfoot[b]

[a]School of Education, Nottingham Trent University, Nottingham, UK; [b]School of Education, Sheffield Hallam University, Sheffield, UK

> Higher education (HE) is often viewed as a conduit for social mobility through which working-class students can secure improved life-chances. However, the link between HE and social mobility is largely viewed as unproblematic. Little research has explored the possible impact of academic failure (in HE) on the trajectories of working-class students or the ways in which working-class students may re-construct their career aspirations as a result of such academic failure. This paper seeks to fill this apparent gap by focusing on a group of non-traditional students enrolled on a BA undergraduate programme in a post-1992 university. Utilising Bourdieu's notion of habitus, the paper identifies how academic failure contributes to possible trajectory interruptions and whether these are temporary or possibly permanent. It specifically focuses on how working-class students interpret and respond to their academic failure and the possible impact this has on their social mobility.

Introduction

There is no doubt that the educational landscape has changed dramatically in recent years. Whilst changes have been evident in the compulsory sector, the widening participation policy agenda has contributed to the mass expansion of higher education (HE) in particular. Such expansion has primarily benefited students from non-traditional backgrounds and yet their experiences within HE are often highlighted as problematic (see, for example, Archer 2003; Ball 2003; Thomas and Quinn 2008).

Educational policy appears to ignore the complex educational experiences of working-class young people. Instead it tends to focus on discourses that highlight the positive outcome HE can provide, particularly that of securing a desired job or 'higher income bracket' (Cabinet Office 2012, 4). However, such policies are entrenched within the rhetoric that such outcomes are available for all students. Platt, for example, states:

> Equality of opportunity is *supposed*∗ to be delivered predominantly through an egalitarian educational system that allows everyone the possibility of achieving the qualifications that will lead them to a 'good job' and a good – or higher – class position. (2011, 41; original emphasis)

In viewing HE as a vehicle through which social mobility can be achieved, universities have an important role in facilitating the aspirations of students who choose to embark on an undergraduate programme. However, evidence would suggest that attending university and obtaining a degree may not be the passport out of poverty (Blythe 2001) and into a 'higher class position' (Platt 2011) that students believe it to be. For example, 'less advantaged (graduate) groups are less likely by 5% to be in employment than most advantaged groups' (Cabinet Office 2012, 44) and 'a large number of the professions remain dominated by a small section of society and … have become less socially representative' (2012, 45).

Whilst the social obligation of education policy-makers is to provide 'equal educational opportunities' (OECD 2010, 1) for all, there thus remains differentiated educational outcomes across all education sectors and employment outcomes according to class (Tomlinson 2008; Reay 2012). This is not solely manifested through academic attainment (for statistics on attainment, see DfE 2012) and low HE participation rates (see HESA 2012), but is also evident in graduate destinations (OECD 2011) and as highlighted above. With an ever-increasing level of pressure placed on undergraduates to secure graduate-based employment, and the pool of graduates seeking such jobs increasing, the risks of attending HE for first-generation students are somewhat magnified.

This context sets the parameters through which young people, and non-traditional students in particular, experience the educational field. Success within this field is dependent on a close alignment to its embedded practices, values and principles and, more precisely, where educational success is about the 'erasure' of 'working classness' (Reay 2001, 334). In effect, HE participation makes unarticulated demands on non-traditional students to move away from the class-based practices that have framed their earlier experiences. This disruption to what is 'known' can be understood as a series of 'trajectory interruptions' (Byrom 2009) through which the habitus of the individual is re-moulded and shaped through the structures evident in education.

However, it is well documented that education is a site of inequality (see, for example, Bourdieu and Passeron 1977; Ball 2003; Reay and Lucey 2003; Platt 2011). Bourdieu (1993) argues that within the field of education there is a complex interplay of relations where people take up positions largely determined by whether they have been 'shaped to enter the field' (Bourdieu 1993, 73). This infers a very different educational experience for working-class students who may struggle to position themselves both socially and academically (Byrom 2009) within an HE quasi-market (Naidoo and Jamieson 2005), and in particular where the process of choice is not equal across social groups.

Data from the DfES (2005) and HESA (2012) continue to evidence lower social class participation rates across the HE sector, but particularly within elite or traditional universities. This situation has been recognised by politicians who acknowledge that 'young people from disadvantaged backgrounds are … less likely to progress to HE, especially in the most selective universities' (Cabinet Office 2012, 26). Whilst some argue that this distribution is caused by low academic aspirations from working-class students (DfES 2003a), there is a much wider body of research that explores the issue in terms of social and academic fit (Reay 1997; Lawler 1999; Archer and Hutchings 2000; Wentworth and Peterson 2001; Bowl 2003; Walkerdine et al. 2003), where many struggle to find their place in an environment that questions their very being – or their constructed class-based habitus.

Whilst Bourdieu has been criticised for being overly deterministic (Giroux 1983), the fact that some working-class students do go into HE would suggest that 'habituses are permeable and responsive to what is going on around them' (Reay 2004, 1104) and 'variable from place to place and time to time' (Bourdieu 1990b, 9). In social mobility terms, and in a Bourdieuian analysis, a working-class habitus requires transformation (Bourdieu 1996) in order for an individual to fit into middle-class contexts. However, what constitutes social class and social mobility is hugely contested (Platt 2011; Saunders 2012); therefore in exploring social mobility and class within education, this paper will take up the perspectives of the students' interviewed where social mobility is largely understood as achieving a job of higher status than their parents. This is an important consideration for students in post-1992 institutions, where their degree carries less weight than those achieved in elite institutions and where research would indicate that Russell Group universities have the highest economic returns (DfES, 2003b).

The extent to which HE provides a space for working-class students to realise their aspirations is reliant on the adaptation of their primary habitus (Reed-Danahay 2005; Mills 2008). Whilst many students appear to manage this process well and complete their degrees (i.e. theoretically, they have been transformed), a number of students experience academic failure that not only emphasises their feelings of being a 'fish out of water' (Reay, Crozier, and Clayton 2010) but brings into question their whole purpose for being in HE in the first place. That is, the direction of travel is problematic. In social mobility terms, academic failure could be interpreted as a 'trajectory interruption' (Byrom 2009) where both the goal of achieving a higher 'class position' (Platt 2011, 41) and habitus transformation is threatened. This paper explores familiar themes in educational research – that of academic failure and fit. However, it extends this beyond statistical information about working-class failure. It focuses instead on the ways in which academic failure impacts upon the career aspirations of working-class students and their reconciliation of the failure. In doing so it poses the following questions:

- How do working-class students experience academic failure?
- To what extent does academic failure impact on career aspirations and potential social mobility?

Method

This paper, although located within a wide body of research concerning academic and social fit, is also situated within policy discourses around widening participation. Students, who identified themselves as being the first in their family to go into HE and who had failed an academic assignment across the three years of an undergraduate joint honours programme, were invited to participate in the research. Despite the identified issues with self-selection within a sample (see, for example, Cohen, Manion, and Morrison 2007), this approach provided us with a longitudinal aspect to the research in which we could consider whether academic failure had contributed to changes of career aspiration over time and thus could have had some influence on an individual's social mobility. Postcode data were collected to ensure the students could be classified as coming from low-participating neighbourhoods.

Much research conducted within this field is qualitative in nature and we take this approach up within this study. Creswell views qualitative research as an 'intricate fabric composed of minute threads, many colours, different textures, and various blends of material' where the fabric 'is not explained easily or simply' (1998, 13). Whilst people may live their lives narratively, as Clandinin and Connelly (2000) state, there are many issues that surround this form of data collection. For example, the stories told within an interview context are both representations and interpretations of previous events that may or may not be accurate. The method therefore, despite reflecting the innate ways in which people reflect upon their experiences, does have some limitations. Thus the methods used within this research seek to uncover the complexities of issues connected with academic failure from the students' perspectives.

In order to explore this issue an online questionnaire was provided for students to complete (57 students completed it, representing a 19% response rate) and individual interviews were conducted with 10 students across three years of the programme.

It should also be noted that the interviews were conducted by two members of the teaching staff who were known to the students and this may have had some impact on the responses received.

In our analytical approach we intend to understand the students' experiences as being part of the 'social world [which] can be represented as a space (with several dimensions)' and where 'agents and groups of agents are thus defined by their relative positions within that space' (Bourdieu 1985, 723–724). Analysis comprised the thematic coding of interview transcripts and open-ended questions from the questionnaire in addition to a frequency count of other questions from the questionnaire.

Findings and discussion

Pertinent to the students' ideas about HE was their unequivocal acceptance of political rhetoric, which would suggest that everyone should have an 'equal chance of getting the job they want or achieving a higher income bracket' (Cabinet Office 2012, 4). It was clear from the questionnaire findings that all of the students believed that they could achieve a job higher in status than that of their parents and that this would be perceived as being socially mobile. However, behind the statistics the very real tensions and self-questioning that follows academic failure illuminates the difficulties associated with processes of social mobility.

What it means to become socially mobile

Habitus as being indicative of class-based practices provides a useful mechanism through which to understand the students' experiences. The students in this study repeatedly suggested that they had come to university to secure a job that was higher in status than that of other family members. Such aspirations indicated a shift in habitus from that of their parents. Whilst it has been argued elsewhere (Byrom 2009) that this shift can be explained through a series of trajectory interruptions, the students in this study appeared to be in the midst of a habitus in tension: they continue to be uncertain of where they are heading despite their desire for a different outcome to that of their parents. Ben illustrates this apparent tension through focusing on his father's regret about not going into HE:

> So I just thought if I don't go to university then ... I used to watch my dad work jobs he hated and I thought ... he always said to me that he regretted not going to university or having the opportunity to, so I had to, to get where I wanted to in life. (Ben, interview, 1 February 2012)

Ben sees university as offering him the route through to better opportunities; however, this journey was proving to be extremely difficult for Ben – he had failed numerous assignments, intercalated for a year and had returned to complete his degree whilst juggling work commitments. In addition, Ben had returned to university reluctantly as he felt that 'he just had to finish it' because he had 'invested so much already'. Theoretically, Ben appears to have reached a phase in habitus transformation where going back was not an option but going forward was particularly difficult, or where the habitus was in conflict with itself (Bourdieu 1990a). Indicative of primary habitus transformation, Ben's story illustrates how problematic the process of social mobility can be for non-traditional students and the dilemma faced when things do not go quite to plan.

Making the decision to go to HE is considered a 'critical phase for social mobility' and decisions at this time have a 'lasting impact on "a young person's" future' (Cabinet Office 2012, 26). With the expansion of HE, the decision not to go to university not only limits the forms of employment available, but inadvertently results in 'othering' (see Walkerdine and Lucey 2001; Walkerdine 2003) where those who choose not to go are discursively constructed as abnormal. The process of 'othering' parents further illustrated the distance between the students' own emerging social status and that of their family based habitus. Rosie knew that she would 'go and get a degree and then go and get a better job, than what my parents could get without a degree' (interview, 20 February 2012). Her academic failure raised some questions in her mind about whether she would be able to avoid a job similar to her father's. Despite Rosie's father working in a factory, it is evident within the family that education is viewed as important. Rosie explains:

> Well it was always held that you study hard, the more you study the better job you can get so getting a degree means a better job. So it has always been like that. (Interview, 20 February 2012)

Rosie's family context is such that there has been a process of transformation from a working-class habitus with the explicit message being conveyed that education was a route into a better job. The emphasis that the family place on obtaining a good education is illustrative of a close alignment with the government rhetoric about education. Byrom (2009, 215) discusses the notion of 'trajectory interruptions' where defining moments (Ball 2003) helped the students occupy different social spaces to their family members. This process of transformation resulted in an emerging secondary habitus – or habitus clivé (Bourdieu 2004, 130, cited in Reed-Danahay 2005, 3) – that enabled the students to accept the particular messages about education they experienced at home (in some cases) but mainly through their respective schools. Thus they experience a social space in which:

[t]he [individual] is 'made up' as a 'successful' social and educational subject – deliberately and knowingly produced, formed, channelled, motivated and constructed through the crafting and purchase of 'opportunities', 'interactions' and experiences. (Ball 2004, 7)

Students get caught up in discourses that present education as an equal playing field where decisions, choices and outcomes are influenced by the individual. Because educational outcomes, and therefore employment opportunities, are based on individual effort and application: 'no one can complain about what happens to them and all can realistically aim for the top' (Platt 2011, 41). Whilst students are enveloped in such discourses, the impact of educational failure becomes harder to reconcile with their career aspirations and their positioning within the field of education. In essence, students begin to fundamentally question whether they should have been at university in the first place, which is a consistent theme found in much of the widening participation literature (see, for example, Michie, Glachan, and Bray 2001: Archer 2003; Archer and Leathwood 2003).

The devastating impact of failure can clearly be seen in Molly's reaction:

I was devastated. I felt like such a failure especially when all of my friends and my boyfriend are such high achievers. I felt ashamed to tell them that I had failed because they are all so much more intelligent, especially because I failed two assignments in the second year alone. (Molly, questionnaire, 10 April 2012)

In comparing her own academic achievements with others, Molly highlights the relational nature of the academic experience. Her reaction is not only indicative of the high stakes at play in obtaining a degree but also of how she understands the 'relative position of players in the field' (Lareau and McNamara Horvat 1999, 39) – that she perceives others as being academically superior. It is evident for many students in the study that the gradual alignment of their respective habituses to the middle-class field was fraught with tension following the academic failure. Whilst habituses can be permeable to change (Reay 2004), the interruption of this process is clearly evident in the self-questioning that followed the students' academic failure.

Rationalisation of failure

Many of the students described how they had not fully prepared for the assignment – citing time management as a major factor in their failure. Whilst Ben (interview, 1 February 2012) talks about the fact that he 'left it to the last minute' and that he 'hadn't given [himself] time to complete it', this seems to mask deeper issues connected with his own perceptions around his ability to do the work:

I struggle[d] with it to be fair. I thought [I'll] just come back to it. I think I was getting frustrated – I think I'll just come back to it and then every time I came back to it, it was the same. You get frustrated, frustrated and put off until eventually the pressure kicks in because the deadline is looming and you are forced to write something. (Ben, interview, 1 February 2012)

He goes on to explain that he felt unprepared to do the work given his academic background:

Because I didn't do A levels, I did BTEC, I think the level of work going from a BTEC National Diploma to an undergraduate degree was a lot bigger than I expected. I don't think I prepared very well. I think now I would have preferred to have done A levels. I think that's a lot more, prepares you for university a lot, the work, a lot better. (Ben, interview, 1 February 2012)

Despite students expressing a lack of familiarity with the assignment requirements, they do not place any blame on the support available to them from tutors. Rachel for example, states that she 'didn't go to her tutor' or access the 'resources around [her]' (interview, 15 February 2012). Bourdieu identifies difficulties in establishing position within fields as individuals attempt to develop an 'inherent part of belonging' (1990b, 67). The introspective personalisation of the academic failure expressed by our students would indicate their continued struggle to 'belong' – the fault lies with themselves and not the institutional practices around them. In not questioning the embedded practices within the institution, important questions surrounding the ways in which students conceptualise their current and future social position are raised.

The literature (for example, Bourdieu and Passeron 1977; Archer and Hutchings 2000; Wentworth and Peterson 2001; Bowl 2003; Walkerdine et al. 2003) identifies numerous issues connected with non-traditional students' fit within education. Whilst Bourdieu raises the question of their participation and educational success in terms of 'transgression' (1990a, 510), the way in which non-traditional students in this study understood their academic failure in relation to the broader context of career aspirations raises some interesting issues. For example, academic failure and low academic performance raised questions about their actual participation in HE for some of the students, as Molly states:

I've never really got amazing marks from any of my assignments. The highest I've got is 60%. Everybody else I know at university achieve much higher grades and are more intelligent so I sometimes feel that I don't deserve to be here and whether it will be worth it in the end, especially if I don't get a high degree. (Molly, questionnaire, 10 April 2012)

Molly goes on to state that she has changed her ideas about possible careers and that teaching is 'not the career path [she wishes] to follow'

(Questionnaire 045, Year 3 student, 10 April 2012). In changing her ideas about her career choice, Molly appears to have been heavily influenced by the academic failure. She appreciates the high stakes that are involved in obtaining a perceived 'high' degree, particularly in the current employment market, and is perhaps realigning her career aspirations accordingly.

For some students, completing the degree becomes a matter of principle. Ben, for example, states that he would complete it because he 'had come so far so [he'd] got to finish it' (interview, 1 February 2012). This is in part explained through Bourdieu's notion of habitus (Bourdieu 1990a). Whilst Ben has to some extent aligned himself with the practices and ethos of the institution, there is a sense in which his emerging habitus (Byrom 2009) is facilitating a shift away from his family-based habitus (Byrom and Lightfoot 2012). It is this shift that is equipping Ben with the resolve to complete his studies – he knows that he will be in a better position than his father had been in.

However, university life for many of the students in this study is fraught with tension where self-questioning about academic ability is a frequent occurrence. Rachel explains:

> I know my writing style is not good … I've always found education hard. I'm not very educationally bright … I've never found uni easy and I've always thought I would drop out. If I look back on it, it probably wasn't the best idea because I'm not very educational. (Rachel, interview, 15 February 2012)

In Rachel's struggle to 'belong', she also demonstrates a strong sense of resilience – where she was 'determined to finish for myself. I don't like dropping out of things. I don't like failing stuff, so I'll finish it, even blood, sweat and tears, I'll finish it' (Rachel, interview, 15 February 2012). It could be that the process of class transformation has left Rachel in a state of 'classlessness' where she has no choice but to go forward given the high risks and costs associated with failure.

Questioning the point of higher education

Whilst the interview data provided some in-depth accounts of how students responded to the academic failure, questionnaire responses appeared to focus on questioning whether university was in fact the right choice for the individual. A total 64.8% of those that replied to the questionnaire had questioned whether they should be at university, particularly in relation to whether it would lead to a specific type of employment and also one that would represent social mobility. The question of whether university was the right choice was further exacerbated by those who had friends in highly paid jobs who had not invested in HE, as illustrated in the following:

> Sometimes wonder if it is worth it when I see people in jobs that I aspire to do having not gone to university. (Questionnaire 07, Year 3 student, 24 April 2012)

> I have questioned whether I should be at uni because the cost to attend is so much and you are not guaranteed a job afterwards. (Questionnaire 09, Year 3 student, 24 April 2012)

> I have questioned whether there is another way into my career path. (Questionnaire 11, Year 2 student, 29 April 2012)

These students' comments are indicative of contextual constraints outside university life. It is evident that they have their future goal in mind as they progress through the course, but their comments also reflect a high level of questioning in relation to being at university: questioning that continues to illustrate discomfort with the decision made to go to HE in the first place. Class transition is a complex process that does not occur through abrupt change. It could be that students who reflected negatively on the purpose of HE were at the early stages of habitus transformation. In addition, their class transformation is more clearly associated with occupation than it is with their educational experiences and the acquiring of increased levels of social and cultural capital. It is widely accepted that the habitus will not stray too far from its roots as Bourdieu states,

> Early experiences have particular weight because the *habitus* tends to secure its own consistency and its defence against change through the selection it makes within new information by rejecting information capable of calling into question its accumulated information, if exposed to it accidentally or by force, and especially by avoiding exposure to such information. (Bourdieu 1990a, 60–61)

The students in this study were juggling competing messages about their HE experience: policy discourses that promoted the positive aspects of university; they did not belong at HE because they had failed academic work; a good degree will lead to improved career options. The students therefore had much work to do to reconcile this complex array of information as they continued to establish a sense of fit in the institution, come to terms with their academic failure and remain mindful of a difficult employment market for which they needed to prepare.

The impact of academic failure appeared to be responded to differently by students. Whilst there appears to be a particular response according to gender, with males tending to remain fixed on their initial career aspirations and females considering alternatives, we do not focus on the gendered elements of their responses here.

Rethinking career options

Whilst there was a sense of resilience from the students, in that they were determined to complete their studies, there was also a sense in which the academic failure contributed to the students' re-considering their career aspirations. Rachel, for example, states:

> Well when I came to uni I wanted to become a teacher so I thought you have to come to uni to become a teacher and ... I decided I didn't want to become a teacher. I took the education because I wanted to become a teacher but I changed my mind on that but I wasn't going to drop out of it because I didn't want to become a teacher anymore I was going to finish it ... it's probably not the best idea for me to go down because I'm not very good at English, so my Mum keeps telling me. (Rachel, interview, 15 February 2012)

Rachel's response reflects Bourdieu and Passeron's (1977) work on reproduction, where structures in education eliminate those who are not 'shaped to enter the field' (Bourdieu 1993, 72). There is a sense in which Rachel is struggling with the competing messages of her prior academic success that secured her place at university and the messages from home – where her mother re-enforces the message that she is not very good at English. Whilst her resilience was sufficient for her to complete the programme, it was not strong enough for her to consider a teaching career. Rachel did not have the family background that could counsel her and advise her on how to deal with the academic failure, nor what possible career options she could consider as alternatives to teaching.

Whilst the academic failure left Rachel undecided about her future career, George used it as an opportunity to completely re-think his career. Transferring from another course invariably forced a different career choice. During a chance conversation with his tutor, George came to the conclusion that he was on the wrong course for him:

> I went and spoke with my Year 2 tutor about the fail and also told him I was coaching 10 hours a week and working with a high profile coach but planning [previous course] doesn't really compliment that so what do I do? He said that he coaches football as a hobby and it was that one sentence that did it for me – because swimming is not a hobby it's a passion so I looked for a course that would complement it. Before it was a complete conflict but now it complements it. (George, interview, 5 February 2012)

The importance of social and cultural capital is evident as George turns to the 'familiar' (swimming; mother) to make sense of the 'unfamiliar' (the previous course; HE). It could be that the beginnings of a 'slow process of autonomisation' within the educational field (Bourdieu 1990a, 67) is at play as George embarks on a different course. For George, the academic failure had a permanent impact on his possible social mobility, but he had to draw from existing social networks through swimming to limit any risks attached to moving course.

Moving on or away from others, particularly where social mobility or class transition is concerned, carries with it emotional risks: it points to disassociation with family members and neighbours. Skeggs (1997, 1) describes this process as becoming respectable. In George's journey to 'respectability', he continued to value the benefit of what HE could provide, but had to align to an alternative career path in order to avoid disrupting the 'distance' travelled to date.

Whilst Rachel and George both re-thought their career options, Dave did not. His response reflected his determination to become a teacher, despite the academic failure.

Remaining fixed on the initial career aspiration

Dave was shocked about his academic failure, because he 'never thought this would happen to me' (interview, 18 January 2012). There is a sense in which Dave shows how he had previously manipulated the education system to ensure he got the grade needed to boost his examination results. However, he had no intention of letting the most recent academic fail get in the way of his plans for his future. He was determined to go into teaching and had applied for postgraduate teaching courses. It becomes clear later in the interview that his determination to succeed is being fuelled by his desire not to lose face with his peer group at home, none of whom had gone to university:

> I'm the only person that a lot of people I know, know who is at university. Does that make sense? Friends and family and stuff – I'm the one that is at university. I'm like perceived as the one who has gone down the academic route sort of thing and … my friends from back home, like would consider me differently now to when we were in school sort of thing. (Dave, interview, 18 February 2012)

It is evident that Dave was feeling the sense of separation from his former existence that comes with habitus transformation. In a Bourdieuian sense, the distance Dave had already travelled (Bourdieu 1998, 6) left him in a transitionary social space where returning to a previous existence, with the concomitant career choices, was not an option. This was not only influenced by the expectations placed on him to be successful where 'they expect me to be earning a lot of money, living in a nice place and driving a nice car', but also the way in which he had to self-regulate in order to develop increased levels of confidence following the failure:

> It did make me question whether I could be a teacher – maybe a little bit, but like I say then when I passed it the second time I thought, I reassured myself

that I could produce good enough work. I just saw it as a bit of a blip. (Dave, interview, 18 February 2012)

Determination and a sense of resilience are amongst capabilities viewed as increasingly important within employment (McNeil, Reeder, and Rich 2012). In addition to not losing face amongst friends from home, it is the drive to avoid working in a job that he felt was not right for him that inspired Dave to continue with his ambition of becoming a teacher:

> Don't know I'm stubborn I'd always tell myself that I'll never do something that I don't want to do like I wouldn't leave uni and work in McDonalds that sort of thing ... I'd hate to go back home and people say like 'I thought you were at uni.' I could never end up doing a job that you could get by not going to university. I just wouldn't turn up, that's how I am sort of thing. (Dave, interview, 18 February 2012)

The academic failure for the above students seemed to remind them that they existed in an environment where having a 'good' degree mattered. Their accounts of how they reacted to and moved on from the academic failure to some extent reflect external constraints where it is becoming increasingly difficult 'to anticipate fluctuations on the stock exchange of scholastic value' (Bourdieu 1998, 25). With student numbers expanding, there are fewer middle-class/professional jobs available. This in itself could impact significantly on the potential for social mobility irrespective of how students seek to reconcile the academic failure and their drive to obtain a good degree.

Conclusion

This paper supports much previous research on the experiences of working-class young people in HE. Whilst disappointed that they had failed a piece of academic work, the strategies for dealing with the failure varied across the group. Whilst habitus is used to understand the behaviour of classified groups (e.g. working or middle class), postcodes are generally used to provide a homogenised group and yet such measures do not account for disparate family histories that have an influence on individuals' behaviour (Byrom 2010). It is through the links with their families that the students appeared to be able to reconcile their failure. Discussions with close family members provided the reassurances needed to continue with the degree programme, despite any reconfiguration of career aspirations.

The educational landscape that has developed into a quasi-market has no place for 'incompetence and weakness' (Douglas 1994, 231), particularly in a context where there is an increased move for universities to provide graduate destination data. This places higher levels of pressure on both staff (to facilitate learning) and students (to obtain good degree classifications and secure graduate-based employment).

Whilst this paper re-visits some familiar themes in educational research, it also provides insights into how students may have to re-think their career options in the light of academic failure. It is clear to the students that the value of their degree is important and yet they are susceptible to the demands of an employment field that demands particular characteristics from graduates: characteristics that may not be easily developed for working-class students who often have more complex living arrangements than traditional (middle-class) students and who are also engaged in a process of transformation or 'transgression' (Bourdieu 1999, 510) from their home-based habitus. Conceptually, habitus offers a useful mechanism through which to understand possible interruptions to social mobility. In examining the students' experiences, it is evident that they are in a precarious position – a no-man's land – where academic failure could result in a form of downward social mobility. Their determination to avoid outcomes similar to their parents is not only illustrative of high levels of resilience, but also the extent to which their habitus has already responded to the field within which it is located. As such, their response to academic failure is as much about 'protection against [possible] downward mobility' (Beck 1992, 94) as it is about securing upward social mobility.

References

Archer, L. 2003. "Social Class and Higher Education." In *Higher Education and Social Class: Issues of exclusion and inclusion*, edited by L. Archer, M. Hutchings and A. Ross. London, RoutledgeFalmer: 5–20.

Archer, L., and M. Hutchings. 2000. "'Bettering Yourself?' Discourses of Risk, Cost and Benefit in Ethnically Diverse, Young Working-Class, Non-participants' Constructions of Higher Education." *British Journal of the Sociology of Education* 21 (4): 555–574.

Archer, L., and C. Leathwood. 2003. "New Times – Old Inequalities: Diverse Working-Class Femininities in Education." *Gender and Education* 15 (3): 227–235.

Ball, S. 2003. *Class Strategies and the Education Market: The Middle Classes and Social Advantage*. London: RoutledgeFalmer.

Ball, S. 2004. *Education For Sale! The Commodification of everything? The Annual Education Lecture 2004*. London, The Institute of Education. http://mykcl.info/content/1/c6/05/16/42/lecture-ball.pdf (Accessed 20/7/12).

Beck, U. 1992. *Risk Society: Towards a New Modernity*. London: Sage Publications.

Blyth, E. 2001. "The Impact of the First Term of the New Labour Government on Social Work in Britain: The Interface between Education Policy and Social Work." *British Journal of Social Work* 31 (4): 563–577.

Bourdieu, P., and J.-C. Passeron. 1977. *Reproduction in Education, Culture and Society*. London: SAGE Publications.

Bourdieu, P. 1985. "The Social Space and the Genesis of Groups." *Theory and Society* 14 (6): 723–744.
Bourdieu, P. 1990a. *Practical Reason*. Stanford, CA: Stanford University Press.
Bourdieu, P. 1990b. *In Other Words: Essays towards a Reflexive Sociology*. Stanford, CA: Stanford University Press.
Bourdieu, P. 1993. *Sociology in Question*. London: SAGE Publications Ltd.
Bourdieu, P. 1996. *The Rules of Art: Genesis and Structure of the Literary Field*. Cambridge: Polity Press.
Bourdieu, P. 1998. *Practical Reason*. Cambridge: Polity Press.
Bowl, M. 2003. *Non-Traditional Entrants to Higher Education: 'They Talk about People like Me'*. Stoke on Trent: Trentham Books Ltd.
Byrom, T. 2009. "'I don't Want to Go to a Crummy Little University': Social Class, Higher Education Choice and the Paradox of Widening Participation." *Improving Schools* 12 (3): 207–224.
Byrom, T. 2010. The Dream of Social Flying: Social Class, Higher Education Choice and the Paradox Of Widening Participation. Saarbrucken: Lambert Academic Publishing.
Byrom, T., and N. Lightfoot. 2012. "Transformation or Transgression? Institutional Habitus and Working Class Student Identity." *Journal of Social Sciences* 8 (2): 126–134.
Cabinet Office. 2012. *Opening Doors, Breaking Barriers: A Strategy for Social Mobility*. London: Cabinet Office.
Clandinin, D., and F. Connelly. 2000. *Narrative Inquiry: Experience and Story in Qualitative Research*. San Francisco, CA: Jossey-Bass.
Cohen, L., Manion, L. et al. 2007. Research Methods in Education. 6th ed. London, RoutledgeFalmer.
Creswell, J. 1998. *Qualitative Inquiry and Research Design: Choosing among Five Traditions*. Thousand Oaks, CA: SAGE Publications Inc.
DfE 2012. GCSE and Equivalent Attainment by Pupil Characteristics in England, 2010/11. London, DfE. http://www.education.gov.uk/rsgateway/DB/SFR/s001057/index.shtml (accessed 24/8/12).
DfES. 2003a. *Widening Participation in Higher Education*. London: DfES.
DfES. 2003b. *The Future of Higher Education* (1–106). London: The Stationery Office.
DfES. 2005. *Higher Standards, Better Schools for All: More Choice for Parents and Pupils. Government White Paper*. London: The Stationery Office.
Douglas, M. 1994. *Risk and Blame: Essays in Cultural Theory*. London: Routledge.
Giroux, H. 1983. *Theory and Resistance in Education: A Pedagogy for the Opposition*. London: Heinemann Educational.
HESA 2012. "PIs: Widening participation of under-represented groups (tables T1, T2)." http://www.hesa.ac.uk/index.php?option=com_content&task=view&id=2060&Itemid=141. (Accessed 24/8/12).
Lareau, A., and E. McNamara Horvat. 1999. "Moments of Social Inclusion and Exclusion Race, Class and Cultural Capital in Family-School Relationships." *Sociology of Education* 72 (1): 37–53.
Lawler, S. 1999. "'Getting Out and Getting Away': Women's Narratives of Class Mobility." *Feminist Review* 63: 3–24.
McNeil, B., Reeder, N. and Rich, J. 2012. "A Framework of Outcomes for Young People." The Young Foundation. https://www.education.gov.uk/publications/eOrderingDownload/Framework_of_Outcomes_for_Young_People.pdf. (Accessed 24/8/12).

Michie, F., M. Glachan, and D. Bray. 2001. "An Evaluation of Factors Influencing the Academic Self-Concept, Self-Esteem and Academic Stress for Direct and Re-Entry Students in Higher Education." *Educational Psychology* 21 (4): 455–472.

Mills, C. 2008. "Reproduction and Transformation of Inequalities in Schooling: The Transformative Potential of the Theoretical Constructs of Bourdieu." *British Journal of the Sociology of Education* 29 (1): 79–89.

Naidoo, R., and I. Jamieson. 2005. "Empowering Participants or Corroding Learning? Towards a Research Agenda on the Impact of Student Consumerism in Higher Education." *Journal of Education Policy* 20 (3): 267–281.

OECD 2010. PISA 2009 "Results: Overcoming Social Background: Equity in Learning Opportunities and Outcomes (Volume II)." OECD Publishing. http://dx.doi.org/10.1787/9789264091504-en (Accessed 24/8/12).

OECD 2011. "Education at a Glance: How Does Educational Attainment Affect Participation in the Labour Market?" OECD Publishing. http://www.oecd.org/education/highereducationandadultlearning/48630772.pdf (Accessed 24/8/12).

Platt, L. 2011. *Understanding Inequalities: Stratification and Difference*. Cambridge: Polity Press.

Reay, D. 1997. "The Double-Bind of the 'Working-Class' Feminist Academic: The Success of Failure or the Failure of Success?" In *Class Matters: 'Working-Class' Women's Perspectives on Social Class*, edited by P. Mahony and C. Zmroczek. London, Taylor and Francis Ltd.

Reay, D. 2001. "Finding or Losing Yourself?: Working Class Relationships to Education." *Journal of Education Policy* 16 (4): 333–346.

Reay, D. 2004. "'It's All Becoming a Habitus': Beyond the Habitual Use of Habitus in Educational Research." *British Journal of Sociology of Education* 25 (4): 431–444.

Reay, D. 2012. "Researching Class in Higher Education." *British Educational Research Association*. Available online at http://www.bera.ac.uk/system/files/Researching%20Class%20in%20Higher%20Education.pdf (accessed 25/8/12).

Reay, D., G. Crozier, and J. Clayton. 2010. "Fitting in' or 'Standing out': Working-Class Students in UK Higher Education." *British Educational Research Journal* 32 (1): 107–124.

Reay, D., and H. Lucey. 2003. "The Limits of 'Choice': Children and Inner City Schooling." *Sociology* 37 (1): 121–142.

Reed-Danahay, D. 2005. *Locating Bourdieu*. Bloomington, IN: Indiana University Press.

Saunders, P. 2012. "Social Mobility Delusions: Why So Much of What Politicians Say about Social Mobility in Britain Is Wrong, Misleading or Unreliable." http://www.civitas.org.uk/pdf/socialmobilitydelusions2012.pdf (accessed 12/7/12).

Skeggs, B. (1997) Skeggs, B. (1997). Classifying Practices: Representations, Capitals Recognitions." In *Class Matters: 'Working-Class' Women's Perspectives on Social Class*, edited by P. Mahony and C. Zmroczek. London: Taylor and Francis Ltd.

Thomas, L., and J. Quinn. 2008. *First Generation Entry into Higher Education: An International Study*. Maidenhead: Open University Press.

Tomlinson, M. 2008. "The Degree is Not Enough': Students' Perceptions of the Role of HE Credentials for Graduate Work and Employability." *British Journal of Sociology of Education* 29 (1): 49–61.

Walkerdine, V. 2003. "Reclassifying Upward Mobility: Femininity and the Neoliberal Subject." *Gender and Education* 15 (3): 237–248.

Walkerdine, V., H. Lucey, and J. Melody. 2001. *Growing up Girl: Psychosocial Explorations of Gender and Class*. Basingstoke: Palgrave.

Walkerdine, V., J. Melody, and H. Lucey. 2003. "Uneasy Hybrids: Psychosocial Aspects of Becoming Educationally Successful for Working-class Young Women." *Gender and Education* 15 (3): 285–299.

Wentworth, P., and Peterson, B. 2001. "Crossing the Line: Case Studies of Identity Development in First-Generation College Women." *Journal of Adult Development* 8 (1): 9–21.

Rural students' experiences in a Chinese elite university: capital, habitus and practices

He Li

School of Foreign Languages, Renmin University of China, Beijing, China

Drawing on a qualitative case study and deploying Bourdieu's thinking tools, this article attempts to understand rural students' subjectivities and practices in a Chinese elite university, relating the types and volumes of capital they possessed to the process of position-takings. It contextualises their experiences against the backdrop of the rural–urban divide in China and the great educational inequality thus entailed. Rurality in the metropolitan space resulted in a strong feeling of being out of place. Lack of the legitimate cultural forms, together with pervasive financial constraints, constituted a major cause of frustration and alienation for these former academic stars. Exclusion and self-exclusion from the 'consecrated' culture, high-status societies and social activities further handicapped their acquisition of valued capitals. Under such conditions, rural participants produced diversified strategies and practices, through which we catch a glimpse of their evolving habitus.

Introduction

The fruits of China's prosperity have not been shared equally among her citizens. To the contrary, the rural–urban divide, described as the 'invisible Great Wall' by Knight and Song (1999), has grown wider: the ratio of average household income per capita in the city to that in the countryside exceeds three to one (Knight and Gunatilaka 2010, 506). A predominantly rural society in tradition, China, in embracing modernisation and urbanisation, has developed urban-biased policies, with the household registration system (*hukou*) at the core. This system, adopted in the late 1950s, categorises the population into agricultural and non-agricultural residents, differentiating their benefits and burdens. Rural residents have been treated as second-class citizens, deprived of many rights and privileges enjoyed by their urban counterparts such as access to quality education, housing and healthcare (Chan and Zhang 1999). China in the market era has witnessed emerging and widening intra-group inequalities as well as a looser migration control. Peasants are nevertheless still trapped in the lowest stratum (Li 2008), not merely reflected in the unusually sharp rural–urban disparities in income but also in the deep-rooted social contempt, with rurality being constructed as backward and inferior (Yin 2008). Although rural and urban residents cannot be conflated into working class and middle class in the western sense, defining class *vis-à-vis* attributes and material conditions, social positions and opportunities, power and exploitation (Wright 2009) is all relevant in this context.

What has implicitly maintained this social gulf is the dual educational system going hand in hand with *hukou*. Public resources are primarily concentrated on educational institutions in cities to foster talents and expertise; by contrast, rural schools are inferior in quality and vocationally oriented in curriculum (Hannum 1999). Unsurprisingly, urban students, the minority of the population, had become the major entrants to higher education even by the mid-1980s (Pepper 1994). Making the uneven more uneven was the introduction of tuition fees and the market orientation in higher education in the 1990s that has placed hurdles in rural children's path to upward mobility. The situation is exacerbated by credential inflation, resulting from the rapid expansion of higher education since 1999. Higher education as a 'positional good' (Hirsch 1977) is prized for its scarcity. More supply inevitably reduces its value and increases the hierarchy to the scarcest credentials. In the epoch of the shrinking job market, a university's prestige weighs heavily in the employment competition. Opportunities to access top-tiered universities, however, are far from equal due to the very unequal selection criteria. Empirical research indicates that, given the same attainment levels, students from big cities are more likely to go to prestigious universities while the rural students are denied access (Yang 2006; Yin 2008). Correspondingly, rural students are increasingly under-represented in leading universities as the process of massification grows (Yang 2006; You 2008). Take Tsinghua, the top elite university in China, for example; only one in seven entrants was of rural origin in the year 2011 (Sun 2012).

Under such conditions, China's higher education has moved toward 'a more social-economically stratified system' with the most prestigious universities 'drawing on the most privileged students economically and academically' (Levin and Xu 2006, 921), while rural students largely cluster in the low-status institutions and majors (Yang 2006). The research therefore focuses on this small group of class defectors who finally go to an elite university 'against all the odds'. What are their experiences in the urban elite milieu? How do their rural origins affect their university life? How do they adapt and transform?

The site I chose to investigate was Stone, a top-tiered university in Beijing.[1] An initial questionnaire served as a tool to gain demographical information as well as informed consent from potential participants. Gaining consent was ongoing, however, and renegotiated between the researcher and the researched throughout the process of fieldwork. Students in different years of study were selected in order to understand their acclimatisation at different stages, with gender, birth province and major being carefully balanced. As sampling was often informed by emerging themes, snowball strategies were also used at the later stage. Although semi-structured interviewing was the major inquiry approach, questions could be very open and subject to readjustment.

Altogether 52 rural participants' educational journeys were investigated; 22 urban students and a small number of administrators and teachers were also interviewed for the sake of relational analysis and data triangulation (Denzin 1970). All interviews were conducted in Mandarin, recorded and later transcribed. Data were analysed with Bourdieu's 'thinking tools', and were translated into English. This article centres on the university experiences of 10 rural students so as to generate an in-depth analysis, while taking other participants' narrations as background data that are integrated into the analysis (Seawright and Gerring 2008). The 10 cases represent the main research themes to emerge across the entire dataset whilst also being diverse in terms of gender, stage of university education, major and birth province.

Misfits in higher education

In a nation with a long meritocratic ideology embodied in elite selection systems, it is only recently that this glaring inequality has captured scholar attention in China. Deng (2012) utilises the concept of cumulative advantage/disadvantage to explain why the proportion of rural students in elite universities has declined, and why rural graduates constitute the majority of the emergent 'ant group' (those low-income, young higher education graduates who cluster and dwell like ants in very tiny spaces in suburban areas of big cities) under the context of soaring housing prices. Besides their low participation in prestigious universities and proletarianisation after graduation, rural students' subjectivities in university have also been analysed in Chinese academia. Zheng (2012) surveys first-year students' self-assessment of individual abilities in 175 higher education institutions and finds that, except for analytical ability, the differences between rural and urban students are statistically significant in other 16 items such as art, information technology, leadership, communication skills, and language competence.

Internationally, there is growing research to explore post-entry experiences of non-traditional students in universities (Archer et al. 2003; Keane 2011; Lehmann 2012; Reay, Crozier, and Clayton 2009, 2010; Watson et al. 2009). Working-class students are found to have to handle class stigma (Granfield 1991), experience a sense of uneasiness and unfamiliarity, and develop various responses in their adaptation to the elite milieu (Reay et al. 2010). In offering important insights into lower social status students' life-world, these studies largely engaged with Bourdieu's theoretical framework, which is also deployed in this research.

In relation to the complex inter-relationship between education and social stratification, very few social theorists have provided more effective explanatory power than Pierre Bourdieu. His work helps us understand the central role the educational system plays in maintaining and reproducing social inequality. For Bourdieu, it is the dominant class who control the economic, social and political resources and whose culture is embodied in educational institutions. This advantage leads to their children's success in education, with social reproduction as a consequence (Harker 1984). Lying at the heart of Bourdieu's social theory is the ecological use of capital, field and habitus. A field can be conceived as a social space with a system of positions. It defines the structure of the social setting in which habitus operates; habitus as 'embodied social structure' (Bourdieu 1984, 467) mediates position and position-taking within the field; capital constitutes desirable resources in the field, differentiating the positions. Differences in habitus are explained by differences in the volume and composition of capital (Bourdieu 1984). The interaction of habitus and cultural capital within and across fields generates the logic of practice (Bourdieu 1990). For Bourdieu, class is relational, defined by agents' relative positions within the space; those 'who occupy similar or neighbouring positions', with similar volume and species of capital, are placed in similar conditions (Bourdieu 1989, 17).

Despite its enormous popularity, Bourdieu's habitus is often accused of determinism; and his cultural reproduction theory is also argued to be a product of particular French conditions, which problematises its use in relation to other societies. Engaging Bourdieu's thinking tools, which are designed 'for and by empirical work' (Bourdieu in Wacquant 1989, 50), demands our sensitivity to cultural specificity, as well as a firm anchor to data. Thinking with Bourdieu in this research is supported by the fact that a growing body of empirical research has demonstrated the relevance of Bourdieu's concepts to Chinese educational inequalities (for example, Liu 2007).

Urban space and institutional habitus: the initial confrontation

Crozier et al. (2008) and Reay et al. (2010) find that working-class students have different experiences in universities of varying status in the United Kingdom, emphasising the importance of institutional habitus. However, the sense of otherness they show across both elite and non-elite contexts was also detected by prior research (see Archer et al. 2003). Literature in China reveals that first-year rural students in general have a far lower level of adaptation than their urban peers, predominantly reflected in their poor interpersonal relations and weak psychological well-being (Yao 2010). This even applies for those in low-status, agricultural higher education institutions (Xu 1998).

However, there is a key difference between western non-traditional students and Chinese rural students. The latter's maladaptation is not only a class issue but also a geographical one, given that China's universities are largely located in big cities, and rural students' subjectivities also involve rural dispositions encountering a metropolitan milieu. Unsurprisingly, anxiety is a feeling shared among the participants who were raised in the countryside, and have now suddenly entered a strikingly new space. Xu (fourth year) felt scared and worried when he found himself among a dense crowd in Beijing Station on his first arrival. Zhang also experienced surprise and fear:

> I felt like a child who had never seen the world. Living in the countryside, I had never been to a big city and my horizon was very narrow ... Everything seemed so new to me. I faced the new world with awe and fear. (Zhang, fourth year)

In Bourdieu's (1984) view, we develop a sense of our place, a perception of where we belong in society and what is, and is not, 'for the likes of us'. The rupture Xu and Zhang experienced in leaving the countryside and moving to the big city created 'an acute sense of self-consciousness' (Crossley 2001, 158) of their rural identity, generating 'disquiet, ambivalence, insecurity and uncertainty' in addition to 'change and transformation' (Reay et al. 2009, 1105). Their dispositions, inculcated by living in a traditional and agricultural world, on entering a totally different space that is modern and populous, resulted in a sense of 'not belonging'. Geographic alienation was only one side of the story; cultural distance loomed even larger, as Han (first year) confided: 'I am quite ignorant about lots of things in daily life, including eating ... This actually humbles me'.

> At that time, I had no courage to speak in public. Coming from a small place, I had lots of misgivings and concerns in big cities, worrying about my poor speech, or worrying about other matters, worrying about other people's opinions. (Dong, fourth year)

Lack of sophisticated urban manners, lifestyles and dispositions thus became a source of anxiety and misery. Rural students' sense of inferiority, as a 'hidden injury of class' (Sennet and Cobb 1973), discloses the universally shared but oppressive perceptual schema of classifying and qualifying persons and objects (Bourdieu 1984), with rurality being derided and stigmatised in the dominant discourse. These former academic successes who had showed high aspirations and self-esteem at the pre-entry stage now underwent a confidence crisis in their early university years. Rural students' feeling of inadequacy in the urban milieu reflected rural–urban inequality in wider society. Their subjectivities were, however, indispensably linked to their immediate surroundings. The analysis is thus situated in university, which is, 'like any other field, the locus of a struggle to determine the conditions and the criteria of legitimate membership and legitimate hierarchy' (Bourdieu 1988, 11). Institutions of different status develop particular values and dispositions, influencing students' strategies and practices and affecting the way they 'see themselves and are seen by others in terms of both their learner and class identities' (Reay et al. 2010, 5). Stone University has been traditionally viewed as a place to educate officeholders or administrators. In recent years, it has also been striving for a world-class standard, with its academic strength particularly in social science, economics, management and humanities. Its position and mission thus defined has developed into a specific institutional habitus, with its own values and orientations embodied in students' collectivity, attitudes and demeanours (Reay, David, and Ball 2005). Stone University's status and institutional habitus has an essential role in defining the types of capital appreciated within the university, determining their exchange values in wider society.

Capital, locations and frustration

To better understand rural students' subjectivities and behaviours, we have to know their position in the field, what volumes and types of capitals they possess and can access. Economic capital, as 'the material residue that resists incorporation into dominant symbolic schema' (McNay 1999, 98), always asserts its power in other fields: financial hardships haunted most rural participants' life, inclining them to refrain from various social gatherings and activities on campus, not to mention some popular but expensive English training outside. In a university where a laptop became a necessity, and where a considerable number of students came from high-status families, Ren's rural roommate was the only one without a personal computer in the dorm; and her priority was to make a living: 'No one sponsors her and she has to totally depend on herself for her education' (Ren, urban, first year).

Their situations seemed deplorable in contrast with the reported wealth-flaunting behaviours of some rich students, such as wearing big brand clothes and frequenting expensive restaurants. The great difference in material wealth is damaging in that it affects not only 'our access to things, relationships, experiences and practices that we have reason to value', but also 'how others value us and respond to us' (Sayer 2005, 1).

Equally, if not more, damaging is a lack of the appreciated cultural forms. As we have glimpsed in the quotes above, rurality constituted an important dimension among 'the magnitude of the cultural obstacles' (Bourdieu and Passeron 1979, 8). Surrounded by urban students with privileged backgrounds, the sense of inferiority was repeatedly reinforced:

> I have been aware of my inadequacies in many respects, especially compared with those around me. Look at their elegant poise and bearings in talking, walking and even eating, you can't help admiring them and feel the great distance from them ... my classmates from big cities can talk with strangers with ease and assurance. But I can't. I'm too shy to do so. (Tang, third year)

Ignorance of the correct way of 'being and doing' 'in the eyes of their judges' (Bourdieu 1984, 511) in day-to-day interactions, as the accounts above indicate, led to a sense of incompetence. Han, Dong and Tang noticed their own ways of eating, walking and speaking as markers of their rural origins were inappropriate in the urban elite context. According to Bourdieu (1984, 466), habitus as mental structure embeds 'values in the most automatic gestures' such as 'ways of walking or blowing one's nose, ways of eating and talking', based on the fundamental social oppositions of the dominant and the dominated. Rural students complied with dominant classifications that reinforced in their subordination. This was visible in their appreciation of urban students' 'grace and ease' contrasting with their depreciation of their own laboriousness and clumsiness. As a consequence, they had to renounce many of their previous experiences and acquisitions.

What constitutes desirable cultural traits was nevertheless not merely constructed in everyday life on campus, but had also been more directly defined by the university since the beginning of their university life:

> In senior middle school, scholastic achievement was given priority. Students had to study very hard. Whereas in university, we are indoctrinated with such an idea that other things are even more important and should be learnt. (Chen, fourth year)

Such 'other things' competing with academic performance turned out to be embodied cultural capital like 'talents in organisation, communication and expression' (Na, fourth year), which were closely related to early socialisation in the urban middle-class families and elite urban schools. We have to bear in mind, however, that rural students generally had excellent grades in school; that is, they possessed scholastic capital – possibly the only form of cultural capital they could access. Soon after they entered university, they found that their type of currency was less valued, with, for example, changed criteria of what constituted English competence (see Li 2010)

What was highly appreciated in this context was different from what they had accumulated before. A 'painful dislocation' (Baxter and Britton 2001, 99) thus occurred. The mismatch of dispositions as academic stars developed earlier in school, and the sense of being cultural incompetents in university resulted in the high levels of stress and identity crises in their early university career:

> In my schooling, few students could surpass me in academic performance and I felt good in every aspect. When I came to Stone University, I suddenly found myself in a reverse position (Sun, third year)

> I was very upset at the beginning, and rang my mom and told her that I felt so inferior to others. My mother's first response was asking if my distress was related to financial difficulties. I told her I never cared about that. Material needs are only secondary to me. What disturbed me most was that I was no longer the best. (Being, first year)

Sun's and Being's identity as successful learners was challenged. Although 'every agent acts according to his position (that is, according the capital he or she possesses) and his habitus, related to his personal history' (Bourdieu 2002, 31), a lack of immediate adaptation to the objective position was evident among these 'wonder' children in the new field. Even though they had positioned themselves low as far as rural–urban relations were concerned, the radical changes of academic positions were still deeply upsetting. Nevertheless, habitus, as Reay et al. (2009, 1104) argue, is 'permeable and responsive to what is going on around them'. The rural exceptions' inclinations to improve themselves through industry were undergoing a re-shaping under 'the pressure of the socially qualified objective situation' (Bourdieu 1977, 26). After the initial encounters and frustrations, they learnt to accommodate themselves to a devalued location through self-regulation. This was even true for Being, who showed a very strong drive to succeed and was one of the most diligent among the participants:

> Now I just want to follow the due course and take it easy … and have a more relaxed attitude toward my scholastic downgrade. (Being first year)

Their adaptation to low locations, however, was not an easy one and was often accompanied by resistance. Some rural participants, after the initial shocks, endeavoured to remould themselves:

> I am trying to make up for my inadequacy in knowledge … When you talk with other students, you will find they know so much about so many things such as the stock market, car, computers etc., etc. (Fan, second year)

Such a 'reflexive transformation of identity' (McNay 1999, 95) was generated from their transformative dispositions, which had been fostered in their earlier years and still exerted power in university.

What cultural activities? The case of Wu

The students' distance from 'legitimate' cultural forms nevertheless made their transformation a bumpy process. According to the principles of class distinction (Bourdieu 1984), high culture is high partly because of its distance from the cultural practices and knowledge of the lower class. Despite rural students' exposure to the elite atmosphere, the cultural activities they routinely engaged in were quite different from those of their privileged urban peers. Wu (fourth year) compared her roommate's 'cultural omnivorousness' with her own narrow range of activities. Her roommate, from an intellectual family, had 'unusual experiences in childhood', had read a wide range of books about which she knew nothing and understood nothing, and participated in 'strange things' of which she doubted the value:

> In the first year, she read lots and lots of books, irrelevant to our major ... chose courses like Tibetan Buddhism and even Beijing Tourism! She also attended various lectures covering a wide range of topics and even courses for postgraduates, visited all the places mentioned in the tourist class, even a very tiny one. She also loves Japanese movies and makes it a point to watch movies with only a very small circle of audience. She seems to have interests in both the highbrow and the middlebrow. (Wu, fourth year)

Wu had not cultivated the taste to appreciate such broad cultural practices, assuming they were solely for showing-off. Neither did she value her own activities:

> I idled my time away, spending all my time doing mathematics and assignments. Two hours' work usually took me a day. I have no idea what I was doing there and how I had killed my time. My GPA is high because I have nothing else to do and haven't spent much time on entertainment. Study, then entertainment: that has been my life here. And my entertainment is to watch soap opera on the computer, which is not at all admirable but a waste of time. (Wu, fourth year)

Wu's roommate strived to accumulate diverse but usually 'consecrated' cultural forms and thus created impressive distinction. What Wu accessed was merely scholastic work and popular culture. And the pursuit of popular culture, such as watching soap operas and playing PC games, was frowned upon by some urban informants despite their own participation. Gang (urban, fourth year), for example, trying to police the boundary, said scornfully: 'those rural students' activities are not at all commendable'. Wu's distance from 'high' culture, together with the cultural boundary, consolidated the internal closure of social groups. Her feelings of being out of place were still strong after almost four years' adjustment:

> Sometimes, I really feel regret about choosing this university and this major. They don't fit for me. Students here are so lively and extrovert. (Wu, fourth year)

To gain recognition, she preferred something solid like science, rather than something far above her reach, so she could achieve success through intensive labour. Recognition and respect mattered a lot. A first-year rural student, mentioning the lack of both she experienced, burst into tears during the interview. Granfield (1991) found that working-class students in an elite American university attempted to conceal their background and blend in. This research also reveals that their disadvantaged background became a burden that rural students tried to disclaim. A case in point was the difficulty in accessing rural participants in my fieldwork. Even if they were willing to, many tended to highlight their identity as a resident of more developed regions over their rural origin. As an urban informant observed: 'I know some rural students are very poor and receive financial aid but they just pretend not to be poor in our daily talk'.

Proximity to poverty might be one reason for their shame about their origins; social contempt could be another. Such a disavowal, as Granfield (1991) argued, is a strategy to handle stigma. Similarly, Skeggs (1997) attributed working-class women's disidentification to negative class labelling. Reflected in this research was rural students' acquisition of a new dress code or lifestyle. Yan (urban, first year) observed her rural roommate: 'in order to buy new clothes, she has to do lots of part-time jobs ... she is so fashionable that she doesn't look like a rural girl at all'. Passing as a privileged member, however, did not gain her approval: 'to be frank, I don't like it at all. It is so vain.'

The students' accounts reveal the power of the dominant culture. Rural students' lack resulted not only in feelings of estrangement, but also in a sense of inferiority. Cultural classifications were incorporated into their mental structure through daily interactions, expressed as shame about their rural origins, and feelings of not fitting in. During the process of adaptation and transformation, barriers occurred in many ways and in different forms, as we will further see below.

Accruing symbolic and social capital: social activities and memberships

In Stone, social activities, mainly in the form of involvement in student societies, are part and parcel of university life, providing an important platform to acquire social and symbolic capital. However, not all memberships in university associations are valuable. Only student leaders in certain groups can benefit to the extent of adding weight to their CV, knowing people in important positions, and developing their organising abilities. As 'communication skills and leadership' are highly appreciated, and sociability is viewed as a necessary trait to participate and achieve highly in student societies, the absence of rural students, who were labelled as deficient, was not a surprise, according to student leaders. If they were ever engaged, as their reports show, they were inclined to join in the less influential and less powerful associations, or held low positions in the hierarchical system.

Position and symbolic violence: the case of Fan

Fan used to only maintain contact with his ex-schoolfellows from the charity school he had attended. But now he tried to extend his social networks to include urban students, as an attempt to integrate himself into the new environment:

> I begin to make friends now, and pay more attention to people around me. I can't always stay in that circle. Recently I have attempted to network and make new friends. It might be good to know people different from me. (Fan, second year)

Fan tried to learn to appreciate the distinctive cultural traits of the student leaders that he had disapproved of:

> Sometimes, you may find that the strength they demonstrate is not what you can learn. When your ability, experience or at least your cognitive ability are inadequate, you may be bewildered by the manners of the president of the student union and even disapprove of them: why does he talk to people in that way? Why has he so many pet phrases, so many foul words …? Now I have the sense that something which seems incomprehensible is exactly his distinctiveness, his charismatic features, his demonstration of his uniqueness. If you look at it from a very vulgar point of view, you won't accept the way he talks and what he says. However, it is exactly where his charm lies. In this way, he can do the job well. If you are in his place, you may not succeed … Now I'm at the phase of learning. (Fan, second year)

Rather than simply displaying unconscious submission by defining himself as unfit for high positions in the student society, Fan had adopted a negative attitude at the beginning towards the president's language style, regarding it as anything but posh. Through critical analysis, he became aware of the way in which student leaders used language to distance themselves from subordinates so as to create prestige and distinction. However, resistance to symbolic violence paradoxically 'can be alienating and submission can be liberating' (Bourdieu and Wacquant 1992, 24). Fan chose to comply with the dominant norms, accepted the 'legitimacy' and 'value' of the president's style, and viewed his previous opinion as 'vulgar', thus subordinating himself to his 'betters' so as to progress up the social ladder. His remarks about what constituted student leadership provide a good example of a paradoxical combination of self-domination and reflexivity. Accordingly, achieving high status in student societies was largely irrelevant to rural students. What was worse, even their engagement was not always welcome, betrayed by an urban student leader' comment, 'the environment doesn't become them' for their 'countrified manner'.

What societies and activities? The cases of Xie and Piao

To buffer the external threat, university students from disadvantaged backgrounds tend to distance themselves for self-protection (Keane 2011). Specifically illustrated in this study was rural students' detachment from social activities and associations. 'I have the time but have never been in any society' was not unusual among rural participants. Xie (third year) also avoided the Student Union and its leaders, believing they were opportunists. He instead chose to mingle with people like him, joining the 'Self-Reliance Association' – an organisation purposely established for the most disadvantaged students. A similar organisation that rural students are more likely to participate in is the work–study division, which offers part-time job opportunities.

Their social engagement is intrinsically linked to their financial constraints, as Ingram, Abrahams, and Beedell (2012) found among working-class students in the United Kingdom. For three years, Piao (fourth year) had been working as a student assistant, a paid post that is only open to students with great hardships. He also took part-time works outside to earn a living: 'In the second year, I worked as a salesman of MP3 and digital cameras' (Piao, fourth year). Although he viewed this as a way to gain social experience, unlike high-status activities, such experience is not a smooth avenue to accumulate valued capital.

Rural students' distancing from mainstream social activities compounded their inadequacy in social capital, resulting from the relative homogeneity of their low-status social connections. Consequently, they tended to be ill-informed and ill-judged in their university career, as Wu (fourth year) confessed in her reflection that, due to the lack of social capital, 'I was so blind at that time and wasted lots of time and made wrong decisions'.

Rural students' strategies, practices and choices

So far I have depicted rural participants' setbacks, their inadequacy in various species of capital. Habitus as 'an open system of dispositions' is 'constantly subjected to experiences and therefore constantly affected by them' (Bourdieu and Wacquant 1992, 133). Their rural habitus oriented them to low positions; their academic habitus, however, inclined them to work hard to move upward. The interactions between position and disposition, between objective constraints and subjective aspirations, produced diverse practices and outcomes. When rural students found themselves under various constraints, what strategies would they adopt? The following section discusses rural students' practices generated by their new 'evolving' habitus, and their 'creative adaptation and multi-faced responses' (Reay et al. 2009, 1103). The discussion is situated in such a context that the decreasing employment opportunities and the oversupply of higher education graduates in China have compelled students to pursue postgraduate degree, which is rapidly becoming a necessity.

Among all the credentials, the strongest are those conferred by internationally well-known universities. Nevertheless, rural students, as this study shows, tended to work immediately after graduation.

What prospects and what practices?

Jiang (third year) was in the School of Science – a newly established institute in Stone, with lots of students from the countryside. Without a postgraduate degree, prospects in the job market would be grim for its students according to both my interviewees and an administrator. However, financial constraints reduced rural students' opportunity to attend graduate school, and they also tended to distance themselves from social activities. Some rural students, male especially, denied various possibilities, adopted a laid-back attitude as Jiang observed, forming a sharp contrast with their industrious dispositions developed in school:

> Male students in our class haven't participated in any student association. They are particularly lazy. Students in science tend to lead a hard academic life with a tight timetable and difficult curriculum. But male students in our class are very famous for idling their time away in PC games. The one who is in our experiment team is the worst, playing games all the time and skipping class and experiments ... I once asked him about his career planning, and he replied that he would find a job first after graduation. He comes from a mountainous area. (Jiang, third year)

Habitus reshaping is an evolving process, with continuous adaptations and position-takings. All rural participants went through transformations, although to different degrees and in different aspects. The male student in Jiang's team conceded to his marginalisation, and gave up his former identity as successful learner. He used PC games as a way to integrate into the urban male group, or to avoid the unhappy reality. Participants were inclined to agree that it was female students who cared more about academic achievement; male students focused more on social aspects, whether it was PC games or other activities. Due to serious sexism in the job market, being a male graduate was unanimously reported to be an advantage and therefore they could afford to be academically less successful.

Another example is Xie (third year). When I first interviewed him, he was a frustrated and stressed first-year student who cared much about his academic performance and sought my advice for improvement. One and a half years later he had changed a lot, not only in his urbanised appearance and manners but also in his much more relaxed attitude towards his scholastic work. After our interview, lunch and a leisurely walk, I asked whether he would work that afternoon as third-year students tended to be very busy. He replied: 'No, I will call it a day and go back to the dorm. Today is Wednesday and Wednesday is also weekend to me.' He joined the Self

Reliance Association, as mentioned earlier, and also participated in a 'university student innovation project' related to rural issues. In these ways, Xie attempted to transform himself and enhance his opportunities, whilst still maintaining a loyalty to his rural roots.

In contrast, female rural students were more likely to commit themselves to study. Being (first year) worked extremely hard to compensate for her want of broader knowledge and reclaim her identity as academic success. Viewed as a 'swot' by her roommate, and an 'exception' by her English teacher, she admitted that 'my only strength is my rigid and industrious habit'. We have to remember, however, that Being was in her first year and her old scholastic habitus still exerted a great influence.

Wei (fourth year) had a strong interest in economics and had wanted to pursue a master's degree in this field. However, her dreams kept on being compromised by reality:

> My family conditions don't allow me to do postgraduate study ... My younger brother is also at university and it is very expensive to support an undergraduate. I felt so sad and sorry to find my mother's newly grey hair; then I told them, 'Alright, I won't go to graduate school'. (Wei, fourth year)

When she found she had no option but to work after graduation, she became resigned and fatalistic about her possibilities: 'In the first two years, I worked hard, but not anymore'.

Zhang (fourth year) also worked hard. As an exception, he was finally recommended to graduate school. Reviewing his trajectory may give us a better understanding of his strategies and practices embedded in habitus:

> The other four (roommates) are all from big cities ... I know my position and then position myself. I come from the countryside. If I want to break away from my rural world completely, I have to study hard. And I'm not good at any other things. They can play video-games well, but I can't because I have never done that before. They can sing songs, have funs, and drink alcohol and go shopping. But I am good at none of these. The only thing left for me to do is to work hard. I know I can't take leisure like others and should study hard: a rural student has to study hard. (Zhang, fourth year)

Zhang positioned himself low among his urban peers. His rural dispositions predisposed him to be diligent. Unlike subjects such as humanities, social science and administration that require a high volume of cultural and social capital, statistics, his major, is a subject in which he was able to achieve high through assiduities. When other forms of capital seemed inaccessible, academic capital became the only form he could accumulate, and scholastic success the only route to change his disadvantaged position and rural identity. His transformative dispositions had been strongly nurtured by his father, a bare-foot peasant doctor, who had been determined to keep his children as far away as possible from the countryside:

> He tells me to keep on moving. He said at the beginning of my university life, 'I don't care what subject you are in, but I do hope you can be a postgraduate.' Therefore, I have been working very hard in the first year when I was aware of the possibility to graduate school, and I obtained good results every term. (Zhang, fourth year)

Zhang wanted to be an academic in the future. Therefore he planned to do a PhD after a master's degree. He did not have to worry as much about financial issues as other rural children because of his relatively well-to-do family conditions and the award of a scholarship. Three of his roommates intended to study abroad. He nevertheless never considered this and perceived studying abroad in the future as impossible, as something beyond his power. Compared with the overseas degrees his urban peers were to pursue, his PhD degree was likely to be depreciated by the time he obtained it. He seemed unaware of this. However, 'I somewhat sense some invisible pressure, including the pressure of studying abroad'.

Their diverse responses and strategies shed some light on how habitus was fashioned and refashioned by objective possibilities, suggesting that resources, whether material or symbolic, always conditioned the degree of these rural children's adaptation and transformation.

What career choices?

Rural students' practices indeed reflected their position-takings in the university field. On the whole, their submission to urban cultural norms was often accompanied by changes, at least at the superficial level, expressed by their adopting some cultural traits (such as appearance) associated with their urban peers. Within various constraints, their adaptation to the new field at different stages varies along a continuum from resignation to their low position to resistance through extreme industry. Even Zhang, who illustrated a strong inclination to transform, still lacked a feel for the game, revealing his rural traces in his practices. The power of a lingering rural habitus, concomitant with objective conditions, can also be detected in their career choices.

Career choices made from necessity is a theme across the samples: they showed more concerns about the immediate financial reward than long-term benefits, choosing jobs their urban counterparts would be reluctant to take. Wei (fourth year) had to give up the job offer in Beijing due to financial considerations, although she was clear that her decision would limit her future advancement:

> At the beginning, I hesitated to choose between the job in Beijing and the job in our province. I know if I choose the latter, it will very difficult for me to go back to Beijing and go abroad in the future. (Wei, fourth year)

As well as the objective constraints, habitus as a 'sense of one's place', 'acquired through the lasting experience of a social position' (Bourdieu 1989, 19), also played a role, influencing students' career aspirations and choices. Jing (fourth year) accepted an offer from a small company with lots of risks and instabilities in the Chinese context. Her explanation illustrates how the objective conditions were internalised into the mental structure, expressed as low career expectation, a view that high-status jobs were not for people like her:

> The job is alright for me. I am not ambitious to set any big goals to do this or that in the future. For me, it doesn't have to be perfect. (Jing, fourth year)

Conclusion

As individuals are 'the product of history' (Bourdieu and Wacquant 1992, 136), investigating the experiences of a group of rural students and their changing positions in an elite university field does not merely help us to understand how their experiences and identities are negotiated, but also reveals social relations in the wider world.

A sense of estrangement and inferiority, stemming from lack of recognition, constituted a salient part of rural students' subjectivities in university. Inadequacy in economic, cultural and social capital placed huge barriers for rural students to overcome. Reay (2005) argues that when habitus encounters a new field, the resulting disjuncture generates not only changes but also emotional burdens. 'Positional suffering', vividly expressed by Being, was even worse than their material suffering as rural students struggled to come to terms with occupying 'an inferior, obscure position in a prestigious and privileged universe' (Bourdieu et al. 1999, 4). Also endemic to their experience in the urban elite environment was the shame of their rural origins and the resulting concealment. Inequality-related shame as a response to class contempt is always accompanied by the lack of valued goods, and works as an important mechanism in reproducing social order (Sayer 2005). To succeed, rural students had to subordinate themselves to urban middle-class norms and underwent difficult adaptations to university life.

Initial disadvantages proved hard to compensate for despite the long exposure to an elite atmosphere. Exclusion in various forms and the entailed self-exclusion hindered rural students' acquisition of valued cultural capital and involvement in student societies to enhance employment opportunities. Even for those who demonstrated a 'transformative' habitus like Zhang, their choices tended to be ill-informed. The case study of a tiny group of 'wonder' children has therefore disclosed the bleak reality of very unequal social relations and a tendency towards a highly closed society in contemporary China.

In relation to Bourdieu's theoretical concepts, this study evidences habitus' dialectic, dynamic aspects: it is not merely reproducing but also transforming, durable but subject to reshaping. These wonder children's inclinations to transform are often overwhelmed by the weight of adverse social, economic, and cultural conditions. This suggests social inequalities cannot be dissolved merely by individual reflexivity. What is equally, if not more, important is access to valued resources. Constructing a more just environment therefore requires changing the unequal social structures with more equalitarian policies. A good place to start is to abolish city-biased systems, allotting a fair share of public resources to rural areas, particularly rural schools. On the other hand, it also helps to widen participation in prestigious universities, to provide substantial financial aid in the form of bursaries and grants to low income rural students, and to develop a more friendly and inclusive ethos in higher education institutions.

Acknowledgements
The author would like to extend gratitude to Professor Diane Reay for her unfailing support in the PhD and postdoctorate research from which this article formed, to anonymous reviewers for their comments, and to participants for sharing their stories and inner world.

Note
1. Stone is a pseudonym, so are the names of the participants in this article.

References
Archer, L., M. Hutchings, and A. Ross, with C. Leathwood, R. Gilchrist, and D. Philips. 2003. *Higher Education and Social Class: Issues of Exclusion and Inclusion*. London and New York: RoutledgeFalmer.
Baxter, A., and C. Britton. 2001. "Risk Identity and Change: Becoming a Mature Student." *International Studies in Sociology of Education* 11 (1): 87–104.
Bourdieu, P. 1977. *Outline of a Theory of Practice*. Cambridge: Cambridge University Press.
Bourdieu, P. 1984. *Distinction, a Social Critique of the Judgment of Taste*. Trans. R. Nice. London: Routledge & Kegan Paul.
Bourdieu, P. 1988. *Homo Academicus*. Trans. P. Collier. Cambridge: Polity.
Bourdieu, P. 1989. "Social Space and Symbolic Power." *Sociological Theory* 7 (1): 14–25.
Bourdieu, P. 1990. *The Logic of Practice*. Stanford: Stanford University Press.
Bourdieu, P. et al. 1999. *The Weight of the World: Social Suffering in Contemporary Society*. Trans. P. P. Furguson et al. Stanford: Stanford University Press.
Bourdieu, P. 2002. "Habitus." In *Habitus: A Sense of Place*, edited by J. Hillier and E. Rooksby, 27–36. Aldershot: Ashgate Publishing House.
Bourdieu, P., and J.-C. Passerson. 1979. *The Inheritors: French Students and their Relation to Culture*. Trans. R. Nice. London: University of Chicago Press.

Bourdieu, P., and L. Wacquant. 1992. *Invitation to Reflexive Sociology*. Chicago, IL: University of Chicago Press.
Chan, K. W., and L. Zhang. 1999. "The Hukou System and Rural-Urban Migration in China: Processes and Changes." *The China Quarterly* 160: 818–855.
Crossley, N. 2001. *The Social Body: Habit, Identity and Desire*. London: Sage.
Crozier, G., D. Reay, J. Clayton, L. Colliander, and J. Grinstead. 2008. "Different Strokes for Different Folks: Diverse Students in Diverse Institutions – Experiences of Higher Education." *Research Papers in Education* 23 (2): 167–177.
Deng, G. 2012. "On the Reproduction of Rural-Urban Inequality in the HE Field [in Chinese]." *Hubei Social Sciences* 6: 158–161.
Denzin, N. K. 1970. *Sociological Methods: A Sourcebook*. London: Butterworths.
Granfield, R. 1991. "Making It by Faking It: Working-Class Students in an Elite Academic Environment." *Journal of Contemporary Ethnography* 20 (3): 331–351.
Hannum, E. 1999. "Political Change and the Urban-Rural Gap in Basic Education in China, 1949-1990." *Comparative Education Review* 43 (2): 193–211.
Harker, R. K. 1984. "On Reproduction, Habitus and Education." *British Journal of Sociology of Education* 5 (2): 117–127.
Hirsch, F. 1977. *The Social Limits to Growth*. London: Routledge and Kegan Paul.
Ingram, N., J. Abrahams, and P. Beedell. 2012. "Students' Engagement in Extra-curricular Activities: Constraints, Freedom and Class Background." In *British Sociological Association (BSA) Annual Conference 2012: Sociology in an Age of Austerity* 2012–04-11, 2012–04-13, Leeds.
Keane, E. 2011. "Distancing to Self-Protect: The Perpetuation of Inequality in Higher Education through Socio-Relational Dis/Engagement." *British Journal of Sociology of Education* 32 (3): 449–466.
Knight, J., and R. Gunatilaka. 2010. "The Rural-Urban Divide in China: Income but Not Happiness?" *Journal of Development Studies* 46 (3): 506–534.
Knight, J., and L. Song. 1999. *The Rural-Urban Divide*. Oxford: Oxford University Press.
Lehmann, W. 2012. "Working-Class Students, Habitus, and the Development of Student Roles: A Canadian Case Study." *British Journal of Sociology of Education* 33 (4): 527–546.
Levin, H. M., and Z. Xu. 2006. "Issues in the Expansion of Higher Education in the People's Republic of China." In *Education, Globalization, and Social Change*, edited by H. Lauder et al., 909–925. Oxford: Oxford University Press.
Li, H. 2010. "Educational Trajectories of Rural Students in an Elite University: English Learning Experience and Beyond." PhD diss. University of Cambridge: UK.
Li, Q. 2008. *Ten Lectures on Social Stratification [in Chinese]*. Beijing: Social Sciences Academic Press.
Liu, H. 2007. "Cultural Capital and Rural Migrant Workers' Integration to Cities [in Chinese]." *Rural Economics*: 122–125.
McNay, L. 1999. "Gender, Habitus and the Field." *Theory, Culture and Society* 16 (1): 95–117.
Pepper, S. 1994. "Editor's Introduction." *Chinese Education & Society* 27 (5): 5–22.
Reay, D. 2005. "Beyond Consciousness? the Psychic Landscape of Social Class." *Sociology* 35 (5): 911–928.
Reay, D., G. Crozier, and J. Clayton. 2009. "'Strangers in Paradise'? Working-Class Students in Elite Universities." *Sociology* 43 (6): 1103–1121.

Reay, D., G. Crozier, and J. Clayton. 2010. "'Fitting in' or 'Standing out': Working-Class Students in UK Higher Education." *British Educational Research Journal* 32 (1): 1–19.

Reay, D., M. David, and S. Ball. 2005. *Degrees of Choice: Social Class, Race and Gender in Higher Education*. Stoke-on-Trent: Trentham Books.

Sayer, A. 2005. "Class, Moral Worth and Recognition." *Sociology* 39 (5): 947–963.

Seawright, J., and J. Gerring. 2008. "Case Selection Techniques in Case Study Research: A Menu of Qualitative and Quantitative Options." *Political Research Quarterly* 61 (2): 294–308.

Sennett, R., and J. Cobb. 1973. *The Hidden Injuries of Class*. New York, NY: Random House.

Skeggs, B. 1997. *Formations of Class and Gender*. London: Sage.

Sun, W. 2012. "Analysis on the Decreasing Ratio of Rural Students in University through the Lens of Communication Theory." *Xinwen Aihaozhe* 2012 (3): 57–58.

Wacquant, L. 1989. "Towards a Reflexive Sociology: A Workshop with Pierre Bourdieu." *Sociological Theory* 7 (1): 26–63.

Watson, J., M. Nind, D. Humphris, and A. Borthwick. 2009. "Strange New World: Applying a Bourdieu Lens to Understanding Early Student Experiences in Higher Education." *British Journal of Sociology of Education* 30 (6): 665–681.

Wright, E. O. 2009. "Understanding Class: Towards an Integrated Analytical Approach." *New Left Review* 60: 101–116.

Xu, X. 1998. "Cultural Conflicts in the Process of Rural University Students' Socialisation [in Chinese]." *Youth Studies* 3: 15–19.

Yang, D. 2006. *Educational Equity in China: Dream and Reality* [in Chinese]. Beijing: Peking University Press.

Yao, H. 2010. "Literature Review on First Year Rural Students' Adaptation to HE." *Journal of Anhui Agricultural Science* 38 (25): 14162–14163.

Yin, P. 2008. *Rural Poverty from Social Exclusion Perspective* [in Chinese]. Beijing: Intellectual Property Press.

You, L. 2008. "Opportunities to Access Higher Education for Rural Children from the Perspective of Massification of HE [in Chinese]." *Academic Journal of Adult Higher Education* 4: 41–45.

Zheng, Ch. 2012. "Differences of Self-evaluation of Individual Abilities between Rural and Urban University Students in China [in Chinese]." *Social Scientist* 4: 110–113.

Cultural capital and distinction: aspirations of the 'other' foreign student

I Lin Sin

Department of Sociology, University of Edinburgh, Edinburgh, UK

This article explores the perceived role of UK international education as foreign cultural capital, obtained outside the UK, in facilitating middle-class social mobility. Drawing on interviews with students in Malaysia, it extends Bourdieu's concept of cultural capital to explain understandings of the rewards and limitations of undertaking UK education externally. I argue that foreign cultural capital has positive exchange value and an under-researched negative value. I discuss how accumulating local cultural capital is a strategic response to the shortcomings of western knowledge, skills and dispositions. Age, ethnicity, gender and nationality add complexities to the conversion of cultural capital into economic and social advantages. I conclude by arguing for more visibility of external modes of UK international education and the positional possibilities they represent to foreign students seeking distinction within the rapidly expanding global academic marketplace.

Introduction

The link between education and middle-class social mobility has long been established, with researchers arguing that elite or more exclusive forms of education can be used as cultural capital to maintain and improve economic and social status (Bourdieu and Passeron 1977; Ball 2003; Devine 2004). Superior knowledge, skills, dispositions and qualifications, key components of cultural capital theorized by Bourdieu (1986), are believed to have exchange value in that they can be converted to economic and symbolic capitals, thus granting privileged access to better jobs, income and status. Much of the existing research, however, has only analysed the exchange value of cultural capital acquired through education in advanced western countries. The transferability and convertibility of cultural capital across different spatial locations have not been explored in detail. The research on which this paper is based contributes to a limited but growing area of research within international education that takes on Bourdieu's invitation (1998) to situate cultural capital in historical and cultural contexts beyond 1950s France. Present literature predominantly focus on how crossing national borders for international education in an advanced western country provides foreign cultural capital for the occupational and status advancement of the middle-class in Asia (Waters 2005, 2006; Sin 2009; Kim 2011; Ong 1999). This paper brings visibility to the often neglected 'other' foreign student who seeks western cultural capital by undertaking foreign tertiary programmes in the home country. Reporting findings from interviews and a focus group with middle-class Malaysian students, it explores the perceived role of cultural capital, obtained through UK offshore or transnational education in Malaysia, in facilitating social reproduction and mobility. The data are derived from my larger study which explores the aspirations and experiences of distinction among Malaysian students and recent graduates of various modes of UK education.

I will discuss the students' understandings of the rewards and shortcomings of undertaking UK education outside the UK. I argue that foreign cultural capital derived from UK international education has a potential positive exchange value, as well as an under-researched negative value. This presented a complex set of positional advantages and disadvantages to the students as they sought to overcome limitations of western cultural capital through selective appropriation of local cultural capital. The students' pursuit for distinction was further enhanced and complicated by ethnicity, age, gender and nationality that shaped their understandings of life chance possibilities in a graduate future.

Context

The growth of the global academic marketplace in the last decade or so has been phenomenal, a huge portion of which is spurred by the expansion of Anglophone universities in the Global North into new modes and partnerships of educational delivery in Asia. Globally, there are approximately 200 overseas branch campuses, termed offshore campuses, of predominantly universities from the West, with an additional 37 or more arriving by 2013 (Katsomitros 2012). Between 2009 and 2011, the number of UK universities with branch campuses overseas nearly doubled to 25 (Sharma 2012). With near market saturation in the Middle East, strategies of UK universities to set up base offshore are shifting to South East Asia (Katsomitros 2012). Malaysia is at the centre of this growth, as numbers of new and upcoming arrivals of UK offshore campuses suggest. In 2011 and 2012, Newcastle University and The University of Southampton respectively opened their purpose-built branch campuses in Malaysia, joining the University of Nottingham that has had offshore campus presence in the country since 2005. Heriot-Watt University and University of Reading will have their purpose-built Malaysian campuses ready in 2014 and 2015, respectively (Nayagam 2011; University of Reading 2011). An offshore programme requires the entire or majority of the time being spent at the UK branch campus in Malaysia. Subject to the student's academic performance, there is opportunity for study exchange to the United Kingdom for usually up to two semesters.

Many UK universities have partnerships with Malaysian private higher educational institutions, delivering mostly transnational and distance or online programmes at undergraduate level that allow students to study entirely or partially in Malaysia for a UK degree. Transnational programmes culminating in joint degrees from the Malaysian private institution and UK partner university are most prominent, with some 49% of 42,535 students pursuing UK studies in Malaysia in 2008/09 enrolled in them (Tan 2010). A typical programme requires the completion of the entire three years of undergraduate studies in Malaysia through what is known as a 3+0 route. A further 31% of the external students in 2008/09 chose the transnational twinning route, which requires studying at least the first year in Malaysia before completing the remaining duration of the programme in the United Kingdom (Tan 2010). Offshore and transnational programmes are marketed as similar to those offered at the parent or partner university in the United Kingdom, especially in terms of course content, academic standards and qualification awarded (British Council 2010). The expanding provision of international education by way of offshore, transnational and distance delivery in Malaysia is enabled by mass structural reforms to the private higher education market since 1996 aimed at addressing three key objectives. They are to cater to the rising demand for tertiary education that Malaysian public universities could not adequately meet, to reverse the massive outflow of economic capital caused by cross-border migration of students for international education and, increasingly, to generate lucrative income revenue by developing Malaysia into a regional and international hub of education (Lee 2004). With more than 48,000 students engaged in UK offshore and transnational education, Malaysia is the leading source of external international students for the United Kingdom (Tan 2010). This figure, which is about four times larger than the Malaysian student population in the United Kingdom (UNESCO Institute for Statistics 2012), shows the popularity of offshore and transnational modes of study among Malaysians seeking international education. It raises the question of the perceived conversion value of cultural capital obtained through UK education outside the United Kingdom and the positional possibilities it brings to these students. This is the central question that frames my research.

Methodology and research design

My methodological approach is guided by interpretivism, which seeks rich understanding through in-depth exploration of the views and experiences of participants (Mason 2002). I used qualitative semi-structured interviewing as the primary method to systematically explore themes and issues that interested me while allowing participants flexibility to introduce topics that were significant to them (Mason 2002). The need to ensure a comfortable, free-flowing setting to encourage informants to reveal details about their personal backgrounds and distinction practices makes one-to-one interviews an appropriate choice. This is a less intrusive method compared with focus group interviews that can, as I found from having administered a semi-structured one with twinning students, limit spontaneity to freely and fully express thoughts.

Between September 2010 and April 2011, I interviewed three samples totalling 36 Malaysian students and graduates who were pursuing or have pursued a UK tertiary education either onshore; that is, physically in the United Kingdom, or in Malaysia through the offshore and transnational modes. My focus in this paper will be on one sample of 14 full-time students of offshore and transnational programmes, aged 19–24, who progressed into tertiary education with no or little experience of full-time, graduate employment. My aim is to explore the anticipation of the advantages and disadvantages of pursuing UK education outside the United Kingdom, as held by young adults still engaged in tertiary studies. I seek to capture impressions and projections of a graduate future and the potential exchange value of competences, experiences, dispositions and credentials derived from UK offshore and transnational education. A student rather than a graduate sample best facilitates this goal as it reduces *post hoc* rationalization and distorted memory of aspirations and experiences leading up to and during tertiary participation.

Theoretical sampling, involving the selection of participants with characteristics that could potentially contribute to developing analysis, theories and explanations (Mason 2002, 138), was employed for the one-to-one interviews. Snowballing was also used for the one-to-one interviews, as it was for the focus group interview. I tapped into the networks of my early participants in the one-to-one interviews to locate further participants. I sought assistance from lecturers, administration staff and student representatives from various private higher learning institutions in Selangor and Kuala Lumpur, which form the central hub of private tertiary education in Malaysia, to establish contact with prospective interviewees. This was especially useful in gaining access to the focus group participants made up of four twinning students who represented the entire intake in their programme.

Although sampling was not intended to be statistically representative, I tried when possible to include students of different ethnicities and academic programmes to potentially obtain a wide and comprehensive coverage of themes and issues. Constraints of time, costs and limited availability of informants of certain characteristics, particularly Malay and the *orang asli* (Malay: 'the original people') ethnic majority students, collectively termed *bumiputera*, who are largely concentrated in the public higher education sector (Aihara 2009), and students enrolled in less conventional subject areas – that is, other than commerce, engineering and technology – limited the extent to which theoretical sampling could be employed for the one-to-one interviews. Table 1 shows the key characteristics of the combined sample of participants from the one-to-one and focus group interviews.

Table 1. Profile characteristics of participants.

Pseudonym	Age	Ethnicity	Gender	Institution	Programme
Wah Seong	22	Chinese	Male	Nottingham (Malaysia)	MSc Civil Engineering
Mushamir	24	Malay	Male	Nottingham (Malaysia)	PhD Electronic & Communication Engineering
Hisham	23	Malay	Male	KDU (3+0) with Keele	BA (Hons) Business Management & Finance
Hui Ching	19	Chinese	Female	KDU (1+2) with Manchester	BA (Hons) Economics
Chloe	19	Chinese	Female	KDU (1+2) with Manchester	BA (Hons) Economics
Sue Ern	19	Chinese	Female	KDU (1+2) with Manchester	BA (Hons) Economics
Salehah	19	Malay	Female	KDU (1+2) with Manchester	BA (Hons) Economics
Francis	23	Indian	Male	KDU (3+0) with UoL	Bachelor of Laws (Hons)
Nadia	19	Malay (mixed)	Female	Nottingham (Malaysia)	BSc (Hons) Applied Psychology & Management
Elaine	22	Sino-Kadazan	Female	Nottingham (Malaysia)	BA (Hons) Business, Economics & Management
Rosli	21	Malay	Male	APIIT (3+0) with Staffordshire	BSc (Hons) Business Computing
Imran	23	Malay	Male	APIIT (3+0) with Staffordshire	BSc (Hons) Business Information Technology
Sze Theng	20	Chinese	Female	ICOM (3+0) with Wolverhampton	BMus (Hons) in Professional Music
Kor Ming	20	Chinese	Male	Taylor's (3+0) with UWE	BA (Hons) Accounting & Finance

Note: APIIT = Asia-Pacific University of Technology and Innovation; ICOM = International College of Music; KDU = *Kolej Damansara Utama*; UoL = University of London; UWE = University of the West of England.

Findings

Affordable accumulation of foreign cultural capital

Studying a UK degree programme entirely or partially in Malaysia was to my participants a cost-efficient way to obtain top-grade tertiary education that they believed surpassed the quality of other sources of education in their home country. The offshore or transnational study arrangement came with incentives of lower tuition fees and less expensive cost of living compared with the onshore mode. One year in a BA Finance, Accounting and Management at Nottingham Malaysia, for example, costs about £6500, compared with approximately £12,000 if the same programme was to be taken in the UK campus (The University of Nottingham 2012a, 2012b). Studying outside the United Kingdom therefore helped ease the financial burden of the interviewees, who generally came from more modest middle-class backgrounds and who lacked accessible economic capital to study entirely overseas. Almost all participants relied on their parents to finance their studies and living expenses.

A UK degree, although pursued in the home country, constituted the same institutionalized cultural capital (Bourdieu 1997) that symbolized and certified the possession of high technical and English proficiency and independent, critical and hands-on knowledge. These are strengths that the participants deemed crucial as they carved out their positional advantage (Brown 2003) in a time of credential inflation (Collins 1979) where more exclusive credentials and characteristics were required to stand out in a congested graduate labour market. There were many instances where the participants stressed the need for economic security and stability in their lives, to which a degree was thought to be the best guarantee and the bare minimum to have to 'become like middle class' (Hisham). A degree was the 'safety net' (Mushamir) to depend on for paid full-time employment. It was a 'security blanket' (Elaine) to absorb any possible setbacks or failures in freelancing and self-employment ventures that a few participants were considering. Furthermore, engaging in UK offshore and transnational education was a strategy to distance the self from a rigid culture of 'spoon feeding' and being 'spoon fed' (Nadia); that is, of rote learning and teaching that were especially prevalent in public institutions. Public university students were described as 'not very rounded' (Elaine), 'very narrow minded' (Mushamir), 'very very shy' (Rosli) and 'brainwash[ed]' (Mushamir) into accepting government propaganda. The participants chose to study in the private sector as they believed their education encouraged them to be 'more outspoken' (Sze Theng), 'more open-minded', 'confident' and to 'think freely' (Imran). The pragmatic motive of building up valuable work skills was tied with the intrinsic motivation for personal development. Pursued for both instrumental and non-pecuniary rewards, a UK external education offered perceived higher valued cultural capital to the interviewees without stretching them too far economically. Similarly, the lower cost of UK transnational education in Hong Kong compared with studies overseas appealed to the transnational students and graduates in Waters and Leung's (2012) study. However, while non-participation in domestic universities left Waters and Leung's (2012) participants with a sense of failure and inferiority, my participants felt none of that as they had better trust in the quality and prestige of UK education relative to a domestic one. The perceived worth of a UK education therefore differed across geographical locations.

High academic and social worth

Underlying my participants' preference for UK education is the belief that it offered high status and recognition, the symbolic capital (Bourdieu 1986) essential to assert superior worth in Malaysia. The interviewees subscribed to a perceived status hierarchy of study destinations and, by extension, educational systems and modes of study. A UK education obtained in the United Kingdom was placed at the top of this hierarchy. Education in the United States and Australia typically occupied the second and third spots, followed by education in a few other advanced countries such as Japan, New Zealand and Singapore. UK offshore and transnational studies were located in the middle ranks of the hierarchy, leading other sources of external international education in Malaysia. Malaysian public education was in most cases positioned at the lower end of the hierarchy. In the same rank or at the bottom was education in or from developing and less developed countries. The ready and unquestioned acceptance of British standards and influences as best is evidence of colonial legacy in Malaysia (Sin 2009), which still thrives more than half a century since independence. The following narratives give a sense of how the participants aspired for prestige by associating their programmes with the symbolic elitism of the United Kingdom:

> I don't know exactly but somehow, you have this perception that the standard of the other universities here [Malaysia] are not as good … So, the UK is like up there, the best. The rankings would be UK and then Monash and then the local universities. Somehow or rather, we do get this impression. Ya, I'm having a UK-based education and it's a lot better than other people are getting … I don't know whether it's because of influence coz not many Malaysian children grew up like, 'Oh, I want to get into a Malaysian university' [laughs], to be honest. (Elaine)

> UK, people will think, more reliable … If you get a degree from Indonesia, people will then, 'Argh' [makes sound to suggest disgust and distrust]. People will think the better one is from the West. I think people look at economy lah. If that country, economy ok, the university has create a name in the world. (Rosli)

Cultural capital obtained through higher education does not have a fixed conversion rate as different sources and modes of study potentially offer varying levels of transferability to economic and social privilege. A UK offshore or transnational education was the consolation prize, 'the next best thing' (Nadia) for my participants who believed that they still enjoyed exclusivity, although not of the highest form that was achievable only by studying onshore. This adds perspective to existing literature (Huang 2002; Waters 2005, 2006; Kim 2011; Sin 2009) on the different gradations of western cultural capital in the global academic field, where the more modest, external, foreign middle-class student experiences and negotiates relative privilege and deprivation.

Less direct experiences of the United Kingodm

The lack or absence of direct exposure to an environment overseas was to the participants the main disadvantage of studying in Malaysia. Embarrassment and inadequateness were felt to some degree as they were unable to directly or substantially experience the academic and wider socio-cultural and physical spaces within the United Kingdom and the surrounding region. Wah Seong had just returned to Malaysia from his one-year study exchange at Nottingham's UK campus when he agreed to be interviewed. He expressed unfulfillment over his inability to study entirely in Nottingham: 'I have sense of regret in me that I can't have the opportunity to graduate in the UK. Ya, coz as much as I want to do the full programme there, it's too costly. It's out of my control'. The twinning students I spoke to in the focus group were set to depart for Manchester the following year. While access to sufficient economic capital enabling their eventual studies overseas could be read as privilege, they saw it as deprivation. They expressed impatience in moving to the United Kingdom where many of their close friends already were:

Chloe: It's more of like all my friends are overseas. I have to go overseas [everyone laughs]. It's not like they will envy me. If I don't go, I will be left out.

Do you feel that way? Do you feel left out?

[Unanimous yes]

Hui Ching: All my friends are overseas. Even like if they're still in Malaysia, … it's because they are doing a twinning programme also. So, they intend to be in the UK eventually.

Salehah: Just that we're going there one year later than them [everyone else laughed].

Although the UK degree certificate, the institutionalized cultural capital, carried a similar university brand name, it is clear that UK education held divergent meanings to the participants, based on the mode through which it was obtained. Limited to no direct knowledge and experience of studies and life in the United Kingdom meant having fewer opportunities to immerse in much desired foreign dispositions and experiences that conferred higher prestige and respectability.

Participants who would complete their education in Malaysia anticipated a lack of appreciation of their mode of study in the labour market, as opposed to their onshore counterparts who were believed to enjoy higher status recognition. Mushamir and Elaine, both students at Nottingham Malaysia, learned of the different and unequal exchange values of a UK education, the former while applying for PhD funding and the latter during an interview for an internship. In both cases, they expressed disappointment over the relatively lower symbolic and economic capital benefits that came with their externally acquired foreign cultural capital:

> People ask you where you study. You answer, 'University of Nottingham'. Then they're like excited and then they say, 'Nottingham, UK?' Then you say, 'Oh no, Nottingham, Malaysia.' They'll go like [gave disappointed look, lowered shoulders and looked downward], 'Oh ...'.
>
> How do you feel when people give you that reaction?
>
> It's quite depressing actually. Because like they don't see you as a Nottingham graduate. They don't see you as a UK degree holder. They see you as a local graduate, you know, something like that. (Mushamir)

> This is the scenario that we were made to feel. Everybody says, 'The degree is the same' and then they are like, ' No' ... the employer would ask you which campus you studied at ... The thing is, you can't really explain that mentality. It's pretty much urm the whole anything from the West is a lot better than here kind of mentality, even though you can't justify it coz it is the same degree, you know. (Elaine)

Elaine's comment especially suggests workings of neo-colonialism in the global education marketplace, which while largely invisible, in that they were hard to pinpoint and articulate, held much of Malaysian society, especially the older generation (Sin 2009), captive to standards in the United Kingdom and by extension in advanced western countries (Sidhu 2006; Alatas 1972). This meant that the onshore mode of international education tended to be regarded as the epitome of excellence and authenticity while the credibility of new and alternative modes of study, such as the participants' that did not require substantial time, if at all, to be spent overseas, was questioned. Not surprisingly, the interviewees acknowledged the probable inconvenience of having to justify and defend the equal worth of their eventual UK institutionalized cultural capital.

Another disadvantage of being geographically distant to the source country of education is the inability to substantially immerse in the adventure and excitement of living out the imaginings the participants had of the United Kingdom. It remains Nadia's dream to study in Durham to absorb its architecture and quaint surroundings:

> Durham, to be really honest, it's because of the campus. They have a world heritage site, the cathedral, in the campus. Ever since I was a kid, I always knew I wanted to study in the UK because of the gorgeous building.

Other features of the wider environment overseas that fascinated the participants were the wider mix of nationalities to interact with, the opportunity to live independently by 'staying in dorms' (Sue Ern), the proximity to Europe that enabled cheaper and more convenient travels and, amusingly, the 'gloomy weather' (Salehah). This suggests wishful desire for educational tourism (Ritchie 2003) where academic pursuits overseas could be accompanied by educational and leisure travel activities. Enhanced embodied cultural capital from this experience could help build better confidence, life-stories and adaptability, leading to higher positional advantage in the Malaysian labour market, as Kor Ming imagined it to be:

> The reason why they [employers] choose overseas is because they [onshore graduates] tend to talk more about themselves ... The self-esteem is higher lah ... let's say your company is dealing in the international market, it's easier for you to adapt to cultures. If let's say it's UK, it'll be an advantage straightaway. You know how to adapt quickly.

All in all, being physically distant from the core of the global knowledge production system – that is, the West – came with perceived limitations in terms of the accumulation of marketable, high-status embodied cultural capital and personal enrichment. As foreign cultural capital does not provide exposure to a prescribed, static set of dispositions and experiences, its conversion into economic and symbolic capitals is not as straightforward and uniform as commonly assumed to be. This brings to light the possible negative effects of cultural capital on middle-class occupational and status advancement.

Proximity to home and culture of complacency

Although the participants aspired to be overseas, remaining in the home country came with the advantage of being able to attend to place-specific needs and responsibilities. The education decision-making process does not solely involve a rational cost–benefit projection of material and social rewards as values and principles can regulate positional strategies (Ball 2003). For instance, the self-imposed obligation to accompany his aging retired parents and not place unnecessary financial burden on them held Wah Seong back from studying completely in the United Kingdom, which he believed had better economic and status opportunities. With personal, familial and emotional considerations factored in, an offshore education, followed by a possible job search in a better-paying neighbouring country, offered a life-chance trajectory that was more geographically and morally suited for him:

> Personal ones. I do not want to be overseas for that long. So I guess the one year exchange programme was perfect.
>
> Why didn't you want to be away longer?
>
> Coz my brother is already working there. He has been away from home for the 6th year now. So, if I'm in the UK as well, my parents, they'll be home alone because there's only me and my brother.
>
> Do they want you to be here?
>
> They didn't say. My parents are retirees already. They're approaching 60. They're not that young anymore. So if I get a job in Singapore, it's not that far away. At least it's not that far.

In another example, although without choice, Nadia remained in the home country, in accordance with the wishes of her single parent and grandparents who wanted to take care of her while she studied: 'I'm still in the comforts of my home. I still live with my family. They don't exactly allow me to stay on campus. I'm the only grandchild, so the family is very protective'. Studying externally provided many participants like Nadia with the comfort and convenience of a home that they shared with their parents out of financial and obligatory reasons.

The perceived downside of being in the home country, however, is that the local environment placed no significant pressure or motivation on the interviewees to quickly absorb and be open to valuable foreign influences and experiences. With the comfort of familiarity with the home surroundings came a tendency to subscribe to a culture of complacency where the local and known were accepted and reproduced while the new and foreign, although welcomed, were not actively sought after. Kor Ming believed that little effort was made by offshore and transnational students to speak formal standard English due to the widespread use of colloquial Malaysian English in the home country: 'If you're in Malaysia, you tend to accept the Malaysian way of speaking. But if you're in UK, you'll tend to adapt very fast'. For Nadia, the centrality of the family in her student life led to taken-for-grantedness that did not push her to think and act independently:

> When you go overseas, you're basically in new territory. You have to be independent. You're forced to be independent ... When there is a problem, you have to fix it whereas if you're staying here, compared to someone who had the education here, you know, you still have your parents with you.

In other cases, limited student diversity, particularly in smaller private institutions without a self-contained campus, limited the participants' exposure to a truly international experience that they associated with a world-class UK education. With only 15 students in his intake, most of whom were locals, there was a lack of opportunity and initiative on Hisham's part to build social capital: 'I can meet the same type of people outside ... Wherever I talk to them, it's always the same things. It's like a tape recorder, so, I don't want to talk again'. For Sze Theng, a transnational music student, a small student population at her institution led to the mundane routine of 'meeting the same few people', which did not inspire her to cultivate a stronger drive for technical excellence:

> If there are more people, you will be more motivated because you see other people practising a lot, studying a lot. It's like my college has so little people ... so the best students, maybe 1 or 2. But those people overseas, maybe there are a number of them, so you have to practise harder to reach that level.

On the whole, the interviewees were tied down to local circumstances, norms and obligations that did not significantly encourage and enable them to seek out a more global experience in their UK education. UK tertiary education does not potentially offer a standard global exchange value as the student's contextual environment frames the degree of possibility and motivation to optimize the enhancement of valued embodied cultural, social and linguistic capital.

Accumulating local cultural capital

A natural inclination towards local ways of knowing, being and speaking when studying in Malaysia is not without positional benefits as the participants highlighted the practical relevance of local cultural capital in the employment arena. Those who would study mostly or entirely in the home country qualified that it would provide them with continuity in the home surroundings, helping them to be more in touch with Malaysian values, norms and expectations that were essential for local employment. Offshore students, in particular, believed that they were receiving a distinct form of education in its own right as they experienced 'the best of both worlds' (Nadia). 'Rather than having [a] Malaysian education or a UK education, you have a UK education in Malaysia', Nadia emphasized, suggesting her relative strength in situating foreign cultural capital into the local context. The participants believed that by being rooted in Malaysia they had better opportunities to enhance local knowledge and social networks:

> I know how to speak, what to say in an interview, as compared to someone educated overseas ... you kind of know the culture, you know the person, you know what people are looking for, you know what kind of products can cater for the Malaysian market. (Elaine)

> It's an advantage because of me not going overseas when I was 18, 19. I get to meet a lot of business people and those are people who are now very close. And because it's local, it's easier to run around, follow them, learn technical skills ... from them. (Kor Ming)

As much as they aspired to study entirely in the United Kingdom, the interviewees realized that local cultural capital held more functional relevance that would give them a head start in the transition into the home labour market. What this means theoretically is that cultural capital of the local and the masses which is less scarce and exclusive can offer wider economic capital opportunities, if not always higher social recognition. Little attention has been given in international education literature to the potential positional rewards of owning common cultural capital. A recent exception is Brooks, Waters, and Pimlott-Wilson's (2012) work on UK students studying abroad, which reveals that the scarcity of overseas-acquired foreign cultural capital was not valued as much in the home labour market as mass local cultural capital obtained domestically.

Aspects of local cultural capital that my interviewees believed were their strong points include spontaneity in using colloquial Malaysian English and willingness to adopt a softer, more submissive interaction style, indicative of Asian reverence for authority and seniority. This is not to say that my informants subscribed to an either/or strategy in which they drew from one consistent source of cultural capital – that is, the local or the foreign – to construct a self-image to project. Their narratives reflect sensitivity and adaptability towards interactional and situational possibilities in their future employment:

> Especially in the Malaysian context, a lot of that is present in the minds of employers that they want someone who is humble and who is pretty down to earth and who is willing to learn, is teachable, as opposed to someone you ... come from [puts on posh Londoner accent], 'Oh, you know, I have a degree from Cambridge and therefore, I can tell you a thing or two about the law'. (Francis)

> Got to check who you meet. Because if you meet a person who is always lower class, if you show that you're too confident too much, they'll call it

arrogant. If you go to a higher person from a higher class and go to him, to them, you're a friend. It means, you know what you are doing, I give you some trust and let's see what you can do ... If I see that the person is from lower, have to go a bit more *pasar* [Malay: market, refers in this context to colloquial, pidgin speech typically used by the lower and modest middle class], so have to talk in a more friendly way. (Hisham)

The key was flexibility, drawing on local knowledge to 'feel on the spot' (Elaine) and display on a case-by-case basis the skills, attributes and dispositions that would provide a good 'fit' (Elaine) with different segments of Malaysian society. This would involve picking up cues from the personality, speech, body language and other personal embodiment of individuals they would come into interaction with and to adjust accordingly. In this sense, the participants planned to personalize their cultural capital by portraying an individualized set of technical competences and inter-personal qualities (Brown and Hesketh 2004, 36) that would provide finer distinctions between the self and similarly qualified credential bearers. Care would be taken to personalize and employ local and foreign embodied cultural capital in appropriate amounts and combinations to build stronger inter-personal relations of trust and inclusiveness across different economic and social divides.

The participants believed that as much as western cultural capital was likely to give a positive impression of a candidate's technical and social competences, it had to be sensibly utilized because a display of excesses could backfire in the conversion to job entry and advancement. Moderation or striking a 'middle ground', as Hisham called it, was important. Rajadurai (2004, 54–55) explains that colloquial Malaysian English, when used in casual and semi-formal interactions, conjures a sense of solidarity and camaraderie among Malaysians, even among those fluent in higher-level standard English. My participants understood this well and were prepared to play down a confident, outspoken approach and English proficiency when interacting with individuals of presumably local or inferior forms of cultural capital ownership and to only shift upwards to assertive, 'formal correct English' (Francis) in high-level interactions. The idea was to put people 'at ease' (Francis), as heavy display of UK cultural capital could be read as plain acts of social snobbery and pretension. The participants believed that humility would give them an added advantage over onshore students whom they generalized as arrogant and unable to adjust to local rules and conditions for economic and social integration. This suggests that securing positional advantage may require not so much a maximization of foreign cultural capital but a careful moderation of its appropriation, use and display to suit the specificities of the local context. Positional competition in higher education is getting more intense but to view it as a war field of vicious players fighting to win entry into elite graduate jobs (Brown, Lauder, and Ashton 2011; Brown and Hesketh 2004) obscures aspects of self-regulation and humility in cultural capital accumulation and activation. Framing this in the context of Asian middle-class social mobility, there is a need to account for how individuals attempt to balance western cultural capital with local awareness and sensitivity to achieve status differentiation without overly flaunting difference at others.

Social divisions and complexities of positional competition

The participants anticipated that status differentiation is made more complex by social divisions such as age, ethnicity, gender and nationality. In relation to age, they believed that the Malaysian work setting typically prioritized and rewarded seniority based on chronological age and length of employment above actual merits and abilities. A young age was anticipated to usually open up situations where the substance of embodied cultural capital – that is, work-related attributes and dispositions – would be scrutinized and any work contribution played down or resisted by those higher in seniority. For example, 24-year-old Mushamir imagined that the Malaysian public work sector tended to favour older and longer-serving employees, thus limiting career advancement opportunities for young credentialled entrants: 'It's very hard to get to the top because they don't care how good you are, how *rajin* [Malay: hard working] you are. They don't care about it. They say you're junior. Let the senior to go [for promotion]'. In certain occupational fields, however, 'a young age would help a lot', 22-year-old Elaine believed as she made reference to her planned entry into food and entertainment within the private sector. She anticipated that a young age, coupled with presentation of a youthful, vibrant disposition, would help create favourable impressions of her knowledge on current consumer trends and patterns:

> Because you have to be on top of things, to know what's new because that is what the entertainment industry is about, everything that is current ... Personality as well because you can be physically young, but if you're not into new things, it won't help as well.

Age, which forms an aspect of physical embodied capital (Bourdieu 1986), was therefore expected by the participants to influence external judgements of their labour-market worth, leading to positional advantage and disadvantage, depending on the context.

The participants believed that ethnicity was just as relevant in determining entry, integration and advancement in the Malaysian labour market. Sin (2009) found in a study of onshore Malaysian students in Manchester that ethnic minority participants, known as non-*bumiputera* Malaysians and made up of the Chinese, Indians and other minority ethnicities, were particularly attracted to employment in the Malaysian private sector due to the anticipated higher income and a more ethnically equitable opportunity structure. State-endorsed ethnic-based affirmative action policies and practices in Malaysia have since 1971 provided privileges in favour of the politically dominant and economically inferior ethnic majority *bumiputera*s in areas such as preferential access to certain public institutions of higher learning, government funding for tertiary studies, public-sector recruitment, professional and managerial employment in the public and, to a lesser extent, private sectors and financial assistance for corporate equity and home ownership (Lee, Gomez, and Yacob 2013). As Mushamir, a Malay *bumiputera* who was bonded to work with the Malaysian government after graduation, acknowledged: 'I think for Malaysia, we all know. For government, of course, they prefer Malay'. Noticeably, all my non-*bumiputera* participants believed that the rules and norms within the *bumiputera*-dominant public employment arena tended to work to the disadvantage of members of their ethnic group while the reverse usually occurred in the private economic sphere that was controlled by Chinese Malaysians. A UK institutionalized cultural capital, when held with the ascribed ethnic membership in Malaysia, was therefore expected to have inclusionary and exclusionary effects on positional chances in the public and private employment sectors.

While nationality was perceived to be irrelevant in influencing chances of permanent employment in Malaysia, it was likely to be an issue if the participants were to look for work in the United Kingdom. They were aware that their eventual qualification, coupled with the geo-political status of Malaysia as a non-European Economic Area country, offered no immediate legitimacy to enter, work and live in the United Kingdom upon graduation. International students based outside the United Kingdom were not eligible for the post-study visa that up to April 2011 was available to onshore international students upon graduation. Given the opportunity, however, many interviewees aspired to work in the United Kingdom for the anticipated better income and work conditions and higher status attached to the experience of work and life in an advanced western country. Essentially, institutionalized foreign cultural capital, obtained offshore or transnationally, is subjected to tighter political–legal conditions and rules that constrain its convertibility into global employment.

With regards to gender, the participants were of the opinion that males would usually gain more immediate symbolic capital (Bourdieu 1986) than females by the simple virtue of being male. For example, 'People think men are more reliable, men can motivate more than girl lah', Rosli, a male student, said in reference to career opportunities in management in Malaysia. Reliability and leadership were presented as masculine and mature dispositions embedded in males. 'Men' in this sense have gender-labelled cultural capital naturally contained in the physical body, which may not require any real activation to yield its exchange value benefits. The use of the word 'girl' rather than women aptly reflects gender and age status gaps in

Malaysia, which the participants believed could potentially add and detract economic and social worth in a way that challenged the stability of UK cultural capital in offering desired employment, trust and recognition. While knowledge, skills and inter-personal qualities can be personalized (Brown and Hesketh 2004, 36) and presented in appropriate amounts and combinations, the social divisions in which the participants were located were, for the most part, visible markers of physical difference that could not be conveniently disguised and altered to generate favourable impressions in all contexts. This essentially presented further complexities to their perceived chances of gaining economic and social advantages.

Conclusion

This article has discussed the perceived role of UK cultural capital, gained through offshore and transnational education, in the occupational and status advancement of middle-class Malaysian students. I argued that cultural capital does not have a constant exchange value across different geographical, interactional and situational contexts. The pursuit for distinction in Malaysia is further complicated by social divisions such as ethnicity, age, gender and nationality. Therefore, an in-depth exploration of the link between cultural capital and distinction has to pay attention to the specificities of the individual, structural and socio-relational contexts in question. My paper extends beyond the scope of existing literature by highlighting the functional value of the more common local cultural capital and the potential negative currency of foreign cultural capital. It problematizes the taken-for-granted singularity of the practice of cultural capital accumulation and activation which comes with the assumption that Asian international students would without question embrace western dispositions and experiences to secure positional advantage. I refute the dominant assumption in the literature that scarcity and exclusivity define the higher worth of cultural capital, showing that local cultural capital owned by the masses can be privileged currency as well. Flexible and moderate appropriation of foreign and local cultural capital, as opposed to maximum utilization of either one, poses the solution for external international students to manage different demands and expectations on them in the home country. My focus on students from generally more modest middle-class backgrounds adds depth and specificity to the investigation of status differentiation among the foreign student middle-class whose heterogeneity has not been given adequate attention. Above all, this article has offered a critical exploration of foreign cultural capital in the global academic marketplace, bringing detail to the intricacies and contradictions surrounding the applicability of western cultural capital in Asia.

My research, however, has limitations which present opportunities for future development. Given resource limitations, I did not interview students of distance learning programmes, but I am aware that virtual education can provide a take on how non-physical and less direct contact with UK cultural capital are experienced and managed to advance life-chance aspirations. Efforts of my participants to claim a bigger slice of positional worth through assertions of localization raises the question as to whether and by how much local cultural capital hold similar meanings for students in the Malaysian public education sector. An investigation into this can potentially offer fresh perspectives on mass and less exclusive forms of cultural capital as a mobilizing and all too assumed debilitating force for economic and social ascent.

The global educational landscape, particularly sites of offshore and transnational education, will continue to expand with the widening of the middle class in rising developing countries in Asia that seeks tertiary education as the means to an affluent life. This brings with it new rules, aspirations and experiences of distinction for the middle class. In light of this unprecedented development, there is much opportunity to critically extend Bourdieu's concept of cultural capital to explicate status differentiation within other key and emerging source markets of external international education. Research in this direction holds the promise of piecing together a rich story of lived experiences of the many intricate layers and relations of hierarchical distinction in the global education marketplace. It is indeed time for the 'other' foreign student to be less foreign in the literature.

Acknowledgements

I would like to thank Ross Bond and Janette Webb of the University of Edinburgh and the reviewers for their helpful comments.

References

Aihara, A. 2009. "Paradoxes of Higher Education Reforms: Implications on the Malaysian Middle Class." *International Journal of Asia Pacific Studies* 5 (1): 81–113.

Alatas, S. H. 1972. "The Captive Mind in Development Studies: Some Neglected Problems and the Need for an Autonomous Social Science Tradition in Asia." *International Social Sciences Journal* 34 (1): 9–25.

Ball, S. 2003. *Class Strategies and the Education Market*. London: RoutledgeFalmer.

Bourdieu, P. 1986. *Distinction: A Social Critique of the Judgement of Taste*. Trans. R. Nice. New York: Routledge.

Bourdieu, P. 1997. "The Forms of Capital." In *Education: Culture, Economy, and Society*, edited by A. H. Hasley, H. Lauder, P. Brown, and A. M. Wells, 40–58. Oxford: Oxford University Press.

Bourdieu, P. 1998. *Practical Reason*. Stanford: Stanford University Press.

Bourdieu, P., and J.-C. Passeron. 1977. *Reproduction in Education, Society and Culture*. London: Sage Publications.

British Council 2010. "UK Qualifications in your own Country." http://www.educationuk.org/Malaysia/A-UK-education/ways-to-study-in-the-uk/uk-qualifications-in-your-own-country.

Brooks, R., J. Waters, and H. Pimlott-Wilson. 2012. "International Education and the Employability of UK Students." *British Educational Research Journal* 38 (2): 281–298.
Brown, P. 2003. "The Opportunity Trap: Education and Employment in a Global Economy." *European Educational Research Journal* 2 (1): 141–179.
Brown, P., and A. Hesketh. 2004. *The Mismanagement of Talent*. Oxford: Oxford University Press.
Brown, P., H. Lauder, and D. Ashton. 2011. *The Global Auction: The Broken Promises of Education, Jobs and Income*. New York: Oxford University Press.
Collins, R. 1979. *The Credential Society: An Historical Sociology of Education and Stratification*. New York: Academic Press.
Devine, F. 2004. *Class Practices*. Cambridge: Cambridge University Press.
Huang, H. 2002. "Overseas Chinese Studies and the Rice of Foreign Cultural Capital in Modern China." *International Sociology* 17 (1): 35–55.
Katsomitros, A. 2012. "International Branch Campuses: Even More Developments. The Observatory on Borderless Higher Education." http://www.obhe.ac.uk/newsletters/borderless_report_march_2012/international_branch_campuses_even_more_developments.
Kim, J. 2011. "Aspiration for Global Cultural Capital in the Stratified Realm of Global Higher Education: Why Do Korean Students Go to US Graduate Schools?" *British Journal of Sociology of Education* 32 (1): 109–126.
Lee, M. 2004. *Restructuring Higher Education in Malaysia*. Penang: Universiti Sains Malaysia.
Lee, H. A. 2013. "Ethnicity, Economy and Affirmative Action in Malaysia." In *Affirmative Action, Ethnicity and Conflict*, edited by E. T. Gomez and R. Premdas, 67–94. Abingdon: Routledge.
Mason, J. 2002. *Qualitative Researching*. 2nd ed. London: Sage Publications.
Nayagam, J. 2011. "Heriot-Watt to Open Doors in Malaysia. The Edge." http://www.theedgemalaysia.com/sports/196437-heriot-watt-to-open-doors-in-msia.html.
Ong, A. 1999. *Flexible Citizenship: The Cultural Logics of Transnationality*. Durham: Duke University Press.
Rajadurai, J. 2004. "The Faces and Facets of English in Malaysia." *English Today* 20 (4): 54–58.
Ritchie, B. 2003. *Managing Educational Tourism*. Clevedon: Channel View Publications.
Sharma, Y. 2012. "Branch Campus Growth has Moved to Asia." University World News. http://www.universityworldnews.com/article.php?story=20120113083126934.
Sidhu, R. 2006. *Universities and Globalization: To Market, to Market*. New Jersey: Erlbaum Associates.
Sin, I.-L. 2009. "The Aspiration for Social Distinction: Malaysian Students in a British University." *Studies in Higher Education* 34 (3): 285–299.
Tan, S.-C. 2010. Tops for TNE. *The Star*, August 1.
The University of Nottingham. 2012a. "Student Fees and Finance." http://www.nottingham.ac.uk/fees/tuitionfees/undergraduatecourses.aspx.
The University of Nottingham, 2012b. "Undergraduate Tuition Fees for 2012–2013." http://www.nottingham.edu.my/Applications/Fees/UG.aspx.
UNESCO Institute for Statistics. 2012. "Higher Education." http://www.uis.unesco.org/Education/Pages/tertiary-education.aspx.
University of Reading. 2011. "Project Timescale." http://www.reading.ac.uk/malaysia/about/uorm-project-timescale.aspx.

University of Southampton. 2012. "Our Malaysian Campus." http://www.southampton.ac.uk/my/campuses/index.page?

Waters, J. 2005. "Transnational Family Strategies and Education in the Contemporary Chinese Diaspora." *Global Networks* 5 (4): 359–377.

Waters, J. 2006. "Geographies of Cultural Capital: Education, International Migration and Family Strategies between Hong Kong and Canada." *Transactions of the Institute of British Geographers* 31 (2): 179–192.

Waters, J., and M. Leung. 2012. "Young People and the Reproduction of Disadvantage through Transnational higher Education in Hong Kong." *Sociological Research Online* 17 (3):1–8.

Meritocracy and the *Gaokao*: a survey study of higher education selection and socio-economic participation in East China

Ye Liu

School of Education, Bath Spa University, Bath, UK

> Meritocracy is a powerful ideology that was used by the Chinese Communist Party during China's transition to a market economy. With the *Gaokao* in particular, higher education selection became an ideal vehicle for the Party to associate itself with the ideology of meritocracy. This article investigates the extent to which higher education selection was based on meritocratic principles in contemporary China. A survey study involving around 960 first-year students was conducted in 2007 in two provinces. The statistical analysis did not suggest a strong socio-economic selection. However, a cultural selectivity was indicated in predicting students' *Gaokao* performance as well as their chances of getting into elite universities. Socio-demographic factors appeared to be more significant than socio-economic status in affecting students' higher education opportunities.

Introduction

Meritocracy has been an enduring theme in modern sociological research. The rise of meritocracy theory was related to dramatic changes in economic, occupational and technological domains after the Second World War in western post-industrial societies (Young 1958; Bell 1973; Goldthorpe 1996). However, there is little empirical evidence to support the notion of a significant trend towards meritocracy in these societies (Breen and Goldthorpe 2001; Whelan and Layte 2002). Intergenerational inheritance has been persistently identified in educational and occupational attainment (Jackson 2007; Arrow, Bowles, and Durlauf 2000). Therefore, meritocracy exists more in belief than reality. The ideology of meritocracy, however, has such an evident attraction that it has been embodied in a variety of political ideologies. It is widely accepted as being an important element of various European centre-left political discourses, particularly of 'New Labour' in

Britain (Goldthorpe and Jackson 2007, 4). The European Union has identified meritocracy as being a key criterion in assessing candidate states for membership of the Union (Vachudova 2005). It has also ostensibly been a key principle in recruitment to jobs in major international organizations such as the IMF and the OECD (Birdsall 2011). Meritocracy exists as a powerful ideology because it represents a type of social selection that, at least nominally, transcends ascriptive boundaries, such as class, gender, ethnicity and nationality, and where there is a positive association between merit and commonly-desired opportunities and rewards.

Meritocracy, as an ideology with powerful political attraction, was also used by the Chinese Communist Party during China's transition to the market society. Dramatic changes that took place in 1978 in China have significance beyond the obvious implications of the Reform and Opening-up. More than 30 years of economic growth, with an annual average rate of 9.6% (Zakaria 2008), was accompanied by enduring social problems, including sharply increasing inequality, environmental pollution, and rudimentary health services. The Chinese Communist Party, however, remained relatively secure in the regime. It has been argued that the Party held society together with a transformed ideology, which involved manipulating feelings of patriotism and rejuvenating traditional values and cultures (Spence 2008; Lall and Vickers 2009). Moreover, the promotion of an education-based meritocracy was an important chapter in this transformed ideology.

This article examines how meritocracy was used by the Chinese Communist Party to deal with dramatic socio-economic and political circumstances during the reform period, and how higher education selection became an ideal vehicle with which the Party could associate itself with the ideology of meritocracy. I begin by outlining the research area, which investigates the relationship between education and meritocracy, before moving on to different theoretical perspectives applied in the Chinese context. I then address some attributes of China as a case for investigating the implications of the ideology of meritocracy. I use a survey study conducted in Anhui and Zhejiang (East China) in 2007 to examine the extent to which contemporary higher education selection was based on meritocratic criteria. This small-scale survey was used as the primary data source mainly because there is a lack of national data on students' socio-economic backgrounds and other demographic information and because it is difficult to collect at a comprehensive level the data that represent all Chinese provinces. This survey study is, of course, inevitably limited as a means of mapping out a general picture of social inequality in higher education in contemporary China. However, the article is able to provide a suggestive analysis with regard to socio-economic participation in higher education in East China. Methodological issues concerning this survey study will be specifically addressed in the following sections. A statistical analysis is then presented to argue the implications of the meritocracy ideology on the Party's overall development strategy and on the life-chances of different social groups.

Education and meritocracy

Meritocracy has been a controversial sociological term. Broadly speaking, meritocracy means 'a large-scale social system in which a positive relationship exists between merit and such commonly desired values as income, power, and prestige' (Krauze and Slomczynski 1985, 623). Merit has been interpreted as educational qualifications (Bell 1973) or intelligence plus effort (Young 1958, 94). Despite the disputed definition of merit, formal education is used as the key variable to measure meritocracy and the educational system is regarded as a selection mechanism that measures and rewards merit (Olneck and Crouse 1979; Goldthorpe 1996). This article focuses primarily on education-based meritocracy instead of a multifaceted social selection, mainly because of the central role of education in examining the process of social status attainment from social origin to destination in the meritocracy thesis (Lipset and Zetterberg 1959; Bell 1973).

Educational meritocracy is often used as a notion with two complementary aspects: how social origin impacts on educational opportunities and achievement; and how merit measured by educational outcomes is related to social destination, which specifically refers to students' destination in types of higher education in this article. As far as meritocratic selection is concerned, educational attainment should not only reflect an individual's ability (or intelligence plus effort) rather than his or her social origin, but it also should promise opportunities and rewards. According to meritocracy theory, an education-based meritocracy can be said to exist where educational attainment is unrelated to social origin and a decisive influence on social destination.

Regarding the first aspect of educational meritocracy – that is, how social origin impacts on education – socio-economic characteristics are treated by Breen and Jonsson (2005) and Jackson (2007) as being the crucial indicator for assessing barriers to meritocratic selection in education. However, these studies mainly focus on western industrial or post-industrial societies. Extending this theoretical perspective to the Chinese context requires highlighting some context-related issues. Most scholarship on educational selection in the context of China has followed the tradition of development theory, which has predominantly focused on gender and regional disparities as key factors that generated glaring inequality in educational attainment (Li and Tsang 2003; Hannum and Wang 2006). Empirical evidence has tested and further confirmed the standpoints of development theory, arguing that the uneven distribution of educational resources and the socially/culturally differentiated expectations of males and females are factors in educational selection based on meritocratic principles (Li and Tsang 2003; Hannum and

Park 2007; Hannum, Wang, and Adams 2008). Little research has been conducted to examine specifically the extent to which socio-economic status impacts on educational selection in contemporary China. Hence, in this article variables such as geographical origin and gender will be used as characteristics of an individual's demographic background along with socio-economic status when evaluating educational selection in China.

Theories on the in/equality of educational opportunities illustrate further the implication of social origin for education. Maximally Maintained Inequality (MMI) theory provides one perspective on the implications of the expansion of educational opportunities for meritocratic selection in education. According to this theory, the effect of social class on educational attainment should decline after a given level of education becomes universal for the upper social class (Raftery and Hout 1993). While they have reached a threshold, the expansion of educational opportunities allows lower social groups to advance. MMI theory argues that socio-economic characteristics impact more significantly on educational attainment at the higher level rather than at the basic level, because this is where the ceiling is reached. However, MMI theory was developed in the context of western industrial societies and may not apply in the same way in the context of China. Universal access to compulsory education in China was provided in urban areas prior to the rural areas. Data on access to compulsory education by the age cohort (7–16 year olds) from 1993 to 2004 show a 10-year lag between the rural and urban areas in terms of enrolment rates; that is, 96% of the rural age cohort in 2004 compared with 95% of the urban cohort in 1993 (CHNS 2004). This urban–rural lag in the provision of universal access to compulsory education complicates the picture of the socio-economic differences in access to educational opportunities.

The lag has significant implications for the patterns of access to post-compulsory education, particularly higher education opportunities. It has been argued that universal access to compulsory education up to secondary schooling provided a crucial demographic base for the expansion of higher education in the experiences of most post-War western societies (Shavit and Blossfeld 1993). In China, higher education has expanded at an unprecedented rate since the mid-1990s, a time prior to rural universal

Table 1. Age participation ratio of students in higher education in China from 1990 to 2006.

	Percentage of 20–24 age group
1990	1.5 (1.58 million)
1998	9.8 (8.5 million)
2006	21 (23 million)

Source: China Statistics Year Book 1991, 1999, 2007 (National Bureau of Statistics 1991, 1999, 2007).

access to compulsory education. Table 1 shows the expansion of student numbers as a percentage of the 20–24 age cohorts from 1990 to 2006. The number of students in higher education increased from 1.58 million in 1990 to over 23 million in 2006, rising from 1.5 to 21% of the 20–24 age cohort. The Chinese pattern of the expansion of educational opportunities, with the rural–urban lag in providing universal access to compulsory education and a massive expansion of higher education, provides an interesting case to examine the arguments from MMI theory.

The second aspect of educational meritocracy – that is, how merit is related to students' destination – is thoroughly elaborated in Effectively Maintained Inequality (EMI) theory. EMI theory, contrary to MMI theory, argues that the effects of social origin on educational attainment would not decrease, even if a given level of education became universal for advantaged social classes. Instead, more advantaged social classes would seek to secure qualitatively better types of education in the face of the expansion of educational opportunities for other groups. A large number of studies have tested the EMI standpoint with empirical evidence (Lucas 2001; Zimdars 2007). A correspondence between students' socio-economic characteristics, such as socio-economic status and parental education, and their destinations, in types of universities, is suggested from research in a variety of social contexts (Ayalon and Yogev 2005; Duru-Bellat, Kieffer, and Reimer 2008).

Elaborating this theoretical standpoint in the context of China requires a specific examination of the pattern of expansion of higher education. The expansion of higher education opportunities has been accompanied by an increasingly stratified system. The project of building 'world-class'[1] universities prioritized the provision of funding and resources to elite universities (Tier One or the 985 universities) and key universities (Tier Two or the 211 universities). Third-tier and fourth-tier universities,[2] particularly vocational and technological institutions at the provincial level, have been poorly staffed and under-funded. They have had to struggle for resources from the government, and consequently are highly subjected to the vagaries of the unfettered market. This mixed pattern of expansion of higher education in China suggests a qualitative difference in addition to the quantitative difference in the expanded higher education system. Hence, this provides an interesting case to test the EMI argument of the qualitative difference by examining the role of education in mediating intergenerational inheritance and the expansion of educational opportunities in realizing a meritocratic selection.

The Chinese context

China offers some attractive attributes as a case through which to examine the links between the expansion of educational opportunities, the ideology of meritocracy and social inequality. Firstly, China's transition from a

Socialist society to a 'Socialist market economy with Chinese characteristics' since 1978 has had direct effects on the means of social selection. Political affiliation and loyalty were characteristics of social selection in a socialist society to maintain the Communist party as the ruling class (Unger 1982, 3). Recruitment to higher education institutions used to give preference to those from the 'red' classes, including workers, peasants and party members (Li and Walder 2001, 1387). The 'Reform and Opening-up' in 1978 not only marked the economic collapse of Communist production in China, but also the decline of the Party's predominantly political affiliation-based social selection. The *Gaokao* was restored as a key mechanism of structuring higher education opportunities, and the academic performance in the *Gaokao*, instead of political affiliation, became the decisive factor in access to higher education. This transition in China offers an unusual opportunity to investigate the extent to which the *Gaokao* selection is based on meritocratic criteria.

Secondly, coinciding with the dramatic economic changes was the emergence of a more stratified social structure. The pre-Reform society was characterized by egalitarian social groups, which included workers, peasants, soldiers and the Party cadres. However, the opportunity structure that had been dominated by the Communist cadres' hierarchy was opened up to a much wider group of institutions and individuals (Nee and Matthews 1996). Those individuals who had seized the new opportunities that emerged from the redistribution of capital and resources during the market transition formed new social groups, such as entrepreneurs, professionals and cadres transformed to businessmen (Huang 1993; Qin 1999; Duckett 2001). The 'homogeneous peasants class' (Parish 1975) became stratified into different types of agricultural workers in the rural areas and, in a more significant way, between these and peasant migrants to urban areas (Harvey 2005). Moreover, the working class was differentiated in many ways, including between wage labour in the private sector, layoff labour, and unprotected labour in the state-owned enterprises (Walker and Buck 2007). The emergence of a stratified social structure during the transition makes China an interesting case for examining the extent to which social origin impacts on opportunity structures.

Hypotheses, data and variables

This article examines the extent to which higher education selection in contemporary China is based on meritocratic criteria. A hypothesis concerning two aspects of education-based meritocracy developed from the previous analysis is that a meritocratic selection would suggest a weak association between a student's social origin and his or her academic performance, and that the academic performance would lead to corresponding destinations in higher education regardless of social origin. First, a series of hypotheses can be formulated regarding the influence of socio-economic background and socio-demographic characteristics on the *Gaokao* performance. Moreover, socio-economic and demographic backgrounds will be examined along with the *Gaokao* performance in relation to students' destination in types of universities.

Because no single set of national data is available to allow a comprehensive examination of undergraduates' socio-economic characteristics, I conducted a survey study involving around 960 first-year undergraduate students in eight different types of universities in two provinces (Anhui and Zhejiang) in 2007.[3] First-hand empirical research is always subject to some methodological limitations. A possible criticism of this study is that all participants have successfully survived in the *Gaokao* competition. It is therefore possible that this analysis is unable to provide a full picture of the survival rates of different social groups in the higher education selection. Hence, prior to investigating the socio-economic characteristics of the surveyed students, it is necessary to provide a general picture of the survival rate of this birth cohort (1986–1989) through various selection points in the education system. This statistical analysis is generated from data provided in the China Statistical Year Book 2006. Among the sampled students, around 90% were born between 1986 and 1989. At the national level, higher education students are those who successfully survived the junior secondary selection and the senior secondary selection. These survivors account for only around 20% of the correspondent age cohort. Moreover, only 11.6% of these survivals secure a Bachelor degree in higher education institutions (see Table 2). Among these four-year programme higher education institutions, the 985 or Tier One universities are highly selective, recruiting only 3.7% of students who survived the competition in the *Gaokao* for four-year programme opportunities. The 211 or Tier Two universities recruited around 11% of such students. Institutions at Tier Three and Tier Four enrolled the

Table 2. Education careers of those born between 1986 and 1988 in China.

Education career	New entrants (×10,000)[a]	Survival rate of age group (%)[b]
Primary schools 1992–1994	2183.2–2537	
Junior secondary schools 1998–2000	1961.4–2263.3	89.8–89.2
Senior secondary schools 2001–2003	558–752.1	25.6–29.7
Higher education 2004–2006	447.3–546.1	20.5–21.53
Bachelor's degree courses 2006	253.1	11.6

Source: National Bureau of Statistics (2007).
Note: [a]Admission numbers are the average of the years concerned.
[b]The survival rate for primary school entrance is calculated as an average of official figures whereas the other three are calculated relative to the first number.

Table 3. Selection rates for different types of higher education institutions with four-year Bachelor programmes in 2006.

Types of university	Selection rate (%)[a]
985 universities	3.7
211 universities	11
All other universities with four-year programmes	85.3

Source: National Bureau of Statistics (2007).
Note: [a]The selection rate was calculated by a number of indicators. The number of new entrants for the 985 universities was added together from the new entry report published by each individual 985 institution. This number was then divided by the number of Bachelor's degree programme entrants for 2006 given in China Statistical Year Book 2007 (National Bureau of Statistics 2007).

majority of students, accounting for around 85% of students who survived the *Gaokao* in 2006 (see Table 3).

The questionnaires were administered in eight higher education institutions in Anhui and Zhejiang. Four universities were chosen in each province. These higher education institutions were selected from each tier of the higher education system. Table 4 demonstrates how these eight universities were distributed to cover all tiers of the higher education system across two provinces. The sampling strategy was designed to correspond to the selection rates of different types of universities shown in Table 3. Over-sampling or under-sampling in a survey study will lead to a distortion of representation of surveyed population and subsequently affects the quality of the data collection. Around 40 students were sampled in the two 985 universities and 400 students were sampled in Tier Three and Tier Four institutions respectively, a ratio of sampling between two types of universities corresponding to the selection rates of the 985 universities and Tier Three and Tier Four universities after the 2006 *Gaokao*. The original number of the participants in this study was 960, with 480 students in Anhui and 480 in Zhejiang. A total 858 of the questionnaires were used in the final analysis after an initial test for credibility of the answers given in each questionnaire.[4] Table 5 shows the original figures of the participants in each university with the final sample figures.

Table 4. Sampling strategy for types of higher education institutions.

	Province A (Anhui)	Province B (Zhejiang)
Tier One (the 985 universities)	1	1
Tier Two (the 211 project)	1	1
Tier Three (comprehensive universities)	1	1
Tier Four (vocational and technical institutions)	1	1
Total number of sampled universities	4	4

Table 5. Sample strategy for numbers of students in different types of universities: 858 out of 960.

	Province A (Anhui)	Province B (Zhejiang)
Tier One (the 985 universities)	14 (out of 20)	16 (out of 20)
Tier Two (the 211 project)	57 (out of 60)	60 (out of 60)
Tier Three (comprehensive universities)	177 (out of 200)	189 (out of 200)
Tier Four (vocational and technical institutions)	173 (out of 200)	172 (out of 200)
Total number of students	421 (out of 480)	437 (out of 480)

The obvious limitation of this survey is the response rate and the representativeness of the surveyed students.[5] The main focus of this study is to examine how socio-economic status affected students' academic performance and how students' academic attainment determines their destinations in different types of university. Hence, the survey study was conducted for the specific purpose of collecting students' information on socio-economic backgrounds. In addition to the survey data, another data source was employed to provide a comparison of the general patterns of the socio-economic composition at the national level. The data on socio-economic status came from Lu Xueyi's statistical study of contemporary social stratification in China (Lu 2010). Details of the comparison are given in this section when they are introduced.

The first independent variable used is socio-economic status. Socio-economic status is certainly the most frequently used term in sociological research, but it is conceptualized differently in different national contexts. The survey used the classification into 10 socio-economic groups developed by Lu Xueyi in his report on contemporary social class in China (Table 6) (Lu 2010). Socio-economic status was re-coded into five categories in the following statistical analysis: leading cadres and managers; private entrepreneurs; professional and clerical employees; working class; and agricultural and unemployed/underemployed workers. Parental educational level is another commonly used indicator of socio-economic characteristics in sociological research (OECD 2007; Duru-Bellat, Kieffer, and Reimer 2008).[6] The details of coding parental educational levels are included in the notes.

Previous discussions suggest geographical origin as a key indicator of socio-economic characteristics in the Chinese context. This study uses three categories defining students' geographical origin of birth – cities, counties and the rural areas. Types of schooling are considered another indicator of socio-demographic characteristics. Schooling has been a key variable in understanding socio-economic participation in higher education in sociological research (Zimdars 2007; Schagen, Davies, and Rudd 2002). Chinese senior secondary schooling is categorized into model/key schools and regular secondary schools.[7]

Table 6. Comparison between the surveyed population and the corresponding composition in the general population.

Lu Xueyi's socio-economic status	Example occupations	Percentage in sample	Percentage in population
01 Leading cadres, governmental officials and executive personnel[a]	Senior carders; senior executives of public and private companies	1.5	3.6
02 Private entrepreneurs	Managers or owners of private companies	4.0	2.6
03 Professionals	Technicians, teachers, doctors	18.4	6.3
04 Clerical workers	Secretaries, *wenshu*, cashiers	9.6	7.0
05 Self-employed (*getihu*)	Small business owners	8.2	9.5
06 Sales and service worker	Waiters/waitresses, business workers	10.6	10.1
07 Manufacturing workers	Manual workers	8.3	14.7
08 Agricultural workers	Peasants, farmers	39.2	50.4
09 Unemployed / underemployed	Jobless	0.2	5.9

Source: Data on socio-economic participation in higher education are generated from my empirical work; data on the composition of the corresponding population come from Lu (2010). Note: [a]The first two socio-economic groups are combined; that is, the leading cadres/governmental officials and executive personnel.

The elaboration of the dependent variables – the *Gaokao* performance and the destination in types of universities – follows the previous discussions on the two aspects of educational meritocracy. First, the *Gaokao* scores will be treated as the measure of an individual's merit in this article. The relation between socio-economic and demographic characteristics and *Gaokao* scores will illustrate the extent to which higher education selection is based on meritocratic principles. The data on the *Gaokao* scores came from the survey study; and answers about the *Gaokao* scores in the questionnaires were tested for their credibility by combining the published information on cutting-off points in each province and the detailed final enrolment reports in each university.[8] The detailed coding of the *Gaokao* scores is explained in the regression analysis section. Second, students' destination in types of universities will be further examined in relation to their *Gaokao* performance as well as their socio-economic and demographic variables. The educational meritocracy hypothesis suggests that students' destination in types of universities should be determined by their *Gaokao* scores regardless of their socio-economic backgrounds. The destination in types of universities will mainly be distinguished between elite universities (the 985 and 211 institutions) and non-elite universities (provincial and vocational institutions).

General pattern of higher education participation by socio-economic status from the survey study

This section presents a descriptive statistical analysis of the general pattern of participation in higher education by different socio-economic groups. Table 6 demonstrates the pattern of socio-economic participation of the surveyed population; and compares this pattern with the corresponding composition of the general population. First, children from two socio-economic groups – leading cadres and managerial personnel – represented 1.5% of the participants in comparison with 3.6% of that group in the whole population. Children of private entrepreneurs accounted for around 4% of the surveyed population, compared with 2.6% in the general population. Children of professionals and clerical workers had a large representation, accounting for nearly one-third of the surveyed students in comparison with the 13.3% of that group in the whole population. Children of working-class parents were under-represented, accounting for around 18% of surveyed students by comparison with the 24.8% of that group in the whole population. This selectivity was most favourable to students from professional families while most unfavourable to students from manufacturing working-class backgrounds. Noticeably, students from agricultural families had a relatively large representation in the survey. However, the agricultural families are still under-represented when compared with their proportion in the whole population. The following sections further discuss the socio-economic patterns that influence the attainment of higher education, by detailing *Gaokao* performance and subsequent destination in higher education.

Models, results and analyses

Table 7 reports the results from a series of simple logistic regression analyses of the log-odds of independent variables on the *Gaokao* performance where the best academic outcome was coded as one, and a low performance in the *Gaokao* coded was as zero.[9]

The logistic regression predicts the log odds that an observation will have an indicator equal to one. The odds of being one of the top performers in the *Gaokao* is defined as the ratio of the probability that a student achieves scores in the highest threshold to the probability that the candidate is on the lower thresholds of the *Gaokao* performance. The best academic performance is understood as the highest threshold of the *Gaokao*. The highest threshold in the 2006 *Gaokao* consists of those who obtained more than 560 points out of a total 750. Model 1 shows the net effect of socio-economic status on *Gaokao* performance. In this model, students from professional backgrounds tended to achieve higher scores than students from agricultural families. Students from leading cadres and business executive backgrounds and from entrepreneur backgrounds do not seem to have significant advantage in the *Gaokao* over students from agricultural families.

Table 7. Simple logit regression for achieving highest thresholds in the 2006 *Gaokao* performance.

	Model 1	Model 2	Model 3	Model 4	Model 5
Socio-economic status (ref.: agricultural and peasants families)					
Leading cadres and managerial class	0.106 (0.047)	0.131 (0.089)	0.095 (00.80)	0.023 (0.043)	0.018 (0.044)
Private entrepreneurs and *getihu*	0.574 (0.094)	0.487 (0.057)	0.065 (0.057)	0.054 (0.051)	0.056 (0.051)
Professionals	1.722*** (0.039)	0.810** (0.068)	0.242 (0.041)	0.278 (0.090)	0.290 (0.049)
Working class	0.231 (0.099)	0.591 (0.108)	0.311 (0.037)	0.333 (0.127)	0.286 (0.123)
Parental educational level (ref: less than schooling level)					
Higher education degree		1.357*** (0.144)	0.681** (0.131)	1.291** (0.157)	0.772* (0.199)
Completed secondary schooling		0.842** (0.085)	0.472 (0.087)	0.849** (0.092)	0.513* (0.192)
Less than secondary schooling		1.138*** (0.083)	0.102 (0.085)	1.119*** (0.092)	0.720** (0.179)
Gender (ref: female)			0.719** (0.034)	0.687* (0.041)	0.512* (0.053)
Geographic origin of birth (ref: the rural areas)					
Cities				0.838*** (0.037)	0.573* (0.114)
Counties				0.084 (0.080)	0.710 (0.158)
Senior secondary schooling (ref: regular schools)					
Model/key schools					1.992*** (0.104)
Chi-square	16.19*	26.91**	35.47**	41.78**	47.31**
Degrees of freedom	4	7	8	11	12
N	858	858	858	858	858

Note: Standard errors are shown in parentheses.
*$p<0.10$, **$p<0.05$, ***$p<0.001$.

Model 2 introduces the indicator of parental educational level on *Gaokao* performance. When including parental educational level, the effect of socio-economic status tended to reduce. Parental educational level has a significant impact on students' performance in the *Gaokao*. Students whose parents had completed higher education generally performed much better in the 2006 *Gaokao* than those whose parents did not. Model 3 demonstrates the gender difference in achieving the highest *Gaokao* performance. Male candidates were more likely to achieve the highest threshold in the 2006 *Gaokao* than were female candidates.

Models 4 and 5 introduce a series of socio-demographic factors as additional predictors that influence academic performance in the *Gaokao*. Model 4 demonstrates a significant impact of the geographical origin on the *Gaokao* performance, even when socio-economic background is included. Specifically, students from cities and counties generally performed better than those from rural area in the 2006 *Gaokao*. When geographical origin was included, the effects of socio-economic characteristics significantly decreased and the impact of parental educational level also tended to reduce. Model 5 introduces types of secondary schooling, and demonstrates that key schools are strongly associated with higher academic performance on the *Gaokao*, even when all the other variables are included.

Students' socio-economic status did not seem to have a consistent impact on academic performance when other socio-demographic factors were included. However, the impact of students' parental educational level was consistently significant when socio-demographic factors were considered. Parental educational level and socio-demographic factors seemed to predict students' academic performance in the *Gaokao* more strongly than students' socio-economic backgrounds. This result seems to contrast with evidence presented in other contexts such as Japan, Korea, and Hong Kong, which suggests families from upper socio-economic status groups tend to invest in private tutoring or other extra-curricular activities to improve their children's academic performance in the national entrance examinations (Bray 2007). A possible explanation for the relatively low impact of socio-economic status compared with parental education level might be that the selection to senior secondary schooling has already filtered out many students from poor rural areas or from lower-working-class backgrounds, but less so where the parents are highly educated. Students who participated in the *Gaokao* competition had already been pre-selected during the transition to senior secondary schools.

Table 8 reports the results of another series of simple logistic regression analyses of the log-odds of the second independent variable, university type. Here, the Tier One (985 institutions) and Tier Two (211 institutions) universities were coded as one, and the non-elite universities, including provincial vocational and technological universities, were coded as zero. Model 1 shows students from different socio-economic backgrounds and their destinations in different types of university. Students from professional backgrounds were much more likely to be accepted to elite universities than those from other social backgrounds. Students from leading cadre or executive manager families did not seem to have strong advantages in getting accepted into elite universities. Model 2 introduces the parental educational level along with socio-economic status. Students whose parents had higher education degrees

Table 8. Simple logit regression of being enrolled into elite universities in the 2006 *Gaokao*.

	Model 1	Model 2	Model 3	Model 4	Model 5	Model 6
Socio-economic status (ref: agricultural and peasants families)						
Leading cadres and managerial class	0.413 (0.25)	0.420 (0.11)	0.151 (0.28)	0.053 (0.041)	−0.132 (0.097)	−0.254 (0.063)
Private entrepreneurs and *getihu*	0.543 (0.087)	0.491 (0.063)	0.064 (0.056)	0.055 (0.058)	−0.156 (0.051)	−0.144 (0.054)
Professional class	0.851*** (0.012)	0.637* (0.021)	0.429 (0.033)	0.271 (0.037)	−0.236 (0.056)	−0.135 (0.064)
Working class	0.613* (0.060)	0.478 (0.064)	0.416 (0.037)	0.187 (0.081)	−0.357 (0.097)	−0.228 (0.111)
Parental educational level (ref: less than schooling level)						
Higher education degree		0.882*** (0.141)	0.631** (0.112)	0.421 (0.158)	0.390 (0.169)	0.234 (0.186)
Completed secondary schooling		0.753*** (0.074)	0.425 (0.071)	0.434 (0.083)	0.461 (0.093)	0.447 (0.106)
Less than secondary schooling		0.532** (0.065)	0.313 (0.042)	0.213 (0.075)	0.275 (0.086)	0.436 (0.095)
Gender (ref: female)			0.578*** (0.043)	0.560** (0.057)	0.504* (0.041)	0.431 (0.058)
The Gaokao scores (ref: lower than highest thresholds)				1.883*** (0.095)	1.782*** (0.098)	1.561*** (0.003)
Geographic origin of birth (ref: the rural areas)						
Cities					1.386*** (0.007)	1.210*** (0.015)
Counties					0.606 (0.052)	0.538 (0.058)
Senior secondary schooling (ref: normal schools)						
Model/key schools						1.566*** (0.023)

(*Continued*)

Table 8. (*Continued*).

	Model 1	Model 2	Model 3	Model 4	Model 5	Model 6
Chi-square	16.31*	19.14**	23.41**	41.78**	43.72**	46.17**
Degrees of freedom	4	7	8	9	11	12
N	858	858	858	858	858	858

Note: Standard errors are shown in parentheses.
*$p<0.10$, **$p<0.05$, ***$p<0.001$.

and senior secondary schooling were more likely to go to elite universities. Model 3 introduces the gender difference: male candidates were more likely to be accepted into elite universities than female candidates.

Model 4 introduces the merit measure – the *Gaokao* performance. The results demonstrate that socio-economic impact was significantly diminished when *Gaokao* performance was considered. Even the impact of parental education level was reduced when the *Gaokao* scores were accounted for. Hence, the *Gaokao* mediated socio-economic effect in predicting their chances of being accepted to elite universities. Model 5 includes the effect of geographical origin on the chances of students getting accepted into elite universities. It is demonstrated that students from cities and counties were more likely to be enrolled in elite universities than those from rural areas. Model 6 predicts the impact of types of senior secondary schooling on elite opportunities, and it is clear that students from key schools were much more likely to get accepted into elite universities than those from regular secondary schools.

Socio-economic effects significantly decreased when their *Gaokao* performance and other socio-demographic factors were included. Similarly, the impact of parental educational level also progressively diminished. There has been a persistently strong link between *Gaokao* performance and chances of being enrolled in elite universities. In this sense, social inequality in the participation in elite universities arises through the influence of geographical origin and secondary schooling being mediated through the *Gaokao*.

Discussion

The analysis of the data from the survey conducted in Anhui and Zhejiang tested the meritocracy hypothesis in the Chinese context. The two aspects of educational meritocracy were addressed in previous analyses. First, differences in students' 'merit' – which were measured by the Gaoako scores – did not necessarily correspond to students' socio-economic backgrounds. Students' parental educational level seemed to predict students' chances of performing well in the *Gaokao* better than their socio-economic status. Students from professional families tended to achieve academically better in the *Gaokao* than those from other socio-economic backgrounds. Students' demographic characteristics, such as geographical origin and gender, and types of schooling, significantly affected their academic performance. These results suggest a strong association between students' parental educational level and socio-demographic backgrounds and their academic outcomes.

Second, the *Gaokao* performance has been demonstrated to be a consistently strong indicator of students' chances of getting accepted into elite universities. In this sense, the *Gaokao* seemed to be a meritocratic selection for elite opportunities. However, given a close association between parental education, demographic factors and the *Gaokao* performance shown previously, the selection system into elite universities might not be entirely based upon meritocratic principles. The *Gaokao* had already filtered out a substantial number of students whose parental educational level was relatively low and who were from rural areas and non-key secondary schools. The competition for getting into elite or key universities is rather a secondary selection, during which the advantages by students gained in the *Gaokao* have become consolidated.

The results from this survey also encompassed certain aspects of the MMI arguments. Consistent with some perspectives of MMI theory, higher education selection in Anhui and Zhejiang demonstrated a certain degree of socio-economic and cultural selectivity. However, the MMI argument does not specify socio-demographic factors as an important dimension to social inequality during the expansion of educational opportunities. The findings from this research suggest the need to include socio-demographic indicators in MMI theory to represent wider social contexts.

Furthermore, consistent with expectations based on EMI theory, the results suggest that students whose parents have higher level of education and those from professional families secured qualitatively better opportunities to elite universities. However, the socio-economic effect significantly diminished when the geographical origin of birth and types of secondary schooling were considered. Geographical origin and secondary schooling conditioned significantly the qualitative differences in participation in types of universities. Hence, the findings in this study call for a more inclusive definition of social class when extending the MMI arguments to research in China.

In summary, this study provides a snapshot of patterns of socio-economic participation in higher education in contemporary East China. The statistical analysis did not suggest a strong socio-economic selection; rather, a certain level of cultural and geographical selectivity was indicated in predicting students' *Gaokao* performance as well as their chances of getting into elite universities. Thus socio-demographic factors appeared to be more significant than socio-economic status in affecting students' higher education opportunities. The *Gaokao* selection system appears to be more meritocratic in relation to socio-economic background than in relation to geographical origins. In addition to this, although this is not shown in my data, it is well known that geographical disparities in resources and schools ensure that many rural children do not reach senior secondary level and therefore have no opportunity to take the *Gaokao* anyway.

This study highlights how socio-demographic disparity is transmitted in the opportunity structures of higher education. Rather than being a system of discovering talents from all social origins, the *Gaokao* particularly favours those from professional families, from urban developed areas and those who attended better secondary schools. The *Gaokao*, with its association with meritocratic selection, justifies the privileges of urban residents and advantaged families in the form of merit outcomes, and further consolidates their advantages by securing opportunities to attend elite universities. Meanwhile, the *Gaokao* punishes those from rural areas for lacking equal educational opportunities and resources at the schooling stage, and justifies their inferior status with demonstrable outcomes in the examinations.

Conclusions

This study raises further questions about the socio-political circumstances that have shaped higher education selection. One of the socio-political consequences of the market reform was worsening social inequality. Social stratification and socio-demographic disparity seem to have been transmitted into opportunity structures through the educational system. The *Gaokao* selection symbolically represents a meritocratic selection that, in fact, legitimized the privileges of those transformed new elites who seized new political and economic power during the market reform, such as professional class and urban elites. Furthermore, the *Gaokao* selection induced lower social groups, such as the working class and peasants who lost their previous social security and welfare during the reform, to believe that they are scholastically inferior in the competition for higher education opportunities. The meritocratic façade of higher education selection has conveniently facilitated the Communist Party's strategy of continuing its market reform and development, while minimizing the actual costs of policy enhancements needed to reduce social inequality. The inconvenient truth behind this façade might be enduring social inequality and divided social interests.

Notes

1. The 985 project was proposed in 1998 by Ministry of Education in the 'Action Plan for Education Revitalization for the 21st Century' to provide generous funding and resources for selected higher education institutions that had the

potential to deliver world-class research excellence. The 211 project was approved by the State Council in 1995 for developing around 100 key universities.
2. Surveyed students were all enrolled in four-year bachelor courses, even in third-tier and fourth-tier universities.
3. Anhui and Zhejiang were chosen out of some methodological considerations.
4. The questionnaires were administrated during class breaks in the compulsory courses, such as Deng Xiaoping Thoughts and English, to include students from a variety of fields of study.
5. The participating students in this survey study represent around 0.4% of the total population of first-year undergraduates enrolled in Bachelor courses in 2007 in these two provinces. The total number of students enrolled in four-year Bachelor courses after the 2006 autumn Gaokao was around 240,000 in two provinces.
6. The parental educational level is coded as: 01 higher education degrees; 02 Completed senior secondary school or vocational, technical secondary school; 03 Not completed senior secondary school; and 04 less than secondary schooling.
7. Shangdong province is an exception, with a lack of the distinction between key/model schools and normal schools.
8. Different thresholds for different types of universities were published by the Ministry of Education at the provincial level annually after the Gaokao. Each university then published their detailed reports on their enrolment, particularly the cutting-off point for each field of study.
9. The best academic performance is understood as the highest thresholds of the Gaokao. The highest thresholds in the 2007 Gaokao are those who obtained more than 560 points out of a total 750. The highest thresholds are understood as cutting-off points for Tier One and Tier Two universities.

References

Arrow, K., S. Bowles, and S. Durlauf, eds. 2000. *Meritocracy and Economic Inequality.* Princeton: Princeton University Press.

Ayalon, H., and A. Yogev. 2005. "Field of Study and Students' Stratification in an Expanded System of Higher Education: the Case of Israel." *European Sociological Review* 21 (3): 227–241.

Bell, D. 1973. *The Coming of Post-Industrial Society. A Venture in Social Forecasting.* London: Heinemann.

Birdsall, N. 2011. "IMF Leadership Selection Survey: Early Results at Odds with European Rush. Center for Global Development." Accessed August 1, 2011. http://blogs.cgdev.org/globaldevelopment/2011/05/imf-selection-survey-early-results-on-selection-system-and-candidates.php.

Bray, M. 2007. *The Shadow Education System: Private Tutoring and Its Implication for Planners.* Paris: UNESCO.

Breen, R., and J. O. Jonsson. 2005. "Inequality of Opportunity in Comparative Perspective: Recent Research on Educational Attainment and Social Mobility." *Annual Review of Sociology* 31: 223–243.

Breen, R., and J. H. Goldthorpe. 2001. "Class, Mobility and Merit the Experience of Two British Birth Cohorts." *European Sociological Review* 17 (2): 81–101.

CHNS (China Health and Nutrition Survey) 2004. "China Health and Nutrition Survey Datasets." Accessed August 10, 2011. http://www.cpc.unc.edu/projects/china/data/datasets.

Duckett, J. 2001. "Bureaucrats in Business, Chinese-Style: the Lessons of Market Reform and State Entrepreneurialism in the People's Republic of China." *World Development* 29: 23–37.

Duru-Bellat, M., A. Kieffer, and D. Reimer. 2008. "Patterns of Social Inequalities in Access to Higher Education in France and Germany." *International Journal of Comparative Sociology* 49: 347–368.

Goldthorpe, J. H 1996. "Problems of 'Meritocracy'." In *Can Education Be Equalized ?*, edited by R. Erikson and J. O. Jonsson, 255–287. Boulder, Colorado: Westview Press.

Goldthorpe, J. H., and M. Jackson. 2007. "Intergenerational Class Mobility in Contemporary Britain: Political Concerns and Empirical findings." *The British Journal of Sociology* 58 (4): 525–546.

Hannum, E., and A. Park. 2007. *Education and Reform in China*. Oxford: Routledge.

Hannum, E., and M. Y. Wang. 2006. "Geography and Educational Inequality in China." *China Economic Review* 17: 253–265.

Hannum, E., M. Y. Wang, and J. Adams. 2008. "Urban-Rural Disparities in Access to Primary and Secondary Education under Market Feform." In *One Country, Two Societies? Rural-Urban Inequality in Contemporary China*, edited by M. K. Whyte, 156–171. Harvard University Press.

Harvey, D. 2005. *A Brief History of Neo-Liberalism*. New York, NY: Oxford University Press.

Huang, P. 1993. "Intellectuals: in Search of Identity." *Chinese Society and Science Quarterly* 2: 113–121.

Jackson, M. 2007. "How Far Merit Selection? Social Stratification and the Labour Market" *The British Journal of Sociology* 58 (3): 367–390.

Krauze, T., and K. M. Slomczynski. 1985. "How Far to Meritocracy? Empirical Tests of a Controversial Thesis" *Social Forces* 63: 623–642.

Lall, M., and E. Vickers. 2009. *Education as a Political Tool in Asia*. Abingdon: Routledge.

Li, B. L., and A. G. Walder. 2001. "Career Advancement as Party Patronage: Sponsored Mobility into the Chinese Administrative Elite, 1949–1996." *American Journal of Sociology* 106: 1371–1408.

Li, D., and M. C. Tsang. 2003. "Household Decisions and Gender Inequality in Education in Rural China." *China: an International Journal* 1 (2): 224–248.

Lipset, S. M., and H. L. Zetterberg. 1959. "Social Mobility in Industrial Societies." In *Social Mobility in Industrial Society*, edited by S. M. Lipset and R. Bendix. Berkeley: University of California Press.

Lu, X. Y. 2010. *Social Structure of Contemporary China*. Beijing: Shehui kexue wenxian chubanshe.

Lucas, S. R. 2001. "Effectively Maintained Inequality: Education Transitions, Track Mobility, and Social Background Effects." *American Journal of Sociology* 106: 1642–1690.

National Bureau of Statistics. 1991, 1999, 2007. "China Statistics Year Book." Beijing: National Bureau of Statistics. Accessed July 2, 2011. http://www.stats.gov.cn/english.

Nee, V., and R. Matthews. 1996. "Market Transition and Societal Transformation in Reforming State Socialism." *Annual Review of Sociology* 22: 401–435.

Olneck, M., and J. Crouse. 1979. "The IQ Meritocracy Reconsidered: Cognitive Skill and Adult Success in the United States." *American Journal of Education* 88: 1–31.

OECD (Organization for Economic Co-Operation and development). 2007. *Education at a Glance*. Paris: OECD.

Parish, W. L. 1975. "Socialism and the Chinese Peasant Family." *The Journal of Asian Studies* 34 (3): 613–630.

Qin, Y. 1999. *China's Middle Classes*. Beijing: China's Planning Press.

Raftery, A. E., and M. Hout. 1993. "Maximally Maintained Inequality – Expansion, Reform, and Opportunity in Irish Education." *Sociology of Education* 66 (1): 41–62.

Schagen, S., D. Davies, P. Rudd, and I. Schagen. 2002. *The Impact of Specialist and Faith Schools on Performance (LGA Research Report 28)*. Slough: NFER.

Shavit, Y., and H. P. Blossfeld, eds. 1993. *Persistent Inequality: Changing Educational Attainment in Thirteen Countries*. Boulder, Colorado: Westview.

Spence, J. 2008. "Confucian ways." Reith Lectures. Accessed May 14, 2008. http://www.bbc.co.uk/radio4/reith2008/transcript1.shtml.

Unger, J. 1982. *Education under Mao: Class and Competition in Canton Schools, 1960–1980*. New York, NY: Columbia University Press.

Vachudova, M. A. 2005. *Europe Undivided: Democracy, Leverage, and Integration after Communism*. Oxford: Oxford University Press.

Walker, R. A., and D. Buck. 2007. "The Chinese Road: Cities in the Transition to Capitalism." *New Left Review* 46: 39–66.

Whelan, C., and R. Layte. 2002. "Late Industrialization and the Increased Merit Selection Hypothesis. Ireland as a Test Case." *European Sociological Review* 18 (1): 35–50.

Young, M. D. 1958. *The Rise of the Meritocracy, 1870–2023. An Essay on Education and Equality*. London: Thames and Hudson.

Zakaria, F. 2008. "Transcript of Interview with Chinese Prime Minister Wen Jiabao." CNN. Accessed November 10, 2009. http://www.cnn.com/2008/WORLD/asiapcf/09/29/chinese.premier.transcript/.

Zimdars, A. 2007. "Challenges to Meritocracy? A Study of the Social Mechanisms in Student Selection and Attainment at the University of Oxford." Unpublished D.Phil Thesis in Sociology in the Division of Social Sciences at the University of Oxford.

Educational expansion and field of study: trends in the intergenerational transmission of educational inequality in the Netherlands

Gerbert Kraaykamp, Jochem Tolsma and Maarten H.J. Wolbers

Department of Sociology, Radboud University Nijmegen, Nijmegen, the Netherlands

> In this paper we study to what extent parental field of study affects a person's educational level and field of study. We employ information on 8800 respondents from the Family Survey Dutch Population (1992–2009). Our results first of all show that, over the last five decades, economic fields of study have become more fashionable among men. In sharp contrast, mainly tracks in agriculture have lost most of their appeal. Among women, medical, economic and socio-cultural fields have gained attractiveness. Second, we established that parental field of study is of significant importance for reaching a high level of education for children, and that the relevance of parental field of study is increasing over the years. Moreover, symmetry in fields could be established when it comes to the intergenerational transmission of field of study. Our results support the idea that educational expansion does not necessarily lead to increasing meritocracy in western societies.

1. Introduction

Educational expansion is one of the most prominent and uncontested developments of modernization in western societies during the last five decades. Not only has the number of men who attained a higher educational level increased in the twenty-first century, but women have obtained dramatically more certificates in higher education (Charles and Bradley 2009). An important consequence of this educational expansion is an inevitable decline of the discriminating character of level of education (van de Werfhorst and Kraaykamp 2001). If ever more people attain a high level of education, a degree in tertiary education may no longer be a clear signal of a person's competence and excellence; the internal heterogeneity of tertiary educated people in terms of social origin, cognitive capacity and motivation increases self-evidently. A number of scholars therefore argue that educational expansion in modern societies has led to an increased significance of horizontal differentiation between fields of study (Davies and Guppy 1997; Kalmijn and van der Lippe 1997; van de Werfhorst 2004; Charles and Bradley 2009; Triventi 2013a). However, in order to be relevant in terms of social inequality, horizontal differentiation in fields of study must have consequences in a hierarchical sense; for example, through the influence of parental field of study on the educational level of attainment of their children, which, in turn, may affect their socio-economic status later in life. Or through the varying academic prestige and economic pay-off with which different fields of study are associated. In particular, given that differentiated occupational returns may be linked to various fields of study, those from upper social classes may take advantage of those educational options which make it possible to enter the labour market with most rewarded credentials (Reimer, Noelke, and Kucel 2008; Triventi 2013b).

Relatively few sociological studies into the popularity and consequences of fields of study have been established. Questions about a (changing) significance of field of study in processes of the intergenerational transmission of inequality have remained under-explored (for exceptions, see van de Werfhorst, de Graaf, and Kraaykamp 2001; de Graaf and Wolbers 2003; Goyette and Mullen 2006; Reimer and Pollak 2010; Triventi 2013a). In this article, we will focus on the importance of parental field of study (besides their level of education) for the educational attainment of their (grown-up) children in the Netherlands. In the process of intergenerational transmission of education, we will first investigate to what extent it is possible to transmit horizontal 'subject-oriented' resources into hierarchical educational resources in the following generation. Next, we will study children's choice for a certain field of study and the determining role of parental field of study (besides their level of education) therein. If field of study has gained importance in the context of educational expansion, it seems necessary to investigate whether intergenerational transmission of field of study can also be established. In this contribution, we will investigate both forms of intergenerational educational inequality proceeding from a time perspective; we will examine to what extent the intergenerational transmission of educational resources in the Netherlands has changed in the course of the past 50 years.

We ask the following questions: 'What have been developments in choices of field of study across birth cohorts in the Netherlands?' and 'How did the intergenerational transmission of educational inequality develop across birth cohorts in the Netherlands if we include – besides level of education – field of study?' To answer these questions, we employ all five available waves from the Family Survey Dutch Population (FSDP; 1992, 1998, 2000, 2003 and 2009). This large-scale, periodically repeated, survey supplies us with representative information on 8800 men and women regarding their own educational career and that of their parents. This allows for making a detailed distinction between educational level and field of study for both children and their parents and, subsequently, to study the intergenerational transmission therein from a time perspective.

The Netherlands provides an interesting testing ground for this issue, because the Netherlands has an occupational labour market rather than a flexible (or an internal) labour market like that of the United Kingdom (Marsden 1986; Brown, Green, and Lauder 2001; Gangl 2001). In the Netherlands, there are many (field-specific) vocational tracks. The curricula of these vocational tracks supply students with (field-specific) skills required for particular jobs. This obviously reduces training costs for employers. Within this institutional context, it is therefore expected that field of study has a more important signalling function than in countries with less extensive systems of vocational training and more on-the-job training. In the Netherlands, children may especially benefit from parents who studied in the same field as these parents may provide crucial information about how labour markets (in this field) work and what are important skills for these types of jobs. In addition, parents who are symmetric with their offspring in field of study are more likely to have relevant social capital, thereby facilitating the school-to-work transition and early career job changes to obtain a better occupational position.

2. Theoretical background and hypotheses

2.1. Intergenerational transmission of educational inequality

The status attainment model of Blau and Duncan (1967) is a classic starting point for studying the intergenerational transmission of social inequality. This approach investigates the degree to which attainment of social status is the result of either 'ascription' or 'achievement'. In other words, to understand differences in socio-economic success in a person's life (usually measured in terms of occupational status), scholars look into the effort and achievement of this person (in terms of level of education) and weigh them against the ascribed characteristics of a person's parental background (parental [or father's] level of education and occupation). The neo-Weberian idea behind this model of status attainment is that within each society a struggle for desirable and scarce (high) positions takes place and that both individuals and their parents mobilize resources in order to reach the highest possible results. A central assumption is that parents actually want and are able to influence the educational and occupational careers of their children. An important consequence of a modernizing labour market, however, is that employers value achieved characteristics increasingly more (and ascribed characteristics less), resulting in more appreciation for personal effort and achievement. The relative importance of individual merit (compared with parental resources) for the achievement of an occupational status therefore increases over time (Shavit and Müller 1998). This process is often referred to in terms of growing openness in modern western countries.

2.2. Inequality in educational level

Numerous studies confirm the importance of parental level of education and occupational status for the success of a child's educational career (Shavit and Blossfeld 1993; Tieben and Wolbers 2010). In this article, we propose to expand research on the intergenerational transmission of educational inequality by taking the field of study of the parents into account besides their educational level. Based on the reasoning that in fields of study useful educational resources can be constructed and cumulated, it is plausible to assume that parents will (consciously or unconsciously) transmit these resources to their children, thereby helping them to achieve an educational level as high as possible.

An important assumption is that fields of study differ in the amount and importance of resources they supply (van de Werfhorst and Kraaykamp 2001; Charles and Bradley 2009) and that these (parental) resources stimulate the attainment of a high educational level for their children to some extent. For this purpose, the cultural reproduction theory (Bourdieu and Passeron 1977), the theory of maximal maintained inequality (Raferty and Hout 1993), and the rational action theory (Goldthorpe 2000) supply us with appropriate suggestions for possible underlying mechanisms (cultural capital, aspirations, risk aversion). Notice that the above reasoning awards a hierarchic meaning to fields of study in the sense that some fields may provide more resources than others.

To gain insight into the relevance of parental field of study in the process of intergenerational transmission of educational inequality, we compare the strength of the relationship between parental field of study and the educational attainment of their children with the strength of the relationship between parental level of education and the educational attainment of their children. One of the main claims at the outset was that, due to educational expansion, the distinctive power of level of education has decreased. Studies by de Graaf and Ganzeboom (1993) and Kraaykamp and van Eijck (2010) confirm this assumption for the Netherlands. In the course of time (i.e. across birth cohorts), parental educational level became less important for the prediction of children's educational success, whereas the hypothesis is that resources acquired in different fields of study have gained importance. Bourdieu's (1986) concept of compensating strategies supports this argumentation. The presumption is that, due to a decreasing influence of parental material wealth on intergenerational transmission of social inequality, alternative resources gain importance over time. The question is whether this phenomenon also occurs in the case of intergenerational transmission of educational inequality. Given the above reasoning, our hypothesis is that the relative importance of parental field of study (i.e. compared with the parental level of education) is larger for the youngest birth cohorts for the explanation of educational attainment of their offspring than for the oldest birth cohorts.

2.3. Inequality in field of study

As we argued earlier, field of study can be interpreted in a hierarchical sense (van de Werfhorst and Kraaykamp 2001; Charles and Bradley 2009). If certain educational specializations provide more resources than others (for instance, in terms of labour-market opportunities), then it is important to investigate to what extent parental education (level and field of study) is related to the field of study choice of their children (Reimer and Pollak 2010; Triventi 2013a). We therefore incorporate an individual's choice for a certain field of study as an outcome in the classic status attainment model. Especially in countries with occupational labour markets, like the Netherlands, field of study is a highly relevant educational outcome, as the field-specific educational credentials are clear signals for future employers and highly rewarded in the allocation of individuals to occupations. Concerning this intergenerational transmission, we also determine the relative importance of parental level of education compared with parental field of study for children's educational field choices.

If certain fields of study constitute more or less potential, status and/or competence, parents from higher social origin probably aspire for their children to choose the most promising and prestigious fields (van de Werfhorst, Sullivan, and Cheung 2003; Goyette and Mullen 2006; Triventi 2013a). More specifically, it seems obvious that members of the higher social strata in society give preference to law school and economic fields of study over, for instance, socio-cultural fields of study for their children (Reimer and Pollak 2010). Various studies indeed support the idea that there are significant differences between fields of study in terms of employment opportunities, occupational status and earnings (Davies and Guppy 1997; Kalmijn and van der Lippe 1997; van de Werfhorst 2004). Therefore, parents are likely to mobilize their own field of study (besides their educational level) to promote that their children select the most 'attractive' fields of study possible. Those who graduated in a prestigious field themselves encourage their children to choose a field of study as 'high' as possible. An alternative explanation for the intergenerational transmission of field of study is, of course, that children perceive their parents as their point of reference (van de Werfhorst, Kraaykamp, and de Graaf 2000). Cultural socialization plays an important role: it is particularly easy for parents to inform their children about, and to make them enthusiastic for, the fields they are acquainted with themselves. This causes symmetry in choices of fields of study between parents and children.

The next issue is whether the intergenerational transmission of field of study has changed over the years. For example, do highly educated parents nowadays direct their children less often to, for instance, a law school than before? And does symmetry in the choice of field of study between parents and children occur at present more often than in the past? Two theoretical arguments can be advanced with regard to the former issue. First, the notion that level of education has lost some of its distinctive power through the process of educational expansion matters (Kraaykamp and Van Eijck 2010). Educational expansion, accompanied by upward social mobility, has caused stronger heterogeneity (in terms of social composition) within the group of highly educated people and thus, indirectly, a decreasing class identification. Consequently, class-specific behaviours have become less common, also in educational decisions. Second, individualization, as described by Beck (1992) and Pakulski and Walters (1996), has contributed to a decreasing social basis for individual preferences and tastes. Especially in the case of more individual choices, like the one for a field of study, it may be expected that parental level of education plays an increasingly smaller role.

With regard to the latter issue – the intergenerational transmission of field of study – there is no reason to assume that parental field of study has become less relevant for children's choice for a particular field of study. Field choices are closely linked to individual preferences for culture, sociability and property, mainly acquired through the process of parental socialization. There is no reason to believe that parents are less involved in upbringing practices nowadays. On the contrary, parents seem to be ever more aware of the fact that they want to pass on valuable assets, norms and competencies to their children. Therefore, they are often actively involved in the stimulation of personal and cultural preferences (Kraaykamp 2009). As a consequence, we assume that the parental transmission of field of study remained more or less stable over the years (van de Werfhorst, Kraaykamp, and de Graaf 2000). Given the above reasoning, we hypothesize for younger birth cohorts that the relative effect of parental field of study (i.e. compared with parental level of education) on field of study choice is stronger than for the older cohorts.

3. Data and measurements

To test our hypotheses we used five waves of the FSDP, a large-scale, periodically repeated survey containing unique retrospective data on the family of origin and on the complete educational and professional careers of both primary respondents and their partners. This survey was established at the beginning of the 1990s by the Department of Sociology at the Radboud University Nijmegen. Data were collected on five occasions; that is, in the years 1992, 1998, 2000, 2003 and 2009 (Ganzeboom and Ultee 1992; de Graaf et al. 1998, 2000, 2003; Kraaykamp, Ruiter, and Wolbers 2009). Throughout these years, the average response varied around 45%. As the interviews for the FSDP on average took more than an hour and both partners had to be interviewed, this response is relatively high. First, a face-to-face interview took place with primary respondents and their partners, followed by a written (or Internet) questionnaire. For each of the measurement years, primary respondents represented a random sample from the Dutch population aged between 18 and 70 years. As primary respondents and their partners grew up in different families, they are treated as independent observations in the current analysis.

We used all five FSDP waves for the empirical analyses. To secure for all respondents that their educational career was completed, we selected respondents of 25 years and older at the moment of interview. We thereby assume that a person's attained level of education and field of study are not subject to great change any more after this age. In total, we analyse 8800 respondents.

By comparing birth cohorts, a much larger period of time can be reviewed than just the period in which the data were collected (between 1992 and 2009). In the descriptive analysis, we distinguished between five cohorts: 1914–1939, 1940–1949, 1950–1959, 1960–1969 and 1970–1984. In the multivariate analysis, we used an individual's actual year of birth, centred around 1960. These centred scores were divided by 10 so that, when studying trends in the effects of parental level of education and field of study, we compare 10-year time spans (like in the descriptive analysis).

The highest attained level of education for individuals was measured as the number of years of education: four years for incomplete primary education, six years for primary education, eight years for lower (secondary) vocational education, 10 years for lower (secondary) general education, 10.5 years for intermediate (secondary) vocational education, 11 years for intermediate (secondary) general education, 12 years for higher (secondary) general education, 15 years for higher (tertiary) vocational education, and 16.5 years for university education.

We distinguished the following 11 fields of study: general, teaching, arts/humanities, agriculture, technical, medical, economic, law, socio-cultural, care, and other. These fields refer to the field of study of the (first) highest attained level of education of individuals.

For the parental level of education and field of study, we took the parent with the highest educational level. We defined the highest attained level of education and the obtained field of study (corresponding to this level of education) of this parent in the same way as we did for respondents.

4. Results

4.1. Descriptive analysis

Table 1 presents historical developments in the obtained field of study for the highest attained educational level for men and women. Educational expansion in this table is observed through the decrease in the percentage of individuals who attended general education. This category covers respondents that attained only primary education or general secondary education. In the oldest birth cohort, 58% of the women only attended general

Table 1. Historical development in obtained field of study.

Field of study		1914–1939	1940–4199	1950–1959	Cohort 1960–1969	1970–1984	Total
General	N (total)	476	674	635	544	317	2646
	% within cohort (men)	36	30	24	23	19	25
	% within cohort (women)	58	50	37	26	16	35
Teaching	N (total)	66	121	170	107	79	543
	% within cohort (men)	5	5	6	2	2	4
	% within cohort (women)	8	10	11	8	7	9
Arts/humanities	N (total)	24	54	65	71	76	290
	% within cohort (men)	1	3	4	2	2	3
	% within cohort (women)	3	4	3	4	6	4
Agriculture	N (total)	57	39	56	89	40	281
	% within cohort (men)	11	4	5	5	3	5
	% within cohort (women)	0	0	1	3	1	1
Technical	N (total)	200	366	409	482	441	1898
	% within cohort (men)	35	40	36	39	44	39
	% within cohort (women)	3	3	2	3	6	4
Medical	N (total)	26	78	205	196	175	680
	% within cohort (men)	1	2	5	3	3	3
	% within cohort (women)	4	7	15	15	17	13
Economic	N (total)	58	139	208	392	346	1143
	% within cohort (men)	7	11	12	18	21	14
	% within cohort (women)	4	6	8	17	18	12
Law	N (total)	12	16	40	67	76	211
	% within cohort (men)	2	2	3	3	2	2
	% within cohort (women)	0	0	1	3	7	2

(Continued)

Table 1. (Continued).

Field of study		Cohort					Total
		1914–1939	1940–4199	1950–1959	1960–1969	1970–1984	
Socio-cultural	N (total)	16	53	104	100	104	377
	% within cohort (men)	1	2	4	3	2	3
	% within cohort (women)	2	4	6	6	10	6
Care	N (total)	87	138	181	182	100	688
	% within cohort (men)	0	1	1	1	1	1
	% within cohort (women)	18	16	16	16	10	15
Other	N (total)	3	5	11	9	15	43
	% within cohort (men)	1	1	1	1	1	1
	% within cohort (women)	0	0	0	0	0	0
Total	N (total)	1025	1683	2084	2239	1769	8800
	N (men)	531	868	1057	1140	890	4486
	N (women)	492	817	1027	1096	879	4311
	% within cohort	100	100	100	100	100	100

Source: FSDP 1992, 1998, 2000, 2003 and 2009; authors' own calculations.

education; in the most recent cohort, this value is down to 16%. For men, the corresponding percentages are 36% and 19%, respectively. In other words, increasingly more people complete some sort of vocational training before leaving daytime education. Prominent fields of study for men are technical and economic studies; the last category showing a strong increase in attendance (from 7 to 21%). For women, the most prevalent fields of study are care and medical studies. Especially, the choice for a medical field of study has grown strongly among women (from 4 to 17%). The figures for other educational fields are smaller in size and show a rather stable pattern over the years (only some percentage points). What is striking is that the choice for an agricultural field of study has decreased for men, while the choices for law and socio-cultural fields of studies have recently increased for women.

Table 2 shows that there is a strong association between the educational level of the parents and the field of study of their children (see the last column). The average parental educational level is lowest for the categories general, care and agriculture (about eight years of education) and highest for law and arts/humanities (around 11 years of education). This variation can, of course, be partly attributed to the observation that there is a positive relationship between parental educational level and the highest attained educational level of their children, combined with the fact that there are differences in the number of fields of study on the different educational levels.

Table 2 also displays that, for each field of study, the average parental educational level has increased over birth cohorts. In total (last row), this increase amounts to about three years of education (from 7.53 years of education in the oldest birth cohort to 10.43 years in the youngest). This indicates once more the enormous educational expansion that has taken place. To take this educational expansion into account, the average parental educational level within birth cohorts has been centred. This means that, within cohorts, the average parental educational level across all fields of study adds up to zero (see the last row) and the average for each specific educational field can be interpreted as a deviation from this cohort average (of zero). In this way, uncontaminated developments in average parental educational level can be investigated for different fields of study, since corrections are made for educational expansion. What then catches the eye is that the average parental educational level of the medical field of study decreases substantially, relatively speaking. For the oldest birth cohort, the average parental educational level was still 2.68 years higher than the average within this cohort. For the most recent cohort, this is only 0.31 years higher. Where in the past especially children of highly educated parents prefer a medical field of study, nowadays this choice is made by children whose parents attained just above average educational levels. Also for the field of teaching, a field of study traditionally chosen by children of highly educated parents, a similar decrease can be verified. The same holds for the arts/humanities and socio-cultural fields, but these

Table 2. Historical development in the average parental level of education within the obtained field of study ($n = 8800$).

Field of study	Average parental level of education	1914–1939	1940–1949	1950–1959	1960–1969	1970–1984	Total
General	Absolute	6.96	7.10	7.43	8.47	9.96	7.78
	Deviation of cohort mean	−0.57	−0.77	−0.81	−0.54	−0.48	−0.66
Teaching	Absolute	9.48	9.52	9.24	9.37	10.34	9.52
	Deviation of cohort mean	1.95	1.66	0.99	0.36	−0.09	0.97
Arts/humanities	Absolute	10.47	10.17	9.79	11.75	11.57	10.86
	Deviation of cohort mean	2.93	2.31	1.54	2.75	1.13	1.99
Agriculture	Absolute	6.34	7.25	7.80	9.10	10.14	8.18
	Deviation of cohort mean	−1.19	−0.61	−0.44	0.09	−0.29	−0.43
Technical	Absolute	7.75	7.95	8.29	8.69	10.39	8.76
	Deviation of cohort mean	0.22	0.08	0.05	−0.32	−0.05	−0.04
Medical	Absolute	10.22	9.18	8.91	9.51	10.75	9.64
	Deviation of cohort mean	2.68	1.32	0.66	0.50	0.31	0.68
Economic	Absolute	8.25	8.44	8.30	9.12	10.16	9.16
	Deviation of cohort mean	0.72	0.57	0.05	0.12	−0.27	0.07
Law	Absolute	8.61	11.05	10.37	10.58	13.22	11.42
	Deviation of cohort mean	1.08	3.18	2.13	1.58	2.78	2.21
Socio-cultural	Absolute	9.80	9.49	9.56	10.60	11.14	10.27
	Deviation of cohort mean	2.27	1.63	1.32	1.59	0.70	1.30
Care	Absolute	6.80	6.94	7.54	7.89	9.42	7.69
	Deviation of cohort mean	−0.74	−0.92	−0.71	−1.11	−1.01	−0.91
Other	Absolute	8.94	6.61	9.26	9.02	7.88	8.39
	Deviation of cohort mean	1.41	−1.25	1.02	0.01	−2.55	−0.68
Total	Absolute	7.53	7.86	8.25	9.01	10.43	8.72
	Deviation of cohort mean	0.00	0.00	0.00	0.00	0.00	0.00

Source: FSDP 1992, 1998, 2000, 2003 and 2009; authors' own calculations.

fields of study continue to demonstrate an above-average educational level of the parents with about one year for the youngest cohort. The average parental educational level in agricultural fields of study, on the contrary, has risen, relatively speaking, over time. Where it used to be a field mainly chosen by children with relatively low-educated parents, this field is now chosen by children with parents with an average level of education. Finally, the study of law remains an elitist choice of study for children as far as the educational level of their parents is concerned.

4.2. *Multivariate analysis*

We employ ordinary least squares regression analysis to study (changing) effects of the parental level of education and field of study on the highest attained educational level of their children (see Table 3). We control for the field of study of the children themselves. Men and women are analysed

Table 3. The (changed) effects of the parental level of education and field of study on the highest attained level of education (linear regression analysis; $n = 8800$).

	Men		Women	
	B	Beta	B	Beta
Constant	8.19**		7.96**	
Level of education, parents (years)	0.32**	0.29	0.26**	0.25
Field of study, parents (deviation contrast)		0.06		0.05
General	0.02		−0.12	
Arts/humanities	0.18		−0.07	
Technical	0.34**		−0.05	
Medical	0.26		−0.29	
Law	0.41		0.21	
Care	−0.27		−0.39*	
Cohort (1960 = 0; per decade)	0.39**	0.15	0.26**	0.10
Cohort×level of education parents	−0.06**	−0.07	0.01	0.01
Cohort×field of study parents		0.09		0.06
General	−0.16†		0.05	
Arts/humanities	0.76**		0.08	
Technical	0.02		0.13†	
Medical	−0.22		0.22	
Law	0.26		−0.58**	
Care	−0.52**		−0.36*	
R^2	0.49		0.66	

Notes: Beta values are based upon constructed sheaf variables; controlled for the field of study of the highest attained level of education. **$p < 0.01$; *$p < 0.05$; †$p < 0.10$ (two-tailed tests).
Source: FSDP 1992, 1998, 2000, 2003 and 2009; authors' own calculations.

separately. All distinguished fields of study are included in the analysis, but only the most relevant fields (arts/humanities, technical, medical, law, care versus general) are presented in the table.

Both models (for men and women) show that both the level of education and the field of study of parents affect the highest attained educational level of their children. The effect of the parental educational level implies that each additional year of education for parents results in an increase of 0.32 years of education for their sons. For daughters, this increase is 0.26 years of education for each year of parental education. The effect of the parental field of study indicates that sons of parents with a technical field of study attain on average the highest educational level. Daughters of parents with a field of study in care are, conversely, on average lowest educated. The results also highlight that the influence of the parental educational level is much stronger than the influence of the parental field of study. The standardized regression coefficients amount to, respectively, 0.29 (0.25) and 0.06 (0.05) for men (women).

In addition, the models show that, as predicted, the intergenerational transmission of level of education for men has declined over time. For men born in 1960 (the mean year of birth in the observed data), the effect of parental educational level on their own educational level amounts to 0.32 years; for each decade of birth later, this decreases with 0.06 years of education. Thus, the effect of the parental educational level for men born in 1984 (the youngest respondents in the data) is 0.25 (0.39 − (2.4 × −0.06)). The observed trend in the effect of parental level of education on their offspring's educational level implies a general decrease of inequality of educational outcomes in the Netherlands.

The influence of the parental field of study on highest attained educational level of children has also changed over time. The effect of parental field on the highest attained educational level for sons with parents who obtained their highest level of education in the fields of care and general education has decreased. On the contrary, for those with parents who obtained their highest qualifications in arts/humanities, the effect has increased. This latter finding means, for example, that sons of parents with a field of study in arts/humanities are nowadays higher educated on average than was the case in former days. For daughters, the effect of parental education in the fields of study of law and care has decreased, but that of parental education in a technical field of study has increased. Given the fact that the influence of the parental educational level has decreased for men (has remained stable for women) and the effect of the field of study of the parents has increased, the relative impact of the parental field of study (compared with the parental level of education) has increased over time. This may seem not surprising when a country, such as the Netherlands, moves to a mass system of higher education.

In Table 4, the effects of parental level of education and field of study on the field of study choice of their children are presented. We control for

Table 4. The (changed) effects of the parental level of education and field of study on the field of study of the highest attained level of (intermediate vocational, higher vocational and university) education (conditional logit analysis; $n = 5033$).

	\multicolumn{5}{c}{b}
	Arts/humanities	Technical	Medical	Law	Care
Men					
Level of education, parents (years)	0.03	0.04**	−0.02	0.05	0.00
Corresponding field of study, parents	−0.40	0.49**	1.17**	0.82†	−8.09
Cohort (1960 = 0; per decade)	−0.62	0.01	0.03	−0.04	0.27
Cohort×level of education, parents	0.04†	0.02†	−0.01	0.04†	0.00
Cohort×corresponding field of study, parents	−1.77**	0.31**	0.06	−0.12	−0.21
Women					
Level of education, parents (years)	0.06	0.04	0.00	0.01	0.00
Corresponding field of study, parents	0.29	0.54**	1.13**	1.35**	0.52†
Cohort (1960 = 0; per decade)	−0.38*	−0.25†	−0.29**	0.10	−0.22*
Cohort×level of education, parents	0.02	−0.10**	0.01	0.04	0.03
Cohort×corresponding field of study, parents	−0.30	0.02	0.05	−[a]	−0.08

Notes: [a]Estimate unreliable not presented; controlled for the highest attained level of (intermediate vocational, higher vocational and university) education.
** $p < 0.01$; * $p < 0.05$; † $p < 0.10$ (two-tailed test).
Source: FSDP 1992, 1998, 2000, 2003 and 2009; authors' own calculations.

the attained level of the children themselves (i.e. intermediate vocational, higher vocational and university). Once again, men and women are analysed separately. The presented estimates are based on a conditional logit analysis. Contrary to the multinomial logit model, in which for each possible combination of educational fields of the parents and of children a separate parameter is estimated, we here only estimate one parameter per educational field. This parameter indicates the (log) odds for a child to pursue the same field (against any other field of study) as its parents. In other words, the effects of all other fields of study combinations are fixed at the value of zero, resulting in a more parsimonious model. In Table 4, once again, only the results of the most relevant fields of study (arts/humanities, technical, medical, law and care) are presented (although the effects of the remaining fields are simultaneously estimated as well). The categories in the dependent variable are contrasted in such a way that they reflect the odds of choosing a certain field of study relative to the choice for any other field of study.

First of all, the results show that parental level of education has only a limited influence on the obtained field of study of the highest attained level of education of individuals. Educational level of the parents only has a positive effect on the choice for a technical field of study for men. Furthermore, a strong intergenerational transmission of field of study emerges. For most fields of study, it holds true that children choose relatively more often the same field of study as their parents than any other one. For sons, this intergenerational resemblance is strongest for the medical field of study. For daughters, this is in law. Thus, parental field of study plays a greater role in the choice for a certain field of study of their children than parental level of education. This also emerges when we compare the fit of the models, in which we either remove the parental level of education or field of study (not shown in Table 4). Both for men and women, the deterioration of the fit (in terms of chi-square value) is bigger when parental field of education is removed from the model than when the level of education of the parents is excluded.

Changes in the influence of the parental level of education and field of study on the obtained field of study of their children are also estimated in Table 4. First of all, the results reveal for men that the effect of the parental educational level on the choice for the fields of arts/humanities, technical and law has increased over birth cohorts, while for women the effect of the parental educational level on the choice for the technical field of study was reduced. Second, the influence of the parental field of study on the field of study of their sons has changed over time for two fields. With regard to arts/humanities, the intergenerational transmission has decreased. Concerning the technical field of study, on the contrary, it has increased. Roughly we can say that the effects of the parental level of education and field of study have increased over time. Unfortunately, it is (statistically) not possible to test whether the relative impact of the parental field of study (compared with the parental level of education) has changed over time. However, the fact remains that when looking at a person's field of study choice, the role of the parental field of study is many times bigger than that of the parental level of education. This finding, once more, underscores that parental resources for their field of study are important in the process of educational and social reproduction, especially in the Dutch context with its mass system of higher education and occupational labour market relying on vocational-specific knowledge and skills.

5. Conclusion and discussion

In this article we have first of all answered the question of how the choice of field of study has developed across birth cohorts in the Netherlands. The results of the empirical analyses, based on the five available waves from the FSDP (1992, 1998, 2000, 2003 and 2009), show that educational expansion has been accompanied by an increasing educational (i.e. vocational) specialization. Currently, the vast majority (i.e. about five-sixths) successfully graduate with a vocational qualification in any of the available fields of study in the Netherlands. At the outset of our observation period (birth cohort 1914–1939) this was only slightly more than one-half. Especially, economic fields of study have become more popular for men, while agricultural and, to a lesser degree, teaching studies have lost popularity. For women, an increase has taken place in the medical, economic and socio-cultural fields of study. In the most recent birth cohort, a decrease can be observed for women in the care field of study.

Second, we have investigated how the intergenerational transmission of level of education and field of study has developed historically in the Netherlands. Educational level of parents determines the level of their children to a considerable extent and there is a strong symmetry in the intergenerational transmission of field of study. What is more interesting is the observation that field of study has an influence on the highest attained level of education of children and that this influence has increased over time. It is found that sons whose parents hold a technical field of study background attain a higher level of education. Daughters with parents who obtained a care field of study attain a lower educational level. We also found that a high parental level of education increases the likelihood for sons to choose a technical field of study. This effect increases over time. For daughters, on the contrary, the effect of the parental educational level on the choice for a technical field of study decreases. Unfortunately, we have no explanation for this trend.

Based on our findings, we suggest the following themes for future research. First, it is important to establish what the benefits of the various fields of study are on the labour market. Now we know that a person's field of study choice is determined by the parental level of education and field of study, we may want to establish whether the prestige and economic pay-off of fields of study differ in the labour market. If particular fields of study give individuals more traction in the labour market than others, field of study is an important channel of social reproduction, given that – as is demonstrated – it is determined by parental background. This can be done by studying differentiation in labour-market rewards of various fields of study; for example, in terms of occupational positions. This would enable us to gain more and new insights into the status attainment process. In particular, it may contribute to our understanding of how families from upper social classes are able to reproduce their advantages to their offspring despite widening educational participation and whether this route is limited to countries with extensive systems of vocational training. Second, it is worthwhile to investigate deeper whether the transmission of educational resources is sex specific. Do fathers transmit their resources relatively more upon their sons than upon their daughters? And are mothers more determinative for the educational choices of their daughters? Third, a closer investigation into the explanation of the observed intergenerational transmission of educational resources is useful. If fields of study can be interpreted hierarchically, the question is which resources lay at their basis. Do only certain fields of study nurture skills and abilities that are useful for educational attainment and returns? And what kind of skills and abilities are these? A direct measurement of the knowledge and skills that are acquired in different educational fields may clarify this.

Earlier research in the Netherlands has shown that the educational expansion has resulted in a decrease of the intergenerational transmission of level of education. This study extends that research to include field of study as an educational resource into the status attainment model. This clearly has led to a more nuanced picture. We foremost have found that field of study is important with regard to the intergenerational transmission of educational inequality and that its relevance has increased over time. The move to a mass system of higher education, with state-funded stipends and where the signalling role of parental level of education has declined, meant that upper-class parents invest more of their time in the transfer of field-specific resources to preserve social reproduction. This illustrates that educational expansion does not necessarily lead to a more meritocratic society in terms of educational outcomes.

References

Beck, U. 1992. *Risk Society: Towards a New Modernity*. London: Sage.
Blau, P. M., and O. D. Duncan. 1967. *The American Occupational Structure*. New York, NY: John Wiley & Sons.
Bourdieu, P., and J. C. Passeron. 1977. *Reproduction in Education, Society and Culture*. London: Sage.
Bourdieu, P. 1986. "The Forms of Capital." In *The Handbook for Theory and Research for the Sociology of Education,* edited by John G. Richardson, 241–258. Westport, CT: Greenwood Publishing Group.
Brown, P., A. Green, and H. Lauder. 2001. *High Skills: Globalization, Competitiveness and Skills Formation*. Oxford: Oxford University Press.
Charles, M., and K. Bradley. 2009. "Indulging Our Gendered Selves? Sex Segregation by Field of Study in 44 Countries." *American Journal of Sociology* 114: 924–976.
Davies, S., and N. Guppy. 1997. "Fields of Study, College Selectivity and Student Inequalities in Higher Education." *Social Forces* 75: 1417–1438.
de Graaf, N.-D., P. M. de Graaf, G. Kraaykamp, and W. C. Ultee, 1998. *Family Survey Dutch Population 1998* [machine-readable data file]. Department of Sociology, Radboud University Nijmegen [producer]. The Hague: Dans [distributor].
de Graaf, N.-D., P. M. de Graaf, G. Kraaykamp, and W. C. Ultee. 2000. *Family Survey Dutch Population 2000* [machine-readable data file]. Department of Sociology, Radboud University Nijmegen [producer]. The Hague: Dans [distributor].

de Graaf, N.-D., P. M. de Graaf, G. Kraaykamp, and W. C. Ultee. 2003. *Family Survey Dutch Population 2003* [machine-readable data file]. Department of Sociology, Radboud University Nijmegen [producer]. The Hague: Dans [distributor].

de Graaf, P. M., and H. B. G. Ganzeboom. 1993. "Family Background and Educational Attainment in the Netherlands of 1891–1960 Birth Cohorts." In *Persistent Inequality*, edited by Y. Shavit and H. P. Blossfeld, 75–100. Boulder: Westview Press.

de Graaf, P. M., and M. H. J. Wolbers. 2003. "The Effects of Social Background, Sex and Ability on the Transition to Tertiary Education in the Netherlands." *The Netherlands' Journal of Social Sciences* 39: 172–201.

Gangl, M. 2001. "European Patterns of Labour Market Entry: A Dichotomy of Occupationalized versus Non-Occupationalized Systems?" *European Societies* 3: 471–494.

Ganzeboom, H. B. G. and W. C. Ultee. 1992. *Family Survey Dutch Population 1992* [machine-readable data file. Department of Sociology, Radboud University Nijmegen [producer]. The Hague: Dans [distributor].

Goldthorpe, J. H. 2000. *On Sociology. Numbers, Narratives, and the Integration of Research and Theory*. Oxford University Press: Oxford.

Goyette, K. A., and A. L. Mullen. 2006. "Who Studies Arts and Sciences? Social Background and the Choice and Consequences of Undergraduate Field of Study." *The Journal of Higher Education* 77: 497–538.

Kalmijn, M., and T. van der Lippe. 1997. "Type of Schooling and Sex Differences in Earnings in the Netherlands." *European Sociological Review* 13: 1–15.

Kraaykamp, G. 2009. *Culturele Socialisatie: En Zegen en een Vloek. Verbreding en Verdieping in het Sociologisch Onderzoek naar Langetermijneffecten van Culturele Opvoeding*. Nijmegen: Radboud University (Inaugural lecture).

Kraaykamp, G., S. Ruiter, and M. H. J. Wolbers. 2009. *Family Survey Dutch Population 2009* [machine-readable data file. Department of Sociology, Radboud University Nijmegen [producer]. The Hague: Dans [distributor].

Kraaykamp, G., and K. van Eijck. 2010. "The Intergenerational Reproduction of Cultural Capital: A Threefold Perspective." *Social Forces* 89: 209–231.

Marsden, D. 1986. *The End of Economic Men? Custom and Competition in Labour Markets*. Brighton: Wheatsheaf.

Pakulski, J., and M. Waters. 1996. *The Death of Class*. London: Sage.

Raferty, A. E., and M. Hout. 1993. "Maximally Maintained Inequality: Expansion, Reform, and Opportunity in Irish Education, 1921–1975." *Sociology of Education* 66: 41–62.

Reimer, D., C. Noelke, and A. Kucel. 2008. "Labor Market Effects of Field of Study in Comparative Perspective: An Analysis of 22 European Countries." *International Journal of Comparative Sociology* 49: 233–256.

Reimer, D., and R. Pollak. 2010. "Educational Expansion and Its Consequences for Vertical and Horizontal Inequalities in Access to Higher Education in Germany." *European Sociological Review* 26: 415–430.

Shavit, Y., and H. P. Blossfeld, eds. 1993. *Persistent Inequality: Changing Educational Attainment in Thirteen Countries*. Boulder: Westview Press.

Shavit, Y., and W. Müller, eds. 1998. *From School to Work. a Comparative Study of Educational Qualifications and Occupational Destinations*. Oxford: Clarendon Press.

Tieben, N., and M. H. J. Wolbers. 2010. "Success and Failure in Secondary Education. Socio-Economic Background Effects on Secondary School Outcome in the Netherlands, 1927-1998." *British Journal of Sociology of Education* 31: 277–290.

Triventi, M. 2013. "Stratification in Higher Education and Its Relationship with Social Inequality. a Comparative Study of 11 European Countries." *European Sociological Review* 29: 489–502.

Triventi, M. 2013b. "The Role of Higher Education Stratification in the Reproduction of Social Inequality in the Labor Market." *Research in Social Stratification and Mobility*, http://dx.doi.org/10.1016/j.rssm.2013.01.003. First published online: February, 8.

van de Werfhorst, H. G. 2004. "Systems of Educational Specialization and Labour Market Outcomes in Norway, Australia and the Netherlands." *International Journal of Comparative Sociology* 45: 315–335.

van de Werfhorst, H. G., N. D. de Graaf, and G. Kraaykamp. 2001. "Intergenerational Resemblance in Field of Study in the Netherlands." *European Sociological Review* 17: 275–293.

van de Werfhorst, H. G., and G. Kraaykamp. 2001. "Four Field-Related Educational Resources and Their Impact on Labor, Consumption and Sociopolitical Orientation." *Sociology of Education* 74: 296–317.

van de Werfhorst, H. G., G. Kraaykamp, and N. D. de Graaf. 2000. "Intergenerational Transmission of Educational Field Resources, the Impact of Parental Resources and Socialisation Practices on Children's Fields of Study in the Netherlands." *The Netherlands' Journal of Social Sciences* 36: 188–210.

van de Werfhorst, H. G., A. Sullivan, and S. Y. Cheung. 2003. "Social Class, Ability and Choice of Subject in Secondary and Tertiary Education in Britain." *British Educational Research Journal* 29: 41–62.

The role of the school curriculum in social mobility

Cristina Iannelli

Moray House School of Education, University of Edinburgh, Edinburgh, UK

> This paper focuses on the role of curricular content on social mobility, an issue largely neglected by social mobility studies. Using data from the National Child Development Study we investigate the extent to which secondary school curricula account for social class differences in the chances of entering into the service class and avoiding a low-skilled occupation. The results show that curriculum matters in the acquisition of different social classes of destination but it matters more for children from advantaged social backgrounds than for children from lower classes of origin. This is because of their higher propensity to choose subjects such as languages, English, mathematics and science, which were found to be highly valued in the labour market. Moreover, net of the effect of origin class and individual ability, all or most of the advantage associated with attendance at selective schools is accounted for by the curriculum studied there.

Introduction

Social mobility studies have investigated extensively the intermediary role of education between social class of origin and destination (Marshall, Swift, and Roberts 1997; Breen 2004; Iannelli and Paterson 2007). Their findings show that relative social class differences in terms of access to the top occupational destinations are still wide and that, despite the growing importance of education for social mobility, we are still far from the advent of a truly 'meritocratic' society. This is because social mobility processes are only partly mediated by education (i.e. a large portion of the social class (dis) advantage cannot be explained by differences in educational attainment) and because inequalities in education are still strong. Thus, children of middle-class families are more likely to achieve higher occupational outcomes than children of working-class families irrespective of their educational qualifications. Moreover, people from lower social classes are less likely to achieve higher educational qualifications and this in turn depresses their chances of reaching high-status occupations.

Some studies have also analysed the role that school types play in the social reproduction of inequalities across generations (Halsey, Heath, and Ridge 1980; Kerckhoff 1993, 1996; Sullivan and Heath 2002; Boliver and Swift 2011). The type of school attended (selective or comprehensive) was found to affect individuals' chances of gaining higher educational qualifications and of being socially mobile. However, this research has not investigated the role of curricular content in social mobility processes. This paper aims at filling this gap through the analysis of the effect of different subjects studied at school (as well as school types) on individuals' destinations and the analysis of the extent to which (im)mobility patterns can be explained by the curriculum studied and the school type attended. Moreover, while social mobility studies have usually analysed mature occupational destinations and, in some cases, first job destinations, the present paper adopts a longitudinal perspective by examining social class of destination at ages 23, 33 and 42.

Curriculum and the reproduction of social inequalities

In the 1970s, research on school curricula found that the content of school programmes played an important part in the reproduction of social inequalities in education. Structural reproduction theorists argued that school curricula were structured in a way that benefited pupils from higher social classes (see Young 1971; Apple 1978; Bernstein 1973–75; Bourdieu 1977). In this view, at the time of entering school, children from higher social classes are already familiar with the world of knowledge to which school is related. They have already acquired the code by which to decipher the meaning of cultural goods in their families. They have a 'readiness' for school that children from lower social classes do not possess because the latter are less exposed to the dominant culture taught in school. Teese and Lamb (2007, 302) summarise this issue well: 'Schooling places poor children in permanent "catch up" mode, while children from better-off families are normally in "extension" mode'.

This initial disadvantage can then be exacerbated by students' allocation to different types of ability and curriculum groupings. Most of the literature on curriculum differentiation has focused on the role of tracking and the distinction between vocational and academic curricula (Oakes 1985; Kerckhoff 1986; Gamoran and Mare 1989; Arum and Shavit 1995). Some scholars have stressed that the dominant groups preserve their privileges by track placement. Even when a certain educational level becomes universal, the more advantaged social classes are able to transmit an advantage to their children by securing them a place in high tracks and/or more prestigious institutions (Lucas 2001). A contrasting viewpoint stresses that low tracks and more vocationally oriented curricula can increase the opportunities of poor and minority groups by providing them with specific, marketable skills (Gambetta 1987; Arum and Shavit 1995). Vocational tracks may provide a 'safety net' to guard people against unemployment or unskilled manual jobs but may also divert them from higher status occupational destinations (Shavit and Müller 2000).

The debate of whether social class differences can be reduced by offering the same curriculum to all or by offering differentiated curricula that take into account personal predispositions and interests is still alive. Noddings (2011), for example, argues that students should be given the freedom to choose courses that interest them and not be forced into college preparatory programmes where they might fail. According to this author, high-quality vocational education, which can provide students with intellectual stimulus as well as practical skills, is a better and a more 'democratic' option. In her reply Reay (2011) expresses concerns, shared by many social stratification researchers, that allocation into vocational and academic programmes is not driven by 'natural inclinations and intrinsic academic dispositions'. The lack of parity of esteem between academic and vocational education in the United Kingdom, as in the United States, makes the coexistence of these two types of education a way of sorting children according to social class lines.

A few studies in social stratification have gone beyond the distinction between academic and vocational tracks in secondary education and have analysed in more detail the role of different fields of study (Van de Werfhorst, Sullivan, and Cheung 2003) and non-hierarchical curriculum differentiation (Ayalon 2006) in the reproduction of social inequalities. Both of these studies found a strong association between social class of origin, subject choices and educational attainment. Moreover, Van de Werfhorst (2002) analysed the mediating role of field of study in the process of intergenerational social mobility in the Netherlands, finding that the major part of intergenerational class (im)mobility is accounted for by class differences in educational choices. Working-class children tend to choose technical and economic subjects that lead to skilled-manual and routine non-manual occupations but which also prevent them from reaching higher social classes. Children from higher social classes choose prestigious fields of study, such as medicine and law, which lead to higher class positions.

Research questions

The present study builds upon two previous pieces of research that also used data from the National Child Development Study (NCDS). Kerckhoff (1993) analysed the structural effects of schools on educational achievement and early job career (by age 23) in Britain. He found that the kind of school attended (selective or comprehensive) and to which ability group the students were assigned had a significant impact on students' academic achievement, even after controlling for their social background and previous academic performance. Moreover, the cumulative effects of being placed in advantaged or disadvantaged locations (at school and in the labour market) made individuals' achievements highly divergent. More recently, Boliver and Swift (2011) found that, controlling for selection into different types of schools, people from low-income and low-social-class families who attended grammar schools were not more likely to be upward mobile than people with the same characteristics who attended comprehensive schools. However, having attended a grammar school made their upward mobility longer in range (i.e. they reached higher income or occupational destinations than if they had attended a comprehensive school). Moreover, studying in a grammar school did not bring more advantages to people originating from lower socio-economic backgrounds than to people from more advantaged backgrounds. Considering grammar and secondary modern schools together, they concluded that the old selective system was no better for social mobility than the comprehensive system which replaced it.

These two studies did not examine whether and how school curricula shape individuals' chances of social mobility. This paper aims to address these issues by answering the following questions:

(1) *To what extent are social class differences in individuals' chances of reaching a service-class position and avoiding a lower social class of destination mediated by the school type attended and the curricula followed?*
(2) *Can school variations in the above chances be attributable to differences in the curriculum taught?*
(3) *Does the effect of schools and curricula change over the life-course?*

Data

The analyses presented in this paper use data from the NCDS. The NCDS is a continuing longitudinal study of all those born in one week in 1958, following them up at ages 7, 11, 16, 23, 33, 42, 46 and 50. The people in the study were in secondary schools between 1969 and 1976 during the period of reorganisation of British secondary education from a selective to a comprehensive system. The coexistence of different secondary school systems at the end of the 1960s provides an excellent opportunity to study the effect of studying different curricula and attending different types of school on individuals' chances of reaching the highest social classes of destination. This is because all respondents went to school in the same period and are likely to have experienced similar labour-market circumstances.[1] Additionally, to be able to look at the long-term effects of curriculum on adult destinations (at age 42) we need to refer to a school system that existed in the past.

Like any longitudinal study, the original NCDS sample (17,416 cases) has reduced over time due to attrition (Table 1). Despite the attrition problem, the NCDS data have managed to maintain a high degree of national representativeness (Nathan 1999). Both Nathan (1999) and Hawkes and Plewis (2006) found that the main factors affecting non-response were low educational attainment, gender, and social class. These variables are included in the analyses and should therefore have allowed us to control for an important part of bias due to attrition (Little and Rubin 1987, 14–15).

The sample in the analyses is composed only of those cases in which information on the dependent variables (i.e. social class of destination) was available at the three time points (Table 1). To avoid any further reduction in the sample we included in the models missing information for the independent variables as additional categories.

Variables

Our dependent variables are respondents' social classes of destination in their current or last job at the ages of 23, 33 and 42. In the NCDS data, respondents' social class was coded into Socio-Economic Groups (SEG). We recoded this information using an approximation to the Erikson, Goldthorpe and Portocarero (EGP) seven-class schema (Heath and McDonald 1987). In the first part of the study the chances of entering a service-class position (Class I–II of the EGP schema) versus the chances of entering the other social classes of destination is analysed. The second part focuses on the chances of ending-up in lower social classes of destination (Class IIIb and VIIa of the EGP schema). We followed Erikson and Goldthorpe (1992), who categorised Class IIIb (lower grade routine non-manual occupations, predominantly female) and Class VIIa (semi-skilled and unskilled manual occupations, not in agriculture, predominantly male) as having the same low occupational status.

The effect of social background on the above destinations was measured by parental social class and education when respondents were age 16. Parental social class was measured as the higher class between father's and mother's. Three classes were distinguished: service class (Class I–II), intermediate class (Class III–V) and working class (Class VI–VII). The informa-

Table 1. Sample sizes.

	Original	At age 23	At age 33	At age 42
Achieved sample	17,416	12,537	11,407	11,419
Sample size in the analyses	–	11,814	10,580	9,590

Note: NCDS data.

tion on mother's and father's age of leaving full-time education was used as a proxy for the highest educational level attended by parents: age 15 or younger indicates attending only an elementary education or some vocational secondary education, age 15–18 indicates attending a proper upper-secondary education, and age 18 or older indicates achieving a senior school certificate and attending university.

Curriculum type studied at school was measured by the number of courses taken in different subjects when respondents were aged 16 (usually ranging from zero to five courses). The subjects analysed are: English, mathematics, languages, arts, social sciences, domestic, commercial, sciences, technical and other. Since English and mathematics were often part of a core curriculum (one English and one mathematics course were required in most cases), we distinguished between: those who did not achieve the minimum required (i.e. achieved either one English or one mathematics course only, or neither); those who achieved the minimum required in these subjects (one of each); and those who achieved more than the minimum. Certain subjects had higher status than others, based on their level of difficulty: classics, modern languages, sciences and mathematics were usually attempted by academically more able pupils in contrast to vocationally oriented subjects, such as domestic, secretarial and technical studies (Kelly 1976; Fitz-Gibbon and Vincent 1994; Sparks 2000).[2]

We distinguished five types of school based on the information collected at the time respondents were aged 16: comprehensive, grammar, secondary modern, independent/direct grant schools (i.e. independent schools that received some public subsidy) and other types of school including missing values. The student composition of these schools was very different. In the selective system, the most academically able pupils (based in principle mainly on the results of tests taken at age 11) went to grammar schools where they were taught a highly academic curriculum. The majority of pupils who failed to gain access to grammar schools went to secondary modern schools, and a small minority (3%) to technical schools. The curriculum offered in these schools was more basic and focused on practical skills. In the mid-1960s, non-selective, neighbourhood-based comprehensive schools were introduced in most of Great Britain. Despite some differences in curriculum arrangements, most comprehensive schools adopted a core curriculum, in which English and mathematics were required subjects, plus five other usually optional subjects (Benn and Simon 1970).

Alongside the above state schools co-existed a number of independent schools (fee-paying) that were entirely free to select their own pupils generally on the basis of academic and financial criteria. Most of these schools were educationally similar to grammar schools but probably with a less selective ability range. (In the NCDS data, the mean ability of pupils who attended grammar schools and independent schools was respectively 57.5 and 52.7, with standard deviations 10.0 and 12.4).

Each type of school had also a clear social class connotation: the proportion of pupils from non-manual families was much higher in independent and grammar schools than in comprehensive and secondary modern schools while higher proportions of pupils from manual families attended secondary modern and comprehensive schools (Kerckhoff et al. 1996, table 11.1, 226).

We used gender and respondents' ability in the statistical modelling as control variables (for space reasons, their coefficients are not presented in the tables). Originally all the analyses were carried out separately for men and women. The general patterns were very similar between the two genders and, for this reason, the pooled sample was analysed. Respondents' ability at age 11 was measured by a test of general ability, recorded on a scale from 0 to 80. To control for this variable is very important since, as discussed above, selection into grammar and independent schools is based on ability.

Analytical strategy

A set of logistic regression models was run to analyse the effect of social background factors on the outcomes (direct effect) and the extent to which 'school types' and 'curricula' mediate the effect of social background (indirect effect). Figure 1 illustrates the analyses conducted.

Changes in the coefficients related to 'social class of origin' and 'parental education' were compared across nested models (without and with 'school types' and 'curricula' among the independent variables) using the KHB method (Karlson, Breen, and Holm 2012) and the statistical software STATA 12. Comparing coefficients across logistic models can be problematic because the variance of the dependent variable changes when new explanatory variables are added, thus affecting the size of the estimates (Long 1997; Mood 2010). Karlson, Breen, and Holm (2012) have provided a method to solve this problem by separating changes in coefficients due to rescaling from changes due to the introduction of more variables in the model. Furthermore this method allows us to decompose the total effect of 'social

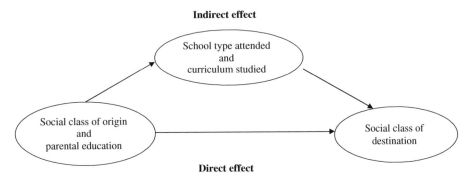

Figure 1. Theoretical model of direct and indirect effects (via school and curriculum) of social background factors on individuals' social class of destination.

class of origin' and 'parental education' into their direct and indirect effects (via 'school types' and 'curricula') (see Tables 5 and 7). Full models are presented only for the outcomes at age 33 (in Tables 4 and 6). As discussed later in the paper, the results for ages 23 and 42 resemble the results at age 33.

Some descriptive statistics

Of the NCDS sample, 33% grew up in a service class family (Class I–II), another 38% in an intermediate social class family (Class III–V) and 29% in a manual class family (Class VI and VII). The general level of parental education was not particularly high: 42% of parents left full-time education at the first possibility (at 15 or younger); another 48% left school at upper-secondary level (at 18 or younger); only 10% of parents left education at higher levels of education (aged older than 18).

At age 23, 27% of respondents occupied a service-class position (Class I–II), another 32% had a routine non-manual occupation (Class III) and around 34% was in a semi-skilled or unskilled manual occupation (Class VI–VII) (Table 2). Respondents' social class clearly improved over the life-course: between ages 23 and 42 the percentage of respondents in Class I almost doubled, and by the age of 42 the percentage of those in the service class (Class I–II) reached 47%.

The majority of respondents in the sample attended comprehensive schools (60%), another 22% secondary modern schools, 12% grammar and 6% independent schools. Table 3 shows large differences among the four school types in the number of courses taken in different subjects by the NCDS members. People who attended grammar and independent schools studied a higher number of languages, sciences, English and mathematics subjects. They also were less likely to study vocationally oriented subjects (i.e. technical, commercial and domestic) and 'other' subjects than people in other schools. A more balanced situation emerges in relation to arts and social sciences.

Table 2. Class of destination by age (percentages).

	Age 23	Age 33	Age 42
Class I	4.7	16.6	20.6
Class II	22.3	19.4	26.7
Class IIIa,b	32.2	28.9	21.7
Class IVa,b,c	3.3	4.7	7.6
Class V	3.9	1.9	5.1
Class VI	16.4	13.7	8.7
Class VIIa,b	17.2	14.9	9.7
Total no. of cases	11,814	10,580	9,590

Note: EGP seven-class schema.

Table 3. Number of subjects studied at age 16 by school type.

	Grammar	Secondary modern	Independent/ direct grant	Comprehensive
Languages	1.26	0.17	1.36	0.46
	(0.02)	(0.009)	(0.04)	(0.009)
Arts	1.19	1.29	1.42	1.12
	(0.03)	(0.02)	(0.04)	(0.01)
Social sciences	0.78	0.83	0.73	0.80
	(0.02)	(0.02)	(0.03)	(0.009)
Domestic	0.24	0.60	0.17	0.44
	(0.02)	(0.02)	(0.02)	(0.009)
Commercial	0.07	0.36	0.04	0.34
	(0.01)	(0.02)	(0.01)	(0.01)
Sciences	1.61	0.86	1.60	1.07
	(0.03)	(0.02)	(0.04)	(0.01)
Technical	0.24	0.70	0.09	0.59
	(0.02)	(0.02)	(0.02)	(0.01)
Other	0.05	0.18	0.05	0.12
	(0.007)	(0.01)	(0.01)	(0.005)
English and mathematics (%)				
Either one English or one mathematics, or neither	0.6	6.0	1.1	3.4
One English and one mathematics	17.0	72.9	21.3	64.0
Two English or/and two mathematics or more	82.3	21.1	77.6	32.5

Note: Data presented as mean (standard error).

Entry into the service class

The first logistic regression analysis examines the effect of social background and school factors on respondents' chances of gaining a service class of destination versus other classes of destination at age 33.

Model 1 in Table 4 analyses the effect of respondents' social class of origin and parental education, net of the effect of gender and ability. This model will be used as a baseline to compare changes in the coefficients related to social background factors in order to explore how much of the effect of these factors on destinations is mediated by the school attended and the curriculum studied. In line with other studies we found that origin class has a strong effect on entry into the service class. People originating from service classes and, to a lesser extent, from intermediate classes are significantly more likely to enter the top social classes than people from lower social classes. Moreover, the higher the parents' education the higher is the children's chance of entering the service class.

Model 2 introduces the effect of school type attended. The results replicate other studies' findings: compared with people from comprehensive

Table 4. Binomial logistic regression of the chances of entering service class (Class I–II) versus all the other classes at age 33.

	Model 1	Model 2	Model 3
Constant	−3.11***	−2.87***	−2.75***
	(0.12)	(0.13)	(0.17)
Parents' social class when respondents were age 16 (Ref. Class VI–VII)			
Class I–II	0.79***	0.73***	0.61***
	(0.07)	(0.07)	(0.07)
Class III–V	0.32***	0.30***	0.25***
	(0.07)	(0.07)	(0.07)
Missing	0.44***	0.40**	0.42**
	(0.13)	(0.13)	(0.13)
Parents' age of leaving full-time education (Ref. age 15 years or younger)			
18 or more years	0.98***	0.84***	0.70***
	(0.09)	(0.09)	(0.10)
15–18 years	0.15**	0.12*	0.07
	(0.06)	(0.06)	(0.06)
Missing	0.19	0.15	0.06
	(0.13)	(0.13)	(0.13)
School type attended at age 16 (Ref. comprehensive)			
Grammar		0.49***	0.04
		(0.08)	(0.08)
Secondary modern		−0.13*	0.13
		(0.06)	(0.07)
Independent/direct grant		0.80***	0.34**
		(0.10)	(0.11)
Other/missing		0.06	0.13
		(0.06)	(0.13)
Number of subjects studied at age 16			
Languages			0.36***
			(0.04)
Arts			−0.03
			(0.03)
Social sciences			−0.02
			(0.04)
Domestic			−0.07
			(0.05)
Commercial			−0.009
			(0.04)
Sciences			0.26***
			(0.03)
Technical			−0.17***
			(0.04)
Other			−0.12
			(0.08)

(*Continued*)

Table 4. (*Continued*).

	Model 1	Model 2	Model 3
Missing			0.12
			(0.13)
English and mathematics, number of subjects (Ref. one English and one mathematics)			
Either one English or one mathematics or neither			0.04 (0.16)
Two English or/and two mathematics or more			0.40*** (0.06)
−2 log likelihood	12,319.892	12,215.200	11,888.241

Total number of cases: 10,580.
All models control for the effect of gender and ability.
*Significant at 0.05 level;
**significant at 0.01 level;
***significant at 0.001 level.

schools, those who attended grammar and independent school had a significant advantage in entering the top-level occupations while those who attended secondary modern schools were at a disadvantage. These school effects are significant even after controlling for social background factors and respondents' ability, and this demonstrates that the student composition of the school cannot fully account for differences in individuals' chances of reaching the top occupations. Moreover, the introduction of school type in the model changes little the coefficients of social class and parental education. Using the KHB method we were able to quantify the extent to which 'school types' mediate the effect of respondents' social class of origin and parental education. The results in Table 5 show that attendance at different types of school contributes little to explaining social class differences in entry to the service class: at age 33 the percentage change in the coefficients of social class due to the introduction of school types is about 6–8% and significant only for the top social classes. School types attended explain more of the effect of parental education: at age 33, 16% of the advantage transmitted by highly educated parents was linked to the school type attended. This may be explained by the high percentage of people with highly educated parents who went to grammar and independent schools (even higher than those from service class of origin).

The questions that now need to be addressed are: do subjects studied at school made a difference in individuals' chances of entering the top social classes? and do subjects explain social class and school differences in the likelihood of their pupils reaching top-class occupations? The results presented in Table 4, model 3, lead us to answer positively to both questions.

Table 5. Percentages of direct and indirect effects of social class of origin and parental education on the chances of entering service class (Class I–II) at different ages.

Social class of origin (Ref. Class VI–VII)	Via school type (model 2, %)			Via school type and curriculum (model 3, %)		
	Age 23	Age 33	Age 42	Age 23	Age 33	Age 42
Class I–II						
Direct effect	94	92	89	80	75	73
Indirect effect	6*	8*	11*	20*	25*	27*
Class III–V						
Direct effect	96	94	92	89	77	77
Indirect effect	4	6	8	11	23	23
Parental education						
(Ref. left at age 15 or younger)						
Left at age 18 or later						
Direct effect	80	84	85	66	67	70
Indirect effect	20*	16*	15*	44*	33*	30*
Left between age 15 and 18						
Direct effect	92	84	84	77	52	63
Indirect effect	8	16	16	23	48	37

Control variables: gender and ability. *Significant at 0.05 level.

The high-status subjects (languages, sciences, English and mathematics), more commonly studied in grammar and independent schools (Table 3), are the ones that appear to give a significant advantage in the chances of attaining a service-class position. On the other hand, the likelihood of entering the same classes is reduced if respondents studied technical (the only significant effect), domestic and arts subjects.

The percentage of 'social class' and 'parental education' effects that is mediated by 'school types' and 'curricula' substantially increases compared with models without curricula (Table 5). In some cases it is three times higher, as for example for Class I–II (25% at age 33). For children of highly educated parents, school and curricula now explain 33% of their advantage in reaching the highest occupational position compared with children of low-educated parents. This testifies that school curricula matter in the transmission of social advantage and may matter even more than the school type attended.

However, schools and curricula are very much interrelated, as shown in Table 3. Indeed the effect of having studied in a grammar school substantially reduces and is not significant any longer when the number of courses taken in different subjects at age 16 is included in the model (Table 4, model 3). Thus, the advantage given by attending this type of school, after having controlled for individual and family characteristics, can be explained by the curriculum studied there. To a lesser extent this is also true for independent schools. However, a significant positive effect of having studied at an independent school on entry to service class remains even after controlling for curriculum type.[3]

After controlling for curriculum type, the negative effect of secondary modern schools disappears (Table 4, model 3). In these schools, curriculum, instead of enhancing occupational opportunities as in the case of selective schools, seems to have depressed occupational attainment (probably due to the predominance of technical and vocational studies). All of these results were confirmed when the logit coefficients were corrected for re-scaling using the KHB method.

Entry into lower social classes

The results of the binomial logistic regression presented in Table 6, model 1, show that, controlling for the effect of gender and ability, parents' social class and education have a strong effect on individuals' chances of ending up in the bottom social classes. These effects go in the opposite direction to that highlighted in the analyses of entry into a service-class position. Thus, having parents from service and intermediate social classes and parents with medium and high levels of education significantly reduces the chances of entering the lower social classes.

Both grammar and independent schools seem to provide a strong 'safety net' against the possibility of ending-up in lower social classes (as the

Table 6. Binomial logistic regression of the chances of entering lower social classes (Class IIIb–VIIa) versus all the other classes at age 33.

	Model 1	Model 2	Model 3
Constant	0.27*	0.12	0.33*
	(0.12)	(0.12)	(0.16)
Parents' social class when respondents were age 16 (Ref. Class VI–VII)			
Class I–II	−0.78***	−0.74***	−0.64***
	(0.08)	(0.08)	(0.09)
Class III–V	−0.43***	−0.42***	−0.38***
	(0.07)	(0.07)	(0.07)
Missing	−0.22	−0.20	−0.20
	(0.14)	(0.14)	(0.14)
Parents' age of leaving full-time education (Ref. age 15 years or younger)			
15–18 years	−0.09	−0.07	−0.05
	(0.06)	(0.06)	(0.06)
18 or more years	−0.44***	−0.30*	−0.19
	(0.13)	(0.14)	(0.14)
Missing	−0.17	−0.16	−0.11
	(0.14)	(0.14)	(0.14)
School type attended at age 16 (Ref. comprehensive)			
Grammar		−0.40***	0.02
		(0.12)	(0.13)
Secondary modern		0.16*	−0.002
		(0.07)	(0.07)
Independent/direct grant		−0.77***	−0.40*
		(0.18)	(0.19)
Other/missing		0.05	0.23
		(0.07)	(0.14)
Number of subjects studied at age 16			
Languages			−0.44***
			(0.06)
Arts			0.001
			(0.04)
Social sciences			−0.006
			(0.05)
Domestic			0.16***
			(0.05)
Commercial			−0.25***
			(0.05)
Sciences			−0.17***
			(0.04)
Technical			−0.12*
			(0.05)
Other			0.05

(*Continued*)

Table 6. (*Continued*).

	Model 1	Model 2	Model 3
			(0.07)
Missing			−0.21
			(0.14)
English and mathematics, number of subjects			
(Ref. one English and one maths)			
Either one English or one mathematics or neither			0.09
			(0.14)
Two English or/and two mathematics or more			−0.40***
			(0.08)
−2 *log likelihood*	9,746.182	9,704.896	9,516.333

Total number of cases: 10,580.
All models control for gender and ability.
*Significant at 0.05 level;
**Significant at 0.01 level;
***Significant at 0.001 level.

significant negative coefficients show in Table 6, model 2). Attendance at selective schools gave a clear advantage in reducing the chances of being in the lower social classes that cannot be explained only by the socially advantaged background of its students. In comparison with people who attended other school types, people who attended independent (and to a lesser extent grammar) schools and did not manage to achieve a service class position may have gained an advantage from the reputation of these schools, and their connections, in avoiding ending up in a low-grade occupation. This is confirmed in model 3: after controlling for curriculum studied, the effect of having attended an independent school substantially reduces but remains significant while the effect of grammar schools disappears.

Once again we found that social class differences in the chances of entering a low-social-class position can be barely explained by the school type attended (at age 33, only between 4 and 7% of the total social class effect, net of the effects of gender and ability). A larger percentage of the difference between highly educated parents and low-educated parents is due to 'school types' (at age 33, 34% of the total effect of having highly educated parents) (Table 7).

The curriculum studied at school is also a strong predictor of low occupational destinations. Having studied languages, sciences, two or more English and/or mathematics subjects reduces the chances of occupying lower social classes. However, commercial and technical subjects also reduce these chances, thus acting as a 'safety net' against ending-up in lower status jobs. Domestic subjects and arts, by contrast, are associated with higher chances of entering unskilled or low-skilled occupations.

Table 7. Percentages of direct and indirect effects of social class of origin and parental education on the chances of entering lower social classes (Class IIIb and VIIa) at different ages.

Social class of origin (Ref. Class VI–VII)	Via school type (model 2, %)			Via school type and curriculum (model 3, %)		
	Age 23	Age 33	Age 42	Age 23	Age 33	Age 42
Class I–II						
Direct effect	95	93	88	82	79	76
Indirect effect	5*	7*	12*	18*	21*	24*
Class III–V						
Direct effect	98	96	95	87	85	87
Indirect effect	2	4	5	13	15	13
Parental education						
(Ref. left at age 15 or younger)						
Left at age 18 or later						
Direct effect	75	66	72	19	39	54
Indirect effect	35*	34*	28*	81*	61*	46*
Left between age 15 and 18						
Direct effect	91	76	81	75	54	66
Indirect effect	9	24	19	25	46	34

Control variables: gender and ability. *Significant at 0.05 level.

A much larger part of the effect of social class and, in particular, of parental education can now be explained by the combined effect of school types and curriculum (Table 7): after controlling for ability and gender, 21% of the total effect of originating from the highest social classes and 61% of the effect of parental education on entry to low occupational classes at age 33 is mediated by these two institutional education factors.

Changes over the life-course

The same outcomes were analysed at ages 23 and 42. The results resembled those presented above. Selective schools, languages, English, mathematics and science subjects had a positive and significant effect on the chances of being in the top social classes and reduced the chances of entering the bottom classes also at early and later stages of respondents' occupational careers. Interestingly, the mediating effect of school types and curricula tends to increase over time in relation to social class of origin but to reduce in relation to parental education (Tables 5 and 7). Thus, when analysing entry to a service class, at age 23, 20% of the advantage of having a parent in the service class was mediated by school types and curricula compared with 27% at age 42 (Table 5). An inverse pattern is visible in relation to parental education: the mediating effect of schools and curricula reduces from 44% at age 23 to 30% at age 42. Similar patterns emerge when analysing entry into the bottom classes. These results suggest that the indirect effects of parental education via school types and curricula are stronger at the beginning of respondents' occupational career than at later stages. The opposite is true for social class of origin: it is in the long run that school and curricular choices emerge more powerfully as transmitters of social advantages.

These results highlight the importance of considering 'social class' not in a uni-dimensional way, through occupational classes or income groups only, but in a multi-dimensional way by including measures of parental education in the study of social mobility. Social (im)mobility processes may differ according to which dimension is considered.

We tested whether the effect of curriculum and school type at age 33 and 42 was simply a result of their effect at age 23 and 33. We added the effect of prior class of destination to model 3. The results, before and after controlling for prior occupational destinations, barely change in the analysis of class of destination at 33, indicating that the effect of studying different subjects and attending various types of schools continues beyond the point of career entry. However, when analysing destinations at age 42 after controlling for destination at age 33, while the effect of subjects remains the same the effect of school types reduces and is no longer significant. These results suggest that the subjects studied at school are very good predictors of individuals' destinations at all three stages of occupational career. On the other hand, the school type attended has a significant short-term and medium-term effect on individuals' occupational destinations but they become less important for explaining later destinations. This may indicate that cognitive effects may be more persistent than institutional status effects. Ishida, Spilerman, and Su (1997) argue that, if education operates as a 'signal' (Thurow 1975), its effect should be stronger at the time of entry into the labour market because employers have little information about entrants' professional ability. However, the long-lasting effects of some school subjects may indicate that they provide skills, such as critical thinking and complex reasoning, which are useful for individuals' future occupational careers.[4]

Conclusions

This study aimed to improve upon the existing social mobility studies through the examination of the intermediary effect of school curriculum on individuals' chances of social mobility. It has addressed this largely unexplored issue and has also investigated the role of curriculum in explaining the advantages associated with attending selective schools.

This paper has demonstrated that at a time in which selective and comprehensive schools coexisted in Great Britain, the curriculum studied affected individuals' chances of entering the top social classes and avoiding lower social classes. Controlling for gender and ability, a very small portion of the effect of origin class could be explained by the school attended. This means that the type of school attended did very little to amplify social class differences in entering a service-class position or in ending-up in a low-skilled occupation. This confirms Boliver and Swift's thesis that a selective system was no better than a comprehensive system for social mobility. However, our analyses show that, taken together, school types and curricula give more than a marginal advantage in reaching the top social classes for those who originated from service-class parents. Moreover, this advantage persists over time, as shown by the results at three time points of individuals' lives.

Another important result is that 'curriculum' also explains the effect of selective schools that could not be explained by the social class and ability of their pupils. In these schools, students were more likely to study a larger number of courses in subjects that have a higher status or are considered more demanding, such as languages, sciences, English and mathematics. On the other hand, in line with other studies, technical and commercial subjects (more frequently studied in secondary modern and comprehensive schools) were found to depress the chances of entering top social classes but also to decrease the chances of ending up in the bottom occupations. Curriculum differences across different types of institutions cannot be understood without referring to the historical and ideological reasons that brought them about. They originate from the nineteenth-century view of education which distinguished a curriculum aimed at educating the future leaders of society (the curriculum of grammar and independent schools) and an 'elementary' curriculum aimed at training the labour force by providing them with basic skills of reading, writing and elementary calculations (the curriculum adopted by secondary modern schools) (Lawton 1975). The introduction of comprehensive schools tried to break those two distinct school traditions by providing a secondary education to pupils of all abilities and levels of attainment, thus reflecting a more egalitarian vision of education that developed in the twentieth century. The curriculum introduced in these schools was often a combination of secondary modern and grammar school curricula (Lawton 1975).

There are a number of implications that can be drawn from the results presented in this paper. Firstly, curriculum differences reproduce social inequalities and affect individuals' chances of social (im)mobility. Secondly, among the school factors, the content taught counts more in the reproduction of social inequalities than the structure of the school system. This casts doubts on the centrality of the debate on 'comprehensive schools versus grammar schools' and it supports the need to focus the discussion on curricular content and inclusive methods of teaching this content. Thirdly, studying core subjects such as languages, English, mathematics and science is important for individuals' long-term occupational opportunities. Whether this is due to their 'higher status' or to the 'skills' that pupils studying those subjects develop could not be assessed here but requires future empirical investigation.[5]

There is no evidence to suggest that nowadays employers in the knowledge economy attribute less value to the more 'traditional' or 'elite' knowledge than they did in the past (Wolf 2002). Data from the British Skill Surveys show that people in professional and managerial occupations are those who mostly use 'generic' skills, in particular literacy skills (professionals), number skills (managers) and 'influence' skills (such as persuading and instructing others, making presentations, writing long reports and analysing complex problems) (Felstead et al. 2007). Interestingly, generic skills are found to be more and more important also among the lower status occupational groups.

Recent debates on school curricula in England focus on the need for extending the study of core subjects. The Wolf (2011) report on vocational education recommends that English and mathematics should be taught in more vocationally oriented programmes as well as in academic programmes. They are argued to be essential for young people's employment and education prospects. In a similar way, the advice given by the panel of experts for the national curriculum review (Department for Education 2011) endorses the importance of keeping English, mathematics and science as core subjects up to age 16. They also highlight that countries which achieve highly according to international standards have 'high expectations for all' and provide support for those struggling to ensure that they master the knowledge required at each stage and they are ready to progress to the next stage. Gamoran (2009) points out that 'raising standards for low achievers' and 'differentiated teaching within mixed-ability grouping' have been found to be viable ways to promote higher achievement for all, regardless of social class or other ascriptive factors. These are not easy solutions; they will require strong policy commitments and highly motivated teachers and pupils.

Acknowledgements

This work was supported by the Economic and Social Research Council (RES-000-27-0176). The author has greatly benefited from comments received from Lindsay Paterson.

Notes

1. It should be recognised, however, that the assignment to different types of school was not at random since assignment into selective schools was based on 'measured ability' and social background factors (see next section) but also because the comprehensive re-organisation occurred at a different speed across the country. Nevertheless, the introduction of respondents' ability, parental education, and parental social class in the analyses will control for a large part of the non-randomness of assignment to school type.
2. For a critique on the possibility of evaluating the level of difficulty of different subjects, see Goldstein and Cresswell (1996).
3. When the same model was run separately for men and women we found that this result applied mainly to women. Women seem to have gained an advantage from attending independent schools that goes beyond the advantage of having studied certain types of subjects in these schools.
4. It may also be argued that the continuing impact of curriculum may be the consequence of employers' preferring the social distinction indicated by participation in a grammar-school curriculum – for example, the capacity to speak specific languages, or the cultural capital associated with knowledge of a canon of literary works. See, for example, Bourdieu (1984).
5. Also requiring further investigation is the possibility that the higher occupational destinations that certain subjects lead to may be linked to the way in which these subjects are taught; for example, the logical sequencing of knowledge acquisition, enquiry-based learning or other pedagogical features.

References

Apple, M. W. 1978. "Ideology, Reproduction, and Educational Reforms." *Comparative Education Review* 22 (3): 367–387.
Arum, R., and Y. Shavit. 1995. "Secondary Vocational Education and the Transition from School to Work." *Sociology of Education* 68 (3): 187–204.
Ayalon, H. 2006. "Nonhierarchical Curriculum Differentiation and Inequality in Achievement: A Different Story or More of the Same?" *Teachers College Record* 108 (6): 1186–1213.
Benn, C., and B. Simon. 1970. *Half Way There: Report on the British Comprehensive School Reform*. Harmondsworth, UK: Penguin Books.

Bernstein, B. 1973–75. *Class, Codes and Control*. London: Paladin and Routledge and Kegan Paul, voll.3.

Boliver, V., and A. Swift. 2011. "Do Comprehensive Schools Reduce Social Mobility?" *British Journal of Sociology* 62 (1): 89–110.

Bourdieu, P. 1977. "Cultural Reproduction and Social Reproduction." In *Power and Ideology in Education*, edited by J. Karabel and A. H. Halsey, 487–511. NY: Oxford University Press.

Bourdieu, P. 1984. *Distinction*. London: Routledge and Kegan Paul.

Breen, R., ed. 2004. *Social Mobility in Europe*. Oxford: Oxford University Press.

Department for Education. 2011. *The Framework for the National Curriculum. A Report by the Expert Panel for the National Curriculum Review*. London: Department for Education.

Erikson, R., and J. H. Goldthorpe. 1992. *The Constant Flux: A Study of Class Mobility in Industrial Societies*. Oxford: Clarendon Press.

Felstead, A., D. Gallie, F. Green, and Y. Zhou. 2007. Skills at work, 1986 to 2006. ESRC Centre on Skills, Knowledge and Organisational Performance based at the Universities of Oxford and Cardiff. Available at: http://www.cardiff.ac.uk/socsi/contactsandpeople/alanfelstead/SkillsatWork-1986to2006.pdf.

Fitz-Gibbon, C. T., and L. Vincent. 1994. *Candidates' Performance in Public Examination in Mathematics and Science*. London: School Curriculum and Assessment Authority.

Gambetta, D. 1987. *Were They Pushed or Did They Jump? Individual Decision Mechanisms in Education*. Cambridge: Cambridge University Press.

Gamoran, A. 2009. *Tracking and Inequality: New Directions for Research and Practice. WCER Working Paper No.2009-6*. Madison: University of Wisconsin.

Gamoran, A., and R. D. Mare. 1989. "Secondary School Tracking and Educational Inequality: Compensation, Reinforcement, or Neutrality?" *American Journal of Sociology* 94 (5): 1146–1183.

Goldstein, H., and M. J. Cresswell. 1996. "The Comparability of External Examinations in Different Subjects." *Oxford Review of Education* 22 (4): 435–442.

Halsey, A. H., A. F. Heath, and J. M. Ridge. 1980. *Origins and Destinations: Family, Class and Education in Modern Britain*. Oxford: Clarendon Press.

Hawkes, D., and I. Plewis. 2006. "Modelling Non-Response in the National Child Development Study." *Journal of the Royal Statistical Society (Series a)* 169 (3): 479–491.

Heath, A. F., and S.-K. McDonald. 1987. "Social Change and the Future of the Left." *Political Quarterly* 58 (4): 364–377.

Iannelli, C., and L. Paterson. 2007. "Education and Social Mobility in Scotland." *Research in Social Stratification and Mobility* 25 (3): 219–232.

Ishida, H., S. Spilerman, and K.-H. Su. 1997. "Educational Credentials and Promotion Chances in Japanese and American Organisations." *American Sociological Review* 62 (6): 866–882.

Karlson, K.B., A. Holm, and R. Breen. 2012. "Comparing Regression Coefficients between Models using Logit and Probit: A New Method." *Sociological Methodology* 42 (1): 274–301.

Kelly, A. 1976. "A Study of the Comparability of External Examinations in Different Subjects." *Research in Education* 16 (1): 37–63.

Kerckhoff, A. C. 1986. "Effects of Ability Grouping in British Secondary Schools." *American Sociological Review* 51 (6): 842–858.

Kerckhoff, A. C. 1993. *Diverging Pathways: Social Structure and Career Deflections*. New York: Cambridge University Press.

Kerckhoff, A. C., K. Fogelman, D. Crook, and D. Reeder. 1996. *Going Comprehensive in England and Wales: A Study of Uneven Change*. London: The Woburn Press.

Lawton, D. 1975. *Class, Culture and the Curriculum*. London: Routledge & Kegan Paul.

Little, R. J. A., and D. B. Rubin. 1987. *Statistical Analysis with Missing Data*. New York: Wiley.

Long, J. S. 1997. *Regression Models for Categorical and Limited Dependent Variables*. Thousand Oaks, CA: Sage Publications.

Lucas, S. R. 2001. "Effectively Maintained Inequality: Education Transitions, Track Mobility, and Social Background Effects." *American Journal of Sociology* 106 (3): 1642–1690.

Marshall, G., A. Swift, and S. Roberts. 1997. *Against the Odds? Social Class and Social Justice in Industrial Societies*. Oxford: Clarendon Press.

Mood, C. 2010. "Logistic Regression: Why We Cannot Do What We Think We Can Do, and What We Can Do about It." *European Sociological Review* 26 (1): 67–82.

Nathan, G. 1999. *A Review of Sample Attrition and Representativeness in Three Longitudinal Studies, Methodology Series 13*. London: Government Statistical Service.

Noddings, N. 2011. "Schooling for Democracy." *Democracy & Education* 19, no.1: Article 1. Available at: http://democracyeducationjournal.org/home/vol19/iss1/1.

Oakes, J. 1985. *Keeping Track*. New Haven, CT: Yale University Press.

Reay, D. 2011. "Schooling for Democracy: A Common School and a Common University? A Response to "Schooling for Democracy." *Democracy & Education* 19, no.1: Article 6. Available at: http://democracyeducationjournal.org/home/vol19/iss1/6.

Shavit, Y., and W. Müller. 2000. "Vocational Secondary Education: Where Diversion and Where Safety Net?" *European Societies* 2 (1): 29–50.

Sparks, B. 2000. "Subject Comparison: A Scottish Perspective." *Oxford Review of Education* 26 (2): 175–189.

Sullivan, A., and A. F. Heath. 2002. *State and Private School in England and Wales. Sociology Working Papers*. Oxford: Nuffield College, Oxford and Department of Sociology, University of Oxford.

Teese, R., and S. Lamb. 2007. "Social Inequalities in Education Enlarging the Scope of Public Policy through Reflection on Context." In *International Studies in Educational Inequality, Theory and Policy, Volume 3 - Inequality: Educational Theory and Public Policy*, edited by R. Teese, S. Lamb, and M. Duru-Bellat, 293–307. Netherlands: Springer.

Thurow, L. C. 1975. *Generating Inequality*. London and Basingstoke: Macmillan Press.

Van de Werfhorst, H. G. 2002. "A Detailed Examination of the Role of Education in Intergenerational Social-Class Mobility." *Social Science Information* 41 (3): 407–438.

Van de Werfhorst, H. G., A. Sullivan, and S. Y. Cheung. 2003. "Social Class, Ability and Choice of Subject in Secondary and Tertiary Education in Britain." *British Educational Research Journal* 29 (1): 41–62.

Wolf, A. 2002. *Does Education Matter? Myths about Education and Economic Growth*. London: Penguin.

Wolf, A. 2011. "Review of Vocational Education – The Wolf Report." Available at: https://www.education.gov.uk/publications/standard/publicationDetail/Page1/DFE-00031-2011.

Young, M. F. D. 1971. *Knowledge and Control*. London: Collier-Macmillan.

Three generations of racism: Black middle-class children and schooling

Carol Vincent[a], Stephen Ball[a], Nicola Rollock[b] and David Gillborn[b]

[a]Department of Humanities and Social Sciences, Institute of Education, University of London, London, UK; [b]School of Education, University of Birmingham, Birmingham, UK

> This paper draws on qualitative data exploring the experiences of first-generation middle-class Black Caribbean-heritage parents, their own parents, and their children. We focus on the different ways in which race and class intersect in shaping attitudes towards education and subsequent educational practices. We argue that the nature of racism has changed, but it still remains, mainly in more subtle, insidious forms. We conclude that race cannot be simply 'added on' to class. Race changes how class works, how it is experienced, and the subjectivites available to individuals. The paper illustrates how the two intersect, in complex ways, in different historical 'moments'.

Introduction

This paper is an account of mobilities – social and spatial – across three generations for which we have data, focusing on the different ways in which race and class intersect in shaping attitudes towards education and subsequent educational practices. We argue, first, that the nature of racism has changed, but it still remains in more subtle, insidious forms. Second, race cannot be simply 'added on' to class analyses. Race/racism changes how class works, how it is experienced, and the subjectivites available to individuals. This paper illustrates how the two intersect, in complex ways, in different historical 'moments'.

In our data, the first generation is the respondents' parents, migrants from the Caribbean to the United Kingdom in the 1950s and 1960s. The respondents themselves are mostly second-generation Black British citizens who have achieved educational and labour market successes, often in challenging circumstances. They have been socially mobile, from the predominantly working-class occupations held by their parents to their current professional employment. They now seek to embed and reproduce their class assets and advantages, through their children, the third generation, and education plays a key role in their thinking and planning for the future. Their strategies with regard to education are directed towards further social mobility for their children into what they perceive to be more secure positions than their own within the middle classes, or at least the social reproduction of their achieved position. 'A thrust inscribed in the slope of the past trajectory', as Bourdieu (1986, 333) puts it. Over and against this, however, they are acutely aware of the racism that still exists in education and employment. Their class position remains 'ill-defined, open, risky and uncertain' (Bourdieu 1986, 345).

We employ an intersectional analysis to explore the ways in which the Black middle class experience various configurations of privilege and disadvantage. Intersectionality emphasises fluidity (Brah and Phoenix 2004, 76), and the importance of different locales, situations, spaces, times, different dispositions and subjectivities, for understanding particular interactions and identities. We have discussed elsewhere the way in which we have framed an intersectional analysis for this research (Vincent et al. 2012b). Specifically, as components of an intersectional analysis, we have used Bourdieu's work on class and social reproduction and the writings of Critical Race Theorists on race, racism and Whiteness, and have applied both to our data. Both allow us to 'see' the world differently; Bourdieu points to the pervasiveness of class privilege and also provides a layered, complex and nuanced understanding of social reproduction. Critical Race Theory (CRT) offers a way to uncover mundane and deeply embedded, racialised assumptions and understandings that normalise and centre White individuals, and marginalise their Black counterparts. An intersectional perspective enables us to keep both bodies of theory in play and to focus in our analysis on the points and moment where race and class come together – without privileging one over the other. This is a task easier to describe than to manage analytically and we discuss some of the difficulties below.

As well as analysing the ways in which race and class shape the priorities, actions, values and beliefs of our cohort of middle-class, middle-age Black adults, we also look before and after them, to their parents and their children, to see what these specific spatial and temporal trajectories reveal about changes in race and racial inequality in England. Mannheim's (1952) paper on the problem of generations considers the impact of generational experience across class and geographical lines. Mannheim argued that a generation could be defined in terms of collective response to a traumatic event or catastrophe that unites a particular cohort of individuals into a self-conscious age stratum; thus generations may exhibit a distinctive consciousness and different situational responses. Racism can be considered in this way. That is to say, for each generation in our study the forms of racism experienced at school and elsewhere differ, as do responses to racism, and the politics of race relations. Mannheim draws attention to what Pilcher (1994, 489) calls the 'dialectic of history and biography', meaning that each social generation has a distinctive historical consciousness. 'In this manner, each social generation, although contemporaneous with other social generations, has a distinctive historical consciousness which leads them to experience and approach the same social and cultural phenomena differently' (1994, 488–489). Neither Mannheim's original paper nor Pilcher's later commentary consider that race might be a factor distinguishing which cultural and social phenomena are particularly affecting for a generation.[1] We also note that Mannheim's focus on the traumatic event, whilst an appropriate way of describing the potential effects of racism on individuals, also acts to suggest that racism is outside of everyday normality. CRT, on the other hand, argues that the longevity and pervasiveness of racism is a result of racist attitudes, preconceptions, and expectations being deeply embedded in routines, 'common sense' and long-established ways of operating.

A significant dimension of generational consciousness is the intersection of opportunity and oppression in relation to education policy. The policy context has changed over time from the assimilationist approaches of the 1960s, through colour-blind, multicultural and anti-racist approaches to education, to the 'aggressive majoritarianism' (Gillborn 2008, 81) of the present day. Education policy rhetorics and practices have differently framed awareness of racial inequality, as well as offering and denying educational opportunities in different ways. In 1965, for example, policies aimed for assimilation, and the dispersal of Black and other minority ethnic children was officially sanctioned as a way of ensuring that Black and minority ethnic children did not become concentrated in particular schools. Through the 1960s and 1970s, there was increasing concern from Caribbean-origin parents concerning the underachievement of their children, reflected and further galvinised by the 1971 publication of Bernard Coard's book *How the West Indian Child is Made Educationally Subnormal in the British School System: The Scandal of the Black Child in Schools in Britain*. During the 1970s, when most of the study's respondents were at school, education policy moved away from an official emphasis on assimilation to one of integration. The first official enquiry into race and education was published as the Rampton Report in 1981, and acknowledged that racism affected Black children's achievements, yet the findings were diluted in the later Swann Report of 1985 and no meaningful action taken. Those of the respondents who were educated at urban schools during the late 1970s and 1980s were sometimes on the receiving end of multicultural education.[2] This was criticised for its superficiality by those arguing for a more robust anti-racist approach (Troyna and Carrington 1990). The latter was taken up in several urban local education authorities in the 1980s. However, the protests against police brutality and economic deprivation in Brixton and Toxteth in 1981 showed how little real progress had been made towards racial equality.

In more general terms, like their White working-class counterparts, the respondents as children were caught up in the messy transition in the 1970s from grammar and secondary modern schooling to comprehensive education. Many of those who did make it to grammar school experienced the alienating and damaging 'dividing practices' described by Jackson and Marden 1962 (see below).

The third generation in our research was born in the shadow of Stephen Lawrence's murder and the inquiry into his death (Macpherson 1999), which highlighted the prevalence of institutional racism in public-sector organisations, and which saw education as the primary means of seeking to address racism in broader society (Macpherson 1999; Rollock 2009). Schools had a short-lived duty (under the Race Relations [Amendment] Act 2000) to record all instances of racial abuse, a responsibility abolished by the current Coalition government. An emphasis on generic equalities and social exclusions has replaced specific concern with racism and sexism, as demonstrated by the abolition of the Commission for Racial Equality and its replacement by a joint Equalities and Human Rights Commission. Overall, there has been a slow, hesitant and partial strengthening of the discourse of racial equality over the past 50 years. However, the CRT concept of interest convergence argues that progressive policies are introduced only where there is some perceived benefit to the White power holders (Bell 1980), and, despite some positive change, progress is still inadequate and incomplete. In 2007, *Tell It Like It Is: How Our Schools Fail Black Children (*Richardson 2007) reprinted Coard's arguments from 1971, to emphasise the slow pace of change and the entrenched nature of racial discrimination in education; despite rhetorical changes over the intervening period, Black children remain less likely to achieve highly in education but more likely to be permanently excluded than their white peers (The Children's Commissioner 2013).

The study

This study draws on 62 semi-structured interviews, 49 with mothers and 13 with fathers, who all self-define as of Black Caribbean heritage. They all have at least one child between eight and 18 years old, and live in England (mostly London). Follow-up interviews were conducted with 15 respondents. We advertised in a variety of professional publications, and recruited parents in professional or managerial occupations (i.e. NS-SEC 1 and 2) using the Standard Occupational Classfication manuals.[3] These occupational groups reflect a particular segment of the middle classes, sometimes called the 'service class' (see Hanlon 1998 for an overview).[4] We also collected information on income, educational qualifications and housing. However, our understanding of class goes beyond these indicators to encompass class as:

an identity and a lifestyle, and a set of perspectives on the social world ... class in this sense is ... an identity based on modes of being and becoming or escape and forms of distinction that are realized and reproduced in specific social locations. (Ball 2003, 6)

Respondents were also asked about their childhood experiences of education and their parents' degree of interaction with their school and/or their learning. Thus we have data on three generations – the parent respondents, their own parents and their children. Interviewees were given the opportunity to express a preference for an interviewer of the same ethnic background; 14 (23%) explicitly stated that they preferred to be seen by Nicola Rollock (the team member of Black Caribbean heritage). As a research team we brought different experiences to our reading of the data. For the White team members, critical questioning of our ethnic privileges and the extent of our 'grasp' of the experience of racism was required. As Agyeman (2008, 82) notes: 'When researching the Other in the role of an outsider, this also means addressing the role of self in research and engaging in critical questioning of one's own role and scope'. Solomona and colleagues refer to the everyday embeddedness of White entitlement as 'the din of common sense' (2005, 157), a common sense that places White people at the centre and Black people at the margin. The interviews sought to reverse this and offered insights into some of the similarities, but, importantly, also the differences between White and Black middle classes. Many of these differences arise from White people rarely having to consider their race, while, as the respondents noted, they were almost always viewed as Black first: 'Before I even open my mouth or do anything you see my colour. So if you have your preconceptions, or whatever it is, they are based on that' (Jean). The 'burden of race' – which simply does not exist for the White majority – is made all the more powerful by its mundane and domestic nature, its embedding into quotidian routines and practices. Referring to a Black contestant's bad behaviour on *Celebrity Big Brother*, Richard explains that 'the majority of [White] people just take that brush and run it across a whole group of us'. Similarly, Cynthia notes: 'I don't think White people are held accountable for the ignorance and stupidity of some White people, whereas I am held accountable for anything that a Black person does – we are [perceived as] all the same'.

Race, racism and intersectionality

The respondents have experienced social mobility, and also some degree of change in the nature of how race and racism are enacted. Over 30 years ago, Barker (1981) characterised contemporary racism as *new* racism, cultural rather than biological, which locates subordinate 'racial' groups as inferior because of their different way of life rather than their skin colour. As Hylton (2009, 5) comments, new racism 'transforms itself into debates about citizenship, immigration, nationhood. [This] results in amorphous types of racism that are difficult to detect and much easier to deny'.

The respondents also identified other forms of subtle (and not so subtle) racism (see below, and Ball et al. 2013; Gillborn et al. 2012; Rollock et al. 2011; Vincent et al. 2012a), such as being perceived as the one who does not quite 'fit in', who is positioned as 'other', and the continued stereotypes of Black people as being prone to aggression, of being uninterested in education, as being from inadequate families. Such persistent racism threatened families' ambitions for their children.

Intersectionality is key to much CRT scholarship; that is, a concern to understand the intersecting, sometimes fluid, relations between different identity categories and inequalities (Crenshaw 1993). However, Critical Race Theorists have expressed doubts about the value of intersectionality. First, as Richard Delgado (2011) argues, intersectionality can be taken to such extreme positions that the constant sub-division of experience (into more and more identity categories) can eventually shatter any sense of coherence, what Preston and Bhopal (2012, 216) refer to as the dangers of 'exploding oppressions into multiplicities'. Identity categories are infinitely divisible, and so there is a risk that the mis-use of intersectionality could lead to the paralysis of critical work amid a 'mosaic of never ending difference' (Gillborn 2012). Second, there is the problem of how and where the emphasis lies in analysis. Acker (2006), for example, proposes a focus on 'gendered and racialized class practices', with class providing her 'entry point' into 'complex ongoing practices'. However, Acker also acknowledges that gender or race could equally well be an 'entry point' to understanding the operation of intersecting power relations. Preston and Bhopal (2012), in contrast to Acker, discuss their commitment to 'foregrounding' race within their analysis. They argue for the space to '"speak" to "race" alone' and 'address its primacy when necessary' (2012, 215). These arguments illustrate the difficulties of our project; of holding both class and race together, trying to understand the workings of both, and their points of interdependence for particular social groups and individuals, in particular situations. The wording that Preston and Bhopal (2012) use – 'its primacy *when necessary*' (emphasis added) – does speak to the way in which intersectionality focuses on fluid, rather than fixed, understandings of the interaction of different social dimensions. We are mindful of this concern and seek to hold race and class in productive tension, as we explore the respondents' transitions and trajectories from Black and working class to Black and middle class.

The educational strategies of the first generation
The majority of respondents explained that their own parents, the first generation in our dataset, had little direct engagement with schools in the

United Kingdom. This was partly because of a different, more distant climate of home–school relations in the 1960s and 1970s, this distance being familiar to respondents' parents from their own schooling in the Caribbean, and partly because of their parents' positioning as predominantly working-class immigrants. Practically (often parents were holding down more than one job or working long hours) and emotionally, intervention into their children's school experience was not generally seen as feasible or appropriate. Grace described her parents as 'placid' and 'accepting'; Richard described his as 'wanting a quiet life', 'fitting in', a response that needs to be contextualised with reference to the crude and overt racism of the 1960s and 1970s. A few had no contact at all with the school, most went to parents' evenings, and almost all conveyed to their children a strong sense of the importance of education and the expectation that they do well at school. A small number were more heavily involved, usually those from more middle-class backgrounds in the Caribbean, whose own education allowed them to be active as well as aspirational around their children's education. Lucy describes her parents:

> My mum was very academic, she was a teacher in Dominica and when she came over here she pursued a career in nursing [...] Dad was a civil servant [...] My parents were fully involved [with school]. You know in terms of primary school where you had activities, my mum and dad would participate [in those] my dad used to teach cricket at school ... Through to secondary school where there were parents' evenings. My parents always attended all those things, you know [curriculum] option meetings ... they were fully involved in my and my brother's education. (Lucy, HR director)

Given provocation, however, some generally non-interventionist parents would act (e.g. Isabelle's parents challenged her placing within the lower status CSE rather than O-level groupings), but for most there was an expectation that the teachers were the experts and knew best. What the respondents' parents did all have was a belief that education was the way forward for their children. They trusted the school system to do its best for their children: 'My parents were accepting of what the [school was] doing and did not question it' (Janet). Josephine's father accepted, for instance, that his daughter needed a remedial speech class whilst she was at primary school because she spoke with a strong Barbadian accent (having spent her early years in Barbados). Most respondents were told by their parents that if they went to school, and paid attention, they would learn, pass examinations and then would have access to a better job and a better life than their parents. This generation, as Esme points out, did not, at first 'appreciate that the system was not on our side'. The awareness that their trust was not repaid grew amongst the first generation, as their children proceeded through the school system.

The majority of the respondents' characterised their own orientation towards their children's education as very different from their parents who had not been 'pro-active', 'hands on' (Isabelle), did not 'intervene' nor have a long-term 'strategy' (Michael). Joan characterised her mother as having the will for her daughter to succeed but not the knowledge of the education system. Joan herself, who works for a local education authority, feels she has both. In this sense they learned *from* and learned to be different *to* their parents. However, it would be misleading to characterise the respondents' parents as simply passive. Their approach was largely one of survival and protecting their families from the racist economic and social conditions they encountered. Another strategy often mentioned was the development of an active and collective aspect to thinking about education. Whilst some respondents said their parents un-reflexively chose local schools, other parents used social networks of neighbours or friends to glean information and help create a climate of expectation. For example, Felicia had a successful educational career as the first Black child at a Jewish primary school, chosen on the advice of a White neighbour. Isabelle describes the encouragement of fellow immigrants from St Vincent in her town to study hard and to reach university. Parents generally emphasised the importance of educational success:

> I did very well at school and [...] my parents ... coined 'Education, education, education' long before Mr. Blair ... they both had this vision of what education could do for their children and they, I wouldn't hesitate from using the word inculcate, they indoctrinated us about the value of education and what we needed to do at school. (Gabriel, education consultant)

The second generation as pupils

Like many respondents Gabriel has good memories of some teachers, but also like many others he was also routinely confronted by racism:

> I have some good memories of teachers [at primary school] who were really keen and interested in the education of all the children ... teachers I still remember to this day. [At grammar school] the racism was ferocious from the other students in the school and some of the teachers, and things like calling me names, like 'gollywog' and 'jungle bunny' putting the blackboard rubber across my brow, marking my face, all day, all day, comments from them [...] Because of the drive from my parents about what education would bring us, and what I had achieved, I stuck it out and I got a good education, but it was at the cost of some pretty horrible experiences.

The chances of White teachers and peers behaving in a racist manner were to some extent arbitrary, but some tendencies are discernible from the data. For example, Ruby had mixed experiences, related largely to the degree to which individual educational settings were ethnically mixed. She was 'dispersed' (bussed to a school outside her immediate locality, a policy designed to hasten the assimilation of Black and ethnic minority children and placate the fears of White parents) to what became a relatively ethnically mixed primary school in a White working-class area and 'has no recollection of racism at all. At all'. She went to a grammar school where she was part of a very small Black minority: '"Wog" was a common phrase at that time wasn't it [the 1970s]? "Oh, no offence" I got fed up of "no offence", five years of "no offence"'. Her sixth-form experience at a different, more ethnically mixed, school was much better. She then went to a London university and 'for the first time [as a young adult] met White people I didn't think were racist'. Similarly Rachel, a student at another London University with a multi-racial intake, found there for the first time 'teachers that care'.

The respondents' stories suggested that the chances of meeting racism increased in some circumstances, and one of these was being a Black minority in a grammar school: 16 out of 62 respondents (26%) attended a grammar school. Much has been written about the experience of White working-class children in grammar schools, their marginalisation and their sense of being 'other' (Lacey 1970; Jackson and Marsden 1962). For the respondents, such class discrimination was compounded by being part of a racial minority. Some, like Gabriel, met physically violent and abusive racism; others experienced acts of racial Othering, for example in the form of repeated questions about skin and hair (see also Rollock 2012). As children, these parents had a sense of isolation. Elizabeth responded to her largely White middle-class grammar school by 'hiding'. Rachel noted:

> I didn't get involved in a lot of stuff at school, a lot of extra curricular stuff because I didn't really feel part of what was going on ... I wasn't properly integrated and I was getting a lot of racial abuse on a daily basis from children.

Isabelle talks about the long-term effect on her of being 'not seen as equal':

> The message I got about being Black [was] I knew there was prejudice and I knew that people would not like me because of the colour of my skin and I don't know how any child recovers from that ... I think to attach a judgment to the colour of my skin, I never got over that, I couldn't get over that.

She describes the embodiment of White privilege in middle-class girls at her grammar school with 'beautiful hair, very healthy looking skin, slender, the way they talked was very refined'; girls who 'didn't talk to you with the same ease with which they spoke to other people, people they related to better'. For Isabelle, such girls grew up to be the mothers outside her daughter's independent school: 'In the playground ... there were lots of parents around with their huge umbrellas when it was raining. I don't know why people in that kind of space have these huge umbrellas ...' Umbrellas here act as a domestic signifier of exclusion and distinction. Isabelle reflects that the success she enjoyed speaking to a school meeting using her professional expertise shows how far she has come from her previously marginalised identity, but that has not made the journey less painful, and she is concerned not to pass on feelings of inferiority to her daughter (also in a minority at her school):

> I talk to her about Blackness to her regularly, but I talk across the spectrum, not just us as victims ... She takes pride in who she is. Her colour doesn't dominate her life. It's who she is but it's not everything to her, she sees herself as [daughter's name] first. I am just amazed.

A sense of being 'other' was also instilled through more subtle signals, which highlighted difference and non-belonging, even through polite and seemingly positive actions. As a working-class Black girl at a largely White middle-class grammar school Lorraine found: 'in many ways I became a teacher's pet because I was the only Black girl in my year, and in some ways people went *over the top* to be nice to me' (emphasis added). The difference in the race and class capitals she bought from home and that of the other children and the school was palpable, and emphasised her difference:

> In primary school you got taunts about race, but not so much in secondary school ... I think class became more of an issue ... In English lessons we'd been asked to bring in newspapers from home to talk about ... when everyone else brought in The Times, I was bringing in, you know the Daily Mirror ... There was quite stunned silences, I really do think my English teacher didn't actually know what to say. [...] No-one said anything horrible but you sensed that this was just not the done thing [...] So much revolved around having read Alice in Wonderland, Wind in the Willows, there were all these references to classic children's literature ... No-one knew about the Anansi[4] tales or anything like that. It was always this sense of being the odd one out, trying hard not to stand out [...] Not letting the race down. I couldn't ever relax while at school. (Lorraine, academic)

It is perhaps unsurprising given the weight and tenor of these experiences, coupled with the low expectations of many teachers, and often poor careers advice, that most respondents did not achieve great educational success at school. Indeed, nearly one-half of the respondents who have a degree achieved that qualification as adult returners (not an unusual path for Black Caribbean graduates; Mirza 2009). Ruby, who did progress onto university at 18, became aware whilst there that as a Black young woman on the 'normal' trajectory (school–A levels–university) she was unusual.

The second generation as parents: the changing but persistent nature of racism

The second generation in this study, the respondents, have succeeded despite racism. They have fulfilled their parents' hope and expectations, but they have not escaped racism, even now. The apparently smooth surface of the professional workplace also revealed flaws. Rachel maintains that as a result of the social conditioning received by White people over hundreds of years, having other White professional colleagues is perceived as 'natural' whilst Black colleagues are somehow mis-placed; Black people in her workplace do not feel accepted and do not get sponsored. Claudette in the civil service and Miles in recruitment also identified pressure to conform to White norms in order to fit in and progress.

The stereotype of Black people as an underclass, uninterested in education, heading lone-mother families, potentially aggressive and potentially violent constantly recurs in the respondents' experiences. Felicia, a barrister, was asked by another barrister whether Jamaicans are pre-disposed to violence. Less overtly prejudiced, but still drawing on stereotypes of Black people as 'other', Derick's teenage daughter is expected by her White peers to know everything about Black music. Some mothers also spoke about the pressure on their teenage daughters to adopt a European light-skinned idea of beauty, by, for example, straightening their hair. This may not be a modern phenomenon, but arguably the increased availability of different forms of media serve to bombard children with images of largely White or light-skinned celebrities. Mothers also referenced the behaviour and self-presentation of the few Black characters in television programmes. The respondents concluded that their experience led them to believe that 'The UK isn't a different place [than in the past] although the same things might be done differently' (Robert).

Richard suggested that relative affluence can help side-step racism, but our analysis suggests that affluence alone is not enough. Most respondents draw on a suite of cultural, social and financial resources, what Lacy (2007, 113) in her study of middle-class African Americans in the Washington suburbs calls 'the mobilisation of class related strategies as a bulwark against racial discrimination'. We have discussed these strategies in detail elsewhere (Rollock et al. 2011). Middle-class capitals help negotiate 'everyday instances of racial discrimination' (Lacy 2007, 111), but are no guarantee against their occurrence. Racism can assail the respondents unexpectedly as they go about their daily routines. Malorie gives the example of her niece, a student, being greeted by monkey noises as she travelled to her university lodging just outside London. June described the racist language used by a man passing her on the street, engaged in a loud conversation on his mobile phone.[5] There is, as both Montgomery (2006) and Lacy (2007) note in their US research, a safety and comfort derived from living with other Black people in multi-racial locations that many of the respondents in our study would not give up, although a few people chose an area for its middle-class affluence, rather than its multi-racial character:

> It's nice where I live, sometimes you think about moving [...] But [if] you move [localitites] ... and as a Black person you think, are there other Black people there? But then I think if there are, are they the type of Black people you want to be associated with? [Laughter] But if there aren't [Black people locally] and you move in, how will people take to you, will you start having issues? Based on a history of never having had any issues, never. [But] there is a possibility [...] You have really got to think about where you are going. (Malorie, local education authority)

As Lacy (2007, 74) found in her Washington study, the respondents assert public, status-based identities calling on their class resources, as 'strategies to sustain problem free interactions'. We have written elsewhere about parents' use of their class resources in relation to successfully navigating their children through the education system. These include long-term planning, an active choice of school, careful monitoring of the child's progress and teacher actions, enrolling children in extracurricular activities, seeking to establish a dialogue of equals with teachers, and using their dress, accent and knowledge about the education system to convince White power-holders of both their respectability and their ambition for their children (also Rollock et al. 2011; Vincent et al. 2013), However, these strategies require considerable parental labour and success is not guaranteed, despite the skill and resources that parents invested in the process.

The strain of living in a society where Whiteness is the norm extracts psychological costs – described by Jean as wearing a 'tight pair of shoes' – which, in some cases, is compounded by their mobility into the middle classes and away from their family origins. Jean is clear that she does not want her children to feel they have to show 'one face out there and a different face at home because I have seen [the costs] so much'. Sandrine develops this theme, noting that with her White middle-class colleagues she is sometimes unwittingly excluded by the conversation; she gives the example of books and plays she is not familiar with, although she notes later that she regularly goes to the theatre, but not necessarily to watch White mainstream productions, and being asked what she did during her gap year when in fact she did a part-time degree as an adult returner whilst working. Here intersectional tensions, and the damage that they can do, come into view. In addition, different forms of *disidentification* are enacted in the tensions between where you are now and where you come from. Both Jean and Sandrine talk about the pressure derived from not being able to be yourself in predominantly White workplaces, but Sandrine does not feel entirely at ease with her family either, not all of whom have been socially mobile. She feels constrained to leave out areas of experience, namely her professional working environment (as a third sector manager), when with her family. It is with her Black work colleagues that she feels the least need for a 'mask'. They share the same class *and* race positions. As Bourdieu (1986, 337) notes: '"Taking off" always presupposes a break, and the discovery of former companions in misfortune is […] one aspect of this'.

> I think the best way I can describe it is that [Black colleagues] understand the masks that we have to put on and take off. So that when you are with them you can take off a mask and you can relate to each other as whole people as oppose to half a person or three quarters of a person. (Sandrine)

As a result of this need to maintain a public identity, the respondents spoke of code switching, speaking differently to different people – with Patois, for example, only used with close colleagues, friends and family:

> [It is] difficult for me coming from a very working class background going to university [Oxbridge] and the [grammar] school that I did, speaking the way I speak [received pronunciation] and being perceived as not working class, not middle class, or a mixture of the two, and I find – even now I adjust my speech depending on who I am talking to … I speak differently, I behave differently, I talk about different things […] That might be one of the advantages of being White, that you don't have to constantly be making those calculations in your head all the time […] It is there in my head twenty-four hours a day: what are people thinking of me as Black person? (Lorraine)

Children's responses – the third generation

We have discussed elsewhere the ambivalence many of the parents displayed when asked about their class identity (Rollock et al. 2012). The majority expressed some reluctance about identifying themselves as 'middle class', despite their professional status. Many felt that 'middle class' was a largely White identity. Even those who did unequivocally identify themselves as middle class had reservations about 'owning' the identity. Robert illustrates this:

> I think we have achieved something for our [teenage] kids because we have got them to a point where it is largely up to them from thereon. … That may be the most important part of middle class-ness I would associate with [the ability to do that for your children]. I am not sure that I buy into being middle class in a lot of other respects … I don't necessarily enjoy a lot of things my White counterparts who are middle class would enjoy. I don't go on holiday to the south of France or Italy. I don't like fine wine and so on […] I still like my Black food, I still like my Black music … I like Black humour and so on. I am married to a Black woman. That is very important to me!

While many parents referred to growing up with mainly Black friendships, they describe almost all of their children as having ethnically mixed friendship groups. Parents were aware that their children's identities are being differently shaped by race and class. The more affluent respondents, especially, having come from economically disadvantaged working-class backgrounds, were very aware that their children were growing up in more secure and comfortable surroundings. The younger generation in some cases also articulate Blackness in ways that differ from their parents, and this can sometimes lead to family perturbations. It should be noted here that our accounts stem from the children's parents and not the young people themselves. Parents were proud and pleased that their children were confident, but their comments on their children's sense of entitlement – which they themselves have worked to develop – were in some cases tinged with ambivalence. This is for two reasons. One is their awareness of the difference between their position – the fragility of being socially mobile and being first-generation middle class, and the sense of 'boundary crossing' that that position elicits – and the more established social position they hope their children will hold. They inhabit this space where class and race intersect differently from their children:

> I never went out to a restaurant when I was young ... My son who is 11 ... We were having a discussion about how, about the fact that he didn't feel that his scallops had been browned off enough ... I didn't even know what a scallop was when I was his age! I had never eaten one, I was highly unlikely to be in a place where I would be getting things like that. And I thought he has been all over the world, he has travelled, and at that age I hadn't done any of that stuff ... He will just grab a menu and go to me 'is that a kind of roux sauce dad?' And I am thinking 'you are 11. You should be eating fishfingers and beans like I was!' (Richard, Director Voluntary organisation)

The second reason for ambivalence is anxiety. The anxiety that their children's security, confidence and promise might be undermined or even destroyed by racism, and furthermore that this is a danger *some* of the children, at the present time, do not see. Both Malorie and Robert noted that their children had called them racist because of their emphasis on race:

> It is difficult to convey ... it is outside of your [said to White interviewer] experience ... but it's really happening, and that's why I am driven to say to [daughter] and my niece and nephew ... 'you need to be aware, you need to be aware that things happen because of the colour of your skin, yes?' And sometimes – it depends how receptive they are to it – but sometimes they just say 'oh, you're racist' (Malorie)

Robert comments that his children have been 'shielded and protected' by their relatively affluent lifestyle. Dawn also notes that her daughter and younger relations 'seem to have bought into whole multiculturalism idea', and Jean further comments that the younger generation is one 'that is sleepwalking into thinking that everything has gone, done, dusted. Whereas I think a lot of the racist stuff that goes on is actually very subtle'.

Concluding thoughts

The first generation in this study came to the United Kingdom with high hopes for their children and found an education system pervaded by crude racisms. While the resources and opportunities to confront these directly were not always available to them, they were able to instil their children with a sense of drive and the possibility of advancement. Now, for the parent respondents, their class resources and accumulated educational assets are key 'to reducing the probability that racial discrimination will determine important outcomes in their lives' (Lacy 2007, 112), and are helping them prepare their children for success in the education and labour markets.

This paper emphasises the particularity of Black experiences of upward social mobility. While they share some of the same insecurities and ambivalences (Reay 2001), respondents' experiences are different to those of White 'border crossers'. They are members of a visible minority, and despite their mobility they also express reservations about being 'middle class' – seeing that designation as owned and protected by a White majority, and membership of a Black middle class as a relatively new and emergent identity. Our intersectional analysis demonstrates that race cannot be simply 'added on' to class, it changes how class works, how it is experienced, and the subjectivites available to individuals. The two intersect, in complex ways, at different historical 'moments', as the data illustrate. As we have suggested above, the intersection for members of the third generation is likely to be different to that lived by their parents and grandparents. These young people are portrayed by their parents as self-confident Black children and young adults, sure of their identity, and accumulating academic qualifications and a range of other skills and capabilities that offer future opportunities. Even those educated in mainly White settings are growing up in a country with a diverse, multi-racial population, and a growing Black middle class. Their experiences of disadvantage and privilege are configured differently and are played out in a different cultural–political context. In this sense they inhabit a different 'generational location', as Mannheim calls it, to their parents. There *is* evidence here of an original and distinctive consciousness and a different dialectic of history and biography. However, it is important to think about what has stayed the same, as well as what has changed, across these three generations. Racism and race inequality has changed but it has not disappeared. For the third generation, racism may be less likely to assail them as explicit vicious abuse, but still retains the potential to undermine, to marginalise and to threaten. There are plenty of examples in our data of moments when racisms of various kinds in the present threaten to negate class resources and block or curtail educational opportunity (see Gillborn et al. 2012; Vincent et al. 2012a). Racism in the labour market persists and there may also be consequences of the current economic crisis that disproportionately threaten this group, particularly the decline in public sector employment (Gillborn 2012; UNISON 2012). While most of the third-generation children are for the most part, with the support of their parents, surviving and thriving in a White dominated society, 'the ever present possibility of [racial] stigmatization' (Lacy 2007, 73) remains.

Notes

1. Several of the respondents mentioned the effect on them of seeing *Roots*, the 1977 television mini series on slavery. Kwame Kwei-Armah, the Black British playwright and actor, who is of the same generation as the respondents in our study has written about his reactions as a child (http://news.bbc.co.uk/1/hi/magazine/6480995.stm).
2. Multicultural education meant 'adding on' references to other cultures in the curriculum, (the 'Three Ss' of saris, samosas, and steel bands, Troyna and Carrington 1990). Anti racist approaches emphasised the explicit promotion of racial equality.
3. Other National Statistics Socio-Economic Classifications (NS-SEC) groups include intermediate workers (e.g. clerical and admin- istrative work), own account workers and those in semi-routine and routine occupations.
4. Anansi, featuring in Caribbean and West African fables, is a clever spider, outwitting those around him.
5. A recent interview with 26-year-old Dominique Walker, whose brother Anthony was murdered in a racist attack on Merseyside, and who is now in the police force, described growing up, a generation after most of our respondents, but sharing some of their experiences of overt racist abuse (http://www.guardian.co.uk/world/2012/jun/10/liverpool-police-dominique-walker-interview).

References

Acker, J. 2006. *Class Questions: Feminist Answers*. Lanham, Maryland: Rowman and Littlefield.
Agyeman, G. 2008. "White Researcher–Black Subjects: Exploring the Challenges of Researching the Marginalised and 'Invisible'." *The Electronic Journal of Business Research Methods* 6 (1): 77–84. www.ejbrm.com.
Ball, S. J. 2003. *Class Strategies and the Education Market*. London: Routledge.
Ball, S., N. Rollock, C. Vincent, and D. Gillborn. 2013. "Social Mix, Schooling and Intersectionality: Identity and Risk for Black Middle Class Families." *Research Papers in Education* 28 (3): 265–288.
Barker, M. 1981. *The New Racism*. London: Junction Books.
Bell, D. 1980. "Brown v. Board of Education and the Interest-Convergence Dilemma." *Harvard Law Review* 93: 518–533.
Bourdieu, P. 1986. *Distinction*. Cambridge, Mass: Harvard University Press.
Brah, A., and A. Phoenix. 2004. "Ain't I a Woman? Revisiting Intersectionality." *Journal of International Women's Studies* 5 (3): 75–86.
Crenshaw, K. 1993. "Mapping the margins: intersectionality, identity politics and violence against women of color." *Stanford Law Review* 43: 1241–1299.

Delgardo, R. 2011. "Rodrigo's Reconsideration: Intersectionality and the Future of Critical Race Theory." 96 *Iowa L. Rev.* 1276.

Gillborn, D. 2008. *Racism and Education: Co-incidence or Conspiracy?* London: Routledge.

Gillborn, D. 2012 "Intersectionality and the Primacy of Racism: Race, Class, Gender and Disability in Education: Keynote Presented at the Annual Conference of the Critical Race Studies in Education Association (CRSEA)." Teacher's College, Columbia University. June 2012.

Gillborn, D., N. Rollock, C. Vincent, and S. Ball. 2012. "'You Got a Pass, So What More Do You Want?' Race, Class and Gender Intersections in the Educational Experiences of the Black Middle Class." *Race Ethnicity and Education* 15 (1): 121–139.

Hanlon, G. 1998. "Professionalism as Enterprise: Service Class Politics and the Redefinition of Professionalism." *Sociology* 32 (1): 43–63.

Hylton, K. 2009. *'Race' and Sport: Critical Race Theory*. London: Routledge.

Jackson, B., and D. Marden. 1962. *Education and the Working Class*. London: Routledge and Kegan Paul.

Lacey, C. 1970. *Hightown Grammar*. Manchester, NH: Manchester University Press.

Lacy, K. 2007. *Blue Chip Black*. Berkeley, LA: University of California Press.

Macpherson, W. 1999. *The Stephen Lawrence Inquiry*. London: The Stationery Office.

Mannheim, K. 1952. *'The Problem of Generations' in Essays on the Sociology of Knowledge*. London: Routledge and Kegan Paul.

Mirza, H. 2009. "Plotting a history: Black and postcolonial new feminisms in 'new times'." *Race, Ethnicity and Education* 12 (1): 1–10.

Montgomery, A. 2006. "Living in each other's pockets": The navigation of social distances by middle class Blacks in Los Angeles." *City and Community* 5 (4): 425–450.

Pilcher, J. 1994. "Mannheim's Sociology of Generations: An Undervalued Legacy." *The British Journal of Sociology* 45 (3): 481–495.

Preston, J., and K. Bhopal. 2012. "Conclusion: Intersectional Theories and 'Race': From Toolkit to 'Mash up." In *Intersectionality and Race in Education*, edited by K. Bhopal and J. Preston. London: Routledge.

Reay, D. 2001. "Finding or Losing Yourself? Working-class Relationships to Education." *Journal of Education Policy* 16 (4): 333–346.

Richardson, B. 2007. *Tell It like It is: How Our Schools Fail Black Children*. London: Bookmark Publications.

Rollock, N. 2009. "Educational Policy and the Impact of the Lawrence Inquiry: The View from another Sector." In *Policing and the Legacy of Lawrence*, edited by N. Hall, J. Grieve, and S. P. Savage. Cullompton, Devon: Willan Publishing.

Rollock, N., et al. 2011. "The Public Identities of the Black Middle Classes: Managing Race in Public Spaces." *Sociology* 45 (6): 1078–1093.

Rollock, N. 2012. "The Invisibility of Race: Intersectional Reflections on the Liminal Space of Alterity." *Race Ethnicity and Education* 15: 65–84.

Rollock, N., C. Vincent, D. Gillborn, and S. Ball. 2012. "Middle Class by Profession: Class Status and Identification Amongst the Black Middle Classes." *Ethnicities*. Published online before print

Solomona, R., J. Portelli, B.-J. Daniel, and A. Campbell. 2005. "The Discourse of Denial: How White Teacher Candidates Construct Race, Racism and 'White privilege'." *Race Ethnicity and Education* 8 (2): 147–169.

The Children's Commissioner. 2013. *They go the extra mile: reducing inequality in school exclusions*. London: The Children's Commissioner.

Troyna, B., and C. Carrington. 1990. *Education, Racism and Reform*. London: Routledge.

Unison. 2012. http://www.unison.org.uk/asppresspack.

Vincent, C., N. Rollock, S. Ball, and D. Gillborn. 2012a. "Being Strategic, Being Watchful, Being Determined: Black Middle-class Parents and Schooling." *British Journal of Sociology of Education* 33 (3): 337–354.

Vincent, C., N. Rollock, S. Ball, and D. Gillborn. 2012b. "Intersectional Work and Precarious Positionings: Black Middle-class Parents and Their Encounters with Schools in England." *International Studies in Sociology of Education* 22 (3): 259–276.

Vincent, C., N. Rollock, S. Ball, and D. Gillborn. 2013. "Raising Middle Class Black Children: Parenting Priorities, Actions and Strategies." *Sociology* 47 (3): 427–442.

Resettling notions of social mobility: locating refugees as 'educable' and 'employable'

Jill Koyama

Educational Policy Studies and Practice, College of Education, University of Arizona, Tucson, AZ, USA

> The global movement of people alters our understandings of social mobility. Here, I draw on ethnographic data collected since January 2011 and utilize the notion of *assemblage* to document and analyze how disparate people, their material objects, and discursive practices are brought together to render refugees as educable, productive, and employable in the United States. I examine the adaptations that result when livelihood paths and educational opportunities become paradoxically diverse due to transnational migrations and are constrained by localized politico-economic environments. My findings complicate the assumption that formal education represents an enduring pathway or necessary precursor to upward social mobility. As refugees are required by resettling agents to become economically self-sufficient as soon as possible, formal education such as English-as-a-second-language courses can limit initial employment opportunities and narrowing families' livelihood strategies upon resettlement, especially during the recent economic downturn.

We live in a time of growing human mobility, with amplified cultural and social diversity, and magnified disparities in economic, educational, and human rights. Our world 'is increasingly crisscrossed by tourists, workers, terrorists, students, migrants, asylum-seekers, scientist/scholars, family members, business people, soldiers, guest workers and so on,' which results in a networked pattern of social life (Hannam, Sheller, and Urry 2006, 2). Those who constitute the global movement represent a multiplicity of aims and aspirations; their 'search for social mobility is constituted by processes, shared by many peoples and communities across the world today, that involve sometimes significant shifts in individuals' spatial and social locations' (Froerer and Portisch 2012, 333). Globalized processes are mediated by local responses, and educational attainment and occupational strategies for transnational migrants are differently conceptualized and enacted within contexts of varying ethnic, religious, gendered, and familial norms.

To locate, analyze, and predict social mobility with long-standing indicators, such as educational attainment, class schemas, and occupational patterns, is complicated by the divergent and fluid nature of networked spaces created by, and contributing to, globalizing movements. Examining the social mobility of those in the twenty-first century, especially those who are 'in transnational motion,' literally migrating through and across countries, the complex of uneven possibilities of educational access and completion, as well as the multiply-situated occupational opportunity and measures of economic success must be considered. When studying immigrants, for instance, legal status may be a better indicator of educational access than parental educational attainment. The skills and occupational knowledge of many immigrants may not transfer into commensurate positions in receiving countries, especially during times of economic downturns. Instead, migrants' abilities to draw upon various social and kin-based networks, as well as to access community resources, may be more important in securing employment and becoming (or more accurately, being perceived as) productive society members (Portisch 2012; Naji 2012). And pathways that circumvent the traditional labor market and defy normative conduits to livelihood opportunities can be more viable for newcomers than traditional school-based education (Fernández-Kelly and Konczal 2005). Migration, itself, can be understood as an important learning opportunity and an essential step to upward social mobility for some.

Aiming to trace and examine the social trajectories of refugees, a specific subset of immigrants, poses additional challenges. Refugees, of whom there are greater than 43.7 million worldwide, are those who are unable or unwilling to return to their countries of nationality because of persecution or a well-founded fear of persecution on account of race, religion, nationality, membership in a particular social group, or political opinion.[1] They endure protracted displacement and forced migration, and often suffer violence and severe poverty prior to and during their resettlement process. The greater than two million refugees who have resettled in the United States since 1975 reflect these hardships. Since the 1990s, most refugees have belonged to what is best described as acute refugee movements, those in which populations flee from violence and war, and are characterized by poverty, limited education, and narrow vocational skills.

For all refugees, displacement and resettlement abruptly disrupt, if not sever, their social, economic, and cultural networks. As stated by Nolan (2006, 183): 'The agency and life choices of the world's refugees are quite different from those of (im)migrants and the social processes that bind the two contexts when physical presence is impossible in the home country.' For those resettled in the United States, their pre-refugee lives are substantially different from their post-resettlement ones. Their prior skills and training often do not easily transfer to the American labor force; their certifications, degrees, and licenses associated with their professions are probably not recognized; and their families' previous social status and educational history do not provide advantages. As noted by the director of the largest resettlement agency in this study, 'refugees are not resettled into the middle class.' Once in the United States, many train for, and work in, menial jobs, struggling to live in urban areas, with unemployment, low-quality schooling, and high rates of crime (McBrien 2005). The recent economic crisis and slow recovery has compounded the challenges for refugees as the resources of local agencies providing assistance with food, rent, transportation, and medical expenses have been stretched thin, and available work is often physically demanding and low-paying.

Here, I trace the refugees' preliminary experiences in education and employment in the United States by probing the processes through which the social, the educational, and the economic are enacted for, and by, them. Drawing on data ethnographically collected since January 2011, I reveal the multiply-situated and varied constructions of refugees as 'educable' and 'employable' persons – and as 'productive members of society' – in a northeastern city characterized by a steadily decreasing native population, a declining body of highly-educated and skilled residents, and a shrinking economy. While I discuss the divergent educational and economic pathways pursued by the refugees, I pay particular attention to resettlement in the United States through authorized local agencies – a process that can have long-term consequences for the social mobility of refugees and their children. Utilizing the notion of *assemblage*, a term often associated with actor-network theory (ANT), I show that it is through resettlement that certain objects, such as medical reports and English tests, combine with case workers' assessments of employability and employers' need for inexpensive labor, to create socio-material renderings or translations of refugees. Local resettlement becomes established as an 'obligatory point of passage' (Latour 1987) that not only mobilizes certain actors – such as refugees, English-as-a-second-language (ESL) teachers, lawyers, and case workers – but also invites them to 'become engaged in new identities and behaviors' (Fenwick and Edwards 2010, 14) in multilateral negotiations and enactments.

I discuss both theoretical and methodological considerations of ANT and assemblage in detail, but first I offer a review of the research on education and social mobility of immigrants. I then complicate the existing literature by providing examples of paradoxes in the findings. For example, highly-educated refugees who worked as doctors, lawyers, and engineers in their countries of origin are designated as 'not currently employable' in their US receiving city. On the other hand, women with no formal education, and who have not worked outside their homes, are designated by refugee agencies as most 'educable' and 'employable,' and are placed in workforce training. I examine the tensions, conflicts, and compromises that result from these situations and analyze them with assemblage thinking to reveal how employable, educable, and societally contributing refugees are not entities that pre-exist, but rather that are produced or constructed in the materially heterogeneous relations of activities, such as ESL classes and workforce training, that are part of resettlement processes.

Literature review: immigrants, education, and social mobility
Among the social science research on migration, inadequate research attention has been given to the experiences and trajectories of especially vulnerable subpopulations of immigrants, including undocumented immigrants, asylum-seekers, and refugees (Pinson and Arnot 2007). Instead, concerns about migration have resulted in numerous studies on immigrant and second-generation incorporation (for example, Alba and Nee 2003; Kasinitz et al. 2008; Portes and Rumbaut 2001). As noted by Froerer (2012, 345): '[R]esearch on social mobility has been dominated by statistical and economic approaches, with analytical focus concentrated on the intergenerational shifts in education and occupational achievements of (especially) male individuals.' Because of this focus, we have a clearer understanding of the educational and occupational attainment of immigrants over three generations. Yet, because the core measures of incorporation used to study the first massive wave of European immigrants remain 'the starting points for understanding immigration assimilation today ...' (Waters and Jiménez 2005, 106), we have mostly failed to challenge traditional models of social mobility that parallel incorporation models (Alba and Nee 2003). Here, then, I briefly review these studies on immigrant incorporation into US society before turning to discuss recent international studies of the educational and employment experiences of migrants that trouble traditional frameworks and understandings of social mobility.

Because Mexicans comprise nearly one-quarter of America's immigrant newcomers and further, because many arrive with low levels of often interrupted education and many enter unauthorized, numerous studies have focused on the social mobility of Mexican immigrants in the United States. The analyses are mixed. While some scholars (Grogger and Trejo 2002) suggest that because Mexican immigrants start so far behind native-born Americans, they are likely to remain at the lower ends of the educational, occupational, and class spectrums. Others demonstrate that Mexican immigrants have made substantial gains in three generations, narrowing education and income gaps with native-born Whites (Bean, Brown, and Rumbaut 2006). The 1.5 and second generations (i.e. those raised or born in the United States of immigrant parents) surpass their native-born peers in school achievement, offering the possibility of future advances in educational and occupational attainment (Farley and Alba 2002). Similar patterns have been shown for West Indians immigrants in New York City (Portes and Rumbaut

2001) and for 1.5-generation and second-generation Mexicans, Chinese, and Vietnamese in Los Angeles (Zhou and Lee 2007). Second-generation Chinese students, according to Kasinitz, Mollenkopf, and Waters (2004), also demonstrate higher high school graduate rates and college attendance than all other ethnic groups, including native-born Whites. Still, for the most studied group – Mexican immigrants – there are concerns. Portes and Rumbaut (2006) find that despite the progress made by the second generation, there are signs – namely high school dropout rates, teen pregnancy, and male unemployment and incarceration – of downward mobility.

However, recent work across international contexts shifts our understandings of the linkages between formal education and social mobility in the work on immigrant incorporation into US society. In this emerging body of scholarship, notions of formal education as precursors to social mobility for immigrants and marginalized ethnic groups are challenged, and diverse ways in which social networks can influence livelihood options are explored. In the aggregate, such studies employ in-depth qualitative methods to examine the pursuit of social mobility by revealing different constraints, challenges, and conditions, including access to formal and informal education, and opportunities to a variety of employment paths (Froerer and Portisch 2012; Rao 2010).

For example, in her study of the upward mobility of women in Sirwa, a marginal Berber region in southern Morocco, Naji (2012), demonstrates that girls' education in weaving as an education in livelihood strategies takes precedence over formal schooling as the girls and young women strive to become legitimate members of female groups. Through her ethnographic work she examines how, for the Sirwa females, marriage and domestic knowledge, including weaving, remains the most common and easiest way to social mobility while 'formal education, with its associated physical mobility can be perceived in opposition to morality and honor' (Naji 2012, 383). Similarly, Valentin's (2012) study of the relationship between migration and education within the context of broader livelihood strategies among Nepalese migrants in India suggests that social and geographical spaces of migration are themselves important components of the educational process. Although the economic and political unrest and instability in Nepal are strong forces behind migration to India, the migratory trajectories, Valentin argues, are enabled and legitimized by the existing social and kin networks established by previous generations of Nepalese migrants. And it is through these same networks that upward social mobility is possible.

The importance of social networks in matters of migration and social mobility are also emphasized in Kasinitz's (2012) review of sociological studies of international migration. He writes that although immigrants are often studied as laborers, and as such people on which the economy depends, they are also people who develop social ties, have relationships, and share spiritual needs and social aspirations – and participate in society in a myriad of ways, all the while consuming and creating culture. It is this 'people' issue that he suggests also informs our post 1980s understanding of how immigrants fit in society and how they utilize their social ties to achieve upward mobility. Putting the notion of assemblage to work aims to reveal the initial social ties that are created and performed during resettlement, and to unsettle the ways in which notions of refugees in this context are continually being selectively adapted, modified, and appropriated to meet the aims of various situations and objectives. This is achieved by tracking the particular, material details of everyday and ongoing practices, situations, activities, and relationships during the ESL and workforce training of resettlement.

Theoretical considerations: assemblage, networks, and relationality

To explore the ways in which refugees are located, mostly by others, along a continuum of social constructions and enactments of what makes one employable and educable, as well as an asset to society, I draw upon the notion of *assemblages* from ANT – a perspective that focuses on how disparate material and discursive practices come together to form dynamic associations that hold (often temporarily) together, to produce agency and perform actions. The theory, which was initially developed (and then challenged and reworked) by Latour (1988, 2005), Callon (1986) and Law (1986) as a theoretical framework of science studies and technology, insists on following the ongoing processes 'made up of uncertain, fragile, controversial, and ever-shifting ties' (Latour 2005, 28) rather than attempting to fit the actors and their activities into pre-determined bounded categories, geographical sites, or groups of analysis, such as social class. Rather than a single, coherent theory, Law suggests that ANT is 'a sensibility to the messy practices of relationality and materiality of the world' (1986, 2); I agree and tend to use assemblage rather than ANT, as it can be to work as a methodological guide as much as a theoretical framing. However, I use them interchangeably when appropriate.

Assemblage thinking is particularly useful in the study of controversies, characterized by the struggle of various groups to establish the authority and legitimacy of ideas and practices (Latour 2005; Venturina 2010). In this study, the controversies explored center on who and what come to decide when refugees are job-ready, when and why they have achieved enough English-language skills, and the path by which they will become incorporated into positions of economic self-sufficiency. In this case, I trace the interactions of those who resettle, train, teach, and hire refugees, as well as the refugees, themselves – as they make sense of their daily situations and take actions through associations with others to become situated in the local economy and society.

Assemblage thinking is productive in examining the relationship between social mobility and education as an accumulation of particular forms of knowledge, practice, and discourse that order people in space, time, and sometimes class (McGregor 2004). Here, the notion of assemblage frames '... how different people, materials, and practices meet to somehow cobble together shared worlds, worlds that are always under negotiation and always dynamic, yet somehow manage to cohere' (Spinuzzi 2003). This approach emphasizes the ways in which social processes materialize or animate knowledge, identities, and action. Using the notion of assemblage, I ask, among other queries, how tools such as job placement/career assessments – that is, the assemblies of texts, aims, histories, resources, and practices that instantiate what we might recognize as assessments – come to reframe refugees as ready for training or employment.

Two particular features of ANT and assemblage make them well suited to trace the ways in which those involved in resettling refugees enlist and join with material objects to make sense of refugees in local educational and livelihood arrangements. First, there is a focus on material objects, in addition to human actors. Objects with subjective investments mediate resettlement practices and 'shape intentions, meanings, relationships, routines' (Fenwick and Edwards 2010, 6). ANT shifts attention from what these non-human actors are to what they can do. For example, the intake assessments can align the placement of refugees in ESL classes, determine their readiness (or non-readiness) for workforce training, organize the use of resettlement agency's space, redistribute resources within the agency, and redefine the role of the case workers.

The second salient feature of ANT is the process through which each entity in an emerging assemblage works upon the other to get things done. The assemblage develops, expands, and contracts through what Latour calls 'translation' – a process in which different actors come together, influence and change one another, and create linkages that eventually form a network of action and material; 'when translation has succeeded, the actor–network is mobilized to assume a particular role and perform knowledge in a particular way' (Fenwick and Edwards 2010, 10). For instance, when an employer encounters the case worker aiming to get the refugees employed, each negotiates the employability of the refugees, their roles in the process, and the expectations of the potential refugee employee. The case worker may report the refugee's English use in a way that is advantageous to securing the position; the employer may downplay his or her intention to limit the refugees' access to additional English classes so that the refugee might remain in an entry level position; and so on. In this study, such negotiations between these sorts of actors are examined, as they 'persuade, coerce, seduce, resist and compromise each other' (Fenwick and Edwards 2010, 4), proposing their own theories of action to explain their behaviors and interactions.

Methodological attentions

Methodologically, there are two approaches to utilizing assemblage and ANT – to follow actors via interviews and ethnographic research, or to first examine material objects such as refugee intake forms and English assessments that serve as intermediaries that pass between actors. In 2010, after I gave a talk on emergent bilingual and immigrant education at my university, I was approached by someone who was working with refugees. She invited me to attend a workshop for agencies and organizations serving English-language learners. There, I met the directors of the two resettlement agencies highlighted in this piece. I 'followed' them and through several interviews with them I was directed to other agencies and organizations that also provided services to refugees. I began to identify, contact, and interview the administrators at these agencies and organizations. Ultimately, I created an interactive database and map that included the locations, services provided, and contact information for each entity. I then returned to the two resettlement agencies and began more in-depth study of their services and the refugees whom they resettle. From there, I traced the interactions of the agencies' staffs who worked hands-on with the refugees as they sought work and education opportunities for the newcomers.

Exploring interactions as a unit of study across a multi-sited field is messy. ANT-inspired ethnographies are unruly because:

> what can be observed locally are the ways in which 'out there' is produced in the patterning of relations between actors or entities in a network. (Clarke 2002, 112)

The work of several scholars (Hamilton 2010; Fenwick and Edwards 2010) who put ANT or assemblage to work in studying education note that what the framework brings to ethnographic methodological approaches is a careful tracing of the 'micro-movements through which little humdrum bits, human and non-human, negotiate their joinings (or their un-joinings) to assemble the messy things we often try to ignore [,take for granted,] or explain away in our everyday words …' (Fenwick and Edwards 2010, 146). The methodological approach of ANT-inspired work resonates with other approaches, including Garfinkel's (1967) ethnomethodology and Dorothy Smith's (2006) institutional ethnography. In each of these, there is also a taking up or following the actor's 'standpoint in the local actualities of the everyday … of looking out beyond the everyday to discover how it came to happen as it does' (Smith 2006, 3). ANT studies also examine how the everyday routines hold together, even if temporarily, how they disconnect, and how they reform in other configurations.

Refugees and Wayside

In 2011, 56,384 persons were admitted to the United States as refugees. New York State received nearly 6.3% or 3529 of the refugees (Martin and

Yankay 2012). The upstate New York city, I call Wayside here, has become the receiving city for approximately 1000 refugees annually since 2005.[2] However, due to the implementation of more stringent screening policies by international institutions, fewer refugees were resettled in 2011. According to the 2010 US Census, Wayside's immigrant and refugee community is 7% (approximately 18,291 people) of the overall population in the city and one-third of the immigrant and refugee population in all of New York State.[3] These refugees originate from countries as diverse as Burma, Somalia, and Iraq. Seventy-three languages are spoken by students in city's public schools and there is an increased diversity of languages and need for English language support. By 2009–2010, the languages spoken by most students receiving language support, after Spanish, were Karen and Somali.

Wayside, a mid-size city characterized by a steadily decreasing native population, a declining body of highly-educated and skilled residents, and a shrinking economy is home to one of the country's largest refugee shelters and a few authorized resettlement affiliates, as well as numerous organizations that provide legal, educational, transportation, health, and spiritual services to refugees and other immigrant newcomers. The federally-approved refugee resettlement agencies, affiliates of national voluntary associations referred to as *vologs*, provide initial resettlement, education, employment immigration-legal, housing, and interpreting services. Individual agencies also have specialized programs, including mental health services. Under the mandates of the US Department of State, these organizations guide refugees as they learn to navigate their initial 90 days in the United States. The agencies in this study focus intensively on the first 30 days of resettlement, during which they secure, among many other things, housing, legal documents, medical examinations, resettlement plans, school enrollment for children, applications for social services, and referrals to ESL classes; they then provide varying services, some grant-funded up to 180 days after arrival.

Data collection and analysis

This paper draws on data collected between January 2011 and June 2012 as part of a continuing ethnographic study of immigrants and refugee networks aimed at tracing and examining the network of services accessed by immigrants and refugees in Wayside to better understand the relationships between the services used and educational choices and work experiences. Data include 15 semi-structured interviews with directors, manager, and program coordinators at the local refugee organizations; semi-structured and informal interviews with the leaders and staff of 25 agencies and organizations that provide services to refugees and immigrant newcomers; business personnel who hire refugees; and 16 refugees who attended ESL and career/workforce training programs at one of the two resettlement agencies highlighted in the study. Language interpreters from local refugee organizations were used when requested by refugee interviewees. All of the interviews used in this paper were audiotaped and later transcribed verbatim. Eight of the refugees were resettled during the study and eight had been resettled in 2010. They were recruited to the study through direct contact and referrals by fellow refugees or staff members at the resettlement agencies. Three public exhibitions/events, in which refugees shared their life-stories, including their resettlement, assisted me in locating the refugee experiences presented in this study as representative of the larger population of refugees' experiences in Wayside.

In addition to the interviews, I observed and participated in weekly ESL classes and two month-long career training programs at both resettlement affiliates. During the study, I served as a volunteer ESL instructor at one (resettlement agency 1) and as a volunteer employment trainer assistant at the other (resettlement agency 2). I also observed the daily work at both agencies one or more days a week throughout the study. I attended multiple community and school meetings, events and activities in which refugees participated, and a variety of government meetings and forums in which issues associated with the Wayside refugee population were discussed.

Data were managed, coded, and analyzed using the software program NVivo 8.0. First-level coding was done according to identifiable ANT translations. For instance, the process through which each refugee was initially translated into an intake assessment, then into a score of the assessment and placed into a particular level of ESL classes, and so forth, was coded. Codes were also made to denote descriptive identifying information, such as demographic information, names of documents, and agency information. Secondary and tertiary coding centered on the knowledges and information that came to be circulated as 'facts,' such as employment rates, job satisfaction, and self-sufficiency, as well as values, perceptions, and ideas about education and employment.

Findings: constructing refugees as educable and ready for employment

At the resettlement agencies, the intake and orientation process, which formalizes the beginning of the refugees' educational and employment trajectories in the United States, includes a review of the refugee's case file, an interview, and a short test of English language skills aimed at measuring word and object recognition. Case workers use the interview information, along with a review of refugees' legal documents and materials from international organizations and *vologs* to identify the 'most employable' members of families. For each adult refugee, an initial written plan that includes employment and education goals, among other objectives, is created from the intake meeting. Human actors within the resettlement agencies and many in associated organizations and government offices 'become mobilized by the non-human text of the "plan" to shape their [future] practices' (Fenwick and Edwards 2010, 118) accordingly.

The enactment of the plan by the multiple actors involves selection, and, in turn, standards. This is most obvious in the placement of each refugee in a section of ESL classes. English is clearly valued over the native languages of the refugees (unless their native languages include English) in the United States, and in ANT terms the learning of language goes through a 'purification,' a process that requires the exclusion of that which is not valued and an excluding of linguistic practices considered non-standard. Further, while the selection and placement process becomes the norm, it is enacted quite variably and with 'a mix of intuition, experience working with so many previous refugees, and a review of some really unrelated pieces of paper that are supposed to document the life of an individual's worth' (interview, director, resettlement agency 2, 5 April 2011). Both the plan and the process it evokes are assembled things, 'lashed up' from numerous elements, and as such each cannot be understood without an examination of 'how it fits into larger arrays of physical objects, social sentiments and ways of being' (Molotch 2005, 1) in a networked whole.

Learning English as an initial step to employment and self-sufficiency

The head ESL instructor at resettlement agency 1 taught advanced ESL classes three afternoons a week and two mornings a week, and managed – or perhaps, more accurately, interacted with – a handful of revolving volunteers. Frequently, there were more than 20 refugees in each class and most refugees took at least two classes a week. On several occasions, the head ESL instructor had no volunteers so he instructed both a beginning and advanced class simultaneously. He stressed learning English as the first step to social mobility; in an interview, he stated:

> English just seems like a good place to start, right? It's not the only thing. There are papers, all kinds of legal documents, and the stuff we all need to live, like safe shelter, food, but English is a long-term kind of commitment to being here ... English works as a step up on the ladder and we're all trying to climb that latter. Refugees too ... (Interview, 8 November 2011)

Managers, caseworkers, and other staff who worked in the resettlement agencies concurred, as did several refugees. Learning English, they agreed, is essential to succeeding. This belief had become a durable and often circulated fact.

However, the emphasis on learning English – or at least learning 'too much' English – was not without conflict and was, on occasion, challenged and partly disassembled. Case workers often removed refugees from ESL classes to take them to job training programs and interviews. When asked about this practice, a former refugee who worked as a case worker responded: 'The goal of resettlement isn't only education. It is getting them into jobs so that they can support themselves and their families' (interview, 15 November 2011), a stance I examine further in the next section. Managers at two of the largest employers of refugees supported this aim. One manufacturing manager stated: 'I want them to learn English, but when they start learning too much English, they begin looking to get out of the factory ... can't blame them, but training new replacements is one of my greatest costs outside materials and shipping' (interview, 17 February 2012). Several managers concurred and candidly identified the greatest risk in hiring refugees as the possibility that once they learned more English, the refugees would find more challenging, higher-paid positions.

One Somalian refugee, Alma, confirmed the managers' concerns. During an interview, she spoke at length about how she had learned English in the refugee camp she had lived in for 18 months, but that her English really improved in the ESL classes she took at the resettlement agency. She was hired less than 90 days after arriving in Wayside and she attributed her job success at a local distribution plant to her ability to speak and write English. She stated:

> I know that my English has gotten better and because of this, I got a higher position at work. I now supervise others, and not all of them are refugees. At first I worked in the back. Now I talk with customers more. (13 January 2012)

Later in the interview, Alma revealed that she had not finished the equivalent of high school and neither had she worked for pay outside of her house in Somalia. She had, like many female refugees, been responsible for the home and the children, while her husband, who was later killed in the resettlement camp in 2008, went 'out to work.' Once he died, she realized that she would be solely responsible for their two children and for migrating to the United States. At that point, in the camp, she decided to attend ESL classes and her instructor recognized her skill in learning languages and began also tutoring her and a few other women after class.

Alma's former case manager confirmed that by the time Alma arrived in the United States she was able to speak a great deal of English and understand much of what was said. Her English skills were, according to the notes the case manager re-read in Alma's intake chart, 'the main reason she's beating the odds.' She continued:

> Her [English] tests look good. There's letters of support from her former camp teacher and a church member where she volunteered. Notes from one of our ESL volunteer teachers. Her writing sample here, from I don't know where, is decent too. She even wrote me a letter introducing herself. It's here too. (Interview, 29 February 2012)

These bits and pieces of material objects, collected from across two or more countries, and then drawn together with actors' interpretations and considerations, outweighed the 'odds' that were against Alma. A single mother who lacked long-term formal education, and endured prolonged periods of poverty – measures often indicating downward social mobility or social reproduction – Alma became rendered as employable. The assemblage of 'evidence' required the casework to respond to Alma as someone ready for work, but this positioning challenged cultural norms and gender roles, which at first put Alma in conflict with the men in her deceased husband's extended family. Ultimately, however, they too came to realize that her status could be beneficial to them as they sought employment and education.

Employment training for 'new work'

As explained by the director of resettlement agency 2, 'The [US] Department of State places tremendous emphasis on the importance of employment of refugees during the early stages of resettlement, usually after the first thirty days' (public presentation, 21 May 2011). Refugees between the ages of 18 and 64 are deemed able to work, unless they have medically diagnosed disabilities, are full-time caretakers for another individual, including a child younger than one year of age, or are women in their last trimesters of pregnancy. According to a case manager at resettlement agency 1:

> Getting refugees to work is the goal. It's pretty difficult to get all of the paperwork documenting that someone is a caretaker. Even being officially recognised as disabled and getting all of the necessary medical appointments and legal documentation of the disability takes time. Basically, the government and the public don't want refugees coming here and then living off the state, so getting them to work and getting them to be self-sufficient is one of our top priorities. (Interview, 4 March 2011)

Both resettlement agencies in this study prepared refugees for work through a variety of specifically targeted career and workforce training activities. They held trainings in developing English skills for employment, writing resumes, dressing for 'success,' getting transportation to work, and practicing interviews. Both agencies sponsored trips to job fairs, developed long-term relationships with potential employers, and collaborated with the local labor department. These employment-focused activities were intricately linked to other legal and medical services that helped prepare the refugees for work in the United States.

At a class focused on career-building/workforce training at agency 2, refugees practiced interviewing. Volunteer interviewers, acting as potential employers, interviewed each refugee and then provided feedback to the interviewees. The mock interviewers and agency staff then debriefed. The following exchange, quoted from the debriefing, exemplifies the complexities of identifying refugees as ready for employment:

> Training manager: Thanks for participating today. You already shared out with the refugees. Thanks for focusing on the positives like they looked you in the eye. Now, we need to talk more about who of the six [refugees interviewed that day], we can recommend for employment now, without more training.
>
> Mock interviewer from labor department: I think they all did an excellent job of wearing appropriate clothing and shaking hands and looking me in the eye, like you said. Dea Phor's answers were okay. They seemed appropriate and what I'd expect from someone whose only been here a month and who knows some English.
>
> Flipping through Dea Phor's file, the training manager agrees: Yes, he tested pretty high on his intake on vocab. and object identification. It says here that he took ESL in camp. I can't really read these intake notes. Maybe he was a camp counselor, but he's never worked outside of the fields.
>
> Mock interviewer from a local grocery chain: I could see him as a stock boy or working janitorial until he gets a bit more comfortable. But he's Buddhist, right? So he can't work around the meat department? ... Anything that might come up about his health?
>
> Dea Phor's case manager: Can't share med. information ...
>
> Mock interviewer: Yeah, right. He looks small, that's all.
>
> Training manager: I don't think he's Buddhist. His sister's Christian. He's pretty average height and weight for Karen. They're hard working even though they seem small to us ...
>
> Dea Phor's case manager: He's already applied for his social security number and passed his medical exam. To me, he's ready for work. He's been taking the advanced ESL class and I've seen him be able to carry on a conversation pretty well. [Name of ESL instructor] told me yesterday that he could leave classes for a job any day now ... (Transcribed fieldnotes, 27 March 2012)

In this assessment, multiple and various ideas and materials were brought to bear on the assessment of Dea Phor's employability. Through multiple translations of different pieces of information, the employment potential of Dea Phor became mired in a display and discussion of assembled 'textual things' (Law and Herrington 2003) – including true and imagined cultural understandings of religion and physical stature, medical records, social security applications, illegible case notes, and so forth. The discussion reveals that different actors had varying expectations and criteria for work readiness, and, further, the very process involved in evaluating the mock interview elicited each actor to construct an account of employability. Through the discussion, Dea Phor's employability became a collection of eclectic facts that was used to determine whether, as he announced during the interviews, he was 'ready for new work.'

Other interviewees that day included Anah, a former government worker from Iraq, who despite his family's prominence and his law degree was determined to be unready for work, according to the training manager and his case manager who considered angry and non-compliant. During the interviews he had given only 'yes' or 'no' answers, if he answered at all, despite being proficient in English. His case manager, an immigrant from the Middle East, had concerns that Anah would not accept a low-wage job. He explained:

> They're here on special visas because they helped the Americans in the war. That's why most of them expected to get here and be treated well with good jobs and homes. But the government doesn't provide for that. They're angry. I don't blame them, really. We treat them like all the refugees, but so they, most of them, refuse to work. They want to go to college ... (Interview, 3 April 2012).

Thus, despite Anah's fluency in English and his long-term high-ranking work, he was situated as currently 'unfit' for employment.

When I asked Anah about employment, he stated:

> I won't work in some menial small job at a packing plant or a grocery store ... It is outrageous to think that this is how I am treated here ... See those other refugees groveling for work? That's not me. (Interview, 1 May 2012)

By the traditional measures – a good education, a law degree, a middle-to-upper class upbringing, and proficiency in English – Anah would probably be a good candidate not only for work, but for future upward social mobility. However, what was to be achieved during the mock interviews had not been met. Standard procedures, such as mock interviews aimed at preparing refugees for jobs, are to result in some ordered, consistent, and comparable conduct 'that occurs at diverse locations and across time, in which a whole constellation of relations meet and weave together in particular ways to constitute practice' (Fenwick and Edwards 2010, 84). They are aimed at delineating levels of competence and there is often not much room explicitly allocated to deviance from expected behaviors.

Yet in an ANT framing, standards and standardized procedures are recognized as a series of negotiations that lead to multiple translations and enactments. As such, there is the possibility that a standard way of doing something toward a set goal may be challenged, undone, and even reconfigured. Such is the case of Anah, who ultimately entered the workforce, but changed the standard procedure while reappopriating some of its required elements. Despite being deemed 'unemployable' by the resettlement agency, he drew upon his family's social status and English skills in his local ethnic community to improve his position. Together, with four other refugee males from Iraq, who had been resettled in 2010, Anah started a small restaurant and taxi service. He recently expanded his ventures to include a small grocery store, as well.

Such alternative pathways were not exclusive to the Iraqi refugees – or to highly-educated refugees of upper-class backgrounds. More than one-half of the refugees interviewed believed that without the ability to speak English well, they would either not find a 'regular' job or they would find only low-paying positions without much room for advancement. Three of the refugee women interviewed worked in Wayside's most celebrated example of refugee entrepreneurship – a cooperative marketplace. At the market, the women work as vendors, selling items they and their neighbors make and items imported from their home regions. A couple of refugees also work as marketplace interpreters. Several others aim to join the collective once the space is expanded in 2012. These examples demonstrate the way in which some refugees, who are considered unprepared for employment in the United States through the standardized channels, reassemble the process to employment.

Concluding thoughts: resettling notions

Examining the textured interactions between human actors, their material objects, and their discursive practices as they assemble the initial resettlement of refugees through ESL classes and workforce training, I have aimed to problematize notions about the relationships between formal education, livelihoods, and social mobility. Adaptations and alternative pathways result when livelihood and educational opportunities become paradoxically diverse due to transnational migrations and are constrained by localized politico-economic environments. My findings complicate the assumption that formal education represents an enduring pathway or necessary precursor to upward social mobility. As refugees are required by resettling agents to become economically self-sufficient as soon as possible, formal education such as ESL courses can limit initial employment opportunities and narrow families' livelihood strategies upon resettlement. Conversely, being proficient in English does not guarantee work placement when it conflicts with the rest of the socio-material assemblage of employability. The relationships between traditional criteria used to measure and predict social mobility are messy, complex, and unsettled in this era of unprecedented movement, especially, perhaps, when aiming to understand the experiences of refugees.

In closing, I must also unsettle the assumptions made about refugees' experiences as part of an American dream. Considering them as global versions of a Horatio Algers narrative obfuscates critical examinations of unequal and conflicting employment and educational opportunities for refugees. I understand this tendency. Americans like stories of success – of pulling oneself up by one's bootstrap, persevering, and ultimately building a comfortable existence. Discourses of moving up the social and economic ladders are part of the durable American story. Because there is a lack of clarity about where to locate refugees among a spectrum of broad American categories – such as race, class, religion, or culture – refugees when resettled in America become thrust into such discourses. As demonstrated by Haines and Rosenblum (2010, 401), 'the conventionalizing and universalizing of the refugee experience with the dehistoricisation and depoliticisation of actual refugees' creates accounts of the refugee experience as ones of hope, resilience, and perseverance, which tidily align with often-cited American values. However, as offered by assemblage thinking in this piece, there are contestations, complications, and multiplicities that demand a more critical examination of the social trajectories of refugees and a resettling – an uprooting, problematizing, and reintegration – of notions of social mobility and its indicators, especially for those who move transnationally.

Notes

1. See http://www.uscis.gov/ilink/docView/SLB/HTML/SLB/0-0-0-1/0-0-0-29/0-0-0-101.html.
2. Pseudonyms for people and places are used throughout the paper. Titles, when used, are generic.
3. See http://quickfacts.census.gov/.

References

Alba, R., and V. Nee. 2003. *Remaking the American Mainstream: Assimilation and Contemporary Immigration*. Cambridge, MA: Harvard University Press.
Bean, F., S. K. Brown, and R. G. Rumbaut. 2006. "Mexican Immigrant Political and Economic Incorporation." *Perspectives on Politics* 4 (2): 309–313.
Callon, M. 1986. "Some Elements of Sociology of Translation: The Domestication of the Scallops and the Fishermen of St. Brieuc Bay." In *Power, Action and Belief: A New Sociology of Knowledge?*, edited by J. Law, 196–223. London: Routledge and Kegan Paul.
Clarke, J. 2002. "A New Kind of Symmetry: Actor-Network Theories and the New Literacy Studies." *Studies in the Education of Adults* 34 (2): 107–122.
Farley, R., and R. Alba. 2002. "The New Second Generation in the United States." *International Migration Review* 36 (3): 669–701.
Fenwick, T., and R. Edwards. 2010. *Actor-Network Theory in Education*. New York: Routledge.
Fernández-Kelly, P., and L. Konczal. 2005. "Murdering the Alphabet: Identity and Entrepreneurship among Second-generation Cubans, West Indians, and Central Americans." *Ethnic and Racial Studies* 28 (6): 1153–1181.
Froerer, P. 2012. "Learning, Livelihoods, and Social Mobility: Valuing Girls' Education in Central India." *Anthropology and Education Quarterly* 43 (4): 344–357.

Froerer, P., and A. Portisch. 2012. "Introduction to the Special Issue: Learning, Livelihoods, and Social Mobility." *Anthropology and Education Quarterly* 43 (4): 332–343.
Garfinkel, H. 1967. *Studies in Ethnomethodology.* Englewood Cliffs, NJ: Prentice Hall.
Grogger, J., and S. Trejo. 2002. *Falling behind or Moving up? The Intergenerational Progress of Mexican Americans.* San Francisco, CA: Public Policy Institute of California.
Haines, D. W., and K. E. Rosenblum. 2010. "Perfectly American: Constructing the Refugee Experience." *Journal of Ethnic and Migration Studies* 36 (3): 391–406.
Hamilton, M. 2010. "Privileged Literacies: Policy, Institutional Process and the Life of the IALS." *Language and Education* 15 (2): 178–196.
Hannam, K., M. Sheller, and J. Urry. 2006. "Editorial: Mobilities, Immobilities and Moorings." *Mobilities* 1 (1): 1–22.
Kasinitz, P. 2012. "The Sociology of International Migration: Where We Have Been; Where Do We Go from Here?" *Sociological Forum* 27 (3): 579–590.
Kasinitz, P., J. H. Mollenkopf, and M. C. Waters. 2004. "Becoming American/Becoming New Yorkers; Immigrant Incorporation in the Majority Minority City." *International Migration Review* 36 (4): 1020–1036.
Kasinitz, P., J. H. Mollenkopf, M. Waters, and J. Holdaway. 2008. *Inheriting the City; the Children of Immigrants Come of Age.* Cambridge, MA: Harvard University Press/Russell Sage Foundation.
Latour, B. 1987. *Science in Action.* Cambridge, MA: Harvard University Press.
Latour, B. 1988. *The Pasteurization of France.* Cambridge: Harvard University Press.
Latour, B. 2005. *Reassembling the Social: An Introduction to Actor-Network Theory.* Oxford: Oxford University Press.
Law, J. 1986. *Power, Action and Belief. A New Sociology of Knowledge?* London: Routledge and Kegan Paul.
Law, J., and K. Hetherington. 2003. "Materialities, Spatialities, Globalities." In *The Spaces of Postmodernism: Readings in Human Geography*, edited by M. Dear and S. Flusty, 390–401. Oxford: Blackwell Publishers/The Sociological Review.
Martin, D. C. and J. E. Yankay. 2012. *Refugees and Asylees: 2011 Annual Flow Report.* United States Department of Homeland Security, Office of Immigration Statistics.
McBrien, J. L. 2005. "Educational Needs and Barriers for Refugee Students in the United States: A Review of the Literature." *Review of Educational Research* 75 (3): 329–364.
McGregor, J. 2004. "Spatiality and the Place of the Material in Schools." *Pedagogy, Culture and Society* 12 (3): 347–372.
Molotch, H. 2005. *Where Stuff Comes from: How Toasters, Toilets, Cars, Computers and Many Other Things Come to Be as They Are.* New York: Routledge.
Naji, M. 2012. "Learning to Weave the Threads of Honor: Understanding the Value of Female Schooling in Southern Morocco." *Anthropology and Education Quarterly* 43 (4): 372–384.
Nolin, C. 2006. *Transnational Ruptures: Gender and Forced Migration.* Aldershot: Ashgate.
Pinson, H., and M. Arnot. 2007. "Sociology of Education and the Wasteland of Refugee Education Research." *British Journal of Sociology of Education* 28 (3): 399–407.

Portes, A., and R. Rumbaut. 2001. *Legacies: The Story of the Immigrant Second Generation*. Berkeley, CA: University of California Press.

Portisch, A. "'Like Unbroken Cream': Education and Livelihoods among the Kazakh of Western Mongolia." *Anthropology and Education* 43 (4): 385–399.

Rao, N. 2010. "Migration, Education and Socio-economic Mobility." *Compare: A Journal of Comparative and International Education* 40 (2): 137–145.

Smith, D. E. 2006. *Institutional Ethnography as Practice*. New York: Rowman and Littlefield.

Spinuzzi, C. 2003. "More than One, Less than Many: A Review of Three 'Post-ANT' books." http://www.cwrl.utexas.edu/currents/fall03/spinuzzi.html.

Valentin, K. 2012. "The Role of Education in Mobile Livelihoods: Social and Geographical Routes of Young Nepalese Migrants in India." *Anthropology and Education Quarterly* 43 (4): 429–442.

Venturini, T. 2010. "Diving in Magma: How to Explore Controversies with Actor-Network Theory." *Public Understanding of Science* 19 (3): 258–273.

Waters, M. C., and T. R. Jiménez. 2005. "Assessing Immigrant Assimilation: New Empirical and Theoretical Challenges." *Annual Review of Sociology* 31: 105–125.

Zhou, M., and J. Lee. 2007. "Becoming Ethnic or Becoming American? Reflecting on the Divergent Pathways to Social Mobility and Assimilation among the New Second Generation." *Du Bois Review* 4 (1): 189–205.

Index

absolute and relative mobility 1, 22, 45–7, 48, 113–14, 159
absolute and relative trends: origins, education and destinations in 1990s and 2000s 135–48
academic failure and working-class students 176–89; findings and discussion 180–8; method 179–80
academy and free schools 51
Acker, J. 298
actor-network theory (ANT): refugees in US 313, 316, 317–27
age and Malaysian work setting 226
agricultural fields of study 261, 263, 267
Agyeman, G. 297
Aihara, A. 216
Alatas, S.H. 220
Alba, R. 314
Allen, K. 91
Allen, M. 56
Andre-Bechely, L. 70
anomic 56
Apple, M.W. 272
'Arab Spring' 56
Archer, L. 176, 178, 182, 183, 195, 196
architecture 121
Arnot, M. 49
Arrow, K. 232
Arum, R. 272, 273
aspirational Britain 27, 29–32, 44–5
assemblage: refugees in US 313, 316–27
assembly line 48–9
Australia 131, 218
Avis, J. 108, 111, 120
Ayalon, H. 236, 273

Ball, S. 32, 44, 51, 55, 69, 80, 112, 176, 177, 181, 212, 222, 297, 298
banking 31, 100
Barker, M. 297
Baxter, A. 199
Bean, F. 314

Beck, U. 189, 257
Bell, D. 43, 48, 131–2, 232, 234, 296
Bell, T. 35
Benn, C. 276
Bernstein, B. 125, 272
Bible 12
Birdsall, N. 233
Black middle-class children and schooling 293–308; race, racism and intersectionality 297–8; study 296–7; educational strategies of first generation 298–300; second generation as pupils 300–2; second generation as parents 303–5; children's responses – third generation 305–7
Blair, Tony 32
Blanchflower, D. 33
Blanden, J. 28, 108, 113, 144, 148
Blau, P.M. 254
Blyth, E. 177
Blyton, P. 55
Boliver, V. 274, 288
Bolton, P. 109
Bond, R. 133
Boudon, R. 49, 56; model of social opportunity: social mobility and post-compulsory education 108–26
bounded rationality 115, 125–6
Bourdieu, P. 37, 46, 52, 68, 88, 89, 92, 93, 94, 103, 104–5, 110–11, 117, 126, 177–8, 180, 181, 183, 184, 185, 186, 187, 188, 189, 195, 196, 197, 198, 199, 200, 203, 204, 208, 212, 213, 217, 218, 226, 227, 229, 255, 272, 294, 305
Bowen, W. 69
Bowl, M. 178, 183
Bragg, Melvyn 31
Brah, A. 294
Brake, M. 92
Brantlinger, E. 70, 71
Bray, M. 244
Breen, R. 46, 48, 116, 133, 135, 144, 148, 232, 234, 271

INDEX

Bristol universities: social class and mobilisation of capitals 87–105
British Household Panel Survey (1991) *see* origins, education and destinations in 1990s and 2000s
British Social Attitudes (BSA) survey (1983–2010): framing higher education 156–74; changing policy context 157–60; data and methods 160–1; discussion and conclusion 172–4; questions and responses in BSA 161–6; self-interest 168, 173, 174; survey responses 167–72
Brooks, R. 224
Brown, Gordon 26–7, 28
Brown, P. 22–3, 43, 46, 47, 48, 49, 50, 52, 53, 54, 58, 66, 88, 89, 90, 98, 105, 109, 111, 115, 121, 149, 217, 225, 228, 254
Browne, L. 91
Browne Report (2010) 51, 159, 172, 173
Brynjolfsson, E. 48
Bukodi, E. 47, 89, 109, 133–4, 139
Burke, P.J. 163
Byrom, T. 177, 178, 180, 181, 184, 188

Calhoun, C. 159
Callon, M. 316
Canada 28, 91, 131
capital, habitus and practices: rural students in Chinese elite university 193–209
capitals, mobilisation of 87–105, 110, 121; extracurricular activities (ECA) 52, 77–8, 89–90, 91–3, 96–8, 104, 105; internships 54, 89, 90–3, 95, 98–103, 104, 105
Causa, O. 28
Cerny, P.G. 51
Chakrabortty, A. 90
Chan, K.W. 193
changes, frequency of job 133
Charles, M. 252, 253, 255, 256
China 48; Hong Kong 218, 244; meritocracy and *Gaokao* (National College Entrance Examinations) 232–48; rural students in elite university: capital, habitus and practices 193–209
Chinese students in US, second-generation 315
Chowdry, H. 87, 89
Clandinin, D. 179
Clarke, J. 318
'class work': producing privilege and social mobility in elite US secondary schools 65–82; class productions in new time and space 67–9; class/ed practices and post-secondary process: State school example 69–74, 78, 79–82; course selection 72–4; critical bifocality 67; fractures in middle/upper middle class: Matthews Academy 74–82; micromanaging college process 75–6;

thinking, plotting, planning 77–80; watching, waiting and deciding when to intervene 70–2
Clegg, Nick 27, 30, 54, 130
Coalition government (2010–2015) 27–8, 44, 49, 51, 87, 130–1, 296
Coard, B. 295, 296
cognitive test scores 119
Cohen, L. 179
Collini, S. 32
Collins, R. 47, 51, 217
comprehensive schools *see* type of school
confidence 15; overseas study 221; rural students in Chinese elite university: crisis in 197–8; self-regulate to develop increased levels of 187–8; social 52; undermined 306
Cookson, P. 69
corporate governance 53
Crenshaw, K. 298
Creswell, J. 179
Critical Race Theory (CRT) 294, 295, 296, 298
critical thinking 288
Crompton, R. 44
Crossley, N. 197
Crozier, G. 196
cultural capital 30, 34, 46, 58, 71, 79, 80, 92, 94, 196; academic failure and working-class students 186; Boudon's model of social opportunity 110, 115, 119, 121, 126; combining social and 90; Malaysia: UK offshore or transnational education 212–29; Netherlands 255; placements in the creative industries 91; rural students in Chinese elite university 199, 206, 208
cultural reproduction theory 255
curriculum 50, 55, 254, 271–90; accelerated 70, 72; analytical strategy 277–8; Boudon's model of social opportunity 118–19; changes over life-course 287–8; China: rural–urban divide 194; China: science 205; data 274–5; lower social classes, entry into 275, 283–7; reproduction of social inequalities 272–3; research questions 273–4; service class, entry into 275, 279–83; some descriptive statistics 278–9; variables 275–7; *see also* Netherlands: educational expansion and field of study

Dahrendorf, R. 55
Davies, S. 253, 256
de Graaf, P.M. 253, 255
de-industrialisation 120
Dearing Report (1997) 159, 172
deficit model 45, 46, 57
Delgado, R. 298
Deng, G. 195
Denzin, N.K. 195
determinism 126, 178, 196

INDEX

Devine, F. 54, 55, 130, 137, 148, 212
disidentification 304–5
displacement and identity confusion 31
dominance effects 114, 121, 124
Douglas, M. 188
Duckett, J. 237
Durkheim, E. 9, 50
Duru-Bellat, M. 236, 240

earnings *see* rewards
economic capital 30, 80, 91, 94, 102, 103, 104; Boudon's model of social opportunity 110, 115, 119, 121, 126; Malaysia: UK offshore or transnational education 217, 219, 220, 224; rural students in Chinese elite university 198, 208
economic fields of study 256, 261, 267
economics, neo-classical 49
economy 32–3, 47, 133, 134, 313
educational expansion and field of study: Netherlands 252–68, 273
egalitarian philosophy 25–6
Ehrenreich, B. 66, 67
Elias, P. 51, 89
emerging economies 48
engineers 55
Erikson, R. 28, 108, 113, 134, 141, 275
Ermisch, J. 108, 109, 119
ethical neutrality 8–9
ethnicity 22, 44, 56, 109, 233; Malaysia: UK offshore or transnational education 215–16, 226–7; *see also* race
European Union 233
extracurricular activities (ECAs) 52, 77–8, 89–90, 91–2, 104, 105; Black children and schooling 301, 304; generating capital through 96–8; methods 92–3

failure and working-class students, academic 176–89
fairness, justice as 54
fairness as social mobility 27, 43–5; fallacy of fairness 46
Farley, R. 314
Felstead, A. 289
Fenwick, T. 313, 317, 318, 321, 325
Fernández-Kelly, P. 312
Fevre, R. 54
field of study *see* Netherlands: educational expansion and field of study
financial crisis (2008) 48, 313
financial services industry 91
Finegold, D. 120
Fitz-Gibbon, C.T. 276
France24 29
Francis, B. 32, 49
Frank, R. 49, 54

free and academy schools 51
Froerer, P. 311, 314, 315
functionalist theory of industrialism 1, 43–4, 54

Gambetta, D. 273
Gamble, A. 51
Gamoran, A. 66, 272, 290
Gangl, M. 254
Ganzeboom, H.B.G. 257
Garfinkel, H. 318
Garrett, D. 144
Gatzambide-Fernandez, R. 77
gender 22, 44, 49–50, 55, 56, 93, 96, 109, 202, 233; academic failure and working-class students 185; British Social Attitudes (BSA) survey (1983–2010): framing higher education 160, 167–8, 172, 173; curriculum 275, 277; internships 99, 100; Malaysia: UK offshore or transnational education 227–8; meritocracy and *Gaokao* (National College Entrance Examinations): East China 234–5, 246, 247; Netherlands: educational expansion and field of study 261, 263–8; origins, education and destinations in 1990s and 2000s 133, 134–49; race and 298; refugees in US 313–14, 322–3, 326; rural students in Chinese elite university 205–6
General Household Survey (2005) *see* origins, education and destinations in 1990s and 2000s
Germany 91
Gillborn, D. 295, 298, 307–8
Giroux, H. 178
Glass, D.V. 42
globalisation 88, 108
Goldthorpe, J. 1, 28, 42, 43, 45–6, 48, 54, 55, 65, 108, 109, 110, 114, 115–16, 120, 125, 133, 134, 135, 140, 144, 159, 161, 232, 233, 234, 255
Goodman, A. 119
Gove, Michael 27, 31–2
Goyette, K.A. 253, 256
grammar schools *see* type of school
Granfield, R. 195, 202
Greece 56
Grogger, J. 314

Habermas, J. 159
habitus 68, 69, 74, 75, 80, 110, 115; HE participation: trajectory interruptions 176–89; rural students in elite Chinese university: capital, habitus and practices 193–209
Haines, D.W. 327
Halsey, A.H. 1, 2–3, 10–22, 34, 42, 44, 50, 132, 133, 135, 148, 157, 272

INDEX

Hamilton, M. 318
Hanlon, G. 296
Hannam, K. 311
Hannum, E. 194, 234, 235
Hansen, M. 116
Harker, R.K. 196
Hartas, D. 30, 32
Harvey, D. 66, 237
Hatcher, R. 32, 111, 116
Hawkes, D. 275
Hayek, F.A. 44, 51
Head, S. 48
Heath, A. 32, 42, 44, 55, 133, 135, 137, 139, 140, 157, 275
Hey, V. 37
higher education 53, 68, 109, 124, 131; academic failure and working-class students 176–89; adult returners 302; British Social Attitudes (BSA) survey (1983–2010): framing 156–74; 'class work' in elite US secondary schools and post-secondary process 65–82; emerging economies 48; grants 159, 161; meritocracy and *Gaokao* (National College Entrance Examinations): East China 232–48; othering: decision not to go to 181; postgraduate degrees 204, 205, 206, 207; rural students in elite Chinese university: capital, habitus and practices 193–209; social class and mobilisation of capitals: recognising and playing the game 87–105; tuition fees 51, 56, 157, 159, 162, 165, 194, 217; *see also* post-compulsory education: Boudon's model of social opportunity
Hills, J. 54
Hindess, B. 161
Hirsch, F. 46, 47, 194
Hoare, A. 166
Hochschild, J. 73
Hoggart, R. 12
Holme, J. 70
Holmes, C. 53, 120
Hong Kong 218, 244
housing 70, 73, 121, 319; China 193, 195
Hoxby, C.M. 66, 68
Huang, H. 219, 237
Hutton, W. 53, 57
Hylton, K. 297–8
hyper-competition 31

Iannelli, C. 271
Ichou, M. 126
identity: confusion 31; crises 199–200; disidentification 304–5
immigration 293, 298–300, 311–12; literature review: immigrants, education and social mobility 314–16; refugees 312–27

income inequality 44, 47, 53–4, 108–9, 125, 144; within occupational categories 55
increasing merit-selection (IMS) 43–4, 46, 47, 50, 52, 54, 57, 132–3
independent schools *see* type of school
India 48, 315
individual nature of social mobility 26, 29, 37, 38–9, 55
individualism 31, 46, 51
inequality of educational opportunity (IEO) and inequality of social opportunity (ISO) 108–26
Ingram, N. 204
international education in Malaysia 212–29
International Monetary Fund (IMF) 233
internships 54, 89, 90–2, 95, 104, 105, 220; barriers to 102–3; Boudon's model of social opportunity 121; generating capital through 98–103; methods 92–3
interrupted trajectories: impact of academic failure on working-class students 176–89; findings and discussion 180–8; method 179–80
intersectionality *see* Black middle-class children and schooling
IQ 133
Ishida, H. 288

Jackson, B. 24, 35, 36–7, 38, 296, 301
Jackson, M. 52, 109, 111, 114, 116, 117, 121, 125, 139, 148, 232, 234
Japan 91, 218, 244
Jones, S. 163
Jonsson, J.O. 43, 91
journalism 131

Kalmijn, M. 253, 256
Karlson, K.B. 277
Kasinitz, P. 314, 315
Katsomitros, A. 213
Kautsky, K. 11–12
Keane, E. 195, 204
Keep, E. 109
Keller, S. 115
Kelly, A. 276
Kerckhoff, A. 65–6, 82, 272, 273–4, 277
Kim, J. 213, 219
Knight, J. 193
Korea 244
Korean News 29
Kraaykamp, G. 255, 257
Krauze, T. 234

Labour government (1997–2010) 87
Lacey, C. 301
Lacy, K. 303, 304, 307, 308
Lall, M. 233

INDEX

Lamaison, P. 94, 104
Lambert, P. 131
Lareau, A. 70–1, 79, 89–90, 105, 182
Latour, B. 313, 316, 317
Lauder, H. 22–3, 49
Law, J. 316, 324
law/lawyers 55, 121, 131, 256, 261, 263, 264, 266, 273, 313
Lawler, S. 37, 178
Lawrence, T. 70
Lawton, D. 289
Lazonick, W. 53
Leathwood, C. 166
Lee, H.A. 227
Lee, M. 214
Lehmann, W. 91, 195
Lennon, John 24, 32–3
level of social mobility in UK 28
Levin, H.M. 194
Levinson, S.C. 163
Li, B.L. 237
Li, D. 234
Li, H. 199
Li, Q. 194
Li, Y. 47, 55, 131, 134, 140
liberal–industrial theory 109, 113, 125
Lipset, S.M. 234
Little, R.J.A. 275
Liu, H. 196
Livingstone, D.W. 49
Lloyd, C. 120
Lockwood, D. 53
Long, J.S. 277
Lu, X.Y. 240
Lucas, S. 66, 236, 272

McBrien, J.L. 313
McDonough, P. 74, 80
McGregor, J. 317
Machin, S. 124
McKinsey & Co 53
McLeod, J. 105
McNay, L. 94, 198, 200
McNeil, B. 188
Macpherson, W. 296
Malaysia: middle class students and foreign education 212–29; context 213–14; findings 217–28; local cultural capital, accumulating 223–6; methodology and research design 215–16; proximity to home and culture of complacency 221–3; social divisions and positional competition 226–8
managers 55
Mannheim, K. 294–5, 307
Manning, A. 28
Mare, R. 114
Marginson, S. 159

Marsden, D. 254
Marshall, G. 43, 44, 45, 54, 132, 133, 137, 140, 271
Martin, D.C. 318
Mason, J. 215
maximally maintained inequality (MMI) theory 235–6, 247, 255
measurement of social background 113
media 29, 173, 303
medicine 121, 131, 261, 266, 267, 273, 313
meritocracy 1, 33, 105, 109, 157–9; Boudon's model of social opportunity 110, 114, 115, 121; China 195, 232–48; increasing merit-selection (IMS) 43–4, 46, 47, 50, 52, 54, 57, 132–3; Netherlands: educational expansion and field of study 254, 268; origins, education and destinations in 1990s and 2000s 131–4, 137, 139, 140, 148; social closure: from meritocracy to performocracy 50–4
meritocracy and *Gaokao* (National College Entrance Examinations): East China 232–48; context 236–7; discussion 246–8; education and meritocracy 234–6; Effectively Maintained Inequality (EMI) theory 236, 247; hypotheses, data and variables 237–41; Maximally Maintained Inequality (MMI) theory 235–6, 247; models, results and analyses 242–6; social stratification 237
Merton, R. 56
Mexican immigrants in US 314–15
Michaels, E. 53
Michie, F. 182
Middleton, Kate 29
migration 293, 298–300, 311–12; literature review: immigrants, education and social mobility 314–16; refugees 312–27
Milburn, A. 91, 130, 131, 156, 157
Mills, C. 178
Mirza, H. 302
Mishel, L. 54
Molotch, H. 321
Montgomery, A. 303
Moore, J. 166
Morocco 315
Mountford-Zimdars, A. 172
Mullen, A. 66
myths, mobility 29–32

Naidoo, R. 178
Naji, M. 315
Nash, R. 111, 116, 117, 125
Nathan, G. 275
National Child Development Study (NCDS) 273, 274–5
National Health Service 174
nationalism 56

INDEX

nationality 227, 228, 233
Nayagam, J. 214
Nee, V. 237
neo-classical economics 49
neo-colonialism 220
neoliberalism 28, 32, 44, 45, 46, 47, 49, 50, 57, 58, 108, 125
Nepalese migrants in India 315
Netherlands: educational expansion and field of study 252–68, 273; conclusion and discussion 266–8; data and measurements 257–8; inequality in educational level 255; inequality in field of study 256–7; intergenerational transmission of educational inequality 254; results 258–66; theoretical background and hypotheses 254–7; *see also* curriculum
New Zealand 218
Noddings, N. 273
Nolin, C. 312
non-understanding, gap of 36–7
Nordic countries 28
norms of upper-middle-class individuals 31

Oakes, J. 272
occupational structure 1, 16, 22, 33, 38, 45, 47, 48; Boudon's model of social opportunity 113, 120; 'knowledge' work 48–9; origins, education and destinations in 1990s and 2000s 139–40; war for talent 53–4
OECD 28, 233
Office for Fair Access 159
older people 163
O'Leary, N. 89
Olneck, M. 234
Olssen, M. 51
Open University 157, 159
opportunity, Boudon's model of social 108–26; educational change and social mobility 122–4; educational opportunity and social mobility 113–17; generating IEO and ISO 118–19; ISO and changes in social structure 119–21; primary and secondary effects of social stratification 114–16; secondary effects, evidence for 116; secondary effects, significance of 116–17; transition from school 111–12
opportunity trap 47, 89, 109
origins, education and destinations in 1990s and 2000s 130–49; absolute trends 135–40; data and methods 134–5; debate on meritocracy 131–4; relative trends 140–8

Pakulski, J. 257
parental field of study *see* Netherlands: educational expansion and field of study
parenting 30, 31

Pareto, V. 9
Parkin, F. 26, 28–9, 35
Parsons, T. 43, 131–2
pay *see* rewards
Payne, G. 26, 27, 42, 45, 57, 130
peer group 187
Penny, L. 50
Pepper, S. 194
performocracy 50–4, 57
personal career: A.H. Halsey 10–22; D. Reay 33–8
personality traits 52, 148, 226
Peters, A.M. 44
Piff, P. 31
Pilcher, J. 295
Pinson, H. 314
Platt, L. 177, 178, 179, 182
playing the game: higher education, social class and mobilisation of capitals 87–105
Polanyi, K. 51
political affiliation and BSA survey (1983–2010): framing higher education 160, 168, 169, 172, 173
political arithmetic tradition 9, 66
Portes, A. 314, 315
Portisch, A. 312
positional competition 46, 47, 50, 51, 53–4, 56; Boudon's model of social opportunity 109, 110, 111, 121; Malaysia 225–8; *see also* 'class work': producing privilege and social mobility in elite US secondary schools; playing the game: higher education, social class and mobilisation of capitals
post-compulsory education: Boudon's model of social opportunity 108–26; educational change and social mobility 122–4; educational opportunity and social mobility 113–17; generating IEO and ISO 118–19; ISO and changes in social structure 119–21; primary and secondary effects of social stratification 114–16; secondary effects, evidence for 116; secondary effects, significance of 116–17; stigma 112; transition from school 111–12; *see also* higher education
Power, S. 51, 148
Pratto, F. 160
Preston, J. 298
private education and Boudon's model of social opportunity 119
private education and BSA survey (1983–2010): framing higher education 160, 168, 172, 173
private school in US: fractures in middle/upper middle class 74–82; class productions in new time and space 67–9; introduction 65–7
privatisation of education 44

336

INDEX

public sector 56; job cuts 33, 308; Malaysia 226; salaries of senior managers 53

Qin, Y. 237
quality-of-life issues 55
quantitative methods 8–10
Quinn, J. 91

race 44, 56; three generations of racism: Black middle-class children and schooling 293–308; *see also* ethnicity
Raferty, A.E. 255
Raffe, D. 111
Raftery, A.E. 235
Rampton Report (1981) 295
Rao, N. 315
rational action/choice theory 161, 255
rationality 115, 125–6
Rawls, J. 54
Reay, D. 3, 30, 31, 33–8, 50, 67–8, 91, 177, 178, 182, 195, 196, 197, 198, 200, 204, 208, 273, 307
recruitment, competency-based 52
redistribution 27, 30, 108
Redmond, P. 90
Reed-Danahay, D. 178, 181
refugees in US 311–27; data collection and analysis 319–20; employment training for 'new work' 323–6; findings 320–1; learning English 321–3, 326; literature review: immigrants, education and social mobility 314–16; methodological attentions 318; theory: assemblage, networks and relationality 316–17
Reich, R.B. 66
Reimer, D. 253, 256
relative and absolute mobility 1, 22, 45–7, 48, 113–14, 159
relative and absolute trends: origins, education and destinations in 1990s and 2000s 135–48
resilience 188, 189, 327
rewards 120, 256; graduate premium 89; income inequalities within occupational categories 55; variability of social 22–3
Richardson, B. 296
Ritchie, B. 221
Robbins Report (1963) 22, 157, 172
Rollock, N. 296, 297, 298, 301, 303, 304, 305
Rose, D. 134
Rose, N. 52
Roulin, N. 52
Royal Wedding (2011) 29
rural students: meritocracy and *Gaokao* (National College Entrance Examinations) 235–6, 242, 244, 246, 247, 248
rural students in Chinese elite university: capital, habitus and practices 193–209;

accruing symbolic and social capital 202–4; capital, locations and frustration 198–200; cultural activities 200–2; method 194–5; misfits in higher education 195–6; strategies, practices and choices 204–8; urban space and institutional habitus: initial confrontation 196–8
Russell Group universities 178

Saunders, P. 28, 133, 178
Savage, M. 33, 54, 133
Sayer, A. 93, 198, 208
Schagen, S. 240
Schoon, I. 137
Scotland 111
Seawright, J. 195
Second World War 10–11, 34, 35
secondary modern schools *see* type of school
secondary to post-secondary pipeline: elite US schools 65–82
selective schools *see* type of school
Sennett, R. 197
Sewell, W. 65
sex discrimination 205
share options 53
Sharma, Y. 213
Shavit, Y. 109, 235, 254, 255, 273
Sidhu, R. 220
Simmel, G. 49, 51
Simmons, R. 112
Sin, I.-L. 213, 218, 219, 220, 226
Singapore 218
Skeggs, B. 35, 52, 187, 202
Smith, D. 318
social capital 30, 78, 90, 91, 94, 101, 102–3, 104, 148; academic failure and working-class students 186–7; Boudon's model of social opportunity 110, 115, 121, 126; Malaysia: UK offshore or transnational education 223, 224; Netherlands 254; rural students in Chinese elite university 202–4, 206, 208; social networks *see separate entry*
social closure: from meritocracy to performocracy 50–1; credentials: declining currency of opportunity 51–2; opportunity and war for talent 53–4
social confidence 52
social congestion 47–50, 56, 57–8, 109
social justice 51, 54–6, 58; and social mobility 26–9, 38; tuition fees 159
Social Mobility and Child Poverty Commission 130–1
social networks 52, 70, 91, 95, 101, 105, 139, 148, 187; Black children and schooling 300; Malaysia: UK offshore or transnational education 224; migrants 312, 315–16;

INDEX

refugees 312; rural students in Chinese elite university 203, 204
social opportunity, Boudon's model of 108–26
socialisation 105, 121, 199, 256, 257
Solomona, R. 297
Souto-Otero, M. 58
Spain 56
Sparks, B. 276
Spence, J. 233
Spinuzzi, C. 317
State school in US: class/ed practices and post-secondary process 69–74, 78, 79–82; class productions in new time and space 67–9; introduction 65–7
statistical modelling 117
statistical training 10
Steedman, C. 34, 35, 37
Stevens, M. 77
Stevenson, J. 90, 91
Stiglitz, J.E. 57
stigma 112, 195, 197, 202, 308
Strand, S. 109
Stuart, M. 90, 91, 92
Sullivan, A. 109, 112, 114, 272
Sun, W. 194
Sutton Trust 131, 160
Swartz, D. 91
Sweden 91
Swift, A. 9, 22–3, 54
symbolic violence 29, 30, 203

Tampubolon, G. 148
Tan, S.-C. 214
Tawney, R.H. 2–3, 9, 21, 22, 24, 25–6, 38
taxation 30
Taylorism 48–9
Tchibozo, G. 90
Teaching and Higher Education Act 1998 159
Teese, R. 272
Thomas, L. 176
Thomas, S.L. 66
Thompson, R. 112
Thurow, L.C. 288
Tieben, N. 255
Timmins, N. 29
Tindall, G. 11
Tomlinson, M. 88, 89, 90, 98, 177
trajectory interruptions: impact of academic failure on working-class students 176–89; findings and discussion 180–8; method 179–80
Triventi, M. 253, 256
Troyna, B. 295
tuition fees 51, 56, 157, 159, 162, 165; China 194; Malaysia: UK offshore or transnational education 217

type of school 119, 273–4, 276–7, 278, 279–81, 283, 288–9; Black children and schooling 296, 300–2; changes over life-course 287–8; entry into lower social classes and 283–7; free and academy schools 51; *see also* 'class work': producing privilege and social mobility in elite US secondary schools; private education

UK education in Malaysia 212–29
unemployment 273, 313, 315; graduates 33; youth 56
unethical behaviour 31
Unger, J. 237
United States 29, 31, 48, 54, 55, 91, 131, 202, 218, 303; academic and vocational education 273; 'class work': producing privilege and social mobility in elite secondary schools 65–82; refugees 311–27
universities *see* higher education

Vachudova, M.A. 233
Valencia, R.R. 42
Valentin, K. 315
Van de Werfhorst, H. 116, 252, 253, 255, 256, 257, 273
Venturini, T. 316
Vincent, C. 294, 298, 304, 308
violence, symbolic 29, 30, 203

Wacquant, L. 126
Walker, R.A. 237
Walkerdine, V. 37, 69, 178, 181, 183
Walsh, V. 37
war for talent 53–4
Waters, J. 213, 218, 219
Waters, M.C. 314
Watson, J. 195
Weber, M. 9
Weis, L. 30, 67, 69
welfare state 37–8, 45
Wentworth, P. 178, 183
Whelan, C. 232
Whitty, G. 50
Wilensky, H. 56
Wilkinson, R. 26
Wolf, A. 33, 112, 149, 289
women 202, 252; academic failure and working-class students 185; British Social Attitudes (BSA) survey (1983–2010): framing higher education 160, 168, 172, 173; internships 99, 100; level of social mobility in UK 28; Malaysia: UK offshore or transnational education 227–8; meritocracy and *Gaokao*: East China 246; migration 313–14, 315; Netherlands: educational expansion and field of study 261, 263–8;

origins, education and destinations in 1990s and 2000s 134–49; refugees in US 313–14, 322–3, 326; rural students in Chinese elite university 205, 206
Wooldridge, A. 53
work experience 90–2, 101, 121; methods 92–3
working-class culture, oppositional 33–4, 35, 38
working-class students and academic failure 176–89; findings and discussion 180–8; method 179–80
World War II 10–11, 34, 35
Wright, E.O. 194

Xu, X. 197

Yang, D. 194
Yao, H. 196
Yin, P. 194
You, L. 194
Young, M. 50, 131, 132, 232, 234, 272

Zakaria, F. 233
Zheng, Ch. 195
Zhou, M. 315
Zimdars, A. 236, 240